WHAT WORKS IN
CHILD WELFARE

EDITED BY
MIRIAM P. KLUGER
GINA ALEXANDER
PATRICK A. CURTIS

FOREWORD BY SENATOR JOHN CHAFEE

CWLA PRESS • WASHINGTON, DC

CWLA Press is an imprint of the Child Welfare League of America. The Child Welfare League of America is the nation's oldest and largest membership-based child welfare organization. We are committed to engaging people everywhere in promoting the well-being of children, youth, and their families, and protecting every child from harm.

CHILD WELFARE LEAGUE OF AMERICA, INC.
HEADQUARTERS
440 First Street, NW, Third Floor, Washington, DC 20001-2085
E-mail: books@cwla.org

CURRENT PRINTING (last digit)
10 9 8 7 6 5 4 3 2 1

Cover design by Tung Mullen
Text design by Pen & Palette Unlimited

Printed in the United States of America

ISBN 0-87868-743-2

Library of Congress Cataloging-in-Publication Data

What works in child welfare / edited by Miriam P. Kluger, Gina Alexander, and Patrick A. Curtis.
    p. cm.
    Includes bibliographical references.
    ISBN 0-87868-743-2
    1. Child welfare—United States. I. Kluger, Miriam P. II. Alexander, Gina. III. Curtis, Patrick A. (Patrick Almond), 1944–

HV741 .W383 2001
362.7′0973—dc21

                          00-058508

Dedication

For Jocelyn, Hannah, Dan, Connor, and Adam

Contents

Contents

List of Tables and Figures

Tables

Figures

Chapter 35

Chapter 36

Acknowledgments

The editors would like to thank several individuals who helped make this project possible. Thanks to Darla Kuh and Julie Crane, Villages of Indiana, for research and all kinds of support. Thanks to Laura Feagans from the Child Welfare League of America, for much help with the figures and illustrations. Special thanks to Madelyn Freundlich for helping us pull together the final manuscript. And to our spouses, thanks for taking care of the kids!

Miriam P. Kluger
Gina Alexander
Patrick A. Curtis

Foreword

Senator John H. Chafee

Since our nation has entered the new millennium, the much-ballyhooed concerns prompted by this milestone, such as combating the year 2000 computer bug, have faded. I submit that the more enduring challenge for the future will be ensuring the well-being of American children and families in an increasingly complex world.

Child welfare advocacy would not be possible without research and evaluation. Studies such as the ones compiled in this volume should be required reading for lawmakers aiming to reconcile state and federal policies with the real-life problems facing our nation's youngest citizens. Analyses of the consequences of existing laws and policies are imperative, for without understanding the consequences, we cannot offer new initiatives or revise unsuccessful ones.

I offer my gratitude and praise to the authors and the Child Welfare League of America for sponsoring such a useful and edifying volume. It will prove helpful to anyone interested in effecting change in this arena. Too often, reports are steeped in jargon impenetrable to all but the experts. This work provides a comprehensive examination of programmatic and clinical interventions shown to be effective with children and families at high risk for neglect and abuse. I think that both laypersons and professionals will find it accessible and engaging.

I have often relied on CWLA and its 1,000-plus member agencies to learn first-hand about the problems facing American children and families. CWLA's extraordinary efforts have spurred marked improvements in child welfare policies that protect abused and neglected children and strengthen vulnerable families. But our work is not done. More than 2.5 million American children remain at-risk for neglect and abuse. Too many children remain in the foster care system, clamoring for a family to provide them with a sense of place and a feeling of permanency in a fragile and disjointed world. As advocates, policymakers, citizens, and neighbors, we must take up their cause, serve as their protectors, and champion their rights.

It seems self-evident that the safety and well-being of children would reign paramount in child welfare decisions. But it was not until November 1997, with the passage of bipartisan legislation I helped author, the Adoption and Safe Families Act, that their primacy was codified into federal law. With the help of advocates like CWLA, this legislation was implemented in an attempt to reduce the number of children in the foster care system and to tighten the timetable that governs the adoption process.

Permanency should remain the watchword that guides our actions and decisions. Whether it is a swift return home, kinship care, or adoption by a loving family, we must streamline the family placement process so that children are not left in a state of limbo, wondering where they will eat their next meal or worrying about whose house they will sleep in tonight. Without the reversal of current trends, a growing number of children will enter adulthood without permanent families or having grown up in households of abuse, neglect, and poverty. What a dangerous foundation to lay at the beginning of a new century!

There is much more work to be done. There are many areas for improvement: we must protect children, diminish the alarming rate at which children are entering the foster care system, ensure that all children have permanent families, increase prenatal care for low-income women, and strengthen efforts to provide all children with health insurance. This anthology is a valuable tool for advocacy, policy, and practices that forge strong children and families for the 21st century.

A Great Friend to Children, Child Welfare, and the Nation

Senator John H. Chafee, 1922–1999

The news of Senator John Chafee's (R-RI) death on October 24, 1999, stunned and saddened us all. The entire country lost a fine and dedicated public servant. It is just beginning to sink in how great a loss his passing is for so many, particularly for those who are most vulnerable and in great need. Senator Chafee was perhaps best known nationally for his work on environmental issues. In the children's services community, we all know he was a champion for much more; he worked effectively in behalf of those who had the least. Senator Chafee did it all without fanfare, simply because it was the right thing to do.

Over the years, the Child Welfare League of America had the privilege of working with Senator Chafee as he fought to protect vulnerable children and families, and to secure health care assistance for those who needed it. When Congress trampled and almost eliminated protections for abused and neglected children during the highly polarized and contentious 1995–1996 welfare debates, Senator Chafee was there, standing firm and building the consensus not to do so. He helped to lead the way to passage of the landmark Adoption and Safe Families Act of 1997 to improve safety and permanency for children who didn't have much of either in their lives. And, regardless of what else he did, Senator Chafee was always looking for—and tended to find or create— ways to guarantee health care coverage for poor children and others without it. CWLA honored Senator Chafee for his tremendous contributions twice, once in 1996 and again last year, but easily could have done so year in and year out.

Up until his death last year, Chafee was hard at work, leading the effort in the Senate to improve services for young people leaving foster care so that they would have a better chance to achieve successful independence. He was the lead sponsor of the Foster Care Independence Act, and the week before his death, he chaired a hearing that explored the problems these young people face and how we can help them.

We will remember Senator Chafee as a tireless public servant with great integrity and common sense, as a leader and consensus builder in Congress, and, most of all, as one of the best friends that children, families, and those who worked with them could ever have had. We all will miss him greatly.

Introduction

Writing this book has been a challenge, beginning with the title, which was originally, "What Works in Child Welfare?" We decided to eliminate the question mark from the title because, despite its limitations, this book is a celebration of what works in child welfare. It is written in a style that makes it accessible to all audiences—researchers, policymakers, CEOs, program managers, and direct service practitioners. The experts who contributed to this book are intellectual leaders in their respective fields, and we are both fortunate and proud to present their work.

Research in child welfare is another case of the glass being half empty versus half full. We do know that some programs and some interventions benefit the children and families served, but rarely do we know how or why they work. For example, we have been asked whether research sheds light on the impact of intensive family preservation services for three versus six months. Unfortunately, given existing resources, research in child welfare cannot answer such a detailed question about models of best practices.

It is no surprise that most research in child welfare occurs when the federal government is willing to pay for it. There is substantially more research, for example, for family preservation services (funded by PL 103–66, 1990 Family Preservation and Support Services Act) than parent aide programs. Public policy, particularly at the federal level, drives research funding but we must find ways for research to influence policy. In an era of accountability, it is also important that research address outcomes and what works, and that this information influences policy and practices.

We also challenge researchers who read this book to share their research. The researchers who contributed to this book did. Not all researchers are advocates per se, but researchers can advocate for the use of empirically based decision-making. Beyond the more traditional channels, some audiences to consider sharing findings with are:

- Children and families, who deal with stress on a daily basis. Is there anything in the research findings that would be directly useful to them?

- Direct service practitioners, who may be looking for ways to change the lives of the families they serve. Given limited resources and the demand for services, what strategies are most effective?

- Program managers/directors, who want to improve the programs they manage. What outcomes should be used? What is a reasonable success rate to anticipate?

- Executive Directors/CEOs, who may be faced with balancing budgets and reducing costs. In deciding to launch a new program, what particular services and strategies hold the most promise with regard to favorable outcomes?

- Board members, who are looking for ways to stay connected and interested in the organization. How do their agency's services or programs fit within the larger child welfare arena?

- Child welfare commissioners, who have the authority to make policy and influence direct practice. What strategies should be promoted at their agencies?

- Foundations/funders, who want to know if their money is being spent as effectively as possible. What are the gaps in services and what kinds of programs should be funded in the future?

- Legislators, who vote to initiate and fund programs on behalf of children and families. Which child welfare bills should they sponsor or endorse?

The book is divided into six major sections; (1) family preservation and family support services; (2) child protective services, including child abuse and neglect prevention and interventions on behalf of child abuse and neglect victims; (3) out-of-home care; (4) adoption; (5) child care; (6) and adolescent services. Each section includes data about effective strategies, conflicting evidence, cost-effectiveness information when available, and a summary table with references for those desiring more detail about the studies mentioned. Note that very little cost-effectiveness data are available, a gap in child welfare research that must be addressed in order to provide important information to policymakers and program managers. Figures and graphs are used whenever possible to illustrate important points. It was a challenge for contributors to write in a nonacademic style, but their willingness to adapt to the requested model was inspiring!

Some sections may overlap somewhat. This seeming redundancy was by design as the sections can be read alone or with other sections in the area. Although readers are certainly welcome to read the book from cover to cover, it is meant as a reference when specific program design, funding, and enhancements are under consideration. The information may also be used as a quick way to become familiar with advances and issues in a particular field. It is our hope that this book will require revision and updating within two years because of new research.

The challenges facing families within the child welfare system are complex, and changes and improvements occur gradually. There are no miracle solutions and, although results are not always overwhelming, behind every percentage change lies the potential for a better life for children and families because the services worked.

Family Preservation and Family Support

What Works in Family Support Services

Elizabeth M. Tracy

The term "family support" refers to a unique set of service delivery features, a philosophy, and a grassroots movement designed to:

- Enhance the strength and stability of families;
- Increase parents' confidence and competence in parenting;
- Afford children a stable and supportive family environment; and
- Enhance child development [Child Welfare League of America 1989; Family Resource Coalition of America 1996].

Family support services differ from family preservation services, which typically are reserved for at-risk or high-risk families. Participants in family support services may receive services without being identified as at-risk and in the absence of problems that threaten family stability.

There is no one format for a family support program, and they are often designed with consumer input to meet needs unique to a setting or population. Comer and Fraser [1998], however, propose that the following interventions may constitute core elements of family support programs:

- Home visiting;
- Child development and screening;
- Parent training and education; and
- Social, emotional, and educational support for parents.

Within these core elements, typical service components include life skills training, individualized case management, parent-child groups and family activities, drop-in times, parent-lending libraries, information and referral services, and concrete support services (such as clothing exchanges, food pantries, and transportation).

Impact of Family Support Programs

A recent review of six family support programs found that "well-conceptualized and implemented family support programs have the capacity to improve family functioning" [Comer & Fraser 1998: 143]. Aspects of family functioning which appeared to maintain gains over a 12-month period included:

- *Improved prenatal care and fewer pregnancy complications.* Leonardson and Wilson [1992] found that teenage parents in a family support program received more prenatal care and reported fewer postpartum emergency room visits than a matched comparison group that had not participated in a support program. Clinton, Elwood, and Parks [1988] found that family support program participants had higher scores on an index of pregnancy self-care and number of prenatal medical visits.

- *Improved parent-child interaction.* Johnson and Walker [1991] found that program participants provided a more educationally stimulating and encouraging home environment for their children as measured by standardized tools and mother-child interactions. Luster, Peristadt, McKinney, Sims, and Juang [1996] reported that teen parents in their home visit group had scores on the Caldwell Home Inventory [Caldwell & Bradley 1984] approximately three points higher than those in the standard program (M = 32.0 and 29.2, respectively).

- *Higher level of parental knowledge.* Pfannenstiel, Lambson, and Yarnell [1991] reported significant increases in parent knowledge of child development. Johnson and Walker [1991] reported more positive attitudes on the part of parents toward their role as teacher of their children and less strict attitudes toward child rearing.

- *Higher level of child development.* Long-term follow-up data from the Yale Child Research Program [Seitz et al. 1985] showed that compared to a control group, participating children scored higher on measures of language and had better school performance and attendance.

In addition to the gains mentioned above, gains in parent education, housing, and income appeared to develop over time, suggesting that some outcomes associated with family support services may be cumulative. For example, one 10-year follow-up [Seitz et al. 1985] showed that family support program participants had obtained higher levels of education and had been able to end their reliance on welfare benefits in greater numbers when compared to a comparison group: 87% of the intervention group parents had become self-supporting compared to 53% of the comparison group.

The Avance Parent-Child Education project found that 60.5% of participating mothers had received their GED as compared with 27.5% of mothers in the comparison group [Comer & Fraser 1998].

These studies also suggest that family support services were more effective for families with young children.

Overall, there is little information concerning the best way to match particular services for different types of families. One family support program, however, found that the intensity of service may be an important feature. Teen parents who received weekly home visits for over a year tended to provide more supportive home environments for their infants than teens who had received only phone and mail support [Luster et al. 1996]. Differences were found in mothers' involvement with and emotional and verbal responsiveness to their children.

Although home visiting over an extended period of time is often a key family support intervention, center-based support, which allows families a respite from harsh home environments, can offer families an alternate form of community and support [Lightburn & Kemp 1994].

Cost-Effectiveness

Although there are few analyses of cost-benefits of family support programs and how best to target such services, proponents of family support point out that early investments have the potential to yield cost savings later in the child's life [Center for Child and Family Policy 1993]. There is some evidence that comprehensive support services delivered early

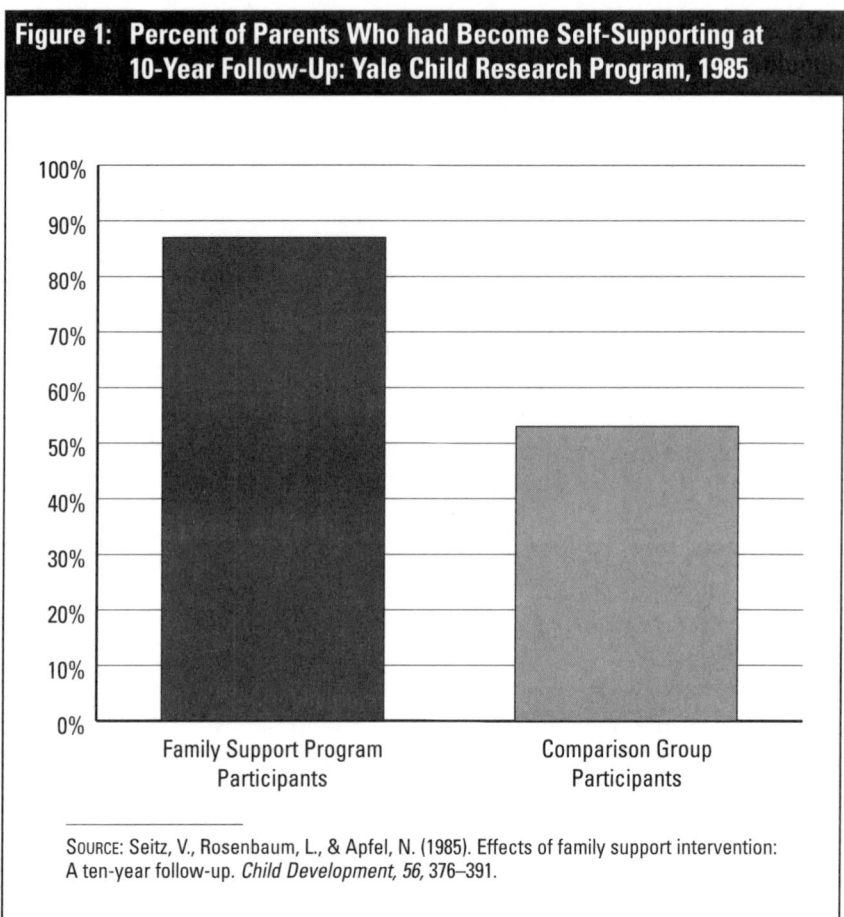

Figure 1: Percent of Parents Who had Become Self-Supporting at 10-Year Follow-Up: Yale Child Research Program, 1985

SOURCE: Seitz, V., Rosenbaum, L., & Apfel, N. (1985). Effects of family support intervention: A ten-year follow-up. *Child Development, 56,* 376–391.

and intensively yield the most benefit and cost savings [Cameron & Vanderwoerd 1997]. The degree to which a family support program addresses broader environmental and developmental concerns of parents also may be a key factor, as suggested by the findings of the Yale Child Welfare Research Program [Seitz et al. 1985].

Conclusion

Family support programs present a number of evaluation challenges due to the comprehensive nature of the services provided, the wide variety of

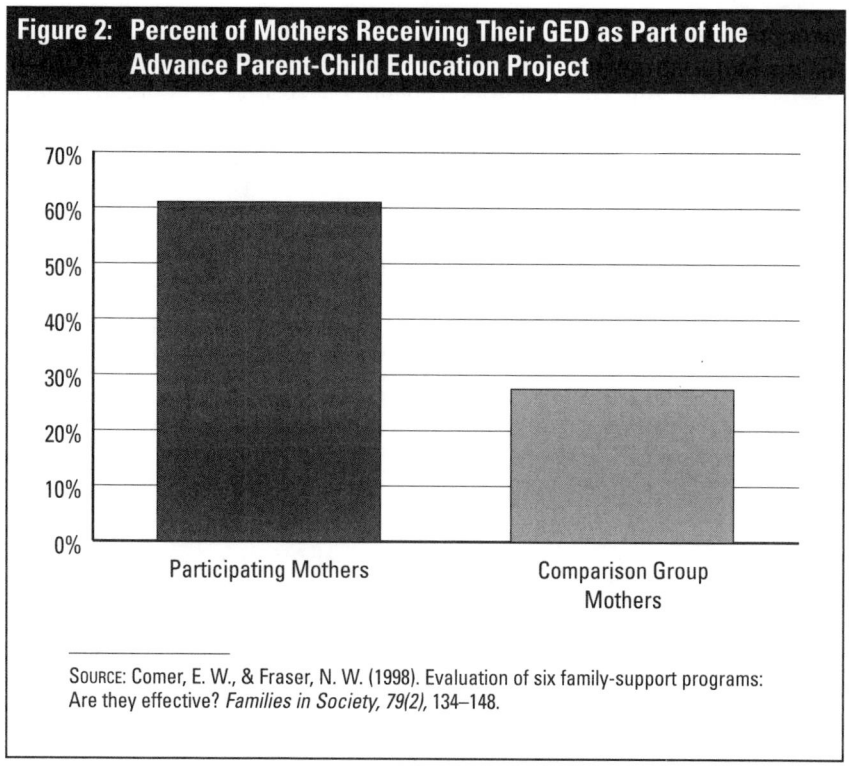

Figure 2: Percent of Mothers Receiving Their GED as Part of the Advance Parent-Child Education Project

SOURCE: Comer, E. W., & Fraser, N. W. (1998). Evaluation of six family-support programs: Are they effective? *Families in Society, 79(2),* 134–148.

families targeted for service, measurement issues in capturing the variety of outcomes intended to derive from family support, and the duration of these outcomes over time [Family Resource Coalition of America 1998]. Although there is still much to be learned about the mechanism of family support, there appears to be sufficient evidence to conclude that family support programs can produce positive changes in parenting behavior and skills, parent-child relations, and some aspects of family self-sufficiency. The long-term service impact, intensity, and timing of service delivery appear to be important factors in influencing outcomes. Tailoring family support programs to meet family and community needs is an important feature to address both in program planning and evaluation.

In addition to further evaluation of outcomes and the long-term impact of family support services, there are other issues to address. One crucial issue is how to involve fathers and other male caregivers in support programs, which are typically oriented toward and used by mothers

[Lightburn & Kemp 1994]. Another challenge is how best to link family support programs and practice technologies with other family services in such areas as community building, school-based intervention, and child welfare practice [Adams & Nelson 1995].

References

Adams, P. & Nelson, P. (Eds.). (1995). *Reinventing human services: Community- and family-centered practice.* Hawthorne, NY: Aldine de Gruyter.

Caldwell, B. & Bradley, R. (1984). *Home observation for measurement of the environment.* Little Rock: University of Arkansas at Little Rock.

Cameron, G. & Vanderwoerd, J. (1997). *Protecting children and supporting families: Promising programs and organizational realities.* Hawthorne, NY: Aldine de Gruyter.

Center for Child and Family Policy. (1993). *Investing in families, prevention and school readiness.* Des Moines, IA: Center for Child and Family Policy.

Child Welfare League of America. (1989). *Standards for services to strengthen and preserve families with children.* Washington, DC: CWLA Press.

Clinton, B., Elwood, P., & Parks, R. (1988). Maternal infant health outreach project. Nashville, TN: Center for Health Services, Vanderbilt University.

Comer, E. W. & Fraser, M. W. (1998). Evaluation of six family-support programs: Are they effective? *Families in Society, 79*(2), 134–148.

Family Resource Coalition of America. (1996). *Making the case for family support.* Chicago: Family Resource Coalition of America.

Family Resource Coalition of America. (1998). *FRCA Report: Family support evaluation,* 16(4). Chicago: Family Resource Coalition of America.

Johnson, D. & Walker, T. (1991). *Final report of an evaluation of the Avance Parent Education and Family Support Program.* San Antonio, TX: Avance.

Leonardson, G. & Wilson, A. (1992). *Evaluation report—Rural America Initiative Project Takoja: Comprehensive teen parent program.* Sioux Falls: University of South Dakota.

Lightburn, A. & Kemp, S. P. (1994). Family-support programs: Opportunities for community-based practice. *Families in Society, 75*(1), 16–26.

Luster, T., Perlstadt, H., McKinney, M., Sims, K., & Juang, L. (1996). The effects of a family support program and other factors on the home environments provided by adolescent mothers. *Family Relations, 45,* 255–264.

Pfannenstiel, J., Lambson, T., & Yarnell, V. (1991). *Second wave study of the Parents as Teachers Program: Final report.* St. Louis, MO: Research and Training Associates.

Seitz, V., Rosenbaum, L., & Apfel, N. (1985). Effects of family support intervention: A ten year follow-up. *Child Development, 56,* 376–391.

What Works in Family Support Services

Study Authors	Survey Sample	Research Design/Outcome Measure	Major Findings
Seitz, V., Rosenbaum, L. & Apfel, N. (1985). Effects of family support intervention: A ten year follow-up. *Child Development, 56,* 376–391.	• Matched comparison group • 10-year follow-up of 15 families	• Child health and development, school performance, parent education, medical care, housing, and community life were examined.	• Participants had a greater number of self-supporting parents and higher level of education. • Children rated higher on school adjustment and attendance.
Pfannenstiel, J., Lambson, T. & Yarnell, V. (1991). *Second wave study of the Parents as Teachers program: Final report.* St. Louis, MO: Research and Training Associates.	• Stratified randomly selected control group • 395 families studied	• Child development and achievement, parent knowledge of child development and child rearing were examined.	• Participants showed improvement on child achievement and parent knowledge of child development.
Johnson, D. & Walker, T. (1991). *Final report of an evaluation of the Avance Parent Education and Family Support Program.* San Antonio, TX: Avance.	• Random assignment • Comparison group • 113 families studied	• Parent-child interaction, parent attitudes, knowledge and child care skills, use of resources were examined.	• Participants provided a more educationally stimulating home environment. • Parents knew of more community resources and had less strict child-rearing attitudes.

2

What Works in Family Preservation Services

Kristine Nelson

In response to a growing number of children in out-of-home care, the Adoption Assistance and Child Welfare Act of 1980 (P.L. 96–272) mandated that states demonstrate "reasonable efforts" to keep children in their own homes or reunify them with their families in order to receive federal reimbursement for foster care. Although the Act was never fully funded, many states instituted intensive family preservation programs to meet this mandate. Funding to states for family support and family preservation services was expanded in the 1993 Family Preservation and Support Services Act (P.L. 103–66) and continued by the 1997 Adoption and Safe Families Act (P.L. 105–89) with its emphasis on child safety and permanency planning.

Intensive family preservation services (IFPS) are normally time-limited (4 to 12 weeks) and comprehensive, with low caseloads (2 to 12 families) to enable frequent contact. The primary outcome measure used in assessing the success of IFPS has been the prevention of out-of-home placement or the return of children to their families after they entered foster care. IFPS research has been criticized for its focus on placement prevention; this outcome, however, does not occur in isolation from other improvements in families' lives: parenting, family functioning, and child safety [Nelson & Landsman 1992]. Reviews of family preservation research also have been critical of the designs of most of the studies.

Impact on Family Preservation

Despite methodological constraints, some of the studies with comparison or control groups have demonstrated significant placement prevention effects [Fraser et al. 1997]. Schwartz, AuClaire, and Harris [1991] studied outcomes for adolescents for whom placement proceedings had been initiated but who were diverted into a family systems-based program. They found that 43.6% were still in their homes at the 12-month follow-up compared to only 8.6% of the overflow comparison group. Pecora and colleagues [1991], also using a matched-pairs case overflow comparison group, found that 55.6% of the adolescents served were still in their homes 12 to 16 months following enrollment in an IFPS program compared to only 14.8% of those receiving standard child welfare services. Feldman [1991] randomly assigned youth in four sites in New Jersey to IFPS or standard services and found a placement prevention rate at the 12-month follow-up of 57.3% in the IFPS group and 43.4% in the control group.

Studies indicate that reductions in out-of-home placement also have been achieved by using IFPS at the outset of child welfare intervention rather than as a last resort. Walton [1997] randomly assigned moderate to high-risk families being investigated for child abuse or neglect to an IFPS worker who, working in conjunction with the child protective service worker, provided an average of two weeks (11.2 hours) of service to each family. When compared to families receiving standard child protective services at the six month follow-up, fewer families receiving IFPS were required to participate in continuing services, more children were maintained in their own homes (85% versus 60%), and the cases in which IFPS were provided remained open for a shorter period of time (see Figure 1).

In Michigan, an evaluation of the statewide Families First program matched 225 children who received an average of 30 days of IFPS with children exiting foster care, under the assumption that children received IFPS as an alternative to placement. At the 12-month comparison, 23.6% of Families First children were placed in foster care compared to 35.1% of the foster care sample who returned to foster care [University Associates 1993]. The difference was even larger when comparing children referred for abuse or neglect: 19.4% of Families First children referred for abuse or neglect and 36% of children in foster care referred for abuse or neglect were placed in, or returned to foster care.

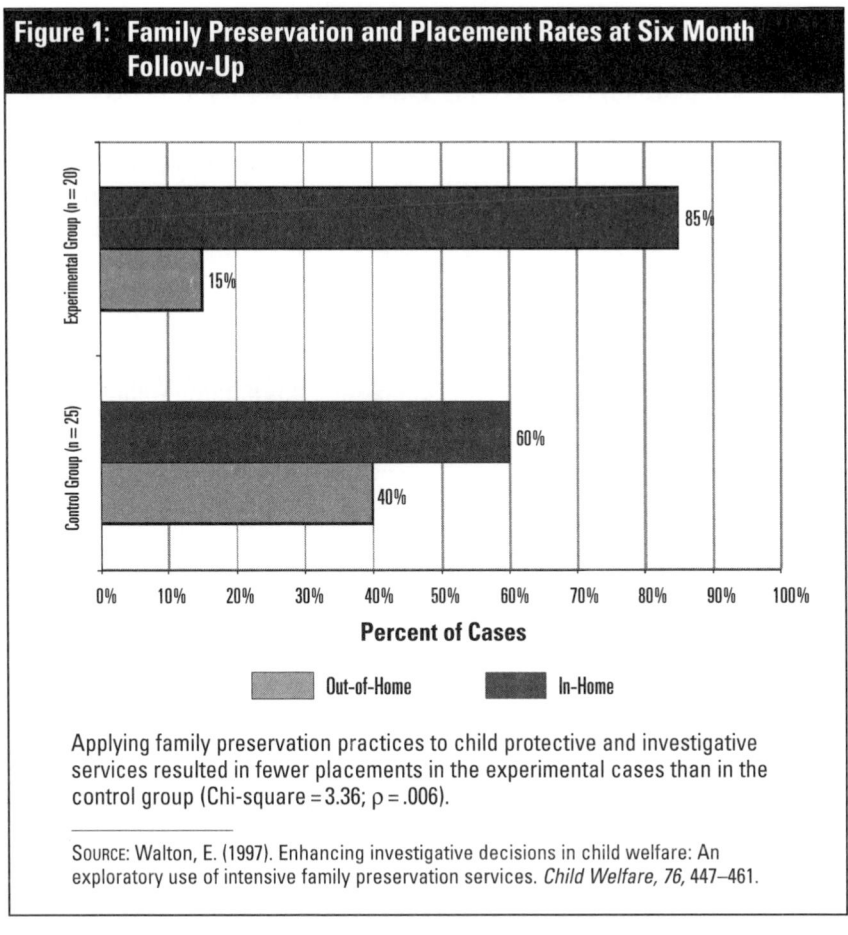

Figure 1: Family Preservation and Placement Rates at Six Month Follow-Up

Applying family preservation practices to child protective and investigative services resulted in fewer placements in the experimental cases than in the control group (Chi-square = 3.36; ρ = .006).

Source: Walton, E. (1997). Enhancing investigative decisions in child welfare: An exploratory use of intensive family preservation services. *Child Welfare, 76,* 447–461.

Impressive findings also have been documented regarding the success of IFPS programs in reunifying children already in foster care. Fraser and his colleagues [1996] provided 90 days of IFPS to families randomly assigned from prescreened foster care caseloads (about two-fifths of all foster cases). IFPS successfully reunited all but two of the families during the service period, whereas almost half of the control children did not return home during the study period. At the end of the 12-month follow-up, 70% of the IFPS children had reunited with their families and remained in the home compared to only 47% of the control group who had reunited with their families and remained in the home.

In addition, IFPS children returned home more quickly and spent fewer days in placement (Figure 2).

In a study of families receiving Family Reunification services for an average of 6.1 months in Michigan, 75% of targeted children who were reunited with their families remained in their homes 12 months following services compared to 65% of children exiting foster care with standard services. At a 30-month follow-up, 68% of the IFPS group remained

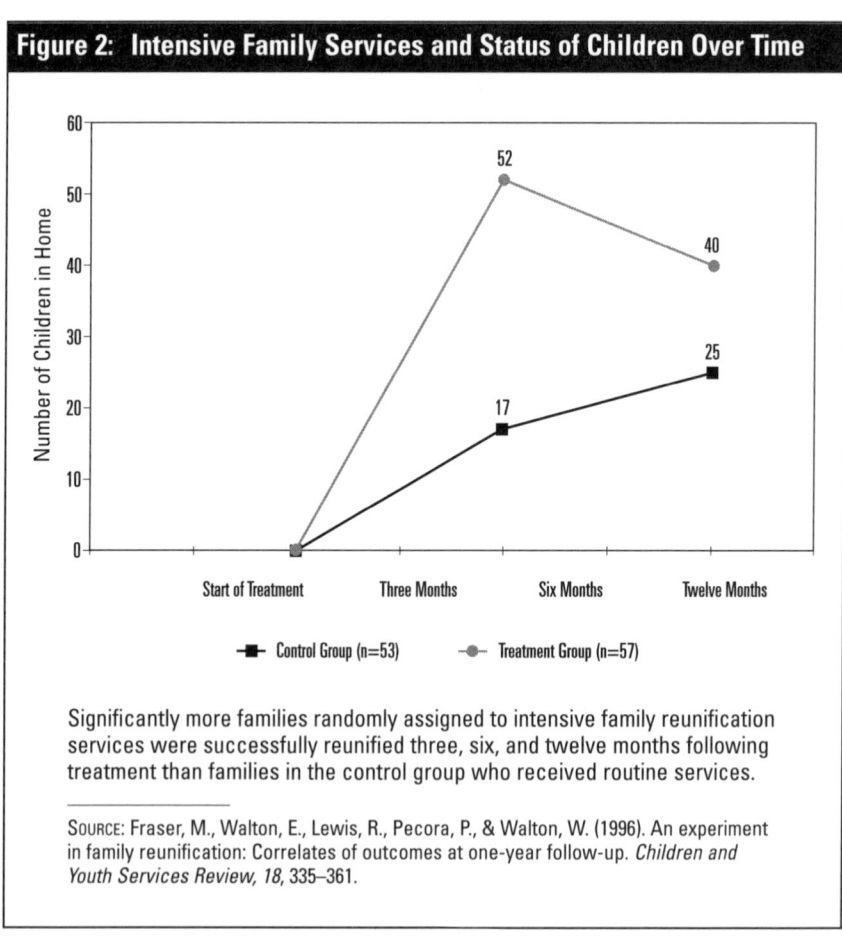

Figure 2: Intensive Family Services and Status of Children Over Time

Number of Children in Home

Start of Treatment · Three Months · Six Months · Twelve Months

—■— Control Group (n=53)   —●— Treatment Group (n=57)

Significantly more families randomly assigned to intensive family reunification services were successfully reunified three, six, and twelve months following treatment than families in the control group who received routine services.

Source: Fraser, M., Walton, E., Lewis, R., Pecora, P., & Walton, W. (1996). An experiment in family reunification: Correlates of outcomes at one-year follow-up. *Children and Youth Services Review, 18*, 335–361.

in their homes compared to 57% of the foster care group [University Associates 1998].

Problems in Determining Success in IFPS

Outcomes Differ by Child's Age

With the exception of the studies by Walton [1997] and University Associates [1993, 1998], the successful placement prevention programs studied have focused on adolescents. Findings regarding IFPS outcomes for families with younger children referred for child abuse and neglect are mixed. Both Yuan and Struckman-Johnson [1991] and Schuerman, Rzepnicki, and Littell [1994] found no difference in placement rates between experimental and control groups of families with younger children receiving IFPS. These studies, however, suffered from three major problems: (1) unlike programs for adolescents, program sites varied greatly in the length and type of services provided; (2) the services were not specifically targeted to children otherwise likely to enter out-of-home care; and (3) the evaluations did not distinguish between families referred for child abuse and those referred for child neglect [Fraser et al. 1997].

Outcomes Differ for Physical Abuse Versus Neglect Cases

Studies which have distinguished physical abuse from neglect have found higher success rates associated with IFPS provided to families referred for physical abuse [Barth & Haapala 1993; Nelson & Landsman 1992; Unrau 1997]. These findings may indicate a need for longer term services with neglect cases.

Recidivism Is not Typically Reported in Studies

Most IFPS studies have not reported re-referrals for child protective services investigations. When they have been tracked, rates of repeated maltreatment have varied from 13% to 25% over six to 12-month follow-up periods. No significant difference in repeat referrals for child maltreatment have been found between IFPS and standard services, indicating that children receiving IFPS are not at higher risk of harm than those receiving standard child welfare services [Schuerman et al. 1994; Yuan & Struckman-Johnson 1991; Walton 1997].

Cost-Effectiveness

The best evidence of the cost-effectiveness of IFPS is from reunification studies, since there is no doubt that the children served were at risk of remaining in out-of-home placements, a more costly service. In the Michigan reunification study, the impact of Family Reunification services on placement costs was studied by comparing the cost of placement for the same children for the 12 months preceding IFPS and the 12 months following IFPS. The average per-child cost for the 2,299 children in the study was $5,326 for the 12 months preceding IFPS and $2,271 for the 12 months following services (Figure 3 shows costs for subgroups of the total population). Subtracting the cost of Family Reunification services from the savings realized in foster care expenditures produced a reduction in costs of $1,099 per child served [University Associates 1998].

Nelson and associates [1996] attempted to determine the cost-effectiveness of three versus six months of IFPS programs that served a combination of placement prevention and reunification cases. For families with adolescents who were motivated to participate in office-based family therapy, three months of IFPS at an average cost of $739 per family was most cost-effective. For families with adolescents in need of in-home services, six months of service at an average cost of $835 per family enabled more intensive work with schools and the community and lowered overall placement costs in the 12 months following intervention by two-thirds ($31,415 versus $109,614). For abuse and neglect cases involving younger children, there was no significant difference in 12-month outcomes between three ($2,284) and six ($3,283) months of in-home services. This IFPS site served a large percentage of families referred for neglect who may have needed more extensive services.

Conclusion

Family preservation and reunification programs provide intensive services that enable children to remain in or return to their families. In studies with comparison groups and consistently implemented service models, significantly more children remained at home or returned to their homes, resulting in considerable savings in foster care costs. Studies that test specific service models for physical abuse or neglect are needed to determine the optimal mix and length of services for different types of cases.

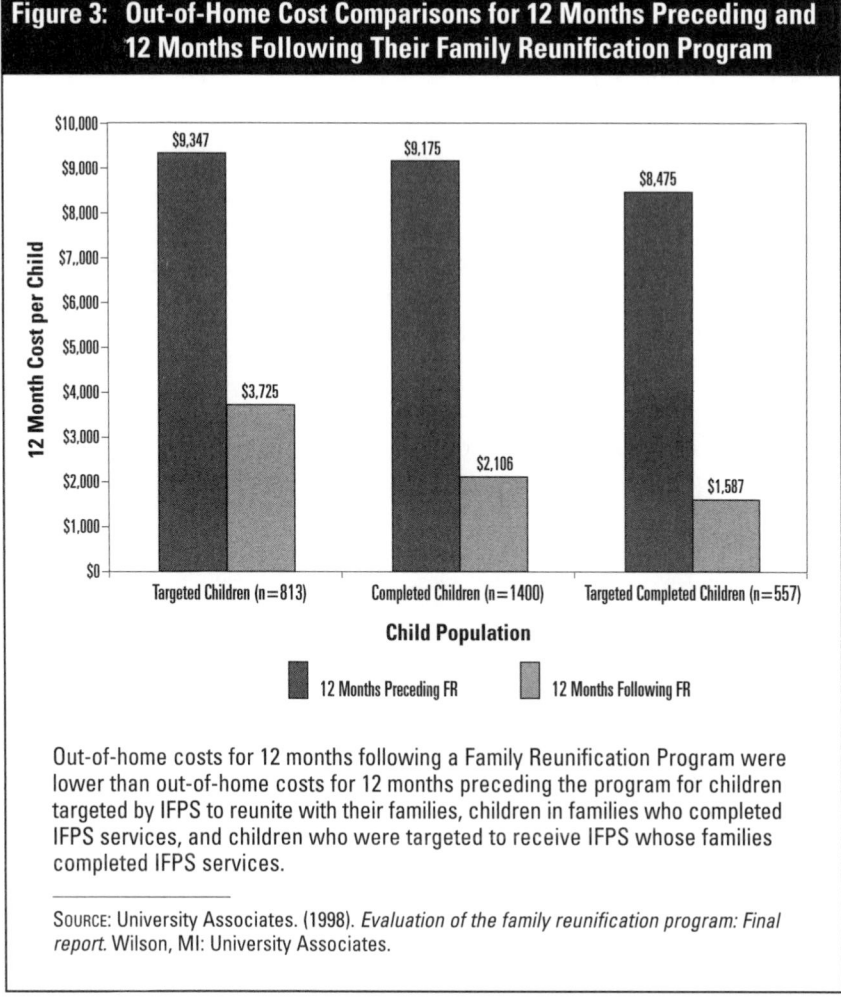

Figure 3: Out-of-Home Cost Comparisons for 12 Months Preceding and 12 Months Following Their Family Reunification Program

Out-of-home costs for 12 months following a Family Reunification Program were lower than out-of-home costs for 12 months preceding the program for children targeted by IFPS to reunite with their families, children in families who completed IFPS services, and children who were targeted to receive IFPS whose families completed IFPS services.

SOURCE: University Associates. (1998). *Evaluation of the family reunification program: Final report.* Wilson, MI: University Associates.

References

Barth, H., & Haapala, D. (1993). Intensive family preservation services with abused and neglected children: An examination of group differences. *Child Abuse & Neglect, 17,* 213–225.

Feldman, L. (1991). Evaluating the impact of intensive family preservation services in New Jersey. In K. Wells & D. Biegel (Eds.), *Family preservation services: Research and evaluation* (pp. 47–71). Newbury Park, CA: Sage.

Fraser, M., Nelson, K. & Rivard, J. (1997). Effectiveness of family preservation services. *Social Work Research, 21,* 138–153.

Fraser, M., Walton, E., Lewis, R., Pecora, P., & Walton, W. (1996). An experiment in family reunification: Correlates of outcomes at one-year follow-up. *Children and Youth Services Review, 18,* 335–361.

Nelson, K. & Landsman, M. (1992). *Alternative models of family preservation: Family-based services in context.* Springfield, IL: Charles C. Thomas.

Nelson, K., Landsman, M., Tyler, M., & Richardson, B. (1996). *Costs and outcomes in two intensive family service programs.* Iowa City, IA: National Resource Center for Family-Centered Practice.

Pecora, P., Fraser, M., Bennet, R., & Haapala, D. (1991). Placement rates of children and families served by intensive family preservation services programs. In M. Fraser, P. Pecora, & D. Haapala (Eds.), *Families in crisis: The impact of intensive family preservation services* (pp. 149–180). New York: Aldine de Gruyter.

Schuerman, J., Rzepnicki, T. & Littel, J. (1994). *Putting families first: An experiment in family preservation.* New York: Aldine de Gruyter.

Schwartz, I., AuClaire, P., & Harris, L. (1991). Family preservation services as an alternative to the out-of-home placement of adolescents: The Hennepin County experience. In K. Wells & D. Biegel (Eds.), *Family preservation services: Research and evaluation* (pp. 33–46). Newbury Park, CA: Sage.

Unrau, Y. (1997). Predicting use of child welfare services after intensive family preservation services. *Research on Social Work Practice, 7,* 202–215.

University Associates. (1993). *Evaluation of Michigan's Families First program: Summary report.* Lansing, MI: University Associates.

University Associates. (1998). *Evaluation of the Family Reunification Program: Final report.* Wilson, MI: University Associates.

Walton, E. (1997). Enhancing investigative decisions in child welfare: An exploratory use of intensive family preservation services. *Child Welfare, 76,* 447–461.

Yuan, Y. & Struckman-Johnson, D. (1991). Placement outcomes for neglected children with prior placements in family preservation programs. In K. Wells & D. Biegel (Eds.), *Family preservation services: Research and evaluation* (pp. 92–118). Newbury Park, CA: Sage.

What Works in Family Preservation Services

Study Authors	Survey Sample	Research Design/Outcome Measure	Findings
Feldman, L. (1991). Evaluating the impact of intensive family preservation services in New Jersey. In K. Wells & D. Biegel (Eds.), *Family preservation services.* (pp. 47–71). Newbury Park, CA: Sage.	• 205 families with children at imminent risk of placement from 4 sites in New Jersey • Randomly assigned to IFPS (96) or standard services (87)	• Data collected from therapists, caregivers, and data systems. • Outcomes included family functioning, social support and placement.	• Family functioning and social support improved in IFPS. • Except in parenting, IFPS group was not significantly different from control group. • At 12-month follow-up, 42.7% of IFPS and 56.7% of control group had been placed at least once.
Fraser, M., Walton, E., Lewis, R., Pecora, P. & Walton, W.(1996). An experiment in family reunification. *Children and Youth Services Review, 18,* 335–361.	• 110 children (24% of those in out-of-home care) were randomly assigned to Family Reunification (FRS) (57) or routine services (53)	• Data collected from caregivers, workers, and state database. • Outcome measures included days until return home, days spent at home, and percent at home at 12-month follow-up.	• 96.5% of FRS (mean = 20.7 days) and 32.1% of controls (mean = 44.6 days) returned home. • FRS group in home 351 days and controls, 310 days. • At follow-up, 70.2% of FRS and 47.2% of controls were in the home.
Nelson, K., Landsman, M., Tyler, M. & Richardson, B. (1996). *Costs and outcomes in two intensive family service programs.* Iowa City, IA: National Resource Center for Family-Centered Practice.	• 460 families were randomly assigned to three or six months of Intensive Family Services in three sites in Oregon and Maryland	• Data collected from caregivers, workers, and state data bases. • Outcome measures included placement, family change, and cost-effectiveness.	• Significant family change occurred in all sites. • Placement rates ranged from 10.3% to 33.3%. • Costs for IFS ranged from $580 to $3,283 per family and for placement from $5,236 to $14,621.

(continued next page)

What Works in Family Preservation Services (continued)

Study Authors	Survey Sample	Research Design/Outcome Measure	Findings
Pecora, P., Fraser, M., Bennet, R., & Haapala, D. (1991). Placement rates of children and families served by intensive family preservation services programs. In M. Fraser, P. Pecora, & D. Haapala (Eds.), *Families in crisis* (pp. 149–180). New York: Aldine de Gruyter.	• 307 families receiving IFPS in four sites in Washington State • 139 families receiving IFPS at two sites in Utah • 26 Utah families referred but not served were used as a comparison group	• Data collected from caregivers, therapists and state data systems. • Outcomes included family change, social support, consumer satisfaction, and placement rates at 12-month follow-up.	• Significant improvement in 21 to 25 risk factors. • Significant reduction in aversive family relations and family problems. • At 12-month follow-up, placement was experienced by 35.5% of Washington families, 47.4% of Utah families, and 85.2% of comparison group families.
Schwartz, I., AuClaire, P. & Harris, L. (1991). Family preservation services as an alternative to out of home placement of adolescents: The Hennepin County experience. In K. Wells & D. Biegel (Eds.), *Family preservation services: Research and evaluation* (pp. 33–46). Newbury Park, CA: Sage.	• 58 adolescents not under court order, but approved for placement, assigned to IFPS as openings occurred • Comparison group of 58 randomly selected from those not assigned to IFPS	• Data collected from case records, social worker interviews, and departmental data files. • Outcomes included shelter, residential treatment, treatment group home placement, number of placements, and potential placement days utilized.	• 56.4% of IFPS group and 90.6% of comparison group were in some type of placement during 12 to 16 month follow-up. • Comparison group had almost twice as many placements and used 46% of expected placement days compared to 21% for the IFPS group.
University Associates. (1993). *Evaluation of Michigan's Families First program: Summary report.* Lansing, MI: University Associates.	• 225 children served by Families First in seven sites in Michigan • Matched on county, age, type of referral, prior CPS involvement, and date of exit to 225 children exiting foster care	• Data collected from case files, referring workers, families, staff, and the state management information system. • Outcomes included family and referring worker satisfaction, placement, and cost.	• High support for program from respondents. • At 12-month follow-up, 23.6% of Families First children had been placed compared to 35.1% of foster care children. • Placement costs averaged $2,123 for the Families First group and $3,302 for the foster care group.

University Associates. (1998). *Evaluation of the Family Reunification Program: Final report.* Wilson, MI: University Associates.	• 705 families referred for family reunification in three sites in Michigan • Criteria included AFDC-FC eligibility and court wardship • 225 children were matched to foster care comparison group from 1993 study	• Data collected from case files, referring workers, families, staff, and the state management information system. • Outcomes included family and referring worker satisfaction, placement, and cost.	• 60%–70% of respondents agreed that program achieved desired outcomes. • At 12-month follow-up, 25% of targeted children and 35.1% of foster care children had been placed. • Placement costs averaged $2,271 for the experimental group and $3,302 for the foster care group.
Walton, E. (1997). Enhancing investigative decisions in child welfare: An exploratory use of intensive family preservation services. *Child Welfare, 76,* 447–461.	• 134 moderate to high risk families referred for child abuse or neglect in Lucas County, OH • Randomly assigned to IFPS (69) and routine CPS (65)	• Data collected from agency information system, caregivers, and staff. • Outcomes included case openings, length open, placement, custody, and referrals.	• 29% of IFPS and 38.5% of controls opened. • IFPS opened an average of 115 days and controls, 170 days. • 15% of IFPS and 40% of controls were placed. • 25% of IFPS and 32% of controls were taken into custody. • Within six-month follow-up, 13% of IFPS and 7.7% of controls were re-referred.

3

What Works in Wraparound Programming

Russell J. Skiba and Steven D. Nichols

The 1980s saw a dramatic increase in the number of children being referred for residential treatment and the cost of such programming. Concerns have been raised about the extent to which gains in emotional and behavioral functioning achieved through residential treatment generalize when a child returns to his or her home community [Epstein et al. 1993]. The National Institutes of Mental Health launched the Children and Adolescent Service System Program (CASSP) in 1984, with the goal of integrating social services into what Stroul and Friedman [1986] termed a "system of care." This approach focuses on developing mental health, education, welfare, and other social services into a coordinated network so that the individual needs of children with emotional and behavioral disorders can be met in their home communities and their family members can be supported as allies in the treatment process.

Out of this system of care framework, some communities and programs have developed a model that has come to be known as "individualized care" [Burchard & Clarke 1990] or "wraparound" [Behar 1985]. Rather than expending local and state resources on expensive residential placements, communities have created a network of coordinated local services which are "wrapped around" the child and family in an effort to maintain the child in the local community. This approach is exemplified by innovative programs such as the Kaleidoscope Program in Chicago [Dennis et al. 1992], the Alaska Youth Initiative [VanDenBerg 1989], and

Project Wraparound in Vermont [Burchard & Clarke 1990]. VanDenBerg and Grealish [1996] have identified a number of principles and procedures that are key to the successful operation of wraparound programming (see Table 1). Wraparound is seen not merely as a change in social service procedure, but more importantly as a shift in philosophy. Values that require services to be strength-based, culturally competent, family-focused, and provide unconditional care are core and must be present for a given service to be technically described as wraparound.

Favorable Outcomes of Wraparound

Outcome studies of wraparound are somewhat limited, perhaps because of the relative newness of the concept. The majority of these outcome studies can be found in a special issue on wraparound services in the *Journal of Child and Family Studies* [Clark & Clarke 1996; Clark et al. 1996; Eber et al. 1996; Evans et al. 1996; Hyde et al. 1996; Rosenblatt 1996; VanDenBerg & Grealish 1996; Yoe et al. 1996]. These studies suggest the following about outcomes of wraparound services:

- *Children and youth served by wraparound options are more likely to transition to living arrangements that are less restrictive and more stable and permanent.* Burchard and colleagues [1993] detail how previously institutionalized youth who received wraparound services were able to succeed in foster care, re-enter regular education, complete their GED, or transition to independent living. Other researchers have reported that youth involved with wraparound care for at least 12 months resided in significantly less restrictive community-based living arrangements [Yoe et al. 1996]. These studies suggest that wraparound may be more effective in maintaining children and youth in less restrictive environments than residential treatment, a more restrictive environment which has yet to demonstrate successful generalization of treatment gains when children and youth move to a community setting.

- *Children and youth receiving wraparound services often show improvements in behavioral adaptation and emotional functioning.* Children and adolescents who receive wraparound services have been found to have significantly fewer problem behaviors overall, and also fewer abuse-related behaviors such as sexual acting out, self-injury, life threat, sexual abuse, and cruelty to animals.

Table 1. Principles and Procedures of Wraparound*

Principles

1. **Community-based:** Wraparound efforts must be based in the community.
2. **Individualized:** Services and supports must be individualized to meet needs of the children and families, not designed to reflect service system priorities.
3. **Culturally competent:** The process must be culturally competent, building on the unique values, strengths, and social and racial makeup of the children and families.
4. **Parent involvement:** Parents must be included in every level of development of the process.
5. **Strength-based:** Participants must work from the strengths of the family and child.
6. **Flexible funding:** Agencies must have access to flexible, non-categorized funding.
7. **Interagency collaboration:** The process must be implemented on an interagency basis and be owned by the larger community.
8. **Unconditional care:** Services must be unconditional. If needs of the child and family change, the child and family must not be rejected from services. Instead, the services must be changed.
9. **Outcome-based:** Outcomes must be measured to prevent the wraparound process from being simply an interesting fad.

Procedures

1. **Development of a community team** that is composed of the key stakeholders in services and supports for children and families.
2. **Identification/referral** by a subcommittee that focuses on identification, referral, and confidentiality issues and processes for wraparound.
3. **Assignment of a resource coordinator** who takes responsibility for managing funds and oversees the "doing" of the wraparound program.
4. **Access, voice, and ownership** in which the parent has valid service options at inclusion points in that process; the parent is heard and listened to at all junctions; and the parent and child agree with and are committed to any plan concerning them.
5. **Strengths discovery** through informal strengths assessment and individualized services and supports based on strengths of the child and family.
6. **Development of child and family team** that includes the child, family, and those close to family (four to 10 members with at least one-half non-professionals).
7. **Development of individualized services and support plan** at meetings of child and family team.
8. **Review of the plan** by the community team for consistency with values, and to develop budget. Community team cannot tinker with plan.
9. **Implementation of the plan** and the child and family team continues to meet.
10. **Measurement of outcomes** to provide feedback on success of the plan.

---

*Adapted from VanDenBerg & Grealish 1966

25

Receiving wraparound services also appears to result in youth internalizing and externalizing problem behaviors. Significant improvement in mood and emotion, behavior, and role performance have also been shown [Evans et al. 1996]. It is important to note, however, that wraparound is not a magic bullet for children with severe emotional and behavioral problems. Despite improvements in functioning, serious school and community-related behaviors such as truancy and police contact often remain [Yoe et al. 1996].

- *Wraparound services rely on and strengthen resources in the local community.* Rather than expending dollars for out-of-state placements, communities may, through wraparound, keep resources within the child's community, thereby strengthening the local economy and increasing local service capacity.

Obstacles to Wraparound

The recency of research data on wraparound precludes strong statements concerning its efficacy. Rosenblatt [1996: 110–111] states that "the results of these studies [on wraparound] can be classified as promising. Still, it is far too early to draw conclusions regarding the ultimate effectiveness of the wraparound process given the current state of knowledge." In addition, there has been a great deal of confusion as a result of an inconsistent definition of "wraparound." Although certain components have been identified as important in the implementation of wraparound [VanDenBerg & Grealish 1996], how many and which components are essential for successful outcomes is not clear. Thus, there is no standard by which programs qualify as wraparound and a variety of alternative service systems may describe themselves as wraparound "regardless of whether they follow the wraparound process or adhere to its underlying principles" [Rosenblatt 1996: 103].

There are other obstacles to wraparound:

- *Interagency collaboration, one of the guiding principles of wraparound, is often very difficult to achieve and maintain.* The most formidable obstacle to changes in service delivery may be the current categorical model that drives services. Resistance may occur when professionals from different disciplines bring different approaches to treatment philosophy and procedures. Bureaucratic constraints—such as supervisory control, organizational incentives, and standard operating procedures—may also decrease motivation to collaborate with other agencies.

- *Despite the importance of flexible funding in wraparound approaches, it is often difficult to change funding practices.* Flexible or pooled funding has been identified as a key component of wraparound, guaranteeing a fiscal base for services. The absence of systematic research investigating outcomes associated with the use of flexible funding [Dollard et al. 1994], however, makes it difficult to convince policymakers to change funding practices and implement wraparound procedures.

- *Research on wraparound programs varies considerably with respect to methodology, sampling, and the outcomes evaluated.* Like many young databases, the quality of research in the area of wraparound varies considerably. As a result, definitive statements regarding its efficacy are premature.

Cost-Effectiveness

One of the central arguments used to promote wraparound is that services in the community are inherently less costly than services in a residential treatment center. Preliminary evidence suggests that community-based alternatives to residential treatment are, in fact, cost-effective. A fiscal evaluation of a statewide program in Indiana estimated that community alternatives, including but not limited to wraparound, were on average only half as costly as either in-state or out-of-state residential programming [Skiba et al. 1998]. In their study of wraparound services provided by Vermont's New Directions initiative, Tighe and Brooks [1995] reported that the mean cost of community-based individualized services per child ($48,427 per year) was significantly less than the average cost of serving one child in an out-of-state residential placement ($58,718 per year).

Conclusion

Wraparound programming appears to be a promising programmatic strategy for delivering services to children and youth with the most serious emotional and behavioral disorders. Preliminary findings suggest that wraparound approaches appear to maintain children with severe disorders in less restrictive settings. Some improvements in behavior have been documented, and the data that exist show wraparound to be a cost-effective alternative to residential treatment. Because of its relative recency, however, there is not yet an extensive database. Thus, there is some danger that the popular use of the term will exceed current knowledge of its effectiveness. As noted by its proponents [VanDenBerg & Grealish 1996], it is critical that any implementation of wraparound be accompanied by an evaluation of its effectiveness.

References

Behar, L. (1985). Changing patterns of state responsibility: A case study of North Carolina. *Journal of Clinical Child Psychology, 14,* 188–195.

Burchard, J. D., Burchard, S. N., Sewell, R. & VanDenBerg, J. (1993). *One kid at a time: Evaluative case studies and description of the Alaska Youth Initiative Demonstration Project.* Washington, DC: Georgetown University, Child Development Center, CASSP Technical Assistance Center.

Burchard, J. D. & Clarke, R. T. (1990). The role of individualized care in a service delivery system for children and adolescents with severely maladjusted behavior. *Journal of Mental Health Administration, 17,* (1) 87–99.

Clarke, R. T., Schaefer, M., Burchard, J., & Welkowitz, J. (1992). Wrapping community-based mental health services around children with severe behavioral disorder: An evaluation of Project Wraparound. *Journal of Child and Family Studies, 1,* 241–261.

Clark, H. B. & Clarke, R. T. (1996). Research on the wraparound process and individualized services for children with multi-system needs. *Journal of Child and Family Studies, 5,* 1–5.

Clark, H., Lee, B., Prange, M., & McDonald, B. (1996). Children lost within the foster care system: Can wraparound service strategies improve placement outcomes? *Journal of Child and Family Studies, 5,* 39–54.

Dennis, K., VanDenBerg, J., & Burchard, D. (1992, April). *The wraparound process.* Presented at the First National Wraparound Conference, Pittsburgh, PA.

Dollard, N., Evans, M., E., Lubrecht, J., & Schaeffer, D. (1994). The use of flexible service dollars in rural community-based programs for children with serious emotional disturbance and their families. *Journal of Emotional and Behavioral Disorders, 2,* 117–125.

Eber, L., Osuch, R., & Redditt, C. A. (1996). School-based applications of the wraparound process: Early results on service provision and student outcomes. *Journal of Child and Family Studies, 5,* 83–99.

Epstein, M. H., Nelson, C. M., Polsgrove, L., Coutinho, M., Cumblad, C., & Quinn, K. (1993). A comprehensive community-based approach to serving students with emotional and behavioral disorders. *Journal of Emotional and Behavioral Disorders, 1*(2), 127–135.

Evans, M., Armstrong, M., & Kuppinger, A. (1996). Family-centered intensive care management: A step toward understanding individualized care. *Journal of Child and Family Studies, 5*, 55–65.

Hyde, K. L., Burchard, J. D. & Woodworth, K. (1996). Wrapping services in an urban setting. *Journal of Child and Family Studies, 5*, 67–82.

Rosenblatt, A. (1996). Bows and ribbons, tape and twine: Wrapping the wraparound process for children with multi-system needs. *Journal of Child and Family Studies, 5*(1), 101–116.

Skiba, R. J., Vesper, N., Ong, K., & Bull, B. (1998). Tracking the costs of wraparound: Statewide system of care expenditures. In C. J. Liberton, K. Kutash, & R. M. Friedman (Eds.), *A system of care for children's mental health: Expanding the research base (7th annual research conference proceedings)* pp. 219–224. Tampa, FL: Florida Mental Health Institute.

Stroul, B. A. & Friedman, R. M. (1986). *A system of care for children and youth with severe emotional disturbances.* (Revised edition). Washington, D C: Georgetown University Child Development Center, CASSP Technical Assistance Center.

Tighe, T. A. & Brooks, T. (1995). Evaluating individualized services in Vermont: Intensity and patterns of services, costs, and financing. In C. J. Liberton, K. Kutash, & R. M. Friedman (Eds.), *The 7th annual research conference proceedings, a system of care for children's mental health: Expanding the research base* (pp. 47–52). Tampa, FL: Florida Mental Health Institute Research and Training Center for Children's Mental Health.

VanDenBerg, J. (1989). *Alaska Youth Initiative (AYI): Program background.* Juneau, AK: Author.

VanDenBerg, J. E. & Grealish, E. M. (1996). Individualized services and supports through the wraparound process: Philosophy and procedures. *Journal of Child and Family Studies, 5*, 7–21.

Yoe, J., Santarcangelo, S., Atkins, M., & Burchard, J. (1996). Wraparound care in Vermont: Program development, implementation, and evaluation of a statewide system of individualized services. *Journal of Child and Family Studies, 5*, 22–39.

What Works in Wraparound Programming

Study Authors	Survey Sample	Research Design/Outcome Measure	Findings
Yoe, J., Santarcangelo, S., Atkins, M. & Burchard, J. (1996). Wraparound care in Vermont: Program development, implementation, and evaluation of a statewide system of individualized services. *Journal of Child and Family Studies, 5,* 22–39.	• 40 children and adolescents with emotional and behavioral disturbances who were already in out-of-home placements or at imminent risk of placement • Children who were enrolled in community-based wraparound care for at least 12 months	• Data were collected via reports of therapeutic case managers at intake and three-month intervals with an assessment of residential, educational, and behavioral outcome data.	After 12 months: • Youth resided in significantly less restrictive community-based living arrangements. • Youth exhibited fewer problem behaviors than at intake. • Youth placed in alternative specialized schools decreased from 30% to 12%. • Significant reductions were found in total problem behavior scores, externalizing behaviors, abuse-related behaviors, and internalizing behaviors. • No significant change was found in public externalizing behaviors (such as police contact, alcohol and substance abuse, truancy, and suicide attempts).

| Clark, H., Lee, B., Prange, M. & McDonald, B. (1996). Children lost within the foster care system: Can wraparound service strategies improve placement outcomes? *Journal of Child and Family Studies, 5,* 39–54. | • 54 children (aged 7–15) were randomly assigned to the Fostering Individualized Assistance Program (FIAP) and 78 children randomly assigned to standard practice (SP) foster care in this controlled study
• All children were behaviorally and emotionally disturbed or were found to be at high risk for such disturbances as assessed in the screening process.
• FIAP applied a wraparound strategy to children and their foster, biological and/or adoptive families, involving clinical case management of a wide range of individualized services. | • Repeated-measures between-groups design; randomly assigned at-risk children in foster care to either the FIAP or SP groups
• Data collected across a number of life domains and from multiple sources; trained interviewers systematically gathered information from children, caregivers, foster care case records and placement payment records, delinquency and incarceration records, and student school records. | • Decreases in the rate of placement changes for the FIAP group; increased rate of placement change for SP group.
• Significant differences in FIAP and SP runaway subsets in length of time spent on runaway (e.g. number of days the child was AWOL from the designated placement), with the FIAP children showing greater improvement.
• During the follow-up period (from entrance into the study to approximately 2 years later) marginally significant increase for both groups in number of days of incarceration: FIAP subset increased to a mean of 23 days per year and SP subset increased to a mean of 91 days per year.
• FIAP children significantly more likely than SP children to achieve a permanency placement in a birth, adoptive, or relative home, or through independent living. |

(continued next page)

What Works in Wraparound Programming (*continued*)

Study Authors	Survey Sample	Research Design/Outcome Measure	Findings
Evans, M., Armstrong, M., & Kuppinger, A. (1996). Family-centered intensive care management: A step toward understanding individualized care. *Journal of Child and Family Studies, 5,* 55–65.	• 42 children with serious emotional disturbance (SED), ages 5–12 years from three rural counties in N.Y. state who were referred for out-of-home placement in treatment foster care	• Study assessed outcomes from two types of foster care: (1) a traditional program—family-based treatment (FBT) and (2) a wraparound program—family-centered intensive case management (FCICM). • Data collected via assessments of children and their families using a battery of instruments administered at baseline, six months of treatment, and one year, including the Family Adaptability and Cohesion Evaluation Scale III (FACES III), Client Description Form (CDF), Child Behavior Checklist (CBCL), and the Child and Adolescent Functional Assessment Scales (CAFAS)	• For FCICM children, significant decreases in symptoms from baseline, at six months, and at one year; no significant decreases in symptoms in FBT group. • No significant changes in CBCL scores over first year of treatment in either group. • For FCICM children, significant improvement in mood and emotions, behavior, and role performance at one year; for FBT children, no such significant progress. • No differences between FCICM and FBT groups in family outcomes as measured by the FACES III.
Clarke, R., Schaefer, M., Burchard, J. & Welkowitz, J. (1992). Wrapping community-based mental health services around children with severe behavioral disorder: An evaluation of Project Wraparound. *Journal of Child and Family Studies, 1,* 241–261.	• 19 families and their children were utilized in home data analyses, and 12 additional children were included in school data analyses • The sample was drawn from Vermont's Project Wraparound, a three year demonstration project in which individualized care was provided with the goal of preventing out-of-home child placements	• Assessment of child adjustment via Child Behavior Checklist (CBCL), Teacher Report Form (TRF), Self-Control Rating Scale (SCRC), and the Connors Hyperkinesis Index (CHI) and assessment of the home environment via the Child Well-Being Scales (CWBS).	• Significant improvement in child behavioral adjustment during 6-month intense home intervention period. • No improvements in school behavior. • Significant positive change on Composite and Parental Disposition scores on the CWBS, but no significant changes in Household Adequacy or Child Performance Subscales.

Child Protective Services:

Preventing Child Abuse & Neglect

4

What Works in Nurse Home Visiting Programs

John Eckenrode

D r. C. Henry Kempe [1976], whose work on the "battered child syndrome" ushered in the modern era of public concern over child abuse and neglect, advocated more than 20 years ago for the use of health home visitors for every new parent as a strategy for preventing child abuse and neglect. More recently, the U.S. Advisory Board on Child Abuse and Neglect [1991] echoed this recommendation by urging the federal government to immediately begin phasing in a national program to prevent child maltreatment. Although such a policy has not yet been implemented in the United States, a renewed interest in home visiting has resulted in numerous efforts at the state and local levels to institute such programs and attempts to coordinate and support these efforts by organizations such as the National Committee to Prevent Child Abuse.

The Benefits of Home Visiting Programs

A growing body of research points to a number of benefits of well-designed and well-administered home visiting programs for both children and parents [Olds & Kitzman 1993; American Academy of Pediatrics 1998]. Greater confidence can be given to outcomes that have been produced from clinical trials involving random assignment of families to home visiting services versus routine community care. For example, in an experimental study of home visiting by nurses in Elmira, N.Y., Olds and his colleagues [1986, 1988] reported that nurse-visited women and children, compared to those not receiving home visits, had:

1. *Improved pregnancy outcomes, including:*

   - Better use of community services (nurse-visited women attended 30% more childbirth education classes);
   - Lower level of smoking (nurse-visited mothers smoked 25% fewer cigarettes);
   - Greater informal support of fathers and companions (10% more fathers accompanied mothers to labor);
   - Among women who smoked, 75% fewer preterm deliveries; and
   - Among young adolescents, babies that were 400 grams heavier.

2. *Improved postnatal outcomes for the mothers and children, including:*

   - 43% fewer subsequent pregnancies after four years;
   - Postponement of the birth of a second child an average of 12 months;
   - 82% more months of working;
   - 84% fewer emergency room visits by children for injuries and ingestions;
   - Among poor, unmarried teen mothers, fewer child maltreatment reports during the first two years (19% for comparison group vs. 4% for nurse-visited families) and safer home environments, including use of more appropriate discipline strategies; and
   - IQ scores that were four to five points higher for children of women who smoked during pregnancy.

These findings have been reinforced in a recent follow-up to the Elmira study that provides some of the first evidence for the long-term effects of prenatal and early infancy home visits by nurses [Olds et al. 1997]. This 15-year follow-up has shown that women who were unmarried and low-income when the study began, and who were nurse-visited during pregnancy and their child's infancy had: 31.8% fewer subsequent pregnancies (Figure 1); a 27 month longer interval between the first and

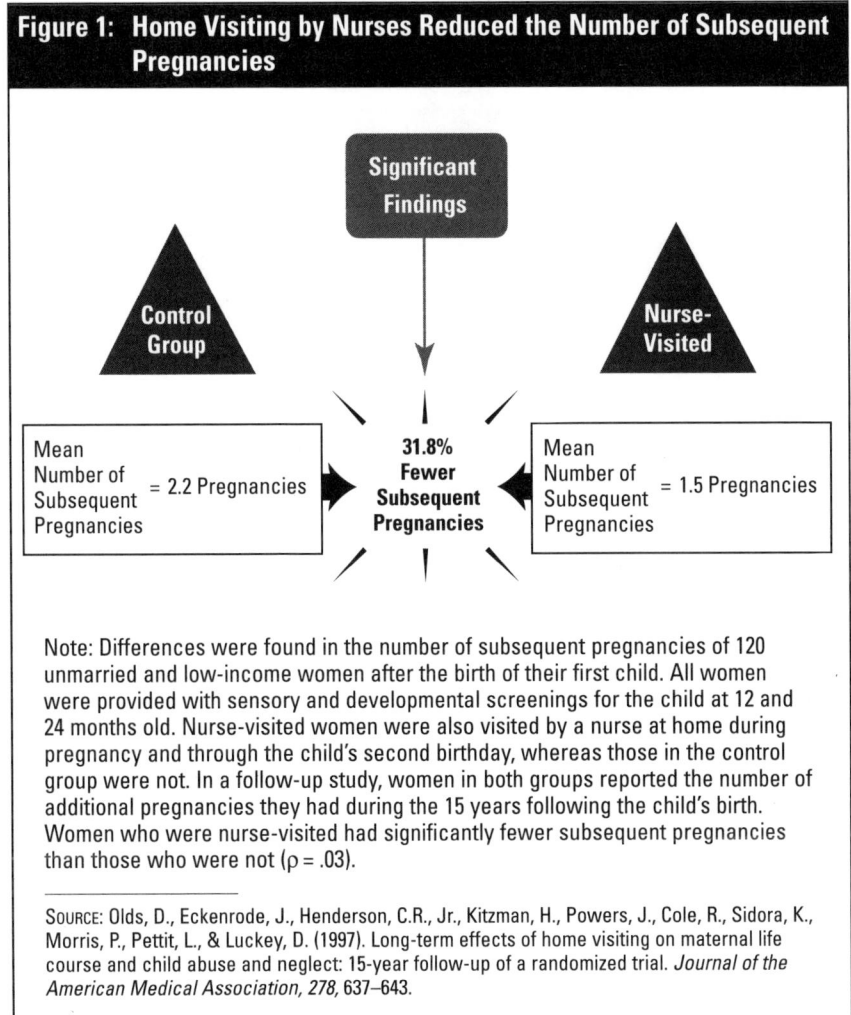

Figure 1: Home Visiting by Nurses Reduced the Number of Subsequent Pregnancies

Significant Findings

Control Group

Nurse-Visited

| Mean Number of Subsequent Pregnancies | = 2.2 Pregnancies |

31.8% Fewer Subsequent Pregnancies

| Mean Number of Subsequent Pregnancies | = 1.5 Pregnancies |

Note: Differences were found in the number of subsequent pregnancies of 120 unmarried and low-income women after the birth of their first child. All women were provided with sensory and developmental screenings for the child at 12 and 24 months old. Nurse-visited women were also visited by a nurse at home during pregnancy and through the child's second birthday, whereas those in the control group were not. In a follow-up study, women in both groups reported the number of additional pregnancies they had during the 15 years following the child's birth. Women who were nurse-visited had significantly fewer subsequent pregnancies than those who were not ($p = .03$).

SOURCE: Olds, D., Eckenrode, J., Henderson, C.R., Jr., Kitzman, H., Powers, J., Cole, R., Sidora, K., Morris, P., Pettit, L., & Luckey, D. (1997). Long-term effects of home visiting on maternal life course and child abuse and neglect: 15-year follow-up of a randomized trial. *Journal of the American Medical Association, 278,* 637–643.

second children; 30 fewer months on welfare (Figure 2); 44% fewer impairments due to drugs and alcohol; and an arrest rate that was one-fifth the rate for mothers in the comparison group.

Over the 15-year period, the number of verified child maltreatment reports on nurse-visited women was almost half that of the women who were not nurse-visited. Among the poor unmarried women, this effect was

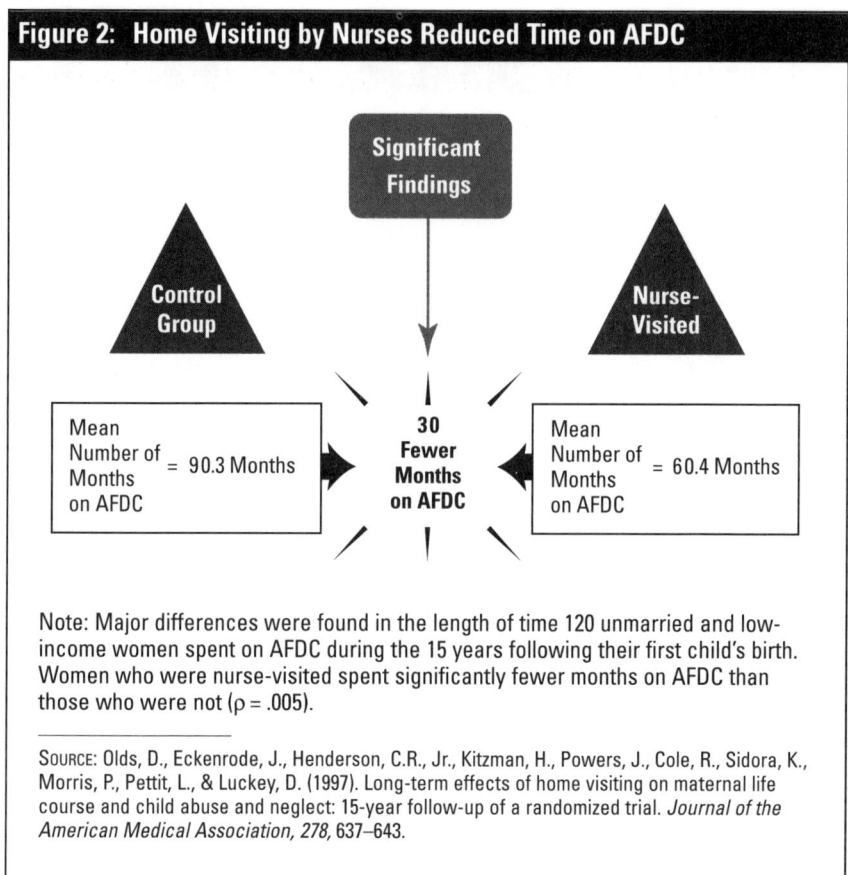

Figure 2: Home Visiting by Nurses Reduced Time on AFDC

Significant Findings

Control Group

Nurse-Visited

Mean Number of Months on AFDC = 90.3 Months

30 Fewer Months on AFDC

Mean Number of Months on AFDC = 60.4 Months

Note: Major differences were found in the length of time 120 unmarried and low-income women spent on AFDC during the 15 years following their first child's birth. Women who were nurse-visited spent significantly fewer months on AFDC than those who were not ($\rho = .005$).

SOURCE: Olds, D., Eckenrode, J., Henderson, C.R., Jr., Kitzman, H., Powers, J., Cole, R., Sidora, K., Morris, P., Pettit, L., & Luckey, D. (1997). Long-term effects of home visiting on maternal life course and child abuse and neglect: 15-year follow-up of a randomized trial. *Journal of the American Medical Association, 278,* 637–643.

even greater. In this group, women not visited had verified child maltreatment reports nearly five times greater than nurse-visited women (Figure 3).

The adolescent children of nurse-visited women also benefited. Children born to mothers who were nurse-visited were, upon reaching adolescence, half as likely to run away or be arrested and only one-fifth as likely to be criminally convicted as adolescents born to mothers who were not nurse-visited. They also reported fewer sexual partners and less alcohol use [Olds et al. 1998].

Figure 3: Home Visiting by Nurses Reduced the Number of Substantiated Reports of Child Abuse and Neglect

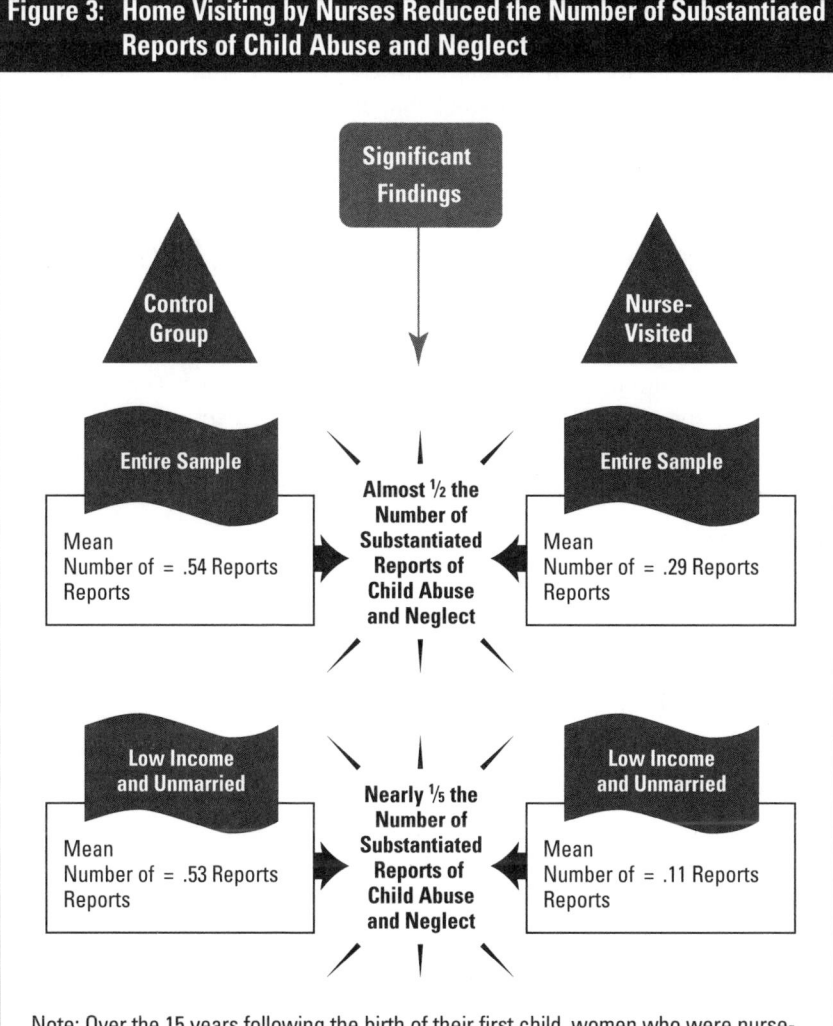

Note: Over the 15 years following the birth of their first child, women who were nurse-visited had significantly fewer substantiated reports of child abuse and neglect than those in the control group (N = 324, ρ < .001). These differences were even more pronounced for low-income and unmarried women (N = 120, ρ < .001). Substantiated reports were taken from state records.

SOURCE: Olds, D., Eckenrode, J., Henderson, C.R., Jr., Kitzman, H., Powers, J., Cole, R., Sidora, K., Morris, P., Pettit, L., & Luckey, D. (1997). Long-term effects of home visiting on maternal life course and child abuse and neglect: 15-year follow-up of a randomized trial. *Journal of the American Medical Association, 278,* 637–643.

The Elmira study has been replicated in an urban, primarily African-American population in Memphis, Tennessee. Early findings suggest some comparability with results from the Elmira study. At 24 months postpartum, for example, nurse-visited mothers had significantly fewer second pregnancies than mothers who were not visited (36% vs. 47%) [Kitzman et al. 1997].

Program Characteristics Associated with Positive Outcomes

Home visiting programs vary considerably in the families served, the timing of visits, the background of the home visitors, the length and number of visits, the amount of supervision that home visitors receive, and the content of the visits [Powell 1993]. Although few experimental studies have directly varied program components, comparisons across studies [Olds & Kitzman 1993] suggest that successful home visiting programs:

- Serve families with the greatest needs;
- Begin during pregnancy;
- Continue through at least the child's second year of life;
- Use nurses as home visitors;
- Provide frequent visits; and
- Employ a comprehensive service model that focuses on numerous aspects of maternal, child, and family health and well-being.

Despite the promising findings from a small number of experimental studies of home visiting, it is also clear that home visiting services alone cannot meet all the needs of families with young children. These services are most likely to succeed when combined with a range of prevention and intervention services in communities [Weiss 1993].

Cost-Effectiveness

Few economic analyses have been conducted of home-visiting programs [Barnett 1993]. There is some evidence, however, that home-visiting programs are cost-effective and that economic benefits build over time. Results from the Elmira study showed that for low-income families, the cost of the program was recovered by the time children reached four years of age. Reductions in welfare services represented the majority of the savings for the nurse-visited women and children. More recently, the Rand Corporation [Karoly et al. 1998] conducted an economic analysis of the Elmira study and estimated that for the highest-risk families in that study, the per-family savings to government was approximately $25,000, compared to the per-family program cost of $6,000 in 1996. Such savings cannot be expected from all home-visiting programs, but these results show that well-designed prevention and early intervention programs yield significant economic benefits to society.

Conclusion

There now appears to be sufficient scientific evidence to suggest that a comprehensive program of home visiting to new parents, especially high-risk parents, by nursing professionals can reduce the incidence of child maltreatment and other adverse child outcomes. There is still, however, much to learn about the characteristics of home-visiting programs that are linked to program success. Over the next few years, there should be better data available to allow an assessment as to whether programs employing paraprofessionals can achieve some of the same benefits seen with programs employing professional home visitors. One of the next major challenges will involve the scaling up of successful experimental programs so that they can be carried out in other communities while not sacrificing the program components that account for their success.

References

American Academy of Pediatrics (1998). The role of home visiting programs in improving health outcomes for children and families. *Pediatrics, 101,* 486–489.

Barnett, W. S. (1993). Economic evaluation of home visiting programs. *The Future of Children, 3,* 93–112.

Karoly, L. A., Greenwood, P. W., Everingham, S. S., Hoube, J., Kilburn, M. R., Rydell, C. P., Sanders, M., & Chiesa, J. (1998). *Investing in our children: What we know and don't know about the costs and benefits of early childhood interventions.* Santa Monica, CA: Rand.

Kempe, C. H. (1976). Approaches to preventing child abuse: The health visitors concept. *American Journal of Diseases of Children, 130,* 941–947.

Kitzman, H., Olds, D., Henderson, C. R., Hanks, C., Cole, R., Tatelbaum, R., McConnochie, K. M., Sidora, K., Luckey, D. W., Shaver, D., Engelhardt, K., James, D., and Barnard, K. (1997). Effect of prenatal and infancy home visiting by nurses on pregnancy outcomes, childhood injuries, and repeated childbearing. *Journal of the American Medical Association, 278,* 644–652.

Olds, D., Eckenrode, J., Henderson, C.R., Jr., Kitzman, H., Powers, J., Cole, R., Sidora, K., Morris, P., Pettit, L., & Luckey, D. (1997). Long-term effects of home visiting on maternal life course and child abuse and neglect: 15-year follow-up of a randomized trial. *Journal of the American Medical Association, 278,* 637–643.

Olds, D., Henderson, C.R., Tatelbaum, R., & Chamberlin, R. (1986). Improving the delivery of prenatal care and outcomes of pregnancy: A randomized trial of nurse home visitation. *Pediatrics, 78,* 65–78.

Olds, D., Henderson, C. R., Tatelbaum, R., & Chamberlin, R. (1988). Improving the life course development of socially disadvantaged mothers: A randomized trial of nurse home visitation. *American Journal of Public Health, 78,* 1436–1445.

Olds, D., Henderson, C. R., Cole, R., Eckenrode, J., Kitzman, H., Pettit, L., Sidora, K., Luckey, D., Morris, P., & Powers, J. (1998). Long-term effects of nurse home visitation on children's criminal and antisocial behavior: 15-year follow-up of a randomized trial. *Journal of the American Medical Association, 280,* 1238–1244.

Olds, D. & Kitzman, H. (1993). Review of research on home visiting. *The Future of Children, 3,* 51–92.

Powell, D. R. (1993). Inside home visiting programs. *The Future of Children, 3,* 23–38.

U.S. Advisory Board on Child Abuse and Neglect. (1991). *Creating caring communities: Blueprint for an effective federal policy on child abuse and neglect.* Washington, DC: U.S. Government Printing Office.

Weiss, H. B. (1993). Home visiting: Necessary but not sufficient. *The Future of Children, 3,* 113–128.

What Works in Nurse Home-Visiting Programs

Study Authors	Survey Sample	Research Design/Outcome Measure	Major Findings
Olds, D., Eckenrode, J., Henderson, C.R., Kitzmar, H., Powers, J., Cole, R., Sidora, K., Morris, P., Pettit, L. & Luckey, D. (1997). Long-term effects of home visitation on maternal life course and child abuse and neglect: 15-year follow-up of a randomized trial. *Journal of American Medical Association, 278,* 637–643.	• 120 low-income, unmarried women who were home-visited by nurses during pregnancy and their child's was an infancy. • Compared to control group that was not nurse-visited	• 15-year follow-up, randomized trial	• Nurse-visited women had 31.8% fewer subsequent pregnancies than control group. • Nurse-visited women were on AFDC 30 fewer months than control group ($p < .005$). • Nurse-visited women had a mean of .29 substantiated child abuse reports compared to a mean of .54 substantiated reports for the control group.

5

What Works in Nonmedical Home Visiting: Healthy Families America

Karen McCurdy

In 1991, the U.S. Advisory Board on Child Abuse and Neglect [Krugman 1993] recommended the implementation of a universal, home-visiting program to reduce incidences of child maltreatment and enhance family functioning. In response to this call, Ronald McDonald's Children's Charities, the National Committee to Prevent Child Abuse and the Hawaii Family Stress Center joined together to develop Healthy Families America (HFA), a national initiative designed to provide universal, community-based, home-visiting services in the context of an integrated social service network. Since its inception in 1992, over 270 HFA programs have been established in 38 states and the District of Columbia, serving close to 18,000 families each year [Daro & Harding 1998].

Each HFA program is built around 11 core elements that have been found or theorized to contribute to enhanced family functioning. Mothers of newborns are invited to receive HFA services on a voluntary basis around the time of the child's birth after an assessment of familial needs. The program offers intensive services (at least weekly for the first year) that are comprehensive, culturally competent, and well-integrated into the community's social service system. Staff receive extensive training and ongoing supervision, and carry limited caseloads to adequately serve families. Both educational credentials and personal characteristics inform staff selection. Although often referred to as a paraprofessional program, a recent survey of HFA home visitors demonstrates great educational variety: 39% of home visitors have some college education, 35% possess a college degree, and 9% received post-secondary education [Daro & Winje 1998]. This model contrasts with the program described in the preceding chapter authored by John Eckenrode which discusses the research on the effectiveness of home visiting by nurses.

Impact of Healthy Families America Programs

A current review of research on HFA programs identifies 15 studies comparing outcomes for visited families to those of nonvisited families [Daro & Harding 1998]. Of these, seven studies have generated preliminary or final reports (See summary table at end of chapter).

Benefits of HFA Programs

Taken together, findings from this body of research note a favorable impact on child health and reductions in abusive and neglectful parenting practices. The key findings are:

- *In states or communities where children have low immunization rates (less than 70%), involvement with a paraprofessional home visitor increases community immunization rates by 10% [Holtzapple 1998; LeCroy et al. 1996; Galano & Huntington undated; Katzev et al. 1998].* Individual children are more likely to receive proper and timely immunizations if the family is involved in an HFA home visiting program. In fact, many HFA programs report rates that meet or exceed 90% of visited children [Daro & Harding 1998].

- *HFA services lead to greater use of preventive health care, including prenatal care [Katzev, et al. 1998]; well-baby visits [Keim 1998]; and involvement with primary health care providers [Duggan et al. 1998].* One study also noted a significant decrease in the number of emergency room visits by families served through HFA [Keim 1998], although two other studies found no impact on the number of ER visits [Center on Child Abuse Prevention Research 1996; Duggan et al. 1998].

- *Prenatal enrollment in HFA services appears to lessen negative birth outcomes for the child.* Research on one program in which services began prenatally found that visited mothers experienced significantly fewer birth complications and pregnancy risks than nonvisited mothers [Galano & Huntington undated].

- *HFA home-visiting programs help to reduce abusive and neglectful parenting behavior.* Of the five studies measuring this outcome, two reported significantly lower verified cases of child maltreatment among visited families [Holtzapple 1998; Krysik et al. 1997], and another noted fewer maternal reports of neglectful behavior by the visited mothers (see Figure 1) [Duggan et al. 1998]. The remaining two studies found lower child abuse and neglect rates among visited as compared to nonvisited families, but these differences were not significant [Center on Child Abuse Prevention Research 1996; Katzev et al. 1998]. Given the increased monitoring of visited families compared to nonvisited families during a time period when many newborns do not come into contact with mandated reporters, these findings are promising.

- *Some evidence suggests that HFA program involvement helps improve specific aspects of parenting.* Visited parents are more likely to report lowered stress [LeCroy et al. 1996], reductions in punitive child-rearing attitudes [Holtzapple 1998; Center on Child Abuse Prevention Research 1996], and increased use of nonviolent discipline methods [Duggan et al. 1998]. These findings are not consistent across all studies as some studies fail to discern impacts on punitive attitudes [Duggan et al. 1998; Galano & Huntington undated] and levels of parental stress [Duggan et al. 1998].

Challenges to HFA Programs

Although these studies suggest that paraprofessional home visiting enhances specific aspects of parenting, HFA has not achieved its desired outcomes in all areas of family functioning. Findings that present challenges to HFA programs include:

- *Visited children looked similar to non-visited children during the first two years of services.* Few child development improvements were seen within two years of birth though some findings suggest that longer-term follow-up is needed before positive effects will be found [Hutcheson et al. 1997; McCurdy 1996].

- *The quantity and quality of maternal support networks showed little change as a result of HFA services.* Although Keim [1998] reports

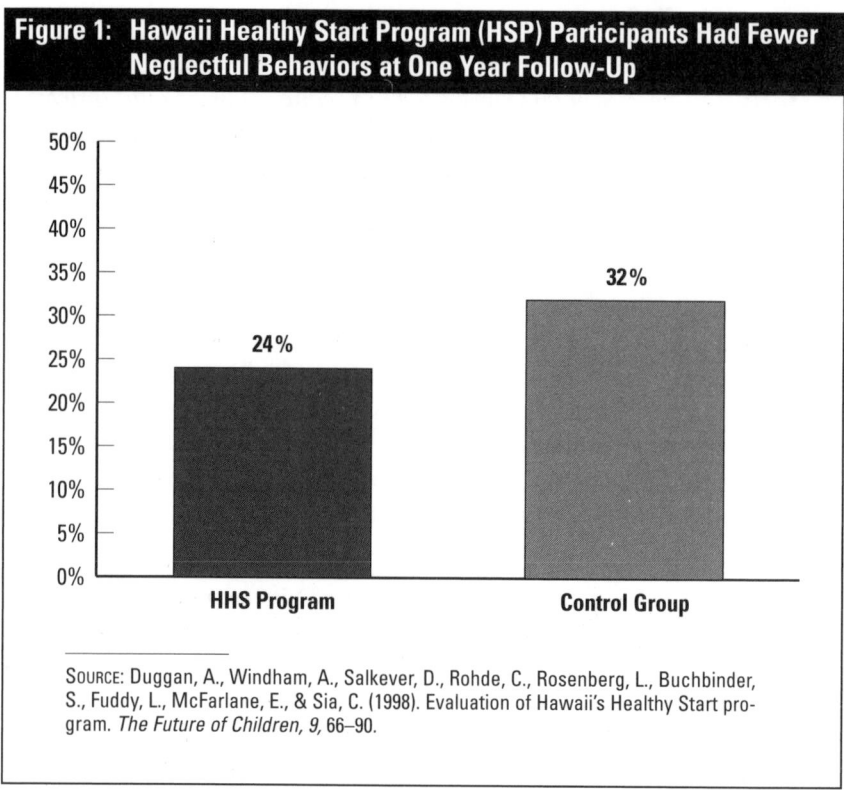

Figure 1: Hawaii Healthy Start Program (HSP) Participants Had Fewer Neglectful Behaviors at One Year Follow-Up

SOURCE: Duggan, A., Windham, A., Salkever, D., Rohde, C., Rosenberg, L., Buchbinder, S., Fuddy, L., McFarlane, E., & Sia, C. (1998). Evaluation of Hawaii's Healthy Start program. *The Future of Children, 9,* 66–90.

that visited mothers take greater advantage of community resources than nonvisited mothers, no significant findings on this outcome emerge from the four studies assessing social support.

- *Paraprofessional home visiting has resulted in mixed outcomes in other areas.* Half of the studies examining the home environment and parent-child relations report improvements [Center on Child Abuse Prevention Research 1996; Galano & Huntington undated; Katzev et al. 1998], and half do not [Holtzapple 1998; Duggan et al. 1998; Keim 1998]. Subsequent pregnancies were reduced at one program [Galano & Huntington undated] but not at another [Center on Child Abuse Prevention Research 1996].

- *Paraprofessional home visiting has faced problems in engaging and retaining eligible families.* Retaining families throughout the HFA program period (three to five years) has proven challenging for many sites, with 20% to 30% of eligible families choosing to forego services [Daro & Harding 1998]. Although such rates are not uncommon in voluntary programs [McCurdy et al. 1995], research needs to investigate the reasons for this retention problem.

Cost-Effectiveness

The seven studies conducted on HFA programs have not provided cost-benefit information.

Conclusion

As one example of a nonmedical home visiting model, Healthy Families America programs help improve child health and family functioning by increasing rates of immunization and preventive health care use and by reducing punitive and neglectful parenting practices. Although these findings are promising, HFA continues to show mixed or no effects in other important areas such as social support, child development, subsequent pregnancies, and the parent-child environment. The absence of cost-effectiveness data, the dearth of follow-up studies, and lower than expected retention rates underscore the need for more research.

References

Center on Child Abuse Prevention Research (1996). *Intensive home visiting: A randomized trial, follow-up and risk assessment study of Hawaii's Healthy Start program.* (NCCAN Grant No. 90–CA–1511). Chicago: National Committee to Prevent Child Abuse.

Daro, D. & Harding, K. (1998). Healthy Families America: Using research to enhance practice. *The Future of Children, 9*(3), 152–176.

Daro, D. & Winje, C. (1998). *Healthy Families America: Profile of program sites.* Chicago: National Committee to Prevent Child Abuse.

Duggan, A., Windham, A., Salkever, D., Rohde, C., Rosenberg, L., Buchbinder, S., Fuddy, L., McFarlane, E., & Sia, C. (1998). Evaluation of Hawaii's Healthy Start program. *The Future of Children, 9*(3), 66–90.

Galano, J. & Huntington, L. (Undated). *Year III evaluation of Healthy Start: 1992–1995.* Abbreviated Version. Williamsburg, VA: William and Mary University.

Holtzapple, E. (1998). Evaluation of Arizona's Healthy Families pilot program. Paper presented at Program Evaluation and Family Violence Research: An International Conference, Durham, NH, July 26–29.

Hutcheson, J., Black, M., Talley, M., Dubowitz, H., & Thompson, B. S. (1997). Risk status and home intervention among children with failure-to-thrive: Follow-up at age 4. *Journal of Pediatric Psychology, 22*(5), 651–668.

Katzev, A., Pratt, C., Henderson, T., & Ozretich, R. (1998). Oregon's Healthy Start effort: 1996–97 status report. Part II — Performance outcomes for children and families. Report to the Oregon Commission on Children and Families. Corvallis, OR: Oregon State University Family Policy Program.

Keim, A. (1998). Healthy Families Walworth County, Wisconsin: A summary of an intensive home visiting project. Paper presented at "Fulfilling the Promise: Getting Parents and Babies Off to a Good Start" Conference, Wisconsin Dells, WI, March 10.

Krugman, R. (1993). Universal home visiting: A recommendation from the U.S. Advisory Board on Child Abuse and Neglect. *The Future of Children, 3*(3), 184–191.

Krysik, J., LeCroy, C., Ashford, J., & Milligan, K. (1997). *Healthy Families Arizona evaluation report.* Prepared for the Arizona Department of Economic Security. Tucson, AZ: LAM Associates.

LeCroy, C., Ashford, J., Krysik, J., & Milligan, K. (1996). Evaluation report for Tucson, Prescott, and Casa Grande sites 1992–1994. Prepared for Arizona Department of Economic Security. Phoenix, AZ: LAM Associates.

McCurdy, K. (1996). Home visiting. Washington, DC: National Center on Child Abuse and Neglect.

McCurdy, K., Hurvis, S. and Clark, J. (1995). Engaging and retaining families in child abuse prevention programs. *The APSAC Advisor, 9*(3), 1, 3–8.

What Works in Nonmedical Home Visiting

Study Authors	Survey Sample	Research Design/ Outcome Measure	Findings
Holtzapple, E. (1998). *Evaluation of Arizona's Healthy Families pilot program.* Paper presented at International Conference, Durham, NH, July 26–29.	• 14 programs in Arizona • Treatment Group = 897 Control Group = 150 • 50% Hispanic, 29% Anglo • Enrolled around birth • Waiting list controls; also compare to community rates for IMZ (Immunization rates)	• Data collected at six and 12 months. • Key outcome measures: Child Health Data, FACES II, Child Abuse Potential (CAP) Inventory, CAN (Child abuse and neglect rates from Child Protective Services records) reports.	• There were significant findings after six months: Child abuse and neglect reports were lower for Healthy Families program families with more than one child and no pre-enrollment reports (3.3% vs. 8.5%). There was also a decrease in CAP scores and higher immunization rates at nine of 14 sites. • There were no significant findings in child abuse and neglect reports for first-time mothers, and on family adaptability and cohesiveness (FACES II).
LeCroy, C., Ashford, J., Krysik, J., & Milligan, K. (1996). *Evaluation report for Tucson, Prescott, and Casa Grande sites, 1992–1994.* Prepared for Arizona Department of Economic Security. Phoenix, AZ: LAM Associates. Krysik, J., LeCroy, C., Ashford, J., & Milligan, K. (1997). *Healthy Families Arizona evaluation report.* Prepared for the Arizona Department of Economic Security. Tucson, AZ: LAM Associates.	• Three programs in Arizona • Treatment Group = 443 Control Group = 136 • Hispanic and Anglo populations, mostly impoverished, single parents • Enrolled around birth • Comparison group of eligible families outside service area on most measures	• Key outcome measures: Parenting Stress Index, CAN reports, IMZ rates. • Data collected at three weeks and six months.	• Significant findings showing advantages for Healthy Families participants were: • Reduced parental stress (Parental Stress Index) Greater parental self-efficacy • Less social isolation • Greater parental attachment • Less depression and better spousal relations Higher immunization rates at birth (99% vs. 74% of state); 97% with complete immunizations at 15 months • Child abuse and neglect rates were lower (4.5% vs. 8.5%).

(continued next page)

What Works in Nonmedical Home Visiting (*continued*)

Study Authors	Survey Sample	Research Design/ Outcome Measure	Findings
Center on Child Abuse Prevention Research. (1996). *Intensive home visitation: A randomized trial, follow-up and risk assessment study of Hawaii's Healthy Start program.* (NCCAN Grant No. 90–CA–1511). Chicago: National Committee to Prevent Child Abuse.	• Two programs in Hawaii • Treatment Group = 157 Control Group = 147 • Multiethnic (Hawaiian, Filipina, Caucasian), impoverished, high psychosocial risk • Enrolled around birth	• Randomized trial; data collected at six and 12 months. • Key outcome measures: — CAP Inventory at 12 months; NCAST Feeding & Teaching; Maternal Social Support Index; HOME Inventory; Confirmed CAN rates (at 18–36 months); Child Health Data; Bayley Scales of Infant Development-II (at 12 months); Michigan Screening Profile of Parenting (MSPP) at six months.	• Significant findings showing advantages for Healthy Families participants at six months: — Higher HOME Inventory Scores; — Greater maternal Involvement; and — Greater maternal sensitivity to cues on subscale (NCAST). — There were no significant findings at six months for ER visits, immunization rates, MSPP, and maternal social support. • Significant findings showing advantages for Healthy Families participants at 12 months: — Reduction in CAP scores NCAST Feeding— increased responsiveness by child. • There were no significant findings at 12 months for — HOME, Bayley, maternal social support, ER visits; immunization rates (82% vs. 82%), and child abuse and neglect rates (3.3% vs. 6.8%).

Duggan, A., Windham, A., Salkever, D., Rohde, C., Rosenberg, L., Buchbinder, S., Fuddy, L., McFarlane, E., & Sia, C. (1998). Evaluation of Hawaii's Healthy Start program. *The Future of Children, 9*, 66–90.	• 6 programs in Hawaii
	• Treatment Group = 373
	  Control Group 1 = 270
	  Control Group 2 = 41
	• Enrolled around birth
		• Randomized trial.
		• Data collected at one and two years.
		• Key outcome measures:
		  — Attachment style questionnaire; Maternal Efficacy; NCAST-Community Life Skills; Conflict Tactics Scale-Revised; HOME Inventory; NCAST Feeding Scale; Maternal Social Support Index; CES-Depression Scale; RAND Social Health Battery; Pre-School Language Scale; Mental Health Inventory.
			• Significant differences showing advantages for Healthy Families participants at one year:
			  — Reduced partner violence;
			  — Better general mental health;
			  — Greater use of nonviolent discipline; and
			  — Fewer maternal reports of neglectful behavior (23% vs. 32%).
			• Significant differences showing advantages for Healthy Families participants at two years:
			  — Has primary health care provider;
			  — Mother works (p = .09);
			  — Less partner violence; and
			  — Greater use of nonviolent discipline.
			• There were no significant findings for
			  — HOME, NCAST, attachment, efficacy, social support, child outcomes, depression, and immunization rates (82% vs. 81% at one year).

(continued next page)

What Works in Nonmedical Home Visiting (*continued*)

Study Authors	Survey Sample	Research Design/ Outcome Measure	Findings
Katzev, A., Pratt, C., Henderson, T., & Ozretich, R. (1998). Oregon's Healthy Start effort: 1996–97 status report. Part II—Performance outcomes for children and families. *Report to the Oregon Commission on Children and Families*. Corvallis, OR: Oregon State University Family Policy Program.	• 13 programs in Oregon • Treatment Group = varies per outcome, around 1,500 for most • Enrolled around birth	• Some comparisons to state wide data and population norms • Key outcome measures: IMZ rates, prenatal care, HOME Inventory, CAN rates.	• Significant findings showing advantages for Healthy Families participants: — Higher immunization rates at two years (96% vs. 67%); — Use of prenatal care for second child vs. first (94% vs. 67%); and — Favorable HOME Inventory scores. — There were no significant findings for child abuse and neglect rates (2.0 vs. 2.7).
Galano, J. & Huntington, L. (Undated). *Year III Evaluation of Healthy Start: 1992–1995. Abbreviated Version.* Williamsburg, VA: William and Mary University.	• two programs in Virginia • Treatment Group = 435 Control Group = 178 • Single mothers, 70% African-American; 26% Caucasian • Enrolled prenatally	• Randomized trial • Data collected at six, 12 and 24 months. • Some comparisons to state rates • 2.3 visits per month • Key outcome measures: CAP Inventory, Child Health Data, NCAST-Difficult Life Circumstances & Community Life Skills, Batelle Developmental Inventory, HOME Inventory, Maternal Social Support Index, NCAST Feeding & Teaching.	• Significant findings showing advantages for Healthy Families participants at six months: — Fewer birth complications (0.2 vs 0.48); — Lower pregnancy risk scores (0.2 vs. 0.8); — Fewer teen repeat births (9% compared to 35.8% in Hampton, 29.8% statewide); — Increase in HOME Inventory at one and two years; — Increase in NCAST; and — Higher immunization rate (92% vs. 74% control group, 60–74% statewide). • There were no significant findings for birthweight, gestational age, maternal social support; Batelle, and CAP.

| Keim, A. (1998). Healthy Families Walworth County, Wisconsin: A summary of an intensive home visitation project. Paper presented at "Fulfilling the Promise: Getting Parents and Babies Off to a Good Start" Conference. Wisconsin Dells, Wisconsin, March 10. | • One program in Wisconsin
• Treatment Group = 34 Control Group = 23
• First-time mothers only; mostly Latina, poor, and adolescent
• Enrolled around birth
• Comparison group with children born prior to program start | • Data collected at one year.
• Two visits per month.
• Key outcome measures:
 — Child Health Data;
 — Maternal Social Support Index;
 — Community Resource;
 — Home Screening Questionnaire. | • Significant findings showing advantages for Healthy Families participants:
 — Greater utilization of community resources
 — More regular child health
 — Less ER care (41% vs. 56%)
 — Trend ($p < .10$) to breastfeed longer.
• There were no significant findings for immunization rates, maternal social support, and Home Screening Questionnaire. |

6

What Works in Child Protective Services Reforms

Amy L. Gordon

From 1986 to 1996, the number of reports of child abuse and neglect increased by approximately 44% [Petit & Curtis 1997; National Committee to Prevent Child Abuse 1997; U.S. Department of Health and Human Services 1997, 1998]. The capacity of the child protective services (CPS) system to adequately respond to this increase has been greatly challenged. As a result, several states and jurisdictions have initiated reforms to improve their approaches to screening and investigating reports of child abuse and neglect.

CPS reforms are generally characterized by replacing a uniform screening approach with a differential and more flexible response to investigating reports of child abuse and neglect. The aim of such efforts is to enhance the public agency's ability to ensure that each child who is at risk of abuse and neglect receives the appropriate level of intervention to prevent further maltreatment. Two primary components of current CPS reforms are the investigation of only those cases that are of a criminal nature and work with law enforcement in these investigations, and the diversion of low and moderate-risk families to community-based services [Farrow 1997; Pelton 1998; Waldfogel 1998; Weber 1998]. A third emphasis of many reforms is establishing partnerships with community-based services in order to serve a greater number of families and promote community involvement in child protection.

Florida, Iowa, Massachusetts, Michigan, Missouri, and Virginia are among the states that have recently implemented CPS reforms. Their primary goals include decreasing the recurrence of child maltreatment, serving a greater number of moderate and low-risk families, and strengthening ties between CPS and the community [Massachusetts Department of Social Services undated; Michigan Department of Children and Families undated; Virginia Department of Social Services, n.d.; Waldfogel 1998]. In addition to these state initiatives, the Edna McConnell Clark Foundation awarded four grants in 1995 to reform CPS Cedar Rapids, Iowa, Jacksonville, Florida, Louisville, Kentucky, and St. Louis, Missouri [Center for the Study of Social Policy 1998]. These initiatives also aim to develop a differential response to families and expand collaboration with community services.

The Child Welfare League of America (CWLA) also has recently initiated demonstration projects in Montgomery County, Maryland, and Alameda County, California, to promote child safety and community involvement in CPS [Kaplan 1999]. The Protecting America's Children initiative will involve working with several other communities nationwide to develop and evaluate comparable child protection reforms at the local level.

The Impact of Dual Response Systems

Florida and Missouri have made the greatest progress to date in evaluating the impact of their CPS reforms [Waldfogel 1998]. Both of these states developed a dual response system with two major components. First, investigations are limited to only the most serious cases—physical or sexual abuse and severe neglect. CPS collaborates with law enforcement in investigating these cases. Social workers assess child and family needs and police officers gather criminal evidence. Second, voluntary family assessments and referrals to community-based services are offered to families whose cases are determined to be less serious. Florida's evaluation occurred in 1996 and assessed reforms piloted in 15 districts [Hernandez & Barrett 1996]. The evaluation gathered information on 850,000 cases using focus groups, interviews, case studies, and case record reviews. Missouri's evaluation compared the outcomes of more than 900 families from 14 pilot counties and 14 comparison counties served from 1994–1997 [Siegel et al. 1998]. Information was gathered from case records, surveys and interviews.

Findings from the Florida and Missouri evaluations suggest that implementation of a dual response system can lead to positive outcomes for children and families [Hernandez & Barrett 1996; Siegel et al. 1998]. The CPS reforms in these two states were found to be related to improvements in child safety, family integrity and satisfaction, and community involvement in child protection.

Findings Related to Child Safety

Major findings on the impact of CPS reforms on child safety are:

- In the 22 months following implementation of the dual response system, Missouri's pilot counties had lower rates of repeated referrals for child abuse or neglect than the comparison counties (38% vs. 40%). Significantly higher rates of re-referrals were found among families with three or more children, families whose children lacked basic necessities or who were not providing adequate supervision and care, and parents who lacked proper educational concern for their children.

- In Missouri, risk assessments conducted at the beginning and end of agency contact indicated that child safety improved for moderate and low-risk families receiving voluntary family assessments and referrals for services.

- CPS investigators in Missouri's pilot counties were more likely to have contacted prosecutors in cases involving serious injury than CPS investigators in comparison counties.

- In Florida, the correlation between the initial decision to remove a child from the home to ensure safety and the final decision to place the child in out-of-home care was higher for pilot counties than for other counties (39% vs. 36%).

Findings Related to Family Integrity and Satisfaction

Key findings on the impact of CPS reforms on family integrity and satisfaction are:

- In Florida, cases in pilot counties were 32% more likely to be dismissed without court involvement than in other counties.

- Case durations (length of time the case was open for investigation) in Florida were shorter in pilot counties than in other counties (56 vs. 72 days).

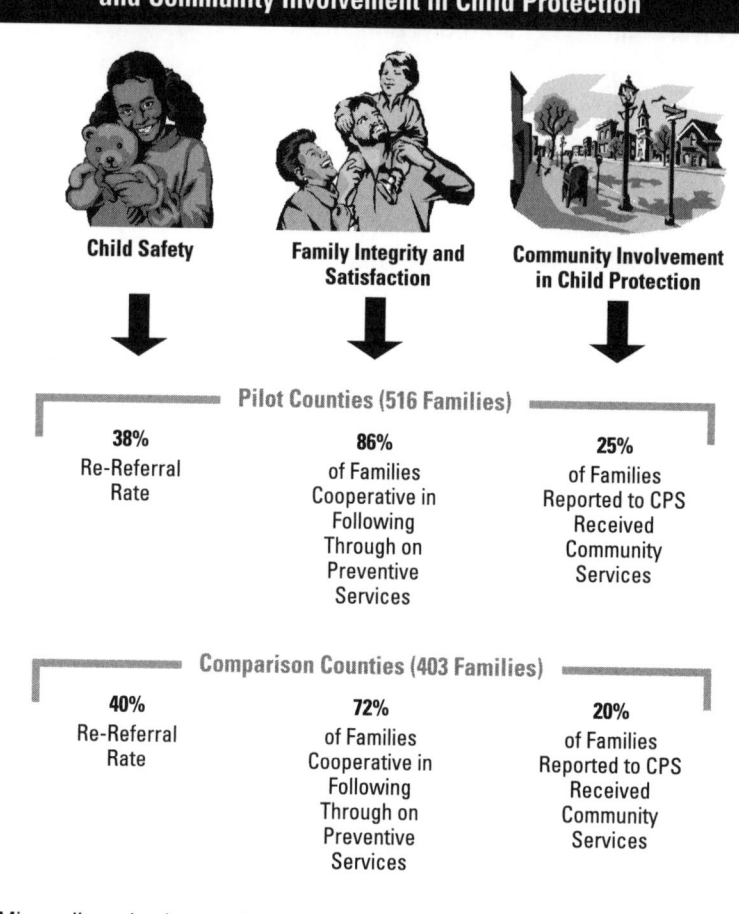

Figure 1: CPS Dual Response System in Missouri Increased Positive Outcomes in Child Safety, Family Integrity and Satisfaction, and Community Involvement in Child Protection

Child Safety

Family Integrity and Satisfaction

Community Involvement in Child Protection

Pilot Counties (516 Families)

38%
Re-Referral Rate

86%
of Families Cooperative in Following Through on Preventive Services

25%
of Families Reported to CPS Received Community Services

Comparison Counties (403 Families)

40%
Re-Referral Rate

72%
of Families Cooperative in Following Through on Preventive Services

20%
of Families Reported to CPS Received Community Services

Missouri's evaluation was based on a quasi-experimental design that compared the outcomes of 14 pilot counties with those of 14 comparison counties. The evaluation used a pre/post-test design, collecting data over a four-year period from 1994–1997 for 516 pilot families and 403 comparison families. Differences between re-referred rates and percentage of families who were cooperative in following through on preventive services were found to be statistically significant at $p < .05$. Methods of data collection included case record reviews, surveys, and interviews.

Source: Siegel, G.L., Loman, A.L., Sherburne, D.S., Aldrich, D., Bergsma, J.L., DeWeese-Boyd, M., Collins, M., Loman, M.J., & McGhee, B. (1998). *Child protection services family assessment and response demonstration impact evaluation: Digest of findings and conclusions.* St. Louis, MO: Institute of Applied Research.

- Missouri experienced a 15% decline (35 days) between 1993 and 1997 in the number of days families in the pilot counties were involved with the agency.
- In Missouri, more families in pilot counties cooperated with services than those in comparison counties (86% versus 72%).
- Family satisfaction in Missouri increased among families in pilot counties as evidenced by their receptivity to services, belief that they improved as a result of services, and their view of the agency as a source of support.

Findings Related to Community Involvement in Child Protection

Major findings on the impact of CPS reforms on community involvement in child protection are:

- In Florida, the use of community-based services increased by 11% from 1991–1995 for families who had been reported to CPS in pilot counties.
- In Missouri, 25% of families in pilot counties received community services as opposed to 20% of families in comparison counties. Families who lacked basic needs, those in which children experienced milder forms of physical abuse, and those in which there were conflicts between parents and older children were the most likely to receive community services.
- Families in Missouri's pilot counties experienced greater timeliness in the initiation of services from the time of the CPS report than those in comparison counties (17 days vs. 35 days).

Conclusion

Evaluations of the Florida and Missouri reforms suggest that implementing a dual response system, in which only the most serious cases are investigated and less serious cases are referred to community-based services, can result in positive changes in child safety, family satisfaction, and community involvement in child protection. Although the evaluation results are modest, they indicate that the CPS reforms in these states were related to lower rates of re-referral, improved family satisfaction, and increased use of community services. Greater impacts may result

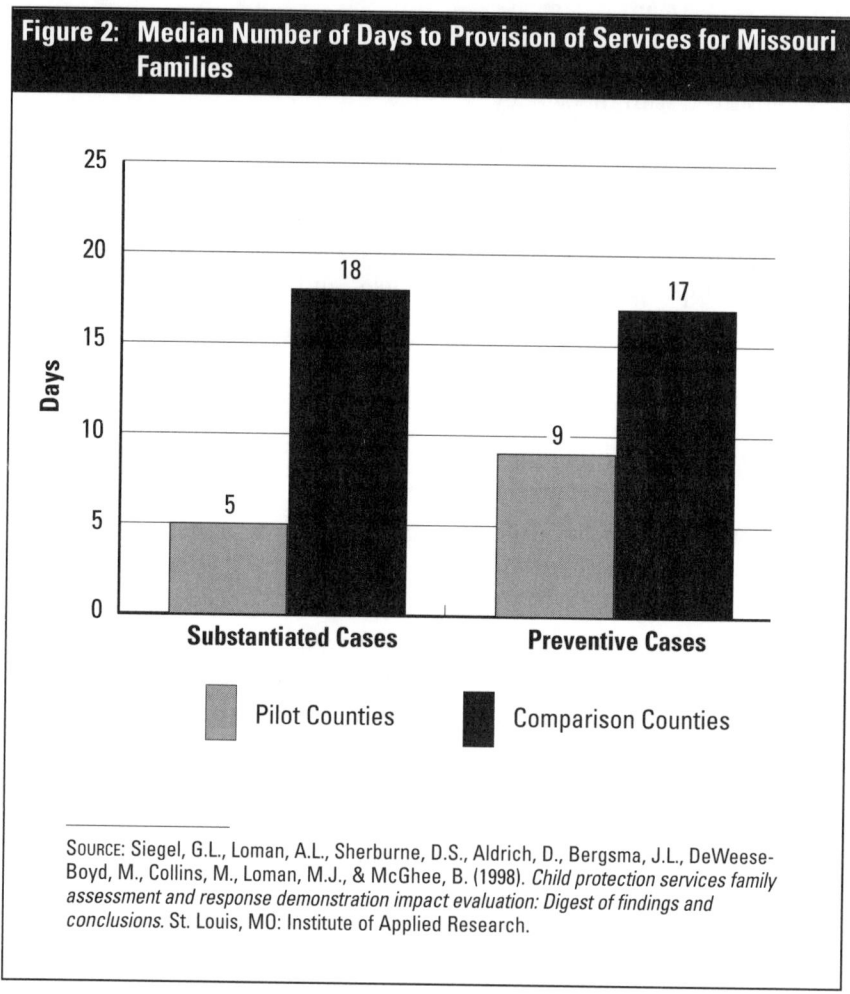

Figure 2: Median Number of Days to Provision of Services for Missouri Families

SOURCE: Siegel, G.L., Loman, A.L., Sherburne, D.S., Aldrich, D., Bergsma, J.L., DeWeese-Boyd, M., Collins, M., Loman, M.J., & McGhee, B. (1998). *Child protection services family assessment and response demonstration impact evaluation: Digest of findings and conclusions.* St. Louis, MO: Institute of Applied Research.

from reforms that include longer demonstration periods and increased resources for hiring more caseworkers, reducing caseloads and providing additional services for families [Siegel et al. 1998]. Further evaluation of CPS reforms is needed to substantiate the findings from Florida and Missouri as well as to identify the specific factors that lead to or hinder success. With the many reform initiatives currently underway, the field of child welfare is well-positioned to evaluate what works in child protective services.

References

Center for the Study of Social Policy. (1998). *The Initiative: What is the Community Partnerships for Protecting Children Initiative?* Online: www.csap.org

Farrow, F. (1997). *Child protection: Building community partnerships getting from here to there.* Boston: John F. Kennedy School of Government, Harvard University.

Hernandez, M. & Barrett, B. A. (1996). *Evaluation of Florida's Family Services Response System.* Tampa: University of Southern Florida's Mental Health Institute.

Kaplan, C. (January 1999). Personal correspondence. Project Manager, Protecting America's Children: It's Everybody's Business. Montgomery County, MD.

Massachusetts Department of Social Services. (undated). *Multidisciplinary assessment teams: An evaluation of the implementation process.* Boston: Massachusetts Department of Social Services.

Michigan Department of Children and Families. (undated). Child protection: *Working together as community partners.* Lansing: Michigan Department of Children and Families.

National Committee to Prevent Child Abuse. (1997). *Current trends in child abuse reporting and fatalities: The results of the 1996 annual fifty state survey.* Chicago: National Committee to Prevent Child Abuse.

Pelton, L. H. (1998). Four commentaries: How we can better protect children from abuse and neglect. *The Future of Children: Protecting Children from Abuse and Neglect,* 8(1), 120–132.

Petit, M. R. & Curtis, P. A. (1997). *Child abuse and neglect: A look at the states—1997 CWLA stat book.* Washington, DC: CWLA Press.

Siegel, G. L., Loman, A. L., Sherburne, D. S., Aldrich, D., Bergsma, J. L., DeWeese-Boyd, M., Collins, M., Loman, M. J., & McGhee, B. (1998). *Child protection services family assessment and response demonstration impact evaluation: Digest of findings and conclusions.* St. Louis, MO: Institute of Applied Research.

U.S. Department of Health and Human Services, National Center on Child Abuse and Neglect. (1997). *Child Maltreatment 1995: Reports from States to the National Child Abuse and Neglect Data System.* Washington, DC: U.S. Government Printing Office.

U.S. Department of Health and Human Services, National Center on Child Abuse and Neglect. (1998). *Child Maltreatment 1996: Reports from States to the National Child Abuse and Neglect Data System.* Washington, DC: U.S. Government Printing Office.

Virginia Department of Social Services. (n.d.). *The multiple response system: A new approach to protect children.* Richmond: Virginia Department of Social Services.

Waldfogel, J. (1998). Rethinking the paradigm for child protection. *The Future of Children: Protecting Children from Abuse and Neglect,* 8(1), 104–119.

Weber, M. W. (1998). Four commentaries: How we can better protect children from abuse and neglect. *The Future of Children: Protecting Children from Abuse and Neglect,* 8(1), 120–132.

What Works in Child Protective Services Reforms

Study Authors	Survey Sample	Research Design/ Outcome Measure	Findings
Hernandez, M., & Barrett, B.A. (1996). *Evaluation of Florida's family services response system.* Tampa, FL: University of Southern Florida's Mental Health Institute.	• 850,000 cases reported to Florida's CPS hotline from 1991–1995	• Pre/post-test design was used to compare baseline and outcome data for counties that successfully implemented reforms with those that did not. • Case record reviews were completed for 850,000 cases. • Focus groups, interviews, and case studies were also conducted as part of the evaluation.	• The correlation between the initial decision to remove a child from the home to ensure his/her safety and the final decision to place the child in out-of-home care was higher for pilot counties than for other counties (39% vs. 36%). ** • Cases in pilot counties were 32% more likely to be dismissed without court involvement. ** • Case durations (length of time case was open for investigation) were shorter in pilot counties than in other counties (56 vs. 72 days). ** • The use of community-based services increased by 11% from 1991–1995 for families in pilot counties who had been reported to CPS. ** ** Statistically significant at $\rho < .01$.

(continued next page)

What Works in Child Protective Services Reforms (continued)

Study Authors	Survey Sample	Research Design/ Outcome Measure	Findings
Siegel, G.L., Loman, A.L., Sherburne, D.S., Aldrich, D., Bergsma, J.L., DeWeese-Boyd, M., Collins, M., Loman, M.J., & McGhee, B. (1998). *Child protection services family assessment and response demonstration impact evaluation: Digest of findings and conclusions.* St. Louis, MO: Institute of Applied Research.	• 14 pilot counties and 14 comparison counties • 516 families from pilot counties and 403 families from comparison counties	• A quasi-experimental design to compare the outcomes of 14 pilot counties with those of 14 comparison counties. • A pre/post-test design, collecting data over a four-year period from 1994–1997 • The primary method of data collection was a review of the case records of 516 families from pilot counties and 403 families from comparison counties. • Surveys and interviews were also conducted as part of the evaluation.	• In the 22 months following implementation of the dual response system, pilot counties had lower rates of repeated referrals for child abuse or neglect than the comparison counties (38% vs. 40%). • In Missouri, risk assessments conducted at the beginning and end of agency contact indicated that child safety improved for moderate and low-risk families receiving voluntary family assessments and referrals for services. • CPS investigators in pilot counties were more likely to have contacted prosecutors in cases involving serious injury than CPS investigators in comparison counties. • Missouri experienced a 15% decline (35 days) between 1993 and 1997 in the number of days families in the pilot counties were involved with the agency. • More families in pilot counties cooperated with services than those in comparison counties (86% vs. 72%). • Family satisfaction increased among families in pilot counties as evidenced by their receptivity to services, belief that they improved as a result of services, and their view of the agency as a source of support. • 25% of families in pilot counties received services as opposed to 20% of families in comparison counties. • Families in pilot counties experienced greater timeliness in the initiation of services from the time of the CPS report than those in comparison counties (17 days vs. 35 days). * Statistically significant at $p < .05$.

7

What Works in Safety and Risk Assessment for Child Protective Services

Dana Hollinshead and John Fluke

R isk assessment has been an integral part of child protective services since the field's inception. The formalization of the process and decision-making inherent in risk assessment, however, took place only a little over a decade ago. In 1984, in response to a rash of child fatalities and a concern about resource and services allocation, Illinois developed a 13-factor model aimed to structure and guide the decisions of child protective services investigators regarding risk [National Resource Center on Child Abuse and Neglect 1994]. Since then, at least 42 states have developed, adopted, or adapted some form of risk assessment and made it an integral part of caseworkers' decision-making practices [Berkowitz 1991; Cicchinelli 1991]. Several states have completed more than one development cycle as the knowledge base concerning risk and safety has improved. While the goals of and approaches to risk assessment vary, at the core is an understanding that the use of risk assessment leads to better decisions concerning the safety of children.

Goals of Risk Assessments

States use risk assessments to address several goals. Among these goals, risk assessments aim to:

- Guide and structure decision-making;
- Predict future harm and classify cases;

- Aid in resource management by identifying service needs for children and families served; and

- Facilitate communication within the agency and other community stakeholders.

The current conceptual environment for risk assessment in Child Protective Services (CPS) agencies includes both assessments for safety (or immediate risk) and risk (which includes immediate risk but also addresses longer-term risk concerns). Other terms have been suggested to describe risk assessment tools including "structured decision-making" and "guided assessment." Both risk and safety assessments are generally referred to as risk assessment.

A conceptual model illustrating the relationship between safety and risk appears in Figure 1. Both types of assessments are found together in unified safety and risk assessment models, but they are sometimes distinct, depending on how an agency has implemented its approach. Some states may have implemented risk assessment only and some have implemented only safety assessment.

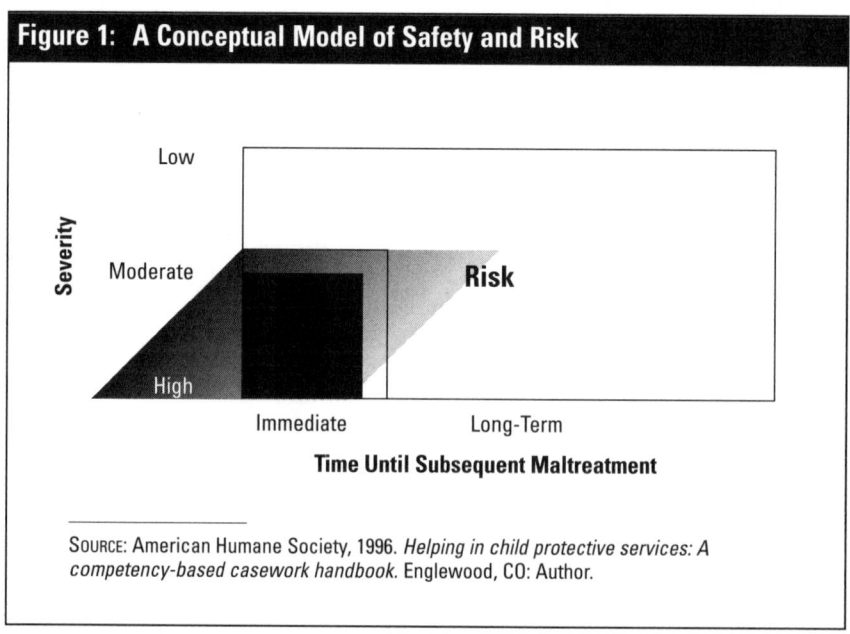

Figure 1: A Conceptual Model of Safety and Risk

Severity: Low, Moderate, High

Risk

Immediate   Long-Term

Time Until Subsequent Maltreatment

SOURCE: American Humane Society, 1996. *Helping in child protective services: A competency-based casework handbook.* Englewood, CO: Author.

Models of Safety Assessment

Safety assessment has been an aspect of risk assessment since the advent of the Child at Risk Field (CARF) in the late 1980s [DePanfillis & Scannapieco 1994]. Although there are many variants of safety assessment in use across many states, almost all can be traced to the original CARF model. Safety assessments are designed to address immediate concerns that are likely to result in harm to children in the very near future. These models usually incorporate factors that are concerned with immediate conditions that might cause harm or permit harm to continue if some action is not taken quickly.

Models of Risk Assessment

Currently, three core models exist in the field of risk assessment: (1) actuarial models, (2) consensus-based models, and (3) composite actuarial-consensus models. Over time, as the research base in the field has developed, distinctions regarding model types have become less meaningful.

- *Actuarial models* are developed by selecting risk factors identified through research as reliable and valid factors associated with risk of future harm (recurrence). These models require case workers to rate each factor using scaled values. In some cases, these factor ratings are applied to a formula that automatically generates an overall risk rating. Often, these models are developed based exclusively on data from the prior experience of the service delivery system.

- *Consensus models* are developed using factors that are identified by seasoned child welfare professionals as being most closely linked to risk of future harm and whether there are empirical data to support these links. Like the actuarial approach, case workers score factors that are based on anchored descriptions. The anchors and the specific factors, however, are not directly supported by specific empirical research.

- *Composite actuarial-consensus models* emphasize factors supported by empirical research but can include factors identified by child welfare professionals as important and relevant to risk of future harm. Where research on specific factors is available, the scales applied in these analyses are used.

Whatever the form chosen, formalized risk assessment appears to support case worker decision-making, provided that attention is paid to adequate implementation [Doueck et al. 1993]. Implementation includes attention to design, training, integration with policy, and ongoing support. With adequate implementation, virtually any model will be effective in identifying risks and supporting appropriate action; without adequate implementation, any model is likely to fail.

Development and Support of Risk Assessment

The development of and support for risk assessment factors and models has evolved through forums, federal grants for research, codification in child welfare best practice, and state initiatives. For over a decade, the American Public Welfare Association (now the American Public Human Services Association) and the American Humane Association (AHA) have cosponsored an annual roundtable focused on practice and research issues in risk assessment. The roundtables have provided a forum for child welfare professionals—including frontline staff, administrators, judges, policymakers, and researchers—from across the country to share their experiences and expertise and identify challenges and ideas for further developing risk assessment. The dual focus of the roundtables has enabled child welfare professionals to bridge the typical gap between practice concerns and research concerns in child protective services and establish consensus on factors related to child risk.

All national CPS best practice standards include the use of risk assessment [AHA 1996; Child Welfare League of America 1999; Council on Accreditation 1996; National Association of Public Child Welfare Administrators 1997]. The federal government, including the National Center on Child Abuse and Neglect (now the Office of Child Abuse and Neglect (OCAN)), has sponsored several forums addressing risk and safety assessment. OCAN also has funded several research grant programs aimed at improving the knowledge base in this area. Further, several states have committed significant resources to develop and evaluate risk assessment models over the past 15 years.

Although formalized risk assessment originally began as an activity within child protective services investigations, its use and focus quickly expanded. In many states, risk assessments are now conducted at other decision points in cases, including decisions regarding the placement of children in out-of-home care, reunification with their families, and case closure. Research to support the development of risk-based tools for decisions about placement of children and successful reunification is underway. Risk assessment tools to address specific problem areas such as substance abuse and domestic violence are also in development. The concept of incorporating risk assessment at decision points throughout the life of a case and to target the assessment to more specific decision-making needs is a fundamental tenet of risk assessment thinking [National Resource Center on Child Abuse and Neglect 1994]. To date, however, the bulk of the research on risk assessment has centered on re-referrals, or recurrence of child abuse and neglect.

Research shows that risk and safety assessments yield positive outcomes for children and families in the child welfare system. For example, the implementation of an immediate safety assessment protocol in Illinois, the Child Endangerment Risk Assessment Protocol, resulted in a 23% decrease of recurrence (substantiated allegations of abuse or neglect) in a six-month period. Three years after the implementation of this tool, the reduction in recurrence rates stood at 28.6% [Fluke et al. 1999a]. Studies of the connection between an overall rating of risk and the likelihood of re-referral reveal that a higher overall risk rating by a case worker was more often associated with re-referral than a lower overall risk rating. A study of risk assessment in Rhode Island revealed that 63% of families classified as high-risk had a subsequent substantiated report of maltreatment and only 6% of families classified at low-risk had a subsequent substantiated report [Wagner & Squadrito 1993]. Further, Johnson [1996] suggests that valid risk assessment accurately predicts maltreatment at a rate of 65%–85%.

The Issue of Predictive Validity

At this time, predictive validity research has established empirical support for some, but not all, factors used by risk assessment models across the nation. The most common measure of the predictive validity of factors is an association between each factor, or combinations thereof, and whether or not a case is re-referred and whether it is subsequently found valid (recurrence) [Fluke et al. 1999b]. Although some factors have yet to be tested, there is recognition that factors supported by broad consensus also should be used to conduct a robust assessment of safety and risk. For example, although there is no empirical support, common sense suggests that "a pattern of escalating severity of harm to a child" indicates a risk and safety concern. It is important to note that risk factors supported by consensus, in addition to factors supported by empirical research, reflect the collective knowledge and experiences of child welfare professionals from across the nation. Even so, the goal of any model implementation process should be to test for empirically supported risk assessment factors as soon as it is feasible.

Conclusion

Although risk and safety assessments have been fundamental features of social work since the field's inception, the formalization and standardization of these practices are fairly new phenomena. While more research is needed on risk and safety assessment, research on the predictive validity of such assessment tools suggests that standardized risk and safety assessments assist social workers in their decision-making and may result in better targeting of services for abused and neglected children and their families.

References

American Humane Association. (1996). *Helping in child protective services: A competency-based casework handbook.* Englewood, CO: Author.

Berkowitz, S. (1991). Key Findings from the State Survey Component of the Study of High-Risk Child Abuse and Neglect Groups. Paper presented by Westat, Inc. and presented to the National Center on Child Abuse and Neglect State Liaison Officers Meeting. Baltimore, MD: Westat, April 3–5.

Child Welfare League of America. (1999). *CWLA Standards of Excellence for Services for Abuse or Neglected Children and their Families.* Washington, DC: Author.

Cicchinelli, L. (1991). *Proceedings of the Symposium on Risk Assessment in Child Protective Services.* Washington, DC: National Center on Child Abuse and Neglect.

Council on Accreditation. (1996). *Council on Accreditation 1997 Standards for behavioral health care services and community support and education services.* New York: Council on Accreditation.

DePanfilis, D. & Scannapieco, M. (1994). Assessing safety of children at risk of maltreatment: Decisionmaking models. *Child Welfare, 73* (3), 229–245.

Doueck, H., English, D., DePanfilis, D., & Moote, G. (1993). Decision-making in child protective services: A comparison of selected risk assessment systems. *Child Welfare* 72(5), 441–452.

Fluke, J., Edwards, M., & Bussey, M. (1999a). Outcome evaluation, CERAP safety assessment: Three-year follow-up. Englewood, CO: American Humane Association.

Fluke, J., Yuan, Y. Y., & Edwards, M. (1999b). Recurrence of maltreatment: An application of the National Child Abuse and Neglect Data System (NCANDS). *Child Abuse & Neglect, 23*(7), 633–650.

Johnson, W. (1996). *Risk assessment research: Progress and future directions.* Unpublished Presentation for the Tenth Annual CPS Risk Assessment Roundtable, San Francisco, CA, June 13–15.

National Association of Public Child Welfare Administrators. (1997). *Draft revised guidelines for a model system of protective services for abused and neglected children and their families.* Washington, DC: American Public Human Services Association.

National Resource Center on Child Abuse and Neglect. (1994). *Risk assessment technical brief.* Englewood, CO: American Humane Association.

Wagner, D. & Squadrito, E. (1993). Results of Rhode Island risk assessment research. In *Seventh National Roundtable on CPS Risk Assessment: Summary of Highlights.* Washington, DC: American Public Welfare Association.

What Works in Safety and Risk Assessment for Child Protective Services

Study Authors	Survey Sample	Research Design/Outcome Measure	Findings
Fluke, J., Edwards, M. & Bussey, M. (1999). *Outcome evaluation, CERAP safety assessment: Three-year follow-up*. Englewood, CO: American Humane Association.	• State database of 349,752 records from the Illinois statewide Child Abuse and Neglect Tracking System (CANTS) spanning 1995–1998	• Analysis of administrative data and use of survival analysis to count recurrence • Outcome measured was short-term (60 day) recurrence (subsequent substantiation of an abuse or neglect allegation).	• Overall reduction from pre-implementation to the end of the third year was 28.6%. The rate of recurrence in 1995 was 2.1% and 1.5% in 1998.
Wagner, D., & Squadrito, E. (1993). Results of Rhode Island Risk Assessment Research. In *Seventh national roundtable on CPS risk assessment; Summary of highlights*. Washington, DC: American Public Welfare Association.	• Random selection of 956 cases (or 35%) from the population of all unduplicated indicated (Rhode Island's term for substantiated) cases in the state of Rhode Island in 1989	• Analysis of administrative data for 24 months following the original indicated report compared with classifications of levels of risk (low, medium, high) assessed at the original report • Outcome measured was follow-up indication rates of abuse or neglect for those families in the sample.	• Risk assessment tools were found to assist workers in discriminating between families who are at high or low risk of future neglect or abuse and apply more accurate service intervention levels. • 63% of families classified as high-risk had a subsequent indicated (substantiated) report of maltreatment and only 6% of those families classified at low-risk had a subsequent indicated (substantiated) report.

8

What Works in Prevention of Child Sexual Abuse: Child-Focused Prevention Techniques

Patricia Goth Mace

In the late 1970s and early 1980s, there was an increasing awareness that the sexual abuse of children in the United States was widespread and pervasive [Finkelhor & Daro 1997]. With this increased awareness came public pressure to respond to the problem [Kaufman & Zigler 1992]. As in other areas of prevention, there has been clear recognition that a diverse set of strategies will be required to eliminate child sexual abuse. Yet, at present, programming to prevent child sexual abuse is "virtually synonymous with group-based instruction for children on personal safety" [Daro 1994: 202].

Instruction on personal safety has typically been school-based and targeted children from preschool to high school, although some programming also has included parents and school personnel. The concepts most commonly discussed in these programs include:

- Children have the right to control who touches their bodies;
- There are different kinds of touches (good, bad, and questionable);
- It is important to tell a responsible adult, even if sworn to secrecy; and
- There are support systems of caring adults who can help if a child has been touched inappropriately [Conte 1993; Daro 1994].

Children are typically taught behavioral strategies that center on saying "no" to a perpetrator, getting away, telling an adult they trust about the abuse, and continuing to tell trusted adults until they are believed.

The Impact of Child Sexual Abuse Prevention Programs

The personal safety instruction approach to the prevention of child sexual abuse has undergone tremendous scrutiny for evidence of its effectiveness. In an effort to synthesize the findings from a large number of diverse studies, the U.S. General Accounting Office (GAO) [1996] summarized 16 review articles covering over 100 studies on education programs to prevent child sexual abuse. The GAO report and other reviews indicate a range of favorable results.

- *Children learn from school-based personal safety programs and families rate them highly.* The GAO report noted that 13 of the 16 reviews it examined concluded that education programs are generally effective in teaching new concepts, and eight of the reviews found that programs are effective in teaching new skills. Rispens, Aleman and Goudena [1997] pooled data from 16 evaluations of school programs on prevention of child sexual abuse and found that such programs were effective in teaching safety concepts and self protection skills. In addition, a national survey of 10- to 16-year-olds and their caretakers found that a majority of both groups described their school-based prevention education programs as helpful (Figure 1). The vast majority of parents and caretakers also felt that as a result of the programs, children were more aware of the problem (92%) and were better prepared to avoid the danger (94%) [Finkelhor & Dziuba-Leatherman 1995].

- *Programs that utilize interactive techniques are most effective.* Those programs that include modeling, role-playing and behavior rehearsal result in greater knowledge gains than those in which children are passive observers [Wurtele et al. 1987; Wurtele et al. 1986]. As Figure 2 shows, children who actively practiced particular skills during safety instruction performed better on post-tests than those who watched an instructor model the skills.

- *Children who have been victimized may disclose their abuse following participation in prevention education.* Educators who teach

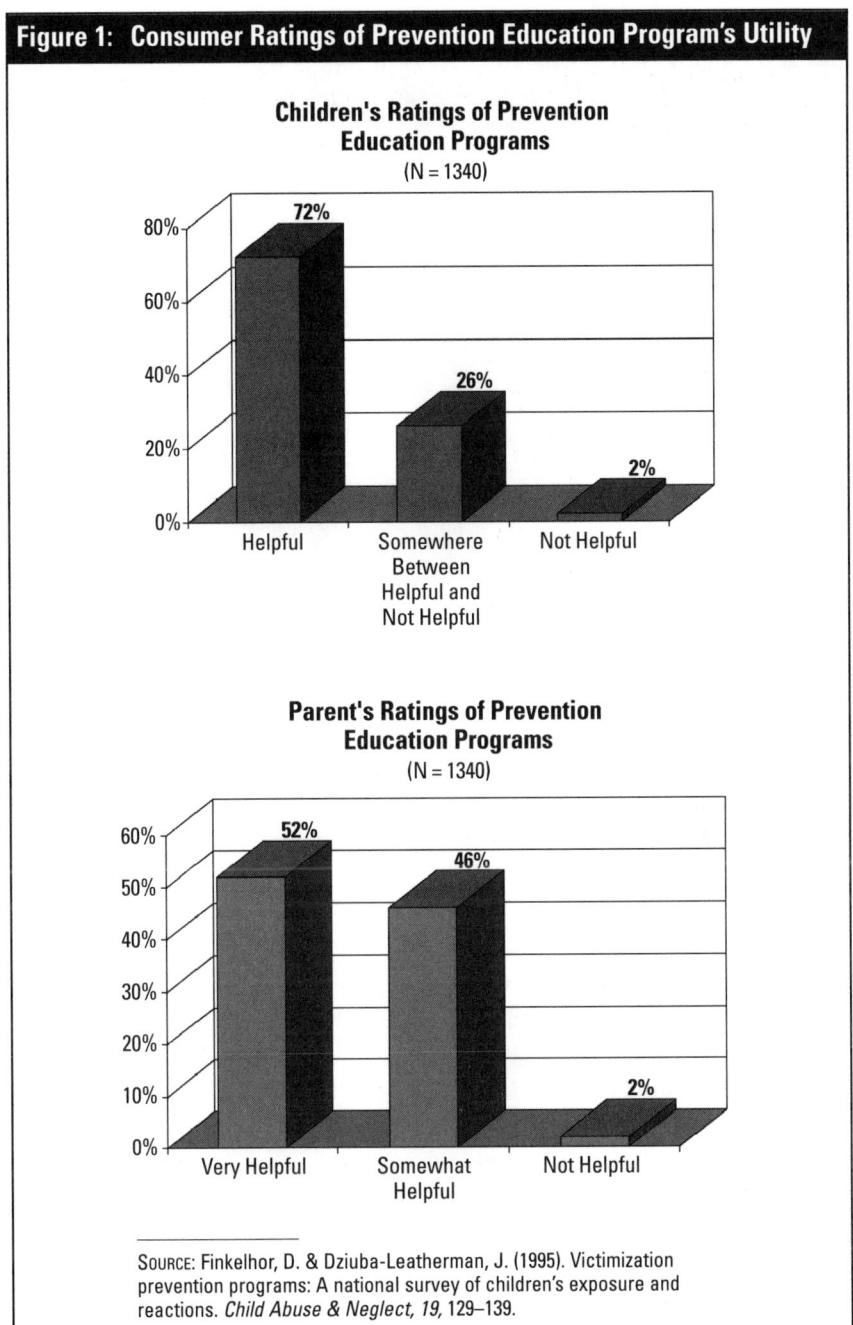

Figure 1: Consumer Ratings of Prevention Education Program's Utility

Children's Ratings of Prevention Education Programs
(N = 1340)

- Helpful: 72%
- Somewhere Between Helpful and Not Helpful: 26%
- Not Helpful: 2%

Parent's Ratings of Prevention Education Programs
(N = 1340)

- Very Helpful: 52%
- Somewhat Helpful: 46%
- Not Helpful: 2%

SOURCE: Finkelhor, D. & Dziuba-Leatherman, J. (1995). Victimization prevention programs: A national survey of children's exposure and reactions. *Child Abuse & Neglect, 19,* 129–139.

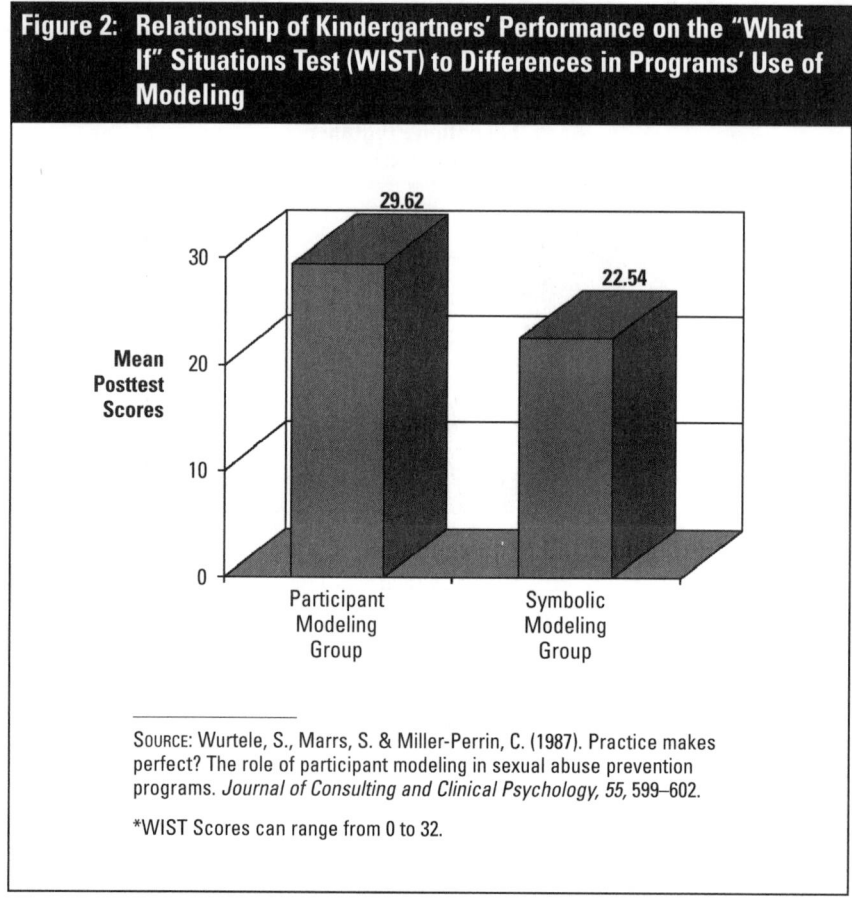

Figure 2: Relationship of Kindergartners' Performance on the "What If" Situations Test (WIST) to Differences in Programs' Use of Modeling

SOURCE: Wurtele, S., Marrs, S. & Miller-Perrin, C. (1987). Practice makes perfect? The role of participant modeling in sexual abuse prevention programs. *Journal of Consulting and Clinical Psychology, 55,* 599–602.

*WIST Scores can range from 0 to 32.

prevention programs report that disclosures of abuse are fairly common after presentations [Finkelhor & Daro 1997; Finkelhor & Strapko 1992]. This example of secondary prevention suggests that programming can contribute to halting abuse at an earlier point in time.

- *Negative effects associated with an instructional approach to child sexual abuse prevention appear to be minimal.* Many evaluations have included assessments of negative behavioral or emotional effects experienced by children following their participation in these programs. Tutty [1997] surveyed parents following their children's participation in a sexual abuse prevention program and found that fewer than 2% reported negative changes in their children's behavior, such as crying more easily, having more nightmares, or seeming more worried that something scary would happen. Finkelhor and Dziuba-Leatherman [1995] found that 8% of children who had participated in a victimization prevention program said it made them worry "a lot," but 53% said it made them worry "a little" about being abused. As shown in Figure 3, however, those children who reported being worried following the program were also more likely to have used the knowledge they were taught than children who did not worry at all (64% compared to 33%). Thus, even some of the work on negative effects might be viewed as the development of appropriate caution on the part of children.

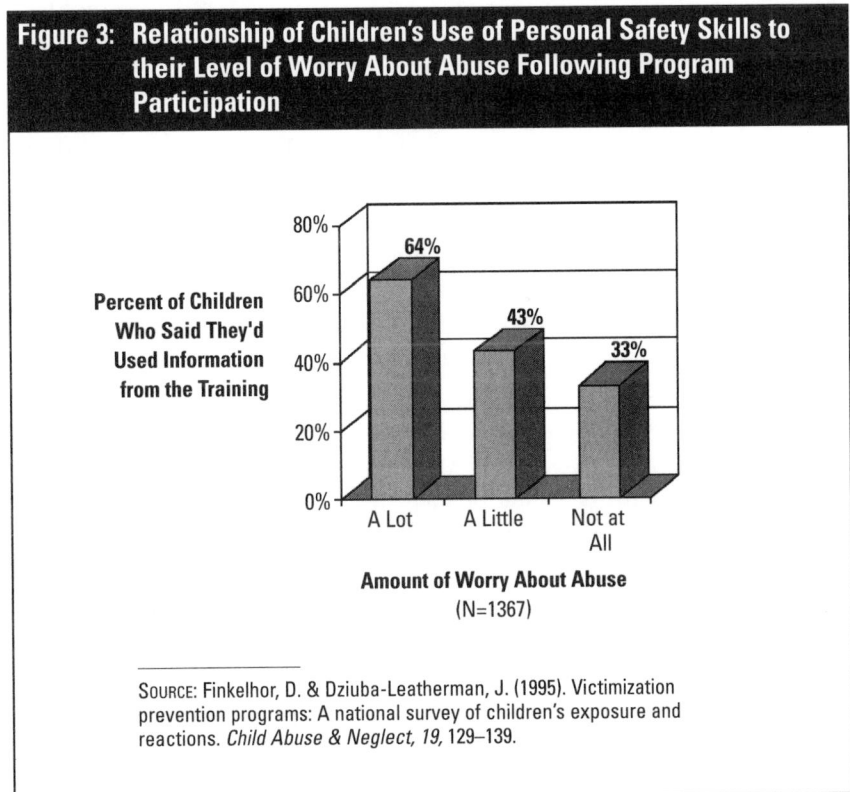

Figure 3: Relationship of Children's Use of Personal Safety Skills to their Level of Worry About Abuse Following Program Participation

Percent of Children Who Said They'd Used Information from the Training

Amount of Worry About Abuse
(N=1367)

SOURCE: Finkelhor, D. & Dziuba-Leatherman, J. (1995). Victimization prevention programs: A national survey of children's exposure and reactions. *Child Abuse & Neglect, 19,* 129–139.

In spite of evidence that child-focused prevention efforts can effectively teach children basic safety concepts, several concerns have been raised regarding the effectiveness of these programs in halting child sexual abuse.

- *There is no direct evidence that school-based safety education programs reduce the incidence of child sexual abuse.* The GAO report [1996] noted that 15 of the 16 reviews it examined pointed to the lack of evidence for incidence reduction. Reppucci and Haugaard [1993: 308] have acknowledged that in order to acquire evidence documenting a link between education and actual prevention of child sexual abuse, complex research designs, lengthy time periods, and "enormous costs involved in evaluating such projects" would be required.

- *Some of the key concepts often included in programs can be difficult for children to learn and remember.* Conte and Fogarty [1990], in their review, summarized findings on the concepts commonly taught in prevention programs. They noted that children usually had an easier time with concrete than abstract concepts; could have difficulty distinguishing between secrets that should be kept and those that should be told; found it difficult to understand that the victim is not to blame; and often had trouble understanding that someone they knew could be a perpetrator of sexual assault. Finkelhor and Strapko [1992] have characterized the idea of a familiar person as a perpetrator as running counter to common social assumptions. Daro [1994] has indicated that the more difficult concepts are more likely to be forgotten on follow-up assessments.

- *The instructional strategy puts the responsibility for prevention on the shoulders of children.* Adults and children may have a false sense of security if they believe that instructing children is sufficient to ensure they are protected [Conte et al. 1989; O'Donohue et al. 1992]. In line with this concern is the belief of professionals in the field that prevention efforts must expand their focus to include potential offenders and community awareness, rather than dedicating energy principally to the child's role in preventing abuse. According to Cohn [1986: 559], "The major responsibility for prevention of sexual abuse should not, indeed cannot, be placed on the victims and potential victims, particularly because they are children. The major focus of prevention efforts should be on potential perpetrators and on the cultural and societal values which allow this problem to persist." Conte and associates [1989] have noted that the perpetrator's advantage in size, strength, and knowledge makes a child vulnerable in spite of careful education and skill development. As research provides a better understanding of the precursors leading to the development of molesting behavior, it should be possible to design effective prevention strategies targeting potential abusers [Finkelhor & Strapko 1992].

Cost-Effectiveness

Child-focused personal safety training is a relatively inexpensive approach to prevention. The Maxine Waters Child Abuse Prevention Training Act (AB 2443), passed in 1984 by the California General Assembly, for example, provided $11.4 million per year for prevention education for all California public school children, at four points in their schooling: preschool, elementary, and junior and senior high school. Daro [1994] calculated that the cost per pupil was less than $7.

The costs associated with mental health treatment and criminal justice services in response to sexual abuse are obviously far greater. Daro [1988] described findings from a National Clinical Evaluation Study that collected information on average costs for various services in 19 clinical demonstration sites. Based on 1983 cost levels, annual costs ranged from $5,000 per family for minimal child sexual abuse prevention services to almost $8,000 per family for therapeutic services utilizing either individual or group counseling. Based on costs in Massachusetts in 1990, estimates of the expenses for investigation, arrest, prosecution, and incarceration of one child sexual abuse offender for an average of seven years without treatment was calculated at $169,029 [Steele 1995]. Given the costs of child sexual abuse to the child victim and to the community, it is clear that effective prevention efforts make financial sense.

Conclusion

Child sexual abuse prevention programming has most frequently been carried out in the form of personal safety instruction for school-age children. Numerous evaluations have demonstrated that it is possible to teach even young children some basic concepts and skills related to personal safety. There is evidence that approaches utilizing more interactive strategies are more effective than approaches in which children remain passive observers. This strategy for sexual abuse prevention also serves as a method of secondary prevention, as children who have been abused may disclose following such programs. The great majority of children who participate in personal safety training are reported to suffer no ill side effects, and even those families who report problems after such programs typically rate the programs positively.

Critics of the personal safety instruction approach consistently have pointed out that there is no evidence that knowledge of safety skills translates into behavior that actually reduces the likelihood of sexual abuse. Also, this approach puts the focus on potential victims rather than prevention of the development of perpetrators. There are concerns that it may not be possible to adequately equip children to prevent their own abuse given the clever manipulations and advantages in strength and knowledge that offenders have. Professionals always have acknowledged the need to address the problem of child sexual abuse in a variety of ways. As Conte [1993: 79] noted, "Sexual abuse prevention programs were never conceived of as the best way to prevent abuse. But, for the time, they may be the best or only way to try."

References

Cohn, A. H. (1986). Preventing adults from becoming sexual molesters. *Child Abuse & Neglect, 10,* 559–562.

Conte, J. R. (1993). Sexual abuse of children. In R. L. Hampton, T. P. Gullotta, G. R. Adams, E. H. Potter III, & R. P. Weissberg, (Eds.), *Family violence prevention and treatment* (pp. 56–85). Newbury Park, CA: Sage.

Conte, J. R. & Fogarty, L. A. (1990).Sexual abuse prevention programs for children. *Education and Urban Society, 22,* 270–284.

Conte, J., Wolf, S., & Smith, T. (1989). What sexual offenders tell us about prevention strategies. *Child Abuse & Neglect, 13,* 293–301.

Daro, D. (1988). *Confronting child abuse: Research for effective program design.* New York: Free Press.

Daro, D. (1994). Prevention of child sexual abuse. *The Future of Children, 4,* 198–223.

Finkelhor, D., Asdigian, N., & Dziuba-Leatherman J. (1995). Effectiveness of victimization prevention instruction: An evaluation of children's responses to actual threats and assaults, *Child Abuse & Neglect, 19,* 141–153.

Finkelhor, D. & Daro, D. (1997). Prevention of child sexual abuse. In Helfer, M., Kempe, R., and Krugman, R. (Eds.), *The battered child* (pp. 615–626). Chicago: University of Chicago Press.

Finkelhor, D. & Dziuba-Leatherman, J. (1995). Victimization prevention programs: A national survey of children's exposure and reactions. *Child Abuse & Neglect, 19,* 129–139.

Finkelhor, D. & Strapko, N. (1992). Sexual abuse prevention education: A review of evaluation studies. In D. J. Willis, E. W. Holden, & M. Rosenberg (Eds.), *Prevention of child maltreatment: Developmental and ecological perspectives* (pp. 150–167). New York: Wiley & Sons.

Kaufman, J. & Zigler, E. (1992). The prevention of child maltreatment: Programming, research, and policy. In D. J. Willis, E. W. Holden, & M. Rosenberg (Eds.), *Prevention of child maltreatment: Developmental and ecological perspectives* (pp. 269–295). New York: Wiley & Sons.

Nibert, D., Cooper, S., & Ford, J. (1989). Parents' observations of the effect of a sexual-abuse prevention program on preschool children. *Child Welfare, 68,* 539–546.

O'Donohue, W., Geer, J., & Elliott, A. (1992). The primary prevention of child sexual abuse. In O'Donohue, W., & Geer, J. (Eds.), *The sexual abuse of children: Clinical issues, Vol. 2* (pp. 477–517). Hillsdale, NJ: Erlbaum Associates.

Reppucci, N. D. & Haugaard, J. J. (1993). Problems with child sexual abuse prevention programs. In R. J. Gelles & D. R. Loseke (Eds.), *Current controversies on family violence* (pp. 306–322). Newbury Park, CA: Sage.

Rispens, J., Aleman, A., & Goudena, P. (1997). Prevention of child sexual abuse victimization: A meta-analysis of school programs. *Child Abuse & Neglect, 21,* 975–987.

Steele, N. (1995). Cost effectiveness of treatment. In B. K. Schwartz & H. R. Cellini (Eds.), *The sex offender: Corrections, treatment, and legal practice* (pp. 4–1 to 4–19). Kingston, NJ: Civic Research Institute, Inc.

Tutty, L. M. (1997). Child sexual abuse prevention programs: Evaluating *Who Do You Tell? Child Abuse & Neglect, 21,* 869–881.

U.S. General Accounting Office (1996). *Preventing child sexual abuse.* GAO/GGD 96–156, Washington, DC: U.S. General Accounting Office.Wurtele, S., Marrs, S. & Miller-Perrin, C. (1987). Practice makes perfect? The role of participant modeling in sexual abuse prevention programs. *Journal of Consulting and Clinical Psychology, 55,* 599–602.

Wurtele, S., Saslawsky, D., Miller, C., Marrs, S., & Britcher, J. (1986). Teaching personal safety skills for potential prevention of sexual abuse: A comparison of treatments. *Journal of Consulting and Clinical Psychology, 54,* 688–692.

What Works in Prevention of Child Sexual Abuse: Child-Focused Prevention Techniques

Study Authors	Survey Sample	Research Design/Outcome Measure	Findings
Finkelhor, D., Asdigian, N., & Dziuba-Leatherman, J (1995). Effectiveness of victimization prevention instruction: An evaluation of children's responses to actual threats and assaults. *Child Abuse & Neglect, 19*, 141–153.	• 2,000 youth between the ages of 10 and 16, generally well-matched to U.S. Census statistics for the population of this age • Sample drawn between May 1992 and February 1993 using random digit dialing and screening for youth in appropriate age range	• Data collected using telephone interviews with youth and their caregivers. • Study assessed all youth respondents' knowledge about sexual abuse. For those who had ever experienced an actual or attempted victimization, data were collected on self-protection strategies employed and self-perceptions of efficacy in response to threats or victimizations.	• Youth who had received more comprehensive abuse prevention training (at least nine of 12 important components as defined by the authors) scored significantly higher on knowledge about sexual abuse; were more likely to use preferred self-protection strategies (for those respondents who had faced attempted or actual victimization); and felt more efficacious in dealing with attempted or actual victimization. • Youth with more comprehensive training did not have significantly lower levels of completed victimizations, and they reported more injuries than other children in sexual victimization attempts.
Wurtele, S.K., Saslawsky, D.A., Miller, C.L., Marrs, S.R., & Britcher, J.C. (1986). Teaching personal safety skills for potential prevention of sexual abuse: A comparison of treatments. *Journal of Consulting and Clinical Psychology, 54*, 688–692.	• 71 children in kindergarten and grades one, five, and six • Sample drawn from a public school in a small rural town in eastern Washington State	• Study compared outcomes for students in four groups based on the type of intervention received: film, Behavioral Skills Training (BST), both film and BST, and control. • Outcomes were performance on the Personal Safety Questionnaire (PSQ) measure of knowledge about sexual abuse, and the "What If" Situations Test measure of children's recognition, refusal, response, and reporting in reaction to four vignettes.	• The two groups that received Behavioral Skills Training (with and without viewing the film) had better post test scores on knowledge about sexual abuse than the control group. • Students who had BST also scored significantly better on the "What If" Situations Test than students in the control group on the post-test. • At three-month follow up, students in all intervention groups scored in the same range and generally maintained the gains they had made on both outcome measures.

Citation	Sample	Methodology	Findings
Nibert, D., Cooper, S., & Ford, J. (1989). Parents' observations of the effect of a sexual-abuse prevention program on preschool children. *Child Welfare, 68*, 539–546.	• 233 parents (34% response rate) whose preschool age children had received a school-based sexual abuse prevention program • Families were from seven Head Start programs in Columbus, Ohio.	• Written surveys were sent home for parents to complete and return to the Head Start centers. • The survey included five questions addressing the program's effects on their children and their likelihood of discussing child sexual abuse with their children.	• 26% of parents reported observing positive behaviors following the intervention, including that their children told them about safety strategies they had learned. • 7% of parents reported problematic behaviors after the program, including discipline problems, sleep disturbances, and bed-wetting. • 66% of parents reported no changes in their children's behavior. • 42% of the children talked about the program with their parents afterwards. • 52% of parents said they discussed child sexual abuse with their children after the program.

Child Protective Services:

Investigating Suspected Child Abuse & Neglect

9

What Works in Protecting Child Witnesses

Kathleen Coulborn Faller

B eginning in the early 1980s children increasingly began testifying as witnesses in court cases. Although children testify to a variety of events they have observed or directly experienced, the most common type of testimony relates to their own sexual abuse [Myers 1996]. They may testify in a range of court proceedings, including juvenile (child protection and delinquency), civil, and criminal court. In most cases, children's testimony is required because only the child and alleged offender have firsthand knowledge of what happened.

All 50 states and the Federal Court Rules of Evidence have legal provisions that speak directly or indirectly to the issue of competency of child witnesses [National Center for the Prosecution of Child Abuse 1997]. Twenty-nine states assume all witnesses are competent regardless of age. Twenty states provide specifically for child witnesses, 13 eliminating some or all competency requirements for children [National Center for the Prosecution of Child Abuse 1997; Whitcomb 1992, 1993]. Six states have special provisions for determining the competency of a child witness, usually a separate hearing and a judicial finding of competence. The general requirements for competency are: (1) sufficient mental capacity to perceive experiences; (2) the ability to recall past events; (3) the ability to differentiate the truth from a lie; and (4) a sense of obligation to tell the truth [Myers 1996 and Whitcomb 1993]. When competency requirements are not specified, the "trier of fact"—the judge or the jury—makes the determination of the witness's competency based upon his or her testimony, rather than a judge determining competency at a separate hearing.

Court Protections for Child Witnesses

There are several special courtroom protections that may be used for child witnesses:

- *The presence of a support person for the child during testimony.* The Federal Court Rules of Evidence and at least 15 states have specific provisions permitting a support person to be present with a child in criminal cases [Whitcomb 1992]. The support person may be present in the courtroom or may sit in close proximity to the child, including in the witness chair with the child sitting on his or her lap. The judge determines who is designated as the support person.

- *Testimony through closed circuit television.* The Federal Court Rules of Evidence and statutes in at least 33 states permit the use of a closed circuit television [National Center for the Prosecution of Child Abuse 1997; Whitcomb 1992, 1993], so that a child may testify from a room outside the courtroom. The child's demeanor can be observed on the television screen by those in the courtroom, and the child is able to view persons in the courtroom on a television monitor. This procedure has been held to technically fulfill the Sixth Amendment guarantee of the right to confront one's accuser.

- *A videotape of the child's account rather than live testimony.* The Federal Court Rules of Evidence and statutes in at least 36 states allow the submission of a videotaped statement [National Center for the Prosecution of Child Abuse 1997; Whitcomb 1992]. The provisions governing the use of videotaped accounts vary by state and by type of court hearing. Generally, evidentiary rules are more relaxed in civil proceedings and at stages of court proceedings other than actual trial. For example, many states allow the admission of a videotape interview of a young child in a child protection proceeding in lieu of the child's testimony. The use of videotapes is more proscribed in criminal cases. An investigatory videotape made by the police may be used at an arraignment or a videotaped deposition (involving direct examination by the attorney for the state and cross-examination by the attorney for the accused) may be substituted for the child's testimony in a preliminary hearing; the child, however, must take the stand at the trial stage.

- *A screen placed between the child and the accused.* Several states allow a child witness to testify from behind a screen [McGough 1994]. A screen prevents eye contact between the child and the accused and minimizes the potential for intimidation of the child that might occur in a direct confrontation.

- *Closing of the courtroom.* The Federal Court Rules of Evidence and statutes in at least 15 states provide for some restrictions on the persons who may be present when a child witness testifies about sexual abuse [Myers 1996; Whitcomb 1992]. All persons other than those directly involved in the case are excluded from the courtroom. This practice protects the child's privacy and helps ensure that the child is not intimidated, either by a large group of people or by particular individuals such as the defendant's family.

- *Use of "props" to facilitate the testimony.* The Federal Court Rules of Evidence and statutes in at least nine states specifically permit the use of anatomical dolls in court [Whitcomb 1992]. Props may also include pictures, drawing materials, nonanatomical dolls, and other demonstration aids. The arguments for the use of props are that children may be more accomplished at showing than telling [Steward et al. 1996] and they may assist children who are reluctant to speak of their experiences.

- *Creation of a "child-friendly" courtroom or atmosphere.* The Federal Court Rules of Evidence and several state laws allow for altering the courtroom for children [McGough 1994], although there is variation among state and local jurisdictions in the specific alterations allowed. Alterations may involve the use of child-sized furniture in the courtroom, allowing the child to testify from a table rather than from the witness box, frequent breaks for the child, and the judge appearing in street clothes rather than his or her robes. The judge also may limit the questions posed to the child by attorneys but not to the point of eliminating cross-examination [Myers 1996].

Related Research

Research has been done on the impact on children of testifying and on the persuasiveness and competency of child witnesses.

Research Findings on the Impact on Children of Testifying

Despite concerns about the impact that testifying may have on children and the belief that child witnesses need special protections, the research is modest and principally consists of the perceptions of "mock jurors." Moreover, the number of criminal trials involving child sexual abuse is quite small, probably less than 10% of known complaints [Goodman et al. 1989; Finkelhor et al. 1988; Whitcomb 1992], and the number of cases in which children actually provide testimony is even smaller [Goodman et al 1989; Whitcomb 1992]. Research is thus limited because of the relative infrequency of child testimony.

Research on the impact of testifying suggests that for most children, court appearances are not positive experiences [Goodman et al. 1989; Tedesco & Schnell 1987]. Negative feelings about testifying are associated with having to face the defendant and cross-examination [Goodman et al. 1989]. The research, however, also indicates that detrimental effects from testimony are usually temporary [Whitcomb 1992] and that it is the waiting process between the decision to go to trial and the actual testimony that creates the most psychic distress [Runyon et al. 1988]. The latter finding lends strong support for expediting the court process to eliminate protracted delays for children.

Research and Court Rulings on the Persuasiveness and Competency of Child Witnesses

There is some research with mock jurors that suggests that they find testimony from a prepared, confident child witness more persuasive than testimony from a hesitant one unless there has been expert testimony indicating that child witnesses should be hesitant [Kovera & Borgida 1996]. In addition, studies indicate that mock jurors find live child testimony more persuasive than videotaped testimony [Kovera & Borgida 1996; Ross et al. 1994; Swim et al. 1993; Tobey et al. 1995].

There have been numerous cases in which the competency of the child witness was at issue. Most cases have affirmed that witness credibility falls within the province of the jury. Despite this finding, a number of important convictions in which child testimony was the cornerstone of the case have been reversed on appeal, generally on the basis that the child's account was contaminated by the investigatory process [State v. Michaels 1993; Commonwealth v. Amirault 1989; State v. Kelly 1996]. These appellate decisions raise the question as to why the judges and juries who heard the children's testimony were not persuaded by the claim that the testimony was tainted, but appeals court judges, who never saw or heard the children, nevertheless were.

Court Rulings on Courtroom Protections for Children

Rulings on Using a Screen Between the Child and the Accused

At least two U.S. Supreme Court cases have affirmed the legality of screening a child witness. In one case, however, *Coy v. Iowa*, the Iowa statute was struck down and a conviction of an alleged sex offender was reversed. This was because the statute had no provision for finding that a child would be traumatized by traditional court testimony. The two 13-year old girls who accused the defendant of sexual abuse arguably could have testified without a screen. The court also reversed the defendant's conviction.

Rulings on Using Closed-Circuit Television

Two U.S. Supreme Court cases have addressed and affirmed the use of closed circuit television [Maryland v. Craig 1990; Globe Newspaper Co. v. Superior Court 1982]. The Supreme Court has held, however, that prior to use of closed circuit television, there must be a finding that the child is unable to testify in open court.

Rulings on Creating a Child-Friendly Courtroom

Few cases have been reversed based upon the courtroom having been made more child-friendly. One of the grounds for reversal in *State v. Michaels* [1993], however, was the action of the judge in allowing the child witnesses to testify sitting on his knee [Myers 1996].

Conclusion

The court environment is strange and potentially intimidating for children. Programs that familiarize them with the court environment and decrease their fear of testifying should be encouraged. When children are witnesses, the goal is to help them give the most accurate, complete and persuasive testimony possible. Special protections for child witnesses may be needed, including the use of closed circuit television. When they are able, children should provide testimony in open court. When they are unable to do so, appropriate child witness protections should be employed such as use of screens, props, and closing of the courtroom, and expert witnesses should explain to juries the necessity of using these protections.

References

Commonwealth of Massachusetts v. Amirault. (1989). 535 N.E.2d. 193.

Finkelhor, D., Williams, L., & Burns, N. (1988). *Nursery crimes.* Newbury Park, CA: Sage.

Globe Newspaper Co. v. Superior Court. (1982). 457 U.S. 596.

Goodman, G., Taub, E., Jones, D., England, P., Port, P., Rudy, L., and Prado, L. (1989). *Emotional effects of criminal court testimony on child abuse victims.* Final report submitted to the National Institute of Justice under Grants #85–IJ–CX–0020.

Kovera, M. & Borgida, E. (1996). Children on the witness stand: The use of expert testimony and other procedural innovations in U.S. child sexual abuse trials. In B. Bottoms & G. Goodman (Eds.), *International perspectives on child abuse and children's testimony* (pp. 201–220). Newbury Park, CA: Sage.

Lawson, L. & Chaffin, M. (1992). False negatives in sexual abuse disclosure interviews: Incidence and influence of caretaker's belief in abuse in cases of accidental abuse discovery by diagnosis of STD. *Journal of Interpersonal Violence.* 7(4), 532–542.

Maryland v. Craig. (1990). 497 U.S. 836.

McGough, L. (1994). *Child witnesses: Fragile voices in the American legal system.* New Haven, CT: Yale.

Myers, J. E. B. (1996). A decade of international reform to accommodate child witnesses. In B. Bottoms & G. Goodman (Eds.), *International Perspectives on Child Abuse and Children's Testimony* (pp. 201–220). Newbury Park, CA: Sage

National Center for the Prosecution of Child Abuse. (1997). *Child abuse and neglect state statute series: Vol. IV. Child witnesses.* Washington, DC: National Center for Child Abuse and Neglect Clearinghouse.

Ross, D., Hopkins, S., Hanson, E., Lindsay, R., Hazen, K., & Eslinger, T. (1994). The impact of protective shields and videotape testimony on conviction rates in a simulated trial of child sexual abuse. *Law and Human Behavior, 18,* 553–566.

Runyon, D., Everson, M., & Hunter, W. (1988). The impact of legal intervention on sexually abused children. *The Journal of Pediatrics, 113,* 647–653.

State of North Carolina v. Kelly (1992). No. 933SC676 (N.C. Super. Ct. 1992).

State of New Jersey v. Michaels. (1993). 625 A.2d 489 (NJ App.).

Steward, M. S. & Steward, D. S., with Farquhar, L., Myers, J., Reinhart, M., Welker, I., Joye, N., Driskill, J., & Morgan, J. (1996). *Interviewing young children about body touch and handling.* Monograph series of the Society for Research on Child Development (SRCD). Chicago: University of Chicago.

Swim, J., Borgida, E., & McCoy, K. (1993). Videotaped versus in-court witness testimony: Does protecting the child witness jeopardize the process? *Journal of Applied Social Psychology, 23,* 603–631.

Tedesco, J., & Schnell, S. (1987). Children's reactions to sexual abuse investigation and litigation. *Child Abuse & Neglect: The International Journal, 11,* 267–272.

Tobey, A., Goodman, G., Betterman-Faunce, J., Orcutt, H., & Sachsenmaier, T. (1995). Balancing the rights of children and defendants: Effects of closed-circuit television on children's accuracy and jurors' perceptions. In M. Zaragoza, J. Graham, G. Hall, R. Hirschman & Y. Ben-Porath (Eds.), *Memory and testimony in child witnesses* (pp. 214–239). Newbury Park, CA: Sage.

Whitcomb, D. (1992). *When the victim is a child* (2nd ed.). Washington, DC: U.S. Department of Justice, National Institute of Justice.

Whitcomb, D. (1993). *Child victims as witnesses: What the research says.* Newton, MA: Education Development Center, Inc.

What Works in Protecting Child Witnesses

Study Authors	Survey Sample	Research Design/Outcome Measure	Findings
Lawson, L. & Chaffin, M. (1992). False negatives in sexual abuse disclosure interviews: Incidence and influence of caretaker's belief in abuse in cases of accidental abuse discovery by diagnosis of STD. *Journal of Interpersonal Violence, 7*(4), 532–542	• 28 cases of children positive for sexually transmitted disease • No prior disclosure of sexual abuse	• Children interviewed in hospital by a specialist in child sexual abuse assessment	• 12 (43%) made verbal disclosures of sexual abuse in the initial interview. • The only factor found predictive of disclosure was caretaker support. 63% of children with a supportive caretaker disclosed; 17% of the children without a supportive caretaker disclosed.
Steward, M. S. & Steward, D. S., with Farquhar, L., Myers, J., Reinhart, M., Welker, I., Joye, N., Driskill, J., & Morgan, J. (1996). Interviewing young children about body touch and handling. Monograph series of the Society for Research on Child Development (SRCD). Chicago: University of Chicago.	• 130 boys and girls • 3–6 years old • Seen in outpatient medical clinic	• Children interviewed shortly after, and at one and six months following medical procedures involving body touch • Children interviewed using four methods: (1) verbal only; (2) anatomical dolls (with props-pictures and doctor toys); (3) anatomical drawings (with props-pictures and doctor toys); and (4) computer assisted interview (with props-pictures and doctor toys).	• Preschool children provide more accurate and complete responses when allowed to use props. • Sexually abused children were significantly more accurate in their reports of genital touch during clinic visits than non-abused children. • Accuracy diminished over time.

10

What Works in Treatment Services for Abused Children

Lucy Berliner and David Kolko

Physical and sexual abuse experiences are associated with a range of emotional and behavioral consequences. The type and severity of problems vary greatly among children. The nature of the abuse—as well as age, gender, ethnicity, prior history, and family characteristics and functioning—have been found to make a difference in how a child is affected. Sexually abused children are more likely to suffer post-traumatic stress symptoms and sexual behavior problems, whereas physically abused children are more likely to have difficulties with social functioning and aggression. Childhood abuse experiences are also risk factors for later psychiatric conditions, antisocial behavior, and relationship impairments.

There is a large body of clinical literature describing treatment approaches. The empirical literature examining the effectiveness of treatment for abused children, however, is relatively sparse, and most of the research has been with sexually abused children. Many of the studies that have assessed sexually abused children before and after treatment report improvement in emotional and behavioral functioning [Finkelhor & Berliner 1995]. Because symptoms generally abate over time with or without intervention, however, these findings cannot be conclusively attributed to effects of therapy. With regard to the treatment of physically abused children, services are often one component of broader interventions that are family-centered but which often emphasize parental treatment. Few studies have evaluated the impact of treating the physically abused child [Kolko 1996a].

There are a number of treatment outcome studies that have used comparison groups and/or random assignment. Most of these treatments consist of well-established cognitive behavioral interventions that are adjusted to be abuse-specific or target abuse-related outcomes.

What Works in Sexual Abuse Treatment

Research findings on the treatment of children who have been sexually abused indicate the following:

- Specific, focused treatments produce superior results compared with nonspecific therapy;
- Post-traumatic stress symptoms improve more when children are the direct recipients of therapy, even if their parents do not receive treatment;
- Parallel treatment for parents improves outcomes; and
- No advantage is found for any particular modality.

[Celano et al. 1996; Deblinger et al. 1996; Cohen & Mannarino 1996, 1998; Finkelhor & Berliner 1995]

Research suggests that the following components characterize effective sexual abuse treatment:

- *Psychoeducation* regarding the nature of sexual abuse, offenders, and the process of victimization.
- *Direct discussion of the traumatic event.* The underlying principle is that gradual exposure to the memories or reminders of the experience reduces negative emotional associations and the need to use avoidance coping.
- *Stress management training.* Relaxation techniques and cognitive coping strategies increase children's capacity to handle negative emotions so that they can participate in direct discussion of the traumatic event. These skills are also transferable to other stressful life experiences.

- *Correcting cognitive distortions.* Negative emotions and maladaptive behavioral responses often are the result of inaccurate and distorted beliefs about the event, the child's role, or the meaning of the experience. Replacing maladaptive attributions allows the experience to be put in a proper perspective.

- *Behavior management training for parents.* Parents who learn to effectively manage abuse-related behavioral reactions help their children recover and are able to reduce negative parent-child interactions.

[American Academy of Child and Adolescent Psychiatry (AACAP) 1998; Berliner 1997]

What Works in the Treatment of Physically Abused Children

Studies suggest that the following are effective in treating physically abused children:

- Therapeutic preschool and day treatment reduces behavior problems for preschool children;

- Peer-based skills training enhances social initiation and positive peer interactions;

- Cognitive-behavioral interventions with parents reduces coercive behavior and improves child functioning; and

- Abuse-informed individual and family therapy reduces violence and improves some child outcomes.

[Kolko 1996b; Fantuzzo et al. 1996; Moore et al. 1998]

Components of effective treatment for physically abused children include:

- Specific discussion of the children's perceptions and attributions of the circumstances of the incident and details of the abuse.

- Psychoeducation for children and parents regarding child abuse law, child safety, and child welfare.

- Child training in self-expression, self-control, and other prosocial skills. Children learn alternative ways to express their feelings and thoughts, especially anger and anxiety, and self-management skills which promotes the ability to solve problems appropriately and effectively.

- Parent training in self-control and methods to enhance child management and development. Once parents have learned psychological skills that enhance control over their own negative affect and maladaptive cognitions they can better use alternative disciplinary strategies that minimize use of physical force.

- Abuse-informed family therapy. A family focus establishes an atmosphere of cohesion and hope, provides the forum for teaching communication and non-coercive problem solving, and develops a system of mutually respected family rules and behavioral contingencies, to facilitate more positive interactions.

[Kolko 1996b, 1996a]

Referral and Utilization of Treatment Services

The evidence suggests that sexually abused children are usually referred for therapy, while physically abused children may only be referred when they have behavior problems or when parents or families are referred for various services. Several studies have examined factors associated with follow-through on referral among sexually abused children. Among the findings are that minority and lower socioeconomic children are less likely to attend treatment [Haskett et al. 1991; Tingus et al. 1996]; school-age children, as opposed to preschoolers and adolescents, are more likely to attend treatment [Tingus et al. 1996]; and system involvement and parental appreciation of the importance of treatment is associated with follow-through on referral [Tingus et al. 1996].

A few studies have assessed the percentage of abused children receiving treatment services. In a sample of child protective services cases, only 24% of sexually abused and 18% of physically abused children had any individual therapy [Kolko et al. 1999]. Among children in out-of-home care, the rates are substantially higher with treatment participation rates of about 77% of sexually abused children and 69% of physically abused children. When families seek victimization-focused therapy for their children, the median number of sessions for sexually abused children is 27, and the median for physically abused is 17. Less than 5% of children participate in long-term therapy (more than 100 sessions) [New et al. 1998].

Conclusion

Research results suggest that there are effective treatments for children who have experienced abuse and that specific, brief, cognitive-behavioral treatments are most effective. Involvement of parents, regardless of whether they are the abusers, enhances outcomes. It is also apparent that many abused children, particularly children of color and children of lower socioeconomic status, do not obtain treatment. System involvement may be helpful because professionals can help parents understand the importance of treatment.

References

American Academy of Child and Adolescent Psychiatry. (1998). Practice parameters for the assessment and treatment of children and adolescents with PTSD. *Journal of the American Academy of Child and Adolescent Psychiatry, 37*(10), Supplement.

Berliner, L. (1997). Trauma-specific therapy for sexually abused children. In D. Wolfe, R. McMahon, & R. Peters (Eds.), *Child abuse: New directions in prevention and treatment across the lifespan* (pp. 157–176). Thousand Oaks, CA: Sage.

Celano, M., Hazzard, A., Webb, C., & McCall, C. (1996). Treatment of traumagenic beliefs among sexually abused girls and their mothers: An evaluation study. *Journal of Abnormal Child Psychology, 24,* 1–16.

Cohen, J. & Mannarino, A. (1996). A treatment outcome study for sexually abused preschool children. *Journal of the American Academy of Child and Adolescent Psychiatry, 35,* 1402–1410.

Cohen, J. & Mannarino, A. (1998). Interventions for sexually abused children: Initial treatment findings. *Child Maltreatment, 3,* 17–26.

Deblinger, E., Lippman, J., & Steer, R. (1996) Sexually abused children suffering posttraumatic stress symptoms: Initial treatment outcome findings. *Child Maltreatment, 1,* 310–321.

Fantuzzo J, Sutton-Smith B, Atkins M., & Meyers R. (1996). Community-based resilient peer treatment of withdrawn maltreated preschool children. *Journal of Child Clinical Psychology, 64,* 1377–1368.

Finkelhor, D. & Berliner, L. (1995). Research on the treatment of sexually abused children: A review and recommendations. *Journal of the American Academy of Child and Adolescent Psychiatry, 34,* 1408–1423.

Haskett, M. E., Nowlan, N. P., Hutcheson, J. S., & Whitworth, J. M. (1991). Factors associated with successful entry into therapy in child sexual abuse cases. *Child Abuse & Neglect, 15,* 467–476.

Kolko, D. J. (1996a). Child physical abuse. In J. Briere, L. Berliner, J. A. Bulkley, C. Jenny, & T. Reid (Eds.), *APSAC handbook of child maltreatment* (pp. 21–50). Thousand Oaks, CA: Sage.

Kolko, D. J. (1996b). Individual cognitive-behavioral treatment and family therapy for physically abused children and their offending parents: A comparison of clinical outcomes. *Child Maltreatment, 1,* 322–342.

Kolko, D. J., Selelyo, J., & Brown, E. J. (1999). The treatment histories and service involvement of physically and sexually abusive families: Description, correspondence, and clinical correlates. *Child Abuse & Neglect, 23,* 459–476.

Moore E., Armsden G., & Gogerty, P. L. (1998). A twelve-year follow-up study of maltreated and at-risk children who received early therapeutic child care. *Child Maltreatment, 3,* 3–16.

New, M., Berliner, L., & Fitzgerald, M. (1998). *Mental health service utilization by victims of crime.* Seattle, WA: Harborview Center for Sexual Assault and Traumatic Stress.

Tingus, K. D., Heger, A. H., Foy, D. W., & Leskin, G. A. (1996). Factors associated with entry into therapy in children evaluated for sexual abuse. *Child Abuse & Neglect, 20,* 63–68.

What Works in Treatment Services for Abused Children

Study Authors	Survey Sample	Research Design/ Outcome Measure	Findings
Celano, M., Hazzard, A., Webb, C., & McCall, C. (1996). Treatment of traumagenic beliefs among sexually abused girls and their mothers: An evaluation study. *Journal of Abnormal Child Psychology, 24*, 1–16.	• Sexual abuse-specific Cognitive Behavioral Treatment (CBT) vs. nonspecific treatment • N = 32	• Randomized clinical trial	For the Cognitive Behavioral Treatment Group, there was: • Increased parental support; and • Increased accurate abuse cognitions.
Cohen, J. & Mannarino, A. (1996) A treatment outcome study for sexually abuse preschool children. *Journal of the American Academy of Child and Adolescent Psychiatry, 35*, 1402–1410.	• Sexual abuse-specific CBT vs. nonspecific treatment • N = 67	• Randomized clinical trial	• For the Sexual abuse-specific CBT group, there was decreased PTSD symptoms, sexual behavior problems, internalizing and externalizing behavior problems.
Cohen, J. & Mannarino, A. (1998) Interventions for sexually abused children: Initial treatment findings, *Child Maltreatment, 3*, 17–26.	• Sexual abuse-specific CBT vs. nonspecific treatment • N = 49	• Randomized clinical trial	For the Sexual abuse-specific CBT group, there was: • Decreased depression; and • Increased social competence.
Deblinger, E., Lippman, J., & Steer, R. (1996) Sexually abused children suffering posttraumatic stress symptoms: Initial treatment outcome findings. *Child Maltreatment, 1*, 310–321.	• Sexual abuse-specific CBT vs. routine community care • N = 100	• Randomized clinical trial	• For the Sexual abuse-specific CBT group, there was decreased PTSD symptoms, depression, and behavior problems.

(continued on next page)

What Works in Treatment Services for Abused Children (*continued*)

Study Authors	Survey Sample	Research Design/ Outcome Measure	Findings
Kolko, D. J. (1996b). Individual cognitive-behavioral treatment and family therapy for physically abused children and their offending parents: A comparison of clinical outcomes. *Child Maltreatment 1*, 322–342.	• Abuse-specific CBT vs. abuse informed family systems vs. routine community care • N = 55	• Randomized clinical trial	For the abuse-specific CBT group, there was: • Decreased child to parent violence; • Decreased externalizing behavior problems; • Decreased parental distress; and • Decreased abuse risk.
Moore, E., Armsden, G., & Gogerty, P. L. (1998). A 12-year follow-up study of maltreated and at-risk children who received early therapeutic child care. *Child Maltreatment 3*, 3–16.	• Therapeutic preschool vs. routine community care (12-year follow-up) • N = 35	• Randomized clinical trial	For the therapeutic preschool group, there was: • Decreased violent delinquency; • Decreased aggression; and • Decreased internalizing behavior problems.

11

What Works in the Treatment of Batterers

Katreena L. Scott and David A. Wolfe

The prevalence and impact of physical abuse perpetrated by men against their spouses is extensive and children are often witnesses to these domestic assaults. National surveys in the United States and Canada estimate that 7% to 14% of women experience physical abuse at the hands of their intimate partners each year, and that over their lifetimes, just under 30% of women are victims of spouse assault [Statistics Canada 1993; Straus & Gelles 1992; Straus et al. 1980]. Children are witness to many assaults against their mothers. In surveys, women indicate that children witnessed their abuse in almost 40% of marriages [Rogers 1994]. Moreover, children are witnesses to approximately two-thirds of spouse assault incidences that come to the attention of the authorities [Manion & Wilson 1995; Prairie Research Associates, Inc. 1994]. Witnessing this abuse is of import as experts agree that children exposed to domestic violence are much more likely to develop behavior problems and are more likely to themselves become abusive as adults [Jaffe et al. 1990; Wolfe et al. 1998].

Intervening with men who are physically abusive towards their partners and/or their children has been a child welfare concern. Men seldom seek out the aid of child and family intervention programs and are often reluctant to take advantage of services offered to them. As a result, their point of entry into the system is often an arrest for domestic violence. To intervene most effectively into men's perpetration of violence within their families, it is important to examine what works in treatment for men who batter their partners. There are two principal approaches to intervention: arrest and treatment.

Arrest

In the mid-1980s, a good deal of attention focused on arrest as a treatment approach for domestic violence offenders as a result of wide publication of findings from the Minneapolis Domestic Violence Experiment [Sherman & Berk 1984]. In this study, Sherman and Berk compared the effectiveness of three types of police response to domestic violence: (1) separating the perpetrator and victim, (2) trying to restore order between the couple, and (3) arresting the perpetrator. Consistent with deterrence theory, the researchers found that men who were arrested had lower rates of violence in the future than men subject to either of the other two interventions. Recognizing the important policy implications of these results, the National Institute of Justice (NIJ) funded replications of the Minneapolis experiment in six new sites. Although the results vary somewhat, several general conclusions can be drawn:

- Arrest, at best, has a small deterrence effect on domestic violence offenses. In the most recent and arguably most complete analysis of the Spouse Assault Replication Program studies funded by NIJ, arrest was found to have a small but consistent deterrent effect on male aggression. There was an average 10% reduction in recidivism for arrested men when compared to nonarrested men [Garner 1998].

- The effect of arrest does not vary greatly according to men's life situations. Although there was some suggestion that arrest had a greater deterrent effect for men who were married and/or employed, subsequent analyses have revealed that the effect of these factors is small and inconsistent [Garner 1998].

- Men's history of assault is, by far, the strongest predictor of future domestic violence. In the most recent meta-analysis, it was reported that the partners of men with a prior criminal record of domestic violence were 30% more likely to report these men for subsequent violence. Men with a prior criminal record were 34% more likely to be re-arrested than men without a prior criminal record of domestic violence [Garner 1998].

Voluntary or Mandated Treatment

A second option for intervening with adult male domestic violence offenders is treatment on a voluntary or mandated basis. Batterer treatment programs originated in the early 1970s as voluntary programs for men whose partners sought shelter services. In recent years, the criminal justice system has made increasing use of treatment programs in the sentencing of men convicted of assaulting their partners.

Most often, intervention involves group programs that combine pro-feminist psychoeducational materials with cognitive-behavioral or psychotherapeutic techniques. Programs vary in length from two to three months to more than a year, and generally include intake assessment, victim contact, orientation classes, group treatment, termination protocols, and follow-up contacts. The value of these programs is still open to question for the following reasons:

- High drop-out rates continue to be problematic for service delivery and program evaluation. Drop-out rates for batterer treatment programs vary from 20% to 80%, depending on how rates are calculated. Gondolf and Foster [1991], for example, reported that of 200 men who contacted a treatment program for information, 45 men attended an intake session and were accepted into the program, 27 attended the first intervention session, and only 2 attended all 32 intervention sessions. Although men court-ordered to attend treatment are somewhat less likely to drop out of programs than are voluntary clients, at least one-third of court-ordered men fail to complete program treatment, underscoring the need for better coordination between the criminal justice system and treatment programs [DeHart et al. 1999; DeMaris 1989; Saunders & Parker 1989].

- Evaluations of batterer intervention programs raise numerous methodological concerns and have yet to provide generalizable conclusions. With few exceptions, evaluations of batterer intervention programs are beset by methodological problems such as small sample sizes, lack of random assignment to treatment and control groups, short or incomplete follow-ups, and unreliable or inadequate information sources. These methodological problems make it difficult to generalize findings to batterers not part of the study.

- Among the few evaluations of batterer intervention programs judged to be methodologically sound, small and generally non-significant differences are found in the recidivism rates of men who attend and who do not attend intervention programs. According to reports of wives and girlfriends, approximately one-third of men referred to treatment programs continue to be physically abusive, regardless of treatment [Gondolf 1998; Levesque & Gelles 1998; Rosenfeld 1992; Tolman & Bennett 1990].

- There is no evidence of greater effectiveness based on the use of a particular theoretical approach, treatment modality (structured vs. non-structured), treatment length, or intervention intensity. In the most methodologically sound investigation of different types of batterer interventions, Gondolf [1998] reported that there were no significant differences in outcomes for men participating in programs that varied in length from three to nine months or in programs that utilized different treatment modalities (didactic or process-oriented). Approximately one-third of men participating in any type of program—ranging between 32% and 39%—re-assaulted in the year following intervention.

- The probability of re-assault is greater for men with prior convictions for assaults against their partners or other and men with drug or alcohol addiction [Shepard 1992].

Conclusion

Men who are physically abusive towards their partners and/or children typically come to the attention of domestic violence specialists. Within this context, men are arrested and/or offered or mandated to participate in treatment designed to prevent the recurrence of abuse. Neither arrest nor treatment (mandatory or voluntary) has been shown to have large effect on men's violent behavior towards members of their families. High drop-out rates underscore the need for better coordination of services between the criminal justice system and treatment programs. One consistent finding is that men who have a history of violent offending and who have abused family members in the past are much more likely to engage in violence in the future, regardless of arrest or treatment. Because research findings on the efficacy of both arrest and treatment are discouraging, there is a strong need to intervene before patterns of abusive behavior develop.

References

DeHart, D. D., Kennerly, R. J., Burke, L. K., & Follingstad, D. R. (1999). Predictors of attrition in a treatment program for battering men. *Journal of Family Violence, 14,* 19–34.

DeMaris, A. (1989, March). Attrition in batterers' counseling: The role of social and demographic factors. *Social Service Review, 143–154.*

Eisikovits, Z. C. & Edleson, J. L. (1989). Intervening with men who batter: A critical review of the literature. *Social Service Review, 3,* 384–414.

Garner, J. (1998). *What are the lessons of the police arrest studies?* Paper presentation at Program Evaluation and Family Violence Research: An International Conference. Durham, New Hampshire.

Gondolf, E. W. (1998). Do batterer programs work?: A 15-month follow-up of multi-site evaluation. *Domestic Violence Report, 3,* 65–79.

Gondolf, E. W. & Foster, R. A. (1991). Pre-program attrition in batterer programs. *Journal of Family Violence, 6,* 337–349.

Jaffe, P., Wolfe, D. A., & Wilson, S. (1990). *Children of battered women.* Newbury Park, CA: Sage.

Levesque, D. & Gelles, R. (1998). *Does treatment reduce recidivism in men who batter? Meta-analytic evaluation of treatment outcome research.* Paper presentation at Program Evaluation and Family Violence Research: An International Conference. Durham, New Hampshire.

Manion, I. G. & Wilson, S. K. (1995). *An examination of the association between histories of maltreatment and adolescent risk behaviours,* Catalogue H72–21/139–1995E, Ottawa, Canada: Minister of National Health and Welfare.

Prairie Research Associates Inc. (1994). *Manitoba Spouse Abuse Tracking Project: Final Report, 1.* Ottawa, Canada: Department of Justice, Canada, WD.

Rogers, K. (1994). Wife assault: The findings of a national survey. *Juristat, 14* (9), Catalogue 85–002. Ottawa, Canada: Canadian Centre for Justice Statistics, Statistics Canada.

Rosenfeld, B. D. (1992). Court-ordered treatment of spouse abuse. *Clinical Psychology Review, 12,* 205–226.

Saunders, D. G. & Parker, J. C. (1989, September). Legal sanctions and treatment follow-through among men who batter: A multivariate analysis. *Social Work Research & Abstracts, Vol. H,* 21–29.

Sherman, L. W. & Berk, R. A. (1984). The specific deterrent effects of arrest for domestic assault. *American Sociological Review, 49,* 261–271.

Shepard, M. (1992). Predicting batterer recidivism five years after community intervention. *Journal of Family Violence, 7,* 167–178.

Statistics Canada. (1993). Violence against women survey. *The Daily, Statistics Canada Cat.* No. 11–001E. Ottawa: Statistics Canada.

Straus, M. A. & Gelles, R. J. (1992). *Physical violence in American families.* New Brunswick, NJ: Transaction Publishers.

Straus, M. A., Gelles, R. J., & Steinmetz, S. K. (1980). *Behind closed doors: Violence in the American family.* New York: Anchor/Doubleday.

Tolman, R. M. & Bennett, L. W. (1990). A review of quantitative research on men who batter. *Journal of Interpersonal Violence, 5,* 87–118.

Wolfe, D. A., Wekerle, C., Reitzel-Jaffe, D., & Lefebvre, L. (1998). Factors associated with abusive relationships among maltreated and non-maltreated youth. *Developmental Psychopathology, 10,* 61–85.

What Works in the Treatment of Batterers

Study Authors	Review Procedures	Findings
Eisikovits, Z. C. & Edleson, J. L. (1989). Intervening with men who batter: A critical review of the literature. *Social Service Review, 3,* 384–414.	• Narrative review of individual, couple, and group treatment	• Existing studies suffer from numerous methodological limitations and no definitive conclusions may be drawn.
Tolman, R. M. & Bennett, L. W. (1990). A review of quantitative research on men who batter. *Journal of Interpersonal Violence, 5,* 87–118.	• 20 studies of various types of intervention including group programs for men and for couples	• The percentage of men achieving nonviolence due to involvement in group treatment varied from 53% to 85%. • Relatively small differences in recidivism rates were found for men in treatment and comparison groups. • There was a tentative conclusion that rates of nonviolence are similar for couples programs.
Rosenfeld, B. D. (1992). Court-ordered treatment of spouse abuse. *Clinical Psychology Review, 12,* 205–226.	• 25 studies of court-ordered treatment	• There was an overall recidivism rate of 27%. • No significant difference was found between treatment completers and drop-outs. • Arrested men dropped out of treatment at similar rates to voluntary clients.
Levesque, D. & Gelles, R. (1998). *Does Treatment Reduce Recidivism in Men Who Batter? Meta-Analytic Evaluation of Treatment Outcome Research.* Paper presentation at Program Evaluation and Family Violence Research: An International Conference. Durham, NH, June 1998.	• 38 outcome studies with single group or between group design	• No differences in treatment and comparison samples were found when relying on partner reports of recidivism. • A difference in favor of the treatment sample was found when relying on official reports of recidivism. • Across types of outcome measures and types of studies, treatment has a small effect on recidivism rates.

12

What Works in Women-Oriented Treatment for Substance Abusing Mothers

Katherine Wingfield and Todd Klempner

Substance abuse by parents is one of the most significant problems facing the child welfare system today. Children whose parents abuse alcohol and other drugs (AOD) are almost three times more likely to be abused and more than four times more likely to be neglected than children of parents who are not substance abusers [Kelleher et al. 1994]. Evidence from several national studies suggest that 40%–80% of all child abuse and neglect cases involve parental misuse of AOD [Young et al. 1998]. Eighty percent of states report that parental substance abuse and poverty are the top two problems among child protective services caseloads [National Committee to Prevent Child Abuse 1998].

Substance abuse treatment is a much-needed but scarce resource for many clients involved with the child welfare system [U.S. Government Accounting Office 1998]. A study of state child welfare agencies by the Child Welfare League of America [1997] estimated that 67% of parents with children in the child welfare system required substance abuse treatment services, but child welfare agencies were able to provide treatment for only 31% of them. Not only do parents have a difficult time obtaining treatment, but available treatment may not match clients' needs. To achieve optimal outcomes for children and families, special attention must be paid to the unique AOD treatment needs of mothers involved with the child welfare system [Nelson-Zlupko et al. 1995].

The Impact of Treatment for Women and their Children

Substance abuse treatment does work. Facilities that provide a continuum of services tailored to meet the special needs of substance-abusing women and their children can do much to improve the life outcomes for these vulnerable families [Center for Substance Abuse Treatment 1998; Young et al. 1998].

- The grant program administered by federal Center for Substance Abuse Treatment (CSAT)—Pregnant and Postpartum Women and Their Infants—incorporates a comprehensive array of services specific to the treatment needs of substance-abusing women and developmentally appropriate services for infants and children. Follow-up data (at a time period of six months to a year after women entered treatment) for 282 women who were enrolled in the program in 1996 demonstrated positive results, including: 67% of the women were not using any drugs, including alcohol; 90% of the women were not involved with the criminal justice system; and 87% of children were living with their mothers [CSAT 1998].

- The STAR program, which is part of the Epiphany Center in San Francisco, provides intensive reunification services to families with infants who have been prenatally exposed to drugs. Between 1994 and 1997, the program reunited 73% of the infants with their families (41% with biological parents; 32% with relatives). The program also includes an array of outpatient services for mothers and follow-up home visits once reunification takes place. [Epiphany Center 1998].

- PAR Village in Florida is a residential center where addicted mothers and their children receive counseling and training in areas ranging from parenting skills to job readiness. A five-year study conducted between 1992 and 1997 followed 52 women and 52 children in treatment (one child of each mother). The study showed that six months after receiving treatment, 65% of participants were drug-free; 87% of the mothers had not been arrested; and 45% of the women had regained custody of their children [Drug Strategies 1998; Operation PAR 1999].

Pregnant and parenting women who use substances require a continuum of culturally competent care that includes a broad range of support services provided over an extended period of time. Ideally, support services should be provided as long as the woman and her family need and can benefit from them. In reality, support services may be available for a period of a few weeks to 18 months. Although there is variation in the types of services and the length of services that women need, data show that the length of stay in treatment has a significant impact on outcomes. PROTOTYPES Women's Center in Pomona, CA, a residential treatment facility serving 80 women and 50 children at a time, conducted follow-up research on 124 women six months after they left the program [Young et al. 1998]. Outcomes were compared based on whether the client stayed for less than 180 days (short stay) or for longer than 180 days (long stay). The results are shown in Table 1.

AOD Treatment Services that Work

A vital component of the continuum of care is the availability of services that are both comprehensive in range yet tailored to meet the special needs of mothers. The continuum includes careful initial assessment through aftercare. CSAT [1993] has outlined five types of services which are often essential for this population.

Table 1. Long vs. Short Term Residential Treatment Outcomes

	Short Stay (<180 days)	Long Stay (>180 days)
AOD abstinence	70%	94%
Employed	48%	63%
No new arrests	72%	96%
Homeless	9%	4%

Health Care Services

Health care services recommended for pregnant and parenting women and their children include: high-risk obstetrical care; postpartum medical and dental checkups for the mother and children; routine checkups and immunizations for all children through a well-baby clinic; and maternal counseling for postpartum depression and guilt regarding the effects of prenatal drug use on the infant. A study done by researchers at John Hopkins University, the National Institute on Drug Abuse (NIDA), and the Maryland State Alcohol and Drug Administration compared the health of babies born to mothers who received treatment with babies whose mothers did not [Svikis et al. 1997]. The treatment group was enrolled in a multi-instructional program which provided both prenatal medical services and AOD treatment services; the control group received no AOD treatment during their pregnancies. Table 2 below details the study's findings.

Alcohol and Other Drug Treatment Services

AOD treatment services needed by pregnant and parenting women include: medically supervised withdrawal executed in collaboration with prenatal care providers; AOD treatment in gender-specific programs that are educationally and culturally sensitive; support and relapse prevention through accessible community groups (such as 12-step programs and

Table 2. Effect of Maternal AOD Treatment on Babies' Health

	Treatment Group	Control Group
Positive drug screen at delivery	37%	63%
Low birthweight infant (< 2500g)	15%	39%
Very low birthweight infant (< 1500g)	0%	17%
Neonatal intensive care unit hospitalization	10%	26%

[Svikis et al. 1997]

support groups); and group and individual counseling that focus on such areas as codependency, self-esteem, sexuality issues, parenting, and relapse prevention. Two such programs are located in Chicago:

- The residential and outpatient program of Chicago's Women's Treatment Center includes services for pregnant women and women with young children. The program offers pregnant women medically supervised detoxification along with a comprehensive list of services. In 1997, all 68 babies delivered while the mother was in treatment were born drug-free [CSAT 1998].

- Haymarket Center also has been successfully providing AOD treatment to women and their children. A post-evaluation of almost 200 clients treated from April 1996 to July 1999 showed that 75% of the women were not using alcohol and over 85% were not using drugs one year after completing treatment [Legal Action Center 1999].

Survival-Related Services

Effective AOD treatment programs provide women (either directly or through referral to other programs) assistance in meeting the family's basic needs. These services may include: assistance in finding drug-free, affordable housing; referrals to emergency shelters; financial assistance through Medicaid and Temporary Assistance to Needy Families (TANF); food assistance through the Special Supplemental Food Program for Women, Infants, and Children (WIC); vocational and job skills training; child care; transportation services; and legal assistance for issues such as family violence, child custody, adoption, and divorce. The National Treatment Improvement Evaluation Study (NTIES) reported the findings of a five-year follow-up to assess the impact of federally funded AOD treatment programs (nonmethadone outpatient, short-term residential, long-term residential, and methadone patient services) on their clients [CSAT 1997]. The study, including 1,374 women, surveyed clients when they entered treatment, completed treatment, and one year post-treatment. Surveys began in June 1993 and finished with a post-treatment survey in October of 1995. A comparison of the women's pre-admittance surveys to the one year post-treatment surveys showed that the number of women employed rose 25%; the women's incomes rose by 6%; and the number of women receiving public assistance decreased by 8% [CSAT 1997].

Psychosocial Services

Women also may have mental health issues that need to be addressed. They may need training in stress and anger management, assertiveness training, relationship and interpersonal skill building, personal care, and psychiatric and other mental health services. An evaluation of the Pregnant and Postpartum Women's Program in Chicago, which provides substance abuse and mental health services, used depression and parenting inventories at admission and discharge to assess the program's impact on their clients' overall psychological functioning and attitudes toward parenting. A depression inventory administered to 77 clients showed dramatically different levels of depression at discharge (45% decrease in their Beck Depression Inventory scores). Additionally, there were significant improvements for 51 women who were evaluated on their attitudes toward parenting and children on the four dimensions of the Adult-Adolescent Parenting Inventory (measuring inappropriate expectations, lack of empathy, physical punishment, and parent-child role reversal) [Oates et al. 1998].

Family and Parenting Services

Family and parenting services may also be needed to improve child safety, promote family reunification and preservation, and enhance general outcomes for children. Such services may include: planning and counseling for reunification with the client's other children who are in foster care; education about child and adult nutritional needs, food purchasing and preparation; education about and training in child growth and development patterns; training in and support for nonpunitive child-rearing practices; assistance with and counseling about maternal and child bonding; and participation in parental support groups. Miracle Village in Cleveland, Ohio, is a residential drug treatment program which engages all family members in treatment. The typical profile of a family enrolled in the program is a 29-year-old mother, addicted to crack, and her three children. The program teaches parenting skills and budgeting and offers wellness classes and family recreational activities. Since the program began in 1992, 305 families, including approximately 900 children, have been served and approximately 100 children in foster care have been reunited with their mothers. Drug-related crime in nearby housing projects has decreased by over 45% since Miracle Village opened [Drug Strategies 1998].

Cost-Effectiveness

Providing substance abuse treatment services to women and their children not only improves outcomes for children and families but also reduces costs to society. It costs $43,200 each year to incarcerate an untreated drug abuser, a figure that does not reflect hidden costs such as foster care and neonatal expenses. This figure compares to an average annual cost of $16,000 for a residential program and an average annual cost of $1,500 for an outpatient program [Operation PAR 1997].

Summit House is a 15-month residential program in North Carolina which serves women whose substance abuse has led to involvement with the criminal justice system and their children. The program has demonstrated significant cost offsets. The average per-day cost for providing services for a mother was $45.37 compared to the cost per day of $72.69 for the same woman in the North Carolina Correctional Institution for Women. The cost per child per day at Summit House was $51.57 compared to an approximate cost per day for the same child in foster care in North Carolina of $116.45 [Summit House 1998].

One prenatal treatment program in Baltimore reported a savings of $18,000–$26,500 per treated mother-infant pair compared with the average cost of treating one drug-exposed infant [Allen & Larson 1998].

Several statewide studies prove cost-effectiveness of AOD treatment [Young et al. 1998]. A California study showed that for every $1 invested in treatment, the state saved $7 [Gerstein et al. 1994]. Oregon determined that $5.60 in AOD-related costs were avoided for every $1 spent on AOD treatment [Finigan 1996].

Conclusion

Alcohol and other drug problems ravage the lives of a majority of the children and families involved with the child welfare system. The heartening news is that many children can remain safe and family breakup can be averted when appropriate treatment is provided. Encouraging outcomes have begun to emerge from the few AOD treatment programs across the United States that focus on women with children. Programs that incorporate a continuum of AOD treatment services that address women's unique health, psychosocial, environmental, and parenting needs as well as the needs of their children have made a significant contribution to promoting self-sufficiency, child safety, and family well-being.

References

Allen, M. L. & Larson, J. (1998). *Healing the whole family: A look at family care programs.* Washington, DC: Children's Defense Fund.

Center for Substance Abuse Treatment. (1993). *Pregnant, substance-using women: Treatment improvement protocol series #2.* Rockville, MD: U.S. Department of Health and Human Services.

Center for Substance Abuse Treatment (1997). *The national treatment improvement evaluation study: Women in treatment.* Rockville, MD: Center for Substance Abuse Treatment.

Center for Substance Abuse Treatment. (1998). *Producing results: A report to the nation 1998.* Rockville, MD: U.S. Department of Health and Human Services.

Child Welfare League of America. (1997). *Alcohol and other drugs: A study of state child welfare agencies' policy and programmatic response.* Washington, DC: Author.

Drug Strategies. (1998). *Keeping score: Women and drugs: Looking at the federal drug control budget.* Washington, DC: Author.

Epiphany Center. (1998). *Epiphany STAR project fact sheet.* San Francisco, CA: Author.

Finigan, M. (1996). *Societal outcomes and cost savings of drug and alcohol treatment in the state of Oregon.* Salem, OR: Department of Human Resources.

Gerstein, D. R., Johnson, R. A., Harwood, H., Fountain, D., Suter, N., & Malloy, K. (1994). *Evaluation recovery services: The California drug and alcohol treatment assessment.* Sacramento, CA: California Department of Alcohol and Drug Programs.

Kelleher, K., Chaffin, M., Hollenberg, J., & Fischer, E. (1994). Alcohol and drug disorders among physically abusive and neglectful parents in a community-based sample. *American Journal of Public Health, 84*(10), 1586–1590.

Legal Action Center. (1999). *Steps to success: Helping women with alcohol and drug problems move from welfare to work.* Washington, DC: Annie E. Casey Foundation.

National Committee to Prevent Child Abuse. (1998). *Current trends in child abuse reporting and fatalities: NCPCA's 1997 annual 50 state survey.* Chicago: Author.

Nelson-Zlupko, L., Kauffman, E., & Dore, M. M. (1995). Gender differences in drug addiction and treatment: Implications for social work intervention with substance-abusing women. *Social Work. 40*(1), 45–54.

Oates, J., Griffith, D., Chandler, J., & Van Biemen, J. (1998). *Final evaluation report for the CSAT funded treatment program for pregnant and postpartum women.* Chicago: Women's Treatment Center.

Operation PAR. (1997). Personal correspondence. Shirley Colletti, President, December.

Operation PAR. (1999). Personal correspondence. Shirley Colletti, President, June.

Summit House. (1998). *Annual report 1997–1998.* Greensboro, NC: Author.

Svikis, D. S., Golden, A. S., Huggins, G. R., Pickens, R. W., McCaul, M. E., Velez, M. L., Rosendale, C. T., Brooner, R. K., Gazaway, P. M., Stitzer, M. L., & Ball, C. E. (1997). Cost-Effectiveness of treatment for drug-abusing pregnant women. *Drug and Alcohol Dependence, 45,* 105–113.

United States General Accounting Office. (1998). *Foster care: Agencies face challenges securing stable homes for children of substance abusers.* Washington, DC: Author.

Young, N. K., Gardner, S. L., & Dennis, K. (1998). *Responding to alcohol and other drug problems in child welfare: Weaving together practice and policy.* Washington, DC: CWLA Press.

What Works in Women-Oriented Treatment for Substance Abuse

Study Authors	Survey Sample	Research Design/Outcome Measure	Findings
Center for Substance Abuse Treatment. (1997). *The national treatment improvement evaluation study: Women in treatment.* Rockville, MD: Center for Substance Abuse Treatment.	• 1,374 women (4,411 total clients) who received federally funded AOD treatment between June 1993 and October 1995 • National sample	• Mainly self-reported data collection with additional data collected from sample drug testing data and sample arrest records • Outcomes measured through pre/post-panel design.	• The number of women employed after treatment rose 25%. • The income of post-treatment women rose 6%. • The number of women receiving public assistance decreased by 8%.
Center for Substance Abuse Treatment. (1998). *Producing results: A report to the nation 1998.* Rockville, MD: U.S. Department of Health and Human Services.	• 282 women and 252 children who were enrolled in Pregnant and Postpartum Women and Their Infants programs funded by CSAT	• Taken from Quarterly Reporting System follow-up data at the end of 1996 • Outcomes measured the effectiveness of CSAT grant programs in reducing substance abuse, reducing crime, increasing employment, and increasing the number of families remaining together.	• 67% of the women were not using any drugs, including alcohol. • 90% of the women were not involved with the criminal justice system post-treatment. • 87% of children were living with their mothers.
Oates, J., Griffith, D., Chandler, J. & Van Biemen, J. (1998). *Final evaluation report for the CSAT funded treatment program for pregnant and post partum women.* Chicago: Women's Treatment Center.	• Conducted from October 1993 through September 1994 • 77 women were measured for scores on the Beck Depression Inventory (BDI) and 51 women measured for scores on the Adult-Adolescent Parenting Inventory (AAPI)	• Outcomes measured were BDI for level of depression, and AAPI for level of agreement with maladaptive parenting behaviors.	• BDI findings: mean depression rating dropped from 11.34 at admission to 5.12 at discharge. • AAPI scores improved from admission to discharge: Inappropriate Expectations scores (23.2 to 25.01); Lack of Empathy (27.75 to 30.85); Physical Punishment (35.82 to 39.49); and Parent Child Role Reversal (25.48 to 29.38).

Reference	Sample	Purpose	Results
Drug Strategies. (1998). *Keeping score: Women and drugs: Looking at the federal drug control budget.* Washington, DC: Drug Strategies.	• A five-year study conducted between 1992 and 1997 of 52 women and 52 children in treatment (one child for each mother)	• Six-month pretest/post-test design • Study measured the effectiveness of the residential treatment center in helping mothers who abused substances.	• Six months after receiving treatment: — 65% of participants were drug-free; — 87% of the mothers had not been arrested; and — 45% of the women regained custody of their children.
Epiphany Center. (1998). *Epiphany S.T.A.R. project fact sheet.* San Francisco, CA: Epiphany Center.	• 59 infants and their 57 birth mothers (there were two sets of twins) who were enrolled in the Epiphany Infant Program	• Study measured how well the program reunified infants with their biological parents or relatives.	• The program reunited 73% of its infants with their families (41% with biological parents; 32% with relatives).
Svikis, D.S., Golden, A.S., Huggins, G.R., Pickens, R.W., McCaul, M.E., Velez, M.L., Rosendale, C.T., Brooner, R.K., Gazaway, P.M., Stitzer, M.L., & Ball, C.E. (1997). Cost-effectiveness of treatment for drug-abusing pregnant women. *Drug and Alcohol Dependence, 45,* 105–113.	• A treatment group of 100 women who were voluntarily admitted to the Center for Addiction and Pregnancy (CAP). Admissions occurred between April 1991 and October 1992 • A control group of 46 women who did not receive drug treatment and were patients at a Baltimore hospital between April 1989 and September 1990—immediately prior to the opening of CAP	• Study measured the effect of prenatal drug treatment on maternal and infant clinical outcomes and cost-effectiveness outcomes.	• 37% of the treatment group had a positive drug screen at delivery compared to 63% of the control group. • 15% of the treatment group delivered a low birthweight infant ($<2500g$) compared to 39% of the control group. • 0% of the treatment group delivered a very low birthweight infant ($<1500g$) compared to 17% of the control group. • 10% of the treatment group required neonatal intensive care hospitalizations compared to 26% of the control group.

(continued next page)

What Works in Women-Oriented Treatment for Substance Abuse (continued)

Study Authors	Survey Sample	Research Design/Outcome Measure	Findings
Young, N.K., Gardner, S.L., & Dennis, K. (1998). *Responding to alcohol and other drug problems in child welfare: Weaving together practice and policy.* Washington, DC: CWLA Press.	• 124 women who had been enrolled in the program	• Six-month follow-up research was conducted comparing outcomes of clients who were in the program under 180 days (short stay) compared to those in treatment over 180 days (long stay).	• 70% of the women who had short stays remained abstinent from AOD use compared to 94% who were classified as having a long stay. • 48% of women with short stays were employed compared to 63% of women with long stays. • 72% of women with short stays had no new arrests compared to 96% of women with long stays. • 9% of women with short stays were homeless compared to 4% of women with long stays.

Section III

Out-of-Home Care

13

What Works in Kinship Care

Jill Duerr Berrick

During the past century, U.S. child welfare practitioners have utilized foster family care as the predominant placement setting for children who must be removed from their parents' homes due to abuse or neglect. During the 1980s, this traditional approach to child placement began to shift with the introduction and then rapid expansion in the use of kinship foster care. Since 1990, kinship care has accounted for almost half of all placements in some states (See Table 1). Kinship foster care involves formal child placement by the juvenile court and the child welfare agency in the home of a child's relative—most frequently the child's grandmother [Hardin et al. 1997]. The relative status of these caregivers sharply distinguishes them from foster family caregivers who, in most instances, are strangers to the child in care.

Kinship foster care has developed swiftly in response to rising child welfare caseloads [Goerge et al. 1995], reductions in the number of available foster family care providers [U.S. Department of Health and Human Services, n.d.], and shifting philosophical notions about family-centered practice in the field of child welfare services [Hegar & Scannapieco 1995].

Child welfare policy vis-à-vis kin differs somewhat by state. In some jurisdictions, kin are only recognized as foster care providers if they meet all of the requirements of conventional foster parents and become fully

Table 1. Kinship Foster Care as a Placement Resource in Selected States, 1990

	Foster Care with Relatives	Foster Family Care with Non-Relatives
Missouri	627	4,380
Illinois	7,653	9,457
California	29,806	32,157
New York	22,937	29,322
Four States Total	61,023	75,316

SOURCE: Hardin, A.W., Clark, R.L. & Maguire, K. (1997). *Informal and formal kinship Care.* Vol.II (p. 33). ASPE Task Order HHS-100-95-0021. Washington, DC: Office of Assistant Secretary for Planning and Evaluation.

licensed [Gleeson & Craig 1994; Hornby et al. 1996]. Elsewhere, kin may be considered children's care providers whether or not they have been formally licensed by the foster care agency [Berrick et al. 1995].

The Benefits of Kinship Care

In light of the continuing expansion of kinship foster care it is relevant to examine the benefits that are afforded children when placed with relatives.

Kinship foster care may be less traumatic than placements in other settings. Children in kinship foster care, as opposed to other kinds of foster care, are more likely to know or be familiar with their kin caregiver prior to placement. This leads some to suggest that the experience of placement may be less traumatic for the youngsters [Child Welfare League of America 1994].

Kinship foster care encourages more visitation and contact with birth parents. Studies have shown that more than half (56%) of children placed with kin saw their parents more than once a month compared to only one-third (32%) of children in nonkin foster care [Berrick et al. 1994; LeProhn 1994] (See Figure 1).

Children in kinship foster care have fewer placement changes during their stays in foster care. In one study, researchers found over half (53%)

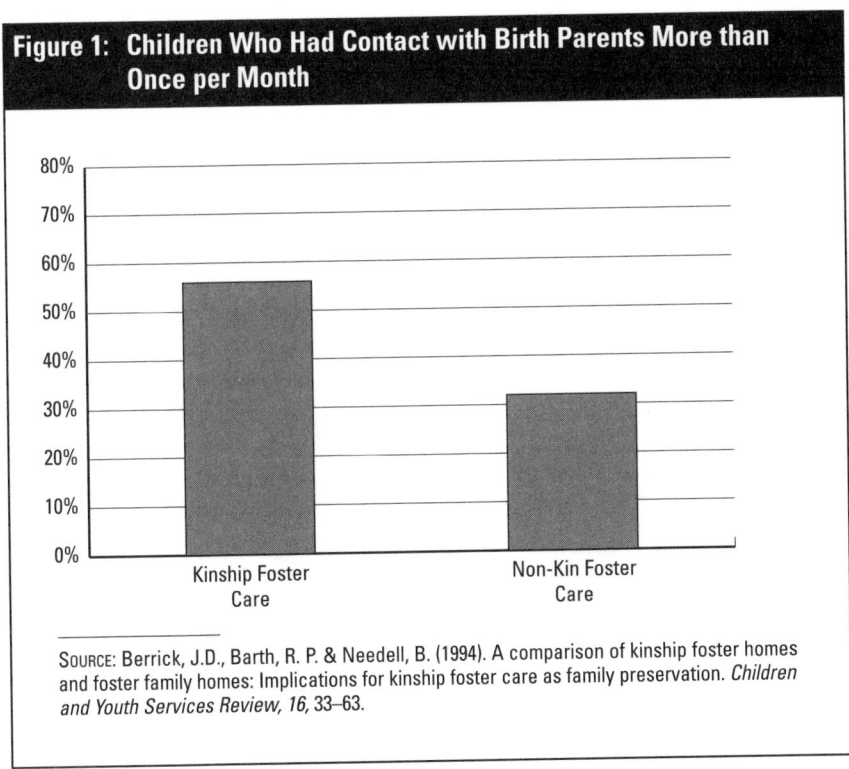

Figure 1: Children Who Had Contact with Birth Parents More than Once per Month

SOURCE: Berrick, J.D., Barth, R. P. & Needell, B. (1994). A comparison of kinship foster homes and foster family homes: Implications for kinship foster care as family preservation. *Children and Youth Services Review, 16,* 33–63.

of children under age six who had been in nonkin foster care for four years had experienced at least three placements compared to 30% of children in kinship foster care [Berrick et al. 1998]. Further, when placement moves cannot be avoided, children in kinship care are more likely to transfer to the home of another relative [Courtney & Needell 1997].

Kinship foster care is associated with more successful reunifications. Children reunified from foster care are less likely to subsequently re-enter care if they were placed with kin. In one study [Berrick et al. 1998], the cumulative probability of returning to care three years after reunification was 16% for children in kinship care and 25% for children in nonkin care. (See Figure 2).

Children in kinship foster care are generally happy with their caregivers. One study examining children's perceptions about residing in foster care showed that children in kinship care were somewhat more likely to indicate that they were "happy" or "very happy" with their caregivers

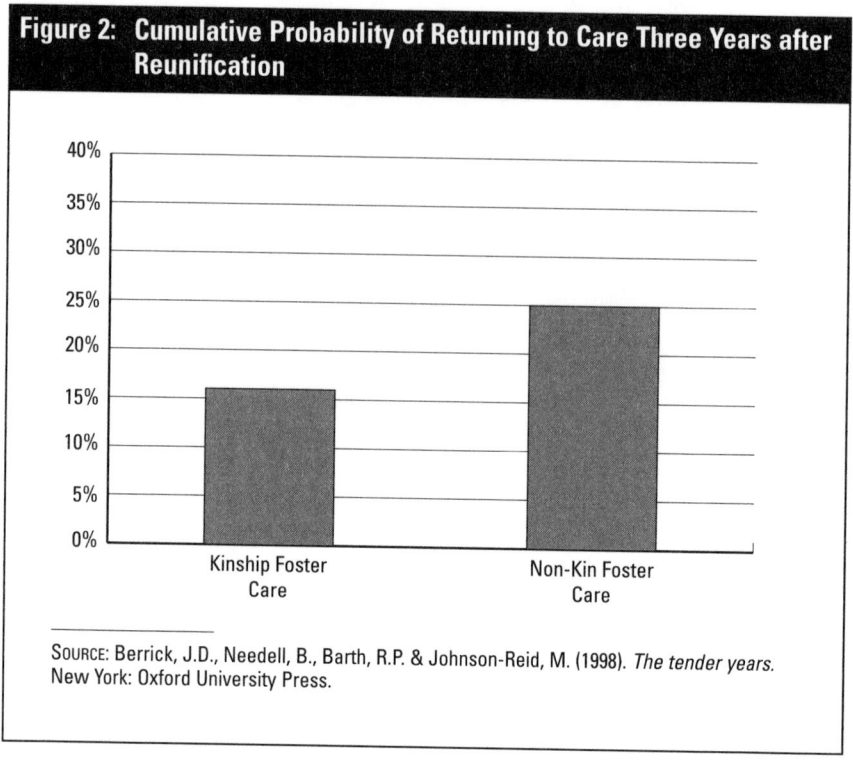

Figure 2: Cumulative Probability of Returning to Care Three Years after Reunification

SOURCE: Berrick, J.D., Needell, B., Barth, R.P. & Johnson-Reid, M. (1998). *The tender years.* New York: Oxford University Press.

compared to children in other forms of care [Wilson 1995]. They also were more likely to say that they "always felt loved" [Wilson 1995].

Although kinship care may provide a variety of benefits to children in care, there is significant evidence to suggest that many of these children may be treated inequitably by the child welfare services system. Kinship foster parents receive less support, fewer services, and less contact with child welfare workers than unrelated foster families [Berrick et al. 1994; Dubowitz 1990; Meyer & Link 1990; Zwas 1993]. Zwas [1993], for example, found that a number of kin either did not receive or experienced delays in receiving Medicaid cards or reimbursement for services that children in their care received. These differences are, in some ways, even more profound because the caregivers may need more from the child welfare system than unrelated foster families. Kinship foster parents are, on average, older and less financially stable; they are more likely to be

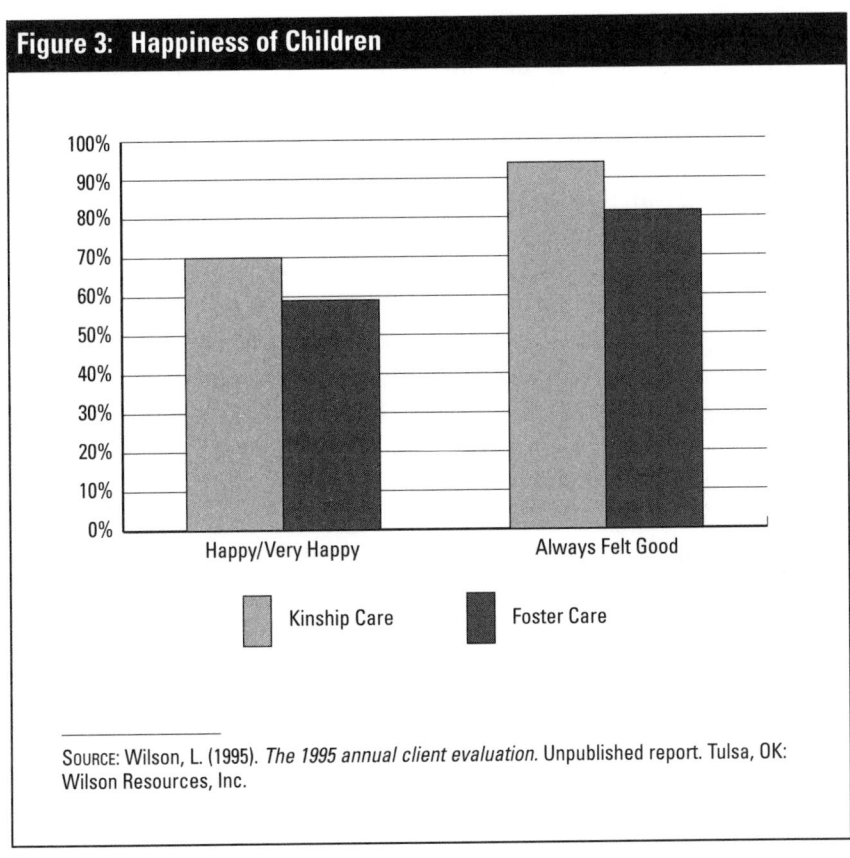

Figure 3: Happiness of Children

Source: Wilson, L. (1995). *The 1995 annual client evaluation.* Unpublished report. Tulsa, OK: Wilson Resources, Inc.

single parents. They have less education; and they are in poorer health [Berrick et al. 1994; Dubowitz 1990; Thornton 1987].

Cost-Effectiveness

Although kinship care affords a number of benefits for children, there is much debate regarding the long-term costs of care. This issue is complicated by the fact that some states pay kinship foster parents the same subsidy as that paid to non-kin; some states pay relatives at the rate of welfare benefits; and other states pay a subsidy in the mid-range between welfare benefits and the foster care subsidy rate [Testa 1997]. These disparities in subsidies result in marked differences in children's long-term living arrangements. In one state, it was found that children whose kin caregivers receive a foster care subsidy are more likely to remain in long-term foster care and are less likely to reunify with birth parents [Berrick & Needell 1999]. In this study, the researchers found that about half of the children whose kinship caregivers were receiving foster care subsidies were reunified with their birth parents within four years compared to two-thirds of children whose kin caregivers were only receiving welfare payments. The lower rates of adoption for children placed with kin [Courtney & Needell 1997] and the limited opportunities for kin to elect legal guardianship (most states do not pay a subsidy to kin who take guardianship) suggest that a study examining the comparative costs of long-term foster care versus subsidized guardianship or adoption may be useful.

Conclusion

Kinship foster care can promote one of the fundamental goals of the child welfare services system—to support families in their efforts to protect children. Children may experience an array of positive outcomes by virtue of their placement with kin, and continued preferences for kin placements will stretch child welfare workers' practice paradigm to be truly family-focused [Jackson 1999]. As this placement alternative grows, child welfare agencies will be challenged to develop policies that promote services to these children and caregivers in order to optimize children's experiences in care.

References

Berrick, J. D., Barth, R. P., & Needell, B. (1994). A comparison of kinship foster homes and foster family homes: Implications for kinship foster care as family preservation. *Children and Youth Services Review, 16*, 33–63.

Berrick, J. D. & Needell, B. (1999). Recent trends in kinship care: Public policy, payments, and outcomes for children. In Curtis, P. A., & Dale, G. (Eds.), *The foster care crisis: Translating research into practice and policy* (pp. 152–174). Lincoln: University of Nebraska Press.

Berrick, J. D., Needell, B., & Barth, R. P. (1995). *Kinship care in California: An empirically-based curriculum.* Unpublished report. Berkeley, CA: Child Welfare Research Center, School of Social Welfare, University of California at Berkeley.

Berrick, J. D., Needell, B., Barth, R. P., & Johnson-Reid, M. (1998). *The tender years.* New York, NY: Oxford University Press.

Child Welfare League of America (1994). *Kinship care: A natural bridge.* Washington, DC: Author.

Courtney, M. E. (1992). *Reunification of foster children with their families: The case of California's children.* Unpublished doctoral dissertation, University of California at Berkeley, Berkeley, CA.

Courtney, M., & Needell, B. (1997). Outcomes of kinship care: Lessons from California. In J. D. Berrick, R. P. Barth, & N. Gilbert (Eds.), *Child welfare research review* (Vol. II) (pp. 130–149). New York: Columbia University Press.

Dubowitz, H. (1990). *The physical and mental health and educational status of children placed with relatives: Final report.* Baltimore: University of Maryland Medical School.

Gleeson, J. P. , & Craig, L. C. (1994). Kinship care in child welfare: An analysis of states' policies. *Children and Youth Services Review, 16,* 17–31.

Goerge, R. M., Wulczyn, F. H., & Harden, A. W. (1995). *An update from the multistate foster care data archive.* Chicago, IL: Chapin Hall Center for Children at the University of Chicago.

Hardin, A. W., Clark, R. L., & Maguire, K. (1997). *Informal and formal kinship care.* ASPE Task order HHS-100-95-0021. Washington, DC: Office of the Assistant Secretary for Planning and Evaluation.

Hegar, R. L., & Scannapieco, M. (1995). From family duty to family policy: The evolution of kinship care. *Child Welfare, 72,* 367–378.

Hornby, H., Zeller, D., & Karraker, D. (1996). Kinship care in America: What outcomes should policy seek? *Child Welfare, 75,* 397–418.

Jackson, S. M. (1999). Paradigm shift: Training staff to provide services to the kinship triad. In R. L. Hegar & M. Scannapiero (Eds.), *Kinship foster care* (pp. 93–111). New York: Oxford.

LeProhn, N. S. (1994). The role of the kinship foster parent: A comparison of the role conceptions of relative and non-relative foster parents. *Children and Youth Services Review, 16,* 107–122.

Meyer, B. S., & Link, M. K. (1990). *Kinship foster care: The double edged dilemma.* Rochester, NY: Task Force on Permanency Planning for Foster Children, Inc.

Testa, M. (1997). Kinship foster care in Illinois. In J. D. Berrick, R. P. Barth, & N. Gilbert (Eds.), *Child Welfare Research Review,* (Vol. II) (pp. 101–129). New York: Columbia University Press.

Thornton, J. L. (1987). *An investigation into the nature of the kinship foster home.* Doctoral dissertation. Wurzweiler School of Social Work, Yeshiva University, New York.

U.S. Department of Health and Human Services (n.d.). *The national survey of current and former foster parents.* Contract Number: 105-89-1602. Washington, DC: U.S. Department of Health and Human Services.

Wilson, L. (1995). *The 1995 annual client evaluation.* Unpublished report. Tulsa, OK: Wilson Resources, Inc.

Wulczyn F. & Goerge, R. M. (1992). Foster care in New York & Illinois: The challenge of rapid change. *Social Service Review, 66,* 278–294.

Zwas, M. G. (1993). Kinship foster care: A relatively permanent solution. *Fordham Urban Law Journal, 20*(2), 343–373.

What Works in Kinship Care

Study Authors	Survey Sample	Research Design/ Outcome Measure	Findings
Berrick, J.D., Barth, R. P. & Needell, B. (1994). A comparison of kinship foster homes and foster family homes: Implications for kinship foster care as family preservation. *Children and Youth Services Review, 16,* 33–63.	• 246 kin caregivers; 354 nonkin caregivers in California	• Cross-sectional mailed survey • Descriptive study regarding the characteristics of caregivers and children in care	• Visitation: 56% of children placed with kin saw parents more than once a month compared to 32% of foster children; 3% of children in foster care saw their parents regularly; 19% of kin children saw a parent a least once a week.
Berrick, J.D. & Needell, B. (1999). Recent trends in kinship care: Public policy, payments, and outcomes for children. In Curtis, P.A., & Dale, G. (Eds.) *The foster care crisis: Translating research into practice and policy* (pp. 152–174). University of Nebraska Press.	• All children who entered care for the first time between 1989 and 1991 and who were placed in kin (n=32,946) and nonkin (n=32,586) foster homes	• Administrative data • Permanency outcomes for children whose kin caregivers received AFDC-FC payments vs. kin caregivers who received AFDC-FG	• AFDC-FC children are about half as likely to be reunified as either AFDC children or children in foster care.

(continued on next page)

What Works in Kinship Care (*continued*)

Study Authors	Survey Sample	Research Design/ Outcome Measure	Findings
Berrick, J.D., Needell, B., Barth, R. P. & Johnson-Reid, M. (1998). *The tender years.* New York, NY: Oxford University Press.	• A cohort of children (n=14,299) who entered care at age 6 or younger	• Administrative data • Examined reunification, re-entry, placement stability, adoption rates, and legal guardianship rates	Four years after initial placement: • Equal proportions of children in kin and nonkin placements were reunified (52%). • 32% of kin vs. 27% of nonkin children were still in care. • 5% of kin vs. 17% of nonkin children were adopted. • 9% of kin vs. 1% of nonkin children were placed in legal guardianship. • 30% of kin vs. 53% of nonkin children had experienced three or more placements while in care. • The probability of re-entry three years after reunification was .13 for infants placed with kin vs. .28 for infants placed with nonkin and was .16 for kin children ages 0–17 and .25 for nonkin children.
Courtney, M. E. (1992). *Reunification of foster children with their families: The case of California's children.* Unpublished doctoral dissertation, University of California at Berkeley, Berkeley, CA.	• 10 % random sample (n=8748) of children who entered foster care in California for the first time between January 1988 and May 1991	• Administrative data	• Children with kin are less likely to reunify during the first year of placement. Reunification rates grow similarly for kin and nonkin after first year in care.

Citation	Sample	Measures	Findings
Courtney, M., & Needell, B. (1997). Outcomes of Kinship Care: Lessons From California. In J.D. Berrick, R. P. Barth, & N. Gilbert (Eds.) *Child Welfare Research Review*, (Vol. II) (pp. 130–149). New York: Columbia University Press.	• Children who entered care in 1988 whose predominant placement was with kin (n = 4644)	• Administrative data • Odds of reunification compared to remaining in long-term foster care	• African American children were much less likely to reunify compared to Caucasian children and somewhat less likely than Hispanic children. • Neglected children placed with kin are about one-quarter less likely to be reunified than physically or sexually abused children placed with kin. • Kin caregivers whose children are AFDC-eligible are about one-third less likely to reunify compared to kin whose children are not AFDC-eligible. • 85% of children initially placed with kin either remain steadily in the same placement or, if moved, move to the home of another relative.
Wulczyn F., & Goerge, R. M. (1992). Foster care in New York & Illinois: The challenge of rapid change. *Social Service Review, 66*, 278–294.	• Administrative records for children entering care in New York, NY and Cook County, IL from 1987 to 1989	• Length of stay in care	• NY: 88% of kin vs. 50% nonkin were still in care by 1990. • IL: 45% kin vs. 40% nonkin were still in care by 1990.

14

What Works in Family Foster Care

Peter J. Pecora and Anthony N. Maluccio

F amily foster care includes single or multiple parent households (relative and nonrelative) that are licensed to care for children who can no longer live with their birth parents. Specific service objectives include the prevention of further child maltreatment; maintenance of family, school, and other connections; minimizing movement from one home to another; stabilization or improvement of the child's emotional, social, and cognitive functioning; and meeting children's immediate health care needs.

Findings from five states (California, Illinois, Michigan, New York and Texas)—which together contain almost half of the nation's foster care population—show the following:

- Foster care caseloads have more than doubled over the past 10 years;
- Admission patterns appear to be far more dynamic than exit patterns, with fluctuations in entry levels tending to dominate short-term changes in the foster care population;
- Much of the recent growth in foster care has involved the placement of children with relatives;
- Two observed episodes of extremely rapid short-term growth in state foster care populations have occurred almost entirely in larger urban centers of the states;

- Entry rates to foster care and the typical length of stay in care showed extensive fluctuations both over time and between population subgroups;
- The number of infants entering foster care has been increasing; and
- Infants are staying in care longer than children who enter at older ages [Goerge et al. 1994; Goerge el al. 1996].

These types of indicators must be developed and continually updated in all states and at the federal level if the field is to be responsive to changes in the population and in service outcomes.

Objectives of Family Foster Care

The key objectives of family foster care are child safety, permanence, and child and family well-being.

Child Safety

Placement in family foster care is intended, at minimum, to help children avoid further child maltreatment. Overall, family foster care has a fairly good track record in protecting children from harm, considering the numbers of children placed and the frequency with which they move in and out of care. Reliable data about rates of child abuse or neglect in larger foster care populations, however, are sparse. As a result, it is difficult to gauge agency performance in this area [Poertner et al. 1999; Zuravin et al. 1997]. The findings from these studies differ, with maltreatment rates by caregivers in out-of-home settings found to range from 3% to 7% [Bolton et al. 1981; Poertner et al. 1999; Ryan et al. 1987].

Permanence

Studies have found that length of stay in foster care is fairly short in most states but varies widely [see Goerge, et al. 1996; Tatara 1997]. For example, the median length of stay in the early 1990s was just under nine months in Texas, 18.1 months in California, and 24.5 months in New York [see Goerge et al. 1996]. This variation is much greater than would be expected as a result of community differences and suggests that much work is needed to refine services in many states to attain more consistent and timely permanent placements for children. A recent evaluation of the Family-to-Family initiatives in Alabama, North Carolina, and Ohio suggests that large scale initiatives can have an impact in key areas of permanency [Usher et al. 1999]. Studies have shown that a range of factors account for achieving permanent placements for children more quickly [Courtney 1994]. One study, for example, found that children whose mothers had prenatal care at any time during pregnancy had a shorter placement duration than children born to mothers without the benefits of prenatal care [Wulcyzn 1992, as cited in Goerge et al. 1994: 532–533].

Child Well-Being

Many youth are served effectively in family foster care, view it as necessary for their well-being, and make significant improvements in behavioral functioning, emotional development, physical health, and academic achievement. One study, for example, found that children living in non-relative family foster care were more likely to say they were "loved" and "safe" than children in group care [Wilson & Conroy 1999]. As shown in Figure 1, children in kinship care were even more likely to report always feeling loved.

The research data, however, also indicate that there is variability in child, youth, and family outcomes achieved, depending upon the particular outcome domain [Alexander & Huberty 1993; Blome 1997; Chernoff et al. 1994; Courtney et al. 1998; Fanshel et al. 1990; Fanshel & Shinn 1978; Frost & Jurich 1983; Jones & Moses 1984; Kluger et al. 1998; Maluccio & Fein 1985; Meier 1965; Robins 1966; Susser et al. 1987; The Pressley Ridge Schools 1997, 1998; Wedeven et al. 1997; Wald et al. 1988; Walsh & Walsh 1990; Widom & Ames 1994.] Complicating much of the outcomes research is the lack of an appropriate control group comprised of persons who have been raised in nonfoster care environments but who are demographically similar to children raised in foster care— that is, they were raised in families of similar income levels and with similar mental health or parenting problems or depending on the study objectives, were placed in other types of out-of-home care such as residential treatment [Buehler et al. 1999; McDonald et al. 1996; Zimmerman 1982]. Nevertheless, it has been shown that youths discharged from foster care grow and function effectively if provided with continuing supports from biological and foster families as well as from child welfare and other service agencies [see Biehal & Wade 1996].

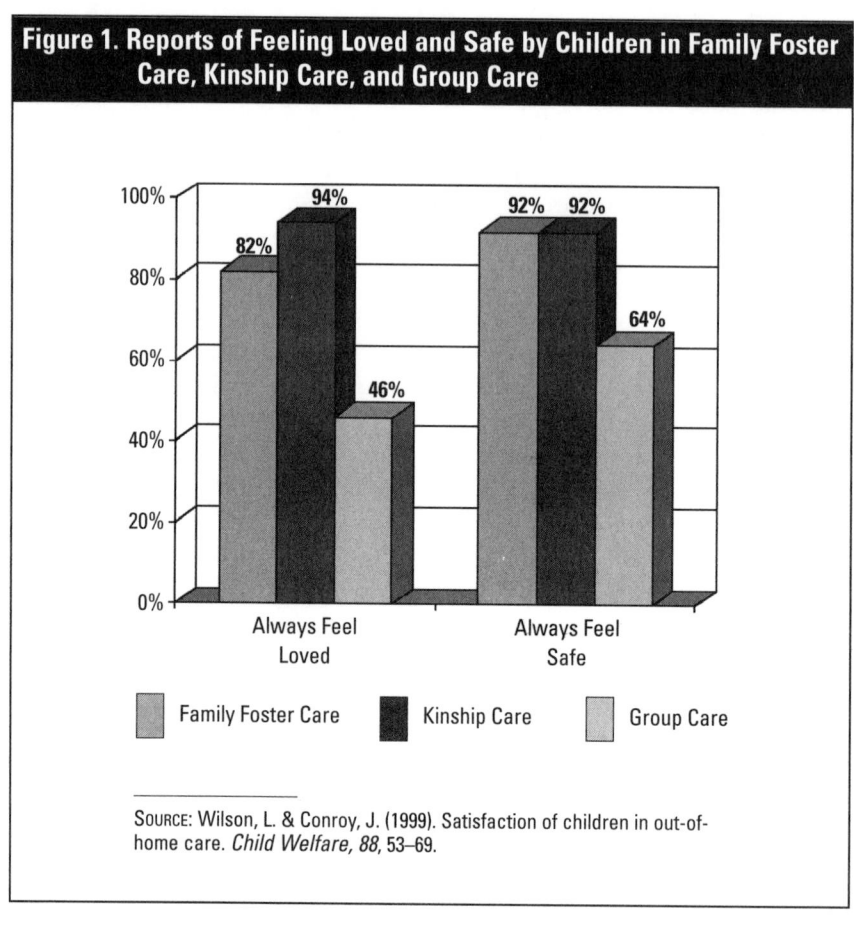

Figure 1. Reports of Feeling Loved and Safe by Children in Family Foster Care, Kinship Care, and Group Care

Always Feel Loved: Family Foster Care 82%, Kinship Care 94%, Group Care 46%

Always Feel Safe: Family Foster Care 92%, Kinship Care 92%, Group Care 64%

SOURCE: Wilson, L. & Conroy, J. (1999). Satisfaction of children in out-of-home care. *Child Welfare, 88,* 53–69.

Major Components of Effective Family Foster Care

There is a lack of rigorous research aimed at evaluating model foster care programs, hampering efforts to refine services and key program components. Despite these limitations, there are components of family foster care that appear promising.

Goal-Oriented Case Planning and Family Involvement

Program effectiveness in family foster care begins with intensive, focused, and goal-oriented case planning that involves the child, birth family and extended family members as appropriate. The process must involve a careful intake study, family-focused assessments, service contracts, and provision of both clinical and concrete services such as employment, housing, and income assistance. Systematic decision-making and the use of time limits are equally crucial. These elements are incorporated in recent developments related to "concurrent planning"—an approach which presently is under study [Curran & Pecora 1999; Emlen et al. 1978; Fein et al. 1990; Katz 1999; Maluccio et al. 1986; Stein et al. 1978].

Providing Youth With Some Voice in Their Care

Children placed in foster care need to have a sense of their future and some role in decision-making [Colton 1989; Festinger 1983; Holdway & Ray 1992; Gil & Bogart 1982; Johnson et al. 1995; Kufeldt 1984; Rice & McFadden 1988; Wilson & Conroy 1999]. Barth and Berry [1987, 1994] reviewed a number of studies regarding preferred permanency planning outcomes (reunification, adoption, guardianship, and long-term foster care) from the child's perspective and found:

- All but one of the children who returned home preferred their present home to their foster home;
- Child satisfaction was highly associated with the child's sense of permanence;
- Children who had multiple placements and who sought a sense of belonging preferred adoption;
- Children living in institutions felt less comfortable, not as happy, less loved, less trusted, and less cared about than did children in other forms of out-of-home care or children reunified with their families; and
- Children who had some choice in their foster care placement were significantly more satisfied with their care than were children who were given no choice.

Facilitating Child Adjustment

Placement is often an emotionally upsetting event for the child, depending upon the home situation they are leaving. The stability of the placement is important for a child's positive self-identity [Cox & Cox

1985; Fanshel & Shinn 1978] and is associated with social worker and foster parent factors such as the ability to balance flexibility and firmness, willingness to be a child advocate, and a sense of humor [Massinga & Perry 1994; Teather et al. 1994]. Practices related to better adjustment for children also include:

- Providing an opportunity for children to share their feelings of confusion and rejection in order to understand the nature of their placement in foster care and to minimize denial, fantasy, and the repression of their pain and suffering [Costin 1979].

- Maintaining some continuity with the prior environment, as children are better able to modify their relationship with their parents if their relationships with them are not denied or they are not expected to abandon them [Fein et al. 1990].

- Promoting identification with birth parents, when appropriate. In one study [Weinstein 1960], it was found that children with the strongest identification with their birth parents had the highest adjustment; children who identified with their birth and foster parents and whose birth parents visited them regularly adjusted well; and children with mixed feelings of identification with birth parents and foster parents and whose birth parents did not visit them adjusted poorly. An overriding factor in most cases was the child's sense of permanence, irrespective of the type of out-of-home placement [Lahti 1982].

- Providing information about the reasons for placement and the meaning of being in foster care. Children who know their birth family makeup, their age when they left home, and where their parents are living adjust and fare better in foster care [Fein et al. 1990].

- Promoting agreement among foster parents, social workers, and birth parents concerning their roles and plans for the child. A coordinated approach results in more cooperation and more effective use of services [Gottsfeld 1970; Maluccio et al. 1986; Maluccio & Whittaker 1988; Palmer 1995].

Agency Investment in Staff Members and an Array of Services

Family foster care works best when there is a determined effort by experienced and trained social workers with reasonable caseloads, and intensive family services are provided early in the child's placement [Kadushin & Martin 1988; Pecora et al. in press; Shapiro 1976]. Social worker visits have been found to be a highly influential factor in the process and outcome of family reunification efforts [Warsh et al. 1994]. Shapiro [1976], for example, found:

- Social worker stability contributed to the discharge of children from foster care during the first two years of placement but not later;
- Social workers with either low or high caseloads tended to discharge children more frequently than those with middle-range caseloads;
- Experienced social workers were more likely to return a child home in the first year of placement but less so as the placement continued;
- Social worker and parental contacts with children were strongly associated with a child's discharge during the first year of placement and less so after one year; and
- During the first year, maternal improvement was related to frequency of contact with the social worker; during the second year, to low caseloads and no worker turnover; and after two years, to none of these measures.

Empathy, positive regard, ability to form a helping relationship, clear communication, cultural competence, and expectations for improvement are important intervention components that are linked with treatment effectiveness. These skills require an investment in social worker recruitment, careful staff screening, and high quality staff development programs. [Cross et al. 1989; Dillon 1994; Iglehart 1992; Shealy 1995; Weisz et al. 1992]. Competency-based approaches to education and training that tie worker performance to the agency's goals and priorities are especially effective [Warsh et al. 1996].

Parental Visitation

Visits with parents and siblings are not only highly correlated with better child functioning at discharge from foster care, but visited children leave family foster care in much higher numbers and more quickly [Fanshel & Shinn 1978]. Especially crucial is early and regular parent-child visits after the child's placement [Hess & Proch 1988].

School and Community Involvement as Part of a System of Care

Preventive supplementary services and more alternatives to foster care are essential. Child placement agencies that have ready access in-house or through a closely linked referral system to a range of service options—such as homemaker, crisis intervention, and emergency housing—are much more likely to develop service plans leading to a child's return home or other permanent placement. Children often need multiple services to meet medical, educational, and psychological needs as well as special educational supports such as tutoring, enrichment, and other educational programs [Aldgate 1990; Biehal & Wade 1996; Winters & Maluccio 1988]. Wraparound and other components of a system of care can help youth obtain the services they need in effective ways [Stroul 1996].

Focus on Independent Living Skills

The disruptions and traumas often suffered by children in foster care may delay or interrupt the development of life skills needed for successful transition to independent living. Programming and services designed to fill these gaps are essential for successful emancipation and social integration. The youth and the foster care agency must take responsibility early in the placement process for jointly developing a self-sufficiency plan—a process that requires the identification of needed attitudes, skills, and behaviors [Barth 1990; Mech 1994; Mech & Rycraft 1996; Nollan 1996; North et al. 1988; Wedeven & Mauzerall 1990]. Recent research finds that preserving or building support networks for youth may be especially important [Buehler et al. 1999; M. E. Courtney, personal communication, March 31, 1999].

Cost-Effectiveness

Very little work has been done on the cost-effectiveness of family foster care, and yet programs that have paid attention to costs have found important benefits from certain kinds of services. Wulczyn, Zeidman, and Svirsky [1997], in their study of a demonstration project in New York City that capitated prospective payments for family foster care, found that greater flexibility in services and lower caseloads resulted in accelerated parent-child reunifications. Fraser and colleagues [1996] also found that intensive family-based service methods were effective in helping children achieve permanent planning outcomes. When projected over time and for larger groups of children, the economic benefits of effective foster care programs can be substantial.

Conclusion

Innovative family foster care practice involves a number of common features: responsive and timely efforts; reasonable worker caseloads; goal- and time-oriented service plans; close intraagency as well as interagency coordination of services; reliance on a variety of services and strategies; and emphasis on family and community-based services. Explicit case planning and case monitoring, special training on permanency planning processes and techniques, and leadership at the supervisory and administrative levels reduce the possibility of foster care drift and increase the probability of early provision of permanent care and positive child development [Berrick et al. 1998; Chamberlain 1994; Goerge et al. 1994; Hudson et al. 1992; Kadushin & Martin 1988; Pecora et al. in press]. At the same time, more research is needed to further refine family foster care programs and delineate key service components, particularly in relation to the diverse children and families served.

References

Aldgate, J. (1990). Foster children at school: Success or failure? *Adoption & Fostering, 14,* 38–69.

Alexander, G. & Huberty, T. J. (1993). *Caring for troubled children: The Villages follow-up study.* Bloomington, IN: The Villages of Indiana.

Barth, R. P. (1990). On their own: The experience of youth after foster care. *Child and Adolescent Social Work, 7*(5), 419–440.

Barth, R. P., & Berry, M. (1987). Outcomes of child welfare services under permanency planning. *Social Service Review, 61*(1), 71–90.

Barth, R. P., & Berry, M. (1994). Implications for research on the welfare of children under permanency planning. In R. P. Barth, J. D. Berrick, and N. Gilbert (Eds.), *Child Welfare Research Review* (Vol. 1) (pp. 323–368). New York: Columbia University Press.

Berrick, J. D., Needell, B. Barth. R. P., & Johnson-Reid, M. (1998). *The tender years: Toward developmentally sensitive child welfare services for very young children.* New York: Oxford University Press.

Biehal, N., & Wade, J. (1996). Looking back, looking forward: Care leavers, families and change. *Children and Youth Services Review, 18*(4 & 5), 425–446.

Blome, W. W. (1997). What happens to foster kids: Educational experiences of a random sample of foster care youth and a matched group of non-foster care youth. *Child and Adolescent Social Work Journal, 14*(1), 41–53.

Bolton, F., Laner, R., & Gai, D. (1981). For better or worse: Foster parents and children in an officially reported child maltreatment population. *Children and Youth Services Review, 3*(1), 37–53.

Buehler, C., Orme, J., Post, J., & Patterson, D. (1999). *The long-term correlates of family foster care.* Knoxville: University of Tennessee.

Chamberlain, P. (1994). *Family connections: Treatment foster care for adolescents with delinquency.* Eugene, OR: Castalia Press.

Chernoff, R., Combs-Orne, T., Risley-Curtiss, C., & Heisler, A. (1994). Assessing the health status of children entering foster care. *Pediatrics, 93*(4), 594–601.

Colton, M. (1989). Foster and residential children's perceptions of their social environments. *British Journal of Social Work, 19,* 217–233.

Costin, L. B. (1979). *Child welfare: Policies and practice.* New York, NY: McGraw Hill.

Courtney, M. E. (1994). Factors associated with reunification of foster children with their families. *Social Service Review, 68*(1), 81–108.

Courtney, M. E., Piliavin I., Grogan-Kaylor, A., & Nesmith, A. (1998). *Foster youth transitions to adulthood: Outcomes 12–18 months after leaving out-of-home care.* Madison, WI: University of Wisconsin-Madison, School of Social Work and Institute for Research on Poverty.

Cox, M., & Cox, R. D. (1985). *Foster care: Current issues, policies and practices.* Norwood, NJ: Ablex Publishing Co.

Cross, T. L., Bazron, B. J., Dennis, K. W., & Issacs, M. R. (1989). *Towards a culturally competent system of care: A monograph on effective services for minority children who are severely emotionally disturbed.* Washington, DC: Georgetown University Child Development Center.

Curran, M. C. & Pecora, P. J. (1999). Assessing youth perspectives of family foster care: Selected research findings and methodological challenges. In P. Curtis, D. Grady, & J. Kendall (Eds.), *The foster care crisis: Translating research into practice and policy.* Lincoln, NE: University of Nebraska Press.

Dillon, D. (1994). Understanding and assessment of intragroup dynamics in family foster care: African American families. *Child Welfare, 73,* 129–139.

Emlen, A., Lahti, J., Downs, G., McKay, A., & Downs, S. (1978). *Overcoming barriers to planning for children in foster care.* Portland, OR: Regional Research Institute for Human Services, Portland State University.

Fanshel, D. & Shinn, E. B. (1978). *Children in foster care: A longitudinal investigation.* New York: Columbia University Press.

Fanshel, D., Finch, S. J., & Grundy, J. F. (1990). *Foster children in life course perspective.* New York: Columbia University Press.

Fein, E., Maluccio, A., & Kluger, M. (1990). *No more partings: An examination of long-term foster family care.* Washington, DC: Child Welfare League of America.

Festinger, T. (1983). *No one ever asked us . . . A postscript to foster care.* New York: Columbia University Press.

Fraser, M. W., Walton, E., Lewis, R. E., Pecora, P. J., & Walton, W. K. (1996). An experiment in family reunification: Correlates of outcome at one-year follow-up. *Children and Youth Services Review, 18*(4–5), 325–362.

Frost, S. & Jurich, A. P. (1983). Follow-up study of children residing in The Villages. Unpublished report. Topeka, KS: The Villages.

Gil, E. & Bogart, K. (1982). Foster children speak out: A study of children's perceptions of foster care. *Children Today 11*(1), 7–9.

Goerge, R. M., Wulczyn, F. H., & Harden, A. (1996). New comparative insights into states and their foster children. *Public Welfare, 54*(3), 12–25, 52.

Goerge, R. M., Wulczyn, F. H, & Harden, A. (1994). *Multi-state foster care data archive: A report on first year results. First Annual Report to the U.S. Department of Health and Human Services.* Chicago: Chapin Hall Center for Children.

Goerge, R., Wulczyn, F., & Fanshel, D. (1994). A foster care research agenda for the 90s. *Child Welfare, 73,* 525–547.

Gottesfeld, H. (1970). *In Loco Parentis: A study of perceived role values in foster home care.* New York: Jewish Child Care Association of New York.

Hess, P. M., & Proch, K. O. (1988). *Family visiting in out-of-home care: Guide to practice.* Washington, DC: Child Welfare League of America.

Holdaway, D. M. & Ray, J. (1992). Attitudes of street kids toward foster care. *Child and Adolescent Social Work Journal, 9*(4), 307–317.

Hudson, J., Nutter, R. W., & Galaway, B. (1992). *Evaluation research on the treatment foster care programs serving youth: A review and suggested directions.* Toronto, Canada: Laidlaw Foundation.

Iglehart, A. P. (1992). Adolescents in foster care: Factors affecting the worker youth relationship. *Children and Youth Services Review, 14,* 305–322.

Johnson, P. R., Yoken, C., & Voss, R. (1995). Family foster care placement: The child's perspective. *Child Welfare, 74,* 959–974.

Jones, M. A. & Moses, B. (1984). *West Virginia's former foster children: Their experiences in care and their lives as young adults.* New York: Child Welfare League of America.

Kadushin, A. & Martin, J. A. (1988). *Child Welfare Services.* (4th ed.). New York: MacMillan

Katz, L. (1999). Concurrent planning: Benefits and pitfalls. *Child Welfare, 78,* 71–87.

Kluger, M., Aprea, D., Mace, P. G., & Charbonneau, B. F. (1998). Factors related to improvements in children's behavior while in specialized foster care. (Mimeograph). Hartford, CT: The Village for Families and Children, Inc.

Kufeldt, K. (1984). Listening to children: Who cares? *British Journal of Social Work, 14,* 257–264.

Lahti, J. (1982). A follow-up study of foster children in permanent placements. *Social Service Review, 56,* 556–571.

Maluccio, A. N. & Whittaker, J. K. (1988). Helping the biological families of children in out-of-home placement. In W. W. Nunnally, C. S. Chilman, & F. M. Cox (Eds.), *Troubled relationships: Families in trouble series,* (Vol. 3) (pp. 205–217). Newbury Park, CA: Sage.

Maluccio, A. N. & Fein, E. (1985). Growing up in foster care. *Children and Youth Services Review, 7,* 123–134.

Maluccio, A. N., Fein, E., & Olmstead, K. A. (1986). *Permanency planning for children: Concepts and methods.* New York: Routledge, Chapman and Hall.

Massinga, R. & Perry, K. (1994). The Casey Family Program: Factors in effective management of a long-term foster care organization. In J. Blacher (Ed.), *There is no place like home* (pp. 113–180). Baltimore, MD: Paul H. Brookes.

McDonald, T. P., Allen, R. I., Westerfelt, A., & Piliavin, I. (Eds.). (1996). *Assessing the long-term effects of foster care: A research synthesis.* Washington, DC: CWLA Press.

Mech, E. V. (1994). Preparing foster youth for adulthood: A knowledge-building perspective. *Children and Youth Services Review, 16*(3/4), 141–145.

Mech, E. V. & Rycraft, J. R. (1996). *Preparing foster youths for adult living: Proceedings of an invitational research conference.* Washington, DC: Child Welfare League of America.

Meier, E. G. (1965). Current circumstances of former foster children. *Child Welfare, 54,* 196–206.

Nollan, K. A. (1996). *Self-sufficiency skills among youth in long-term foster care.* Unpublished doctoral dissertation, University of Washington, Seattle.

North, J., Mallabar, M., & Desrochers, R. (1988). Vocational preparation and employability development. *Child Welfare, 67,* 573–586.

Palmer, S. E. (1995). *Maintaining family ties: Inclusive practice in foster care.* Washington, DC: Child Welfare League of America.

Pecora, P. J., Whittaker, J. K., Maluccio, A. N., & Barth, R. P., with R. Plotnick. (In press.) *The child welfare challenge* (2nd ed.). Hawthorne, NY: Walter de Gruyter.

Poertner, J., Bussey, M., & Fluke, J. (1999). How safe are out-of-home placements? *Children and Youth Services Review, 21*(7), 549–563.

Rice, D. L. & McFadden, E. J. (1988). A forum for foster children. *Child Welfare, 67*, 231–243.

Robins, L. N. (1966). *Deviant children grown up: A sociological and psychiatric study of sociopathic personality.* Baltimore, MD: Williams and Wilkins.

Ryan, P., McFadden, E., & Wiencek, P. (1987). *Analyzing abuse in family foster care.* Final report to the National Center on Child Abuse and Neglect on Grant #90CA097. Washington, DC.

Shapiro, D. (1976). *Agencies and foster children.* New York: Columbia University Press.

Shealy, C. N. (1995). From Boys Town to Oliver Twist: Separating fact from fiction in welfare reform and out-of-home placement of children and families. *American Psychologist, 50*(8), 565–580.

Stein, T. J., Gambrill, E. D., & Wiltse, K. T. (1978). *Children in foster homes: Achieving continuity of care.* New York: Praeger.

Stroul, B. (1996). *Children's mental health: Creating systems of care in a changing society.* Baltimore, MD: Paul H. Brookes Publishing Co.

Susser, E. Struening, E. L., & Conover, S. (1987). Childhood experiences of homeless men. *American Journal of Psychiatry, 144*, 1599–1601.

Tatara, T. (1997). U. S. child substitute care flow data and the race/ethnicity of children in care for FY 1995, along with recent trends in the U.S. child substitute care populations. *VCIS Research Notes, 113.* Washington, DC: American Public Welfare Association.

Teather, E. C., Davidson, S., & Pecora, P. J. (1994). *Placement disruption in foster care.* Seattle: The Casey Family Program.

The Pressley Ridge Schools (1997). *Snapshot: Outcomes 1996.* Pittsburgh, PA: Pressley Ridge.

The Pressley Ridge Schools (1998). *Snapshot: Measuring outcomes 1997.* Pittsburgh, PA: Pressley Ridge.

Usher, C. L., Wildfire, J. B., & Gibbs, D. A. (1999). Measuring performance in child welfare: Secondary effects of success. *Child Welfare, 88*(1), 31–51.

Wald, M. S., Carlsmith, J. M., & Leiderman, P. H. (1988). *Protecting abused and neglected children.* Stanford, CA: Stanford University Press.

Walsh, J. A. & Walsh, R. A. (1990). *Quality care for tough kids.* Washington, DC: Child Welfare League of America.

Warsh, R., Maluccio, A. N., & Pine, B. A. (1994). *Teaching family reunification: A sourcebook.* Washington, DC: Child Welfare League of America.

Warsh, R., Pine, B. A., & Maluccio, A. N. (1996). *Reconnecting families: A guide to strengthening family reunification services.* Washington, DC: Child Welfare League of America.

Wedeven, T. & Mauzerall, H. (1990). Independent living programs: Avenues to competence. In A. N. Maluccio, R. Krieger, & B. A. Pine (Eds.), *Preparing adolescents for life after foster care: The central role of foster parents* (pp. 91–105). Washington, DC: Child Welfare League of America.

Wedeven, T., Pecora, P. J., Hurwitz, M., Howell, R., & Newell, D. (1997). Examining the perceptions of alumni of long-term family foster care: A follow-up study. *Community Alternatives: International Journal of Family Care, 9(1),* 88–105.

Weinstein, E. A. (1960). *The self-image of the foster child.* New York: Russell Sage Foundation.

Weisz, J. R., Weiss, B., & Donenberg, G. R. (1992). The lab versus the clinic: Effects of child and adolescent psychotherapy. *American Psychologist, 47,* 1878–1585.

Widom, C. S. & Ames, M. A. (1994). Criminal consequences of childhood sexual victimization. *Child Abuse & Neglect, 18(4),* 303–318.

Wilson, L. & Conroy, J. (1999). Satisfaction of children in out-of-home care. *Child Welfare, 88(1),* 53–69.

Winters, W. & Maluccio, A. N. (1988). School, family and community working together to promote social competence. *Social Work in Education,* 207–217.

Wulczyn, F., Zeidman, D., & Svirsky, A. (1997). HomeRebuilders: A family reunification demonstration program. In J. D. Berrick, R. P. Barth, & N. Gilbert (Eds.), *Child welfare research review* (pp. 252–271). New York: Columbia University Press.

Wulczyn, F. H. (1992). *Status at birth and infant foster care placement in New York City.* Albany: New York State Department of Social Services.

Zimmerman, R. B. (1982). Foster care in retrospect. *Studies in Social Welfare, 14,* New Orleans: Tulane University.

Zuravin, S., Benedict, M., & Somerfield, M. (1997). Child maltreatment in family foster care: Foster home correlates. In J. Duerr Berrick, R. P. Barth, & N. Gilbert (Eds.), *Child welfare research review* (pp. 189–200). New York: Columbia University Press.

What Works in Family Foster Care

Study Authors	Survey Sample	Research Design/Outcome Measure	Findings
Fanshel, D. & Shinn, E. B. (1978). *Children in foster care: A longitudinal investigation.* New York: Columbia University Press.	• Longitudinal study of children placed in foster care in New York City	• A total of 624 children who entered foster care in 1966 were selected using a sequential sampling design to stratify by age and gender.	• At the end of five years, 36.4% of the children were still in foster care, largely through a lack of systematic case management and accountability and not through design. • 57.7% of the children had not been visited by their parents. Children with higher birth parent contact functioned better and returned home in higher numbers and earlier. • Foster care provided children with some positive benefits in terms of IQ score gains. It was not a predictor of problems in school performance or emotional adjustment.

(continued next page)

What Works in Family Foster Care (*continued*)

Study Authors	Survey Sample	Research Design/Outcome Measure	Findings
Stein, T. J., Gambrill, E. D. & Wiltse, K. T. (1978). *Children in foster homes: Achieving continuity of care.* New York: Praeger.	• Evaluation of a demonstration project to increase the permanency planning outcomes for children placed in Alameda County, California • Housing, financial assistance and intensive casework services were provided within a goal and time-oriented framework and as outlined in contractual agreements with the parents, case worker and project director	• A quasi-experimental design was used: 56 experimental group cases, and 40 control group cases were identified from cases that referral agency staff volunteered and could be served due to caseworker openings from one of four foster care units (three units contributed to the experimental group and one unit contributed to the control group).	• Significantly more experimental group cases compared to control group cases were closed through return home, guardianship, or adoption (26% vs. 18%). Cases where the children were returned home with court dependency to be terminated soon were also more likely to be closed (31% vs. 22%). • At time of project termination, 79% of the experimental group children were either out of foster care or plans were underway to discharge them compared to 40% of the control group children. The additional specificity in the case plans that resulted from the use of service contracts was noted.

Wulczyn, F., Zeidman, D., & Svirsky, A. (1997). Home rebuilders: A family reunification demonstration program. In J. Duerr Berrick, R. P. Barth & N. Gilbert (Eds.) *Child welfare research review* (pp. 252–271). New York: Columbia University Press.	• Evaluation of the Home Rebuilders demonstration project to achieve early the permanency planning outcomes for children placed in New York City • Exclusionary criteria included children ages 12 and older; children who remained in foster care for less than 90 days, had been in foster care before, or had siblings who had experienced prior care; children who were placed in training schools, state hospitals or institutions for the severely developmentally delayed; children who were in adoptive homes; and children whose parents had paid for the total cost of care.	• Agencies received a prospectively fixed payment intended to cover all the costs of foster care for a three-year period. • Typical categorical restrictions on how foster care costs were claimed were waived to enable a wide variety of foster care, discharge planning and aftercare activities. • Caseload sizes were reduced. • Children were selected randomly into the experimental and control groups.	• At the end of the first year, 79% of the Home Rebuilders children remained in care compared to 85% of the control group, indicating an accelerated return rate. • In addition, 380 Home Rebuilders children were returned home, compared with 224 children who would have returned home using a projected "baseline" rate (an estimate of how many children would still be in care if not for the project based on historical agency data). The 380 figure also compares favorably to a "projected" number of children (309) which was based on a target for the HomeRebuilders group at a 10% return rate.

15

What Works in Treatment Foster Care

Patricia Chamberlain

Treatment foster care (TFC) is a family-based alternative to residential, institutional, and group care for children and adolescents with significant behavioral, emotional, and mental health problems. TFC has been variously referred to as specialized foster care, therapeutic foster care, and foster family-based treatment. All terms refer to the same service; the term TFC will be used here.

The TFC model has been broadly defined as "a service which provides treatment for troubled children within the private homes of trained families" [Rivera & Kutash 1994: 69]. TFC first appeared in the United States in the mid-1970s as an alternative to institutional placement, and since that time has grown rapidly as a child welfare, mental health, and juvenile justice system service model. TFC is currently one of the most widely used forms of out-of-home placement for children and adolescents with severe emotional and behavioral disorders and is considered the least restrictive form of residential care [Kutash & Rivera 1996; Stroul 1989].

TFC differs from most residential and group care settings in several important ways:

- Community families are recruited, trained, and supported to provide the placements;
- Children generally attend public schools;

- No more than two youngsters are placed in a home;
- Most TFC programs include a family therapy component with the biological parent(s) or aftercare resource; and
- TFC is significantly less costly than group care.

Treatment teams typically consist of several program staff working together under the direction of a case manager or clinical supervisor. TFC families are trained, supported, and closely supervised to participate also as key players in the treatment team. Team members provide therapy and/or skills training for youth and their biological or adoptive families or other aftercare placement resources. The goals are to facilitate the post-placement transition and to support the aftercare setting so that youth can maintain the gains they made in TFC over the long term. Consultants may be used in a number of areas—such as education or psychiatric treatment—depending on the specific needs of the child. The TFC model allows children and families to receive intensive, coordinated, multisystemic services while the child lives in a relatively nonrestrictive setting.

A principle advantage of the TFC model is that treatment services can be tailored to fit the needs of the individual and his or her family. Another advantage is that in TFC, youth are placed in a normalizing family setting rather than with other youngsters who have similar problems.

Research Evidence on TFC

Studies have found that:

- TFC programs serve children and adolescents who have problems similar to those who are being served in group and residential care settings [Meadowcroft et al. 1994].
- The majority of TFC placements are completed as planned, suggesting that TFC is a viable placement alternative for children and adolescents with severe emotional and/or behavioral problems [Meadowcroft et al. 1994].
- While in TFC placements, most youth improve on behavioral indicators of adjustment [Clark et al. 1993]. In several studies, youth in TFC have shown better adjustment at follow-up in terms of post-

discharge stability of living situation and restrictiveness of placement setting than youth served in congregate care settings [Chamberlain & Reid 1998; Hawkins et al. 1989].

- Of the children and adolescents in TFC, 60%–89%, are discharged to less restrictive living settings following TFC placement [Fanshel et al. 1990].

In one study comparing the effectiveness of TFC to group or residential care for serious adolescent offenders, adolescents who participated in TFC had a significantly greater drop in criminal activity (over 50%) at one and two-year follow-ups according to both official record data and self-reports of criminal activities [Chamberlain & Reid 1998]. Figure 1 depicts arrest rates for youth in TFC and in group care at the one-year follow-up period. In the Chamberlain and Reid study, significantly more TFC youth completed their programs than did youth in group/residential care. TFC youth were incarcerated for 60% fewer days in the follow-up period than youth in group/residential care, and more TFC youth were discharged from out-of-home care to live with their families [Chamberlain & Reid 1998].

Research Evidence in Support of Other Treatment Strategies

Evans and colleagues [1994] compared outcomes for 6- to 12-year-olds, who were seriously emotionally disturbed, and placed in TFC, with outcomes for a similar group of children who remained at home and whose families received intensive case management. They found that home placement youth did as well as those placed in TFC. In that study, however, families of youth in TFC did not receive family therapy as part of their TFC program.

Other studies have highlighted the importance of working with adults who will provide aftercare services to youth who were placed outside of their homes. Hoagwood and Cunningham [1992], for example, examined outcomes by school district for 114 children and adolescents who had been placed in residential care in a large southwestern state. They found that the availability of community-based services during the transition from residential care to home was the single best predictor of positive child adjustment at discharge.

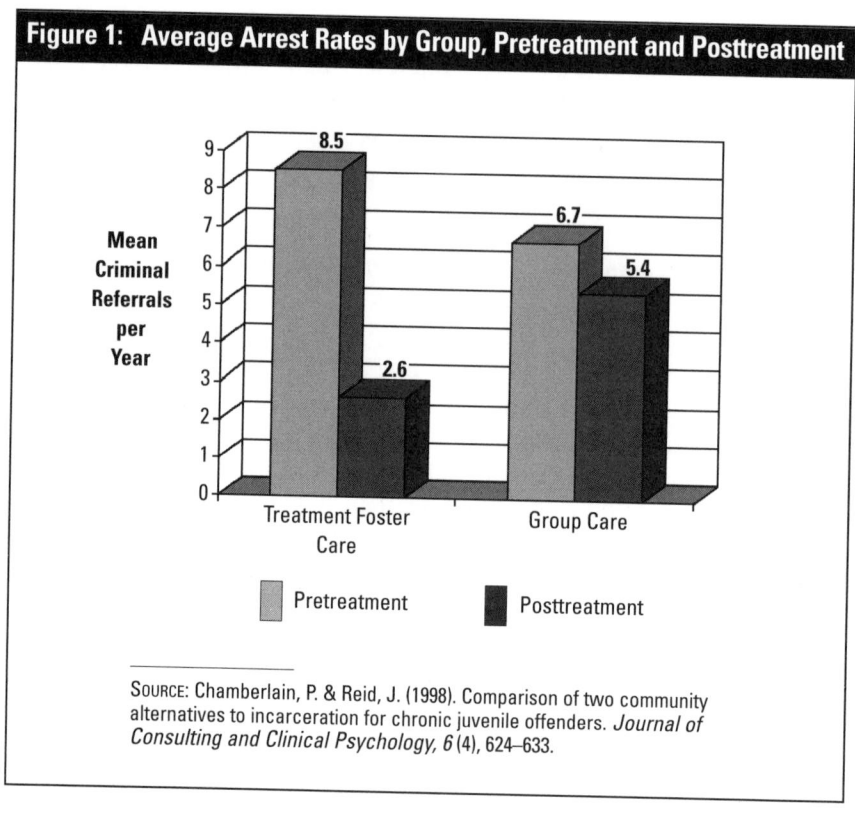

Figure 1: Average Arrest Rates by Group, Pretreatment and Posttreatment

Mean Criminal Referrals per Year

Treatment Foster Care — Pretreatment: 8.5, Posttreatment: 2.6

Group Care — Pretreatment: 6.7, Posttreatment: 5.4

■ Pretreatment   ■ Posttreatment

SOURCE: Chamberlain, P. & Reid, J. (1998). Comparison of two community alternatives to incarceration for chronic juvenile offenders. *Journal of Consulting and Clinical Psychology, 6* (4), 624–633.

Cost-Effectiveness

It is generally accepted that TFC costs less than residential care, which has undoubtedly influenced the proliferation of TFC programs throughout the United States during the past decade.

Estimates are that TFC programs require one-fifth to one-third less funding than residential centers or group homes who serve comparable populations [Kutash & Rivera 1996]. One study found that the Oregon TFC model, which targets serious and chronic juvenile offenders, was among the approaches that resulted in the greatest savings to state taxpayers [Aos et al. 1999]. In two years, program costs were recouped through savings in reduced arrest and incarceration rates and decreased costs for the criminal justice system and victims [Washington State Institute for Public Policy 1998].

Conclusion

TFC programs provide an alternative to more restrictive group and residential care placements for various populations of youngsters, including those with serious emotional and behavioral problems, delinquency, and developmental disabilities. Research indicates that despite wide variance in program models in terms of population served and components included, the TFC use of professionally trained and supported community families has been a consistently effective approach. Studies have shown that when compared to residential and group care, outcomes for youngsters participating in TFC are favorable. More research, however, is needed on the effectiveness of the TFC model for specific types of youngsters and the role of TFC programs within the continuum of child welfare services.

References

Aos, S., Phipps, P., Barnoski, R., & Lieb, R. (1999). *The comparative costs and benefits of programs to reduce crime: A review of national research findings with implications for Washington State*. Olympia: Washington State Institue for Public Policy.

Chamberlain, P., & Reid, J. (1998). Comparison of two community alternative to incarceration for chronic juvenile offenders. *Journal of Consulting and Clinical Psychology, 6*(4), 624–633.

Clark, H., Boyd, L., Redditt, C., Foster-Johnson, L., Hardy, D., Kuhns, J., Lee, G., & Stewart, E. (1993). An individualized system of care for foster children with behavioral and emotional disturbances: Preliminary findings. In K. Kutash, C. Liberton, A. Algarin & R. Friedman (Eds.), *5th annual research conference proceedings for a system of care for children's mental health* (pp. 365–370). Tampa: University of South Florida, Florida Mental Health Institute, Research and Training Center for Children's Mental Health.

Evans, M. E., Armstrong, M. I., Dollard, N., Kuppinger, A. D., Huz, S., & Wood, V. M. (1994). Development and evaluation of treatment foster care and family-centered intensive case management in New York. *Journal of Emotional and Behavioral Disorders, 2*(4), 228–239.

Fanshel, D., Finch, S., & Grundy, J. (1990). *Foster children in a life course perspective.* New York: Columbia University Press.

Hawkins, R., Almeida, C., & Samet, M. (1989). Comparative evaluation of foster family-based treatment and five other placement choices: A preliminary report. In A. Algarin, R. Friedman, A. Duchnowski, K. Kutash, S. Silver, & M. Johnson (Eds.), *Children's mental health services and policy: Building a research base* (pp. 98–119). Tampa, FL: Research and Training Center for Children's Mental Health, University of South Florida, Florida Mental Health Institute.

Hoagwood, K. & Cunningham, M. (1992). Outcomes of children with emotional disturbance in residential treatment for educational purposes. *Journal of Child and Family Studies, 1*(2), 129–140.

Kutash, K. & Rivera, V. R. (1996). *What works in children's mental health services?* Baltimore, MD: Paul H. Brookes Publishing Co.

Meadowcroft, P., Thomlinson, B. & Chamberlain, P. (1994). Treatment foster care services: A research agenda for child welfare. *Child Welfare, 33*(5), 565–581.

Rivera, V. R., & Kutash, K. (1994). Therapeutic foster care services. In V. R. Rivera & K. Kutash (Eds.), *Literature series on the components of a system of care* (pp 81–99). Tampa: Research and Training Center for Children's Mental Health, Florida Mental Health Institute, University of South Florida.

Stroul, B. (1989). *Community-based services for children and adolescents who are severely emotionally disturbed: Therapeutic foster care.* Washington, DC: CAASP Technical Assistance Center, Georgetown University Child Development Center.

Washington State Institute for Public Policy. (1998). *Watching the bottom line: Cost-effective interventions for reducing crime in Washington (Seminar 3162).* Olympia, WA: The Evergreen State College.

16

What Works In Family Reunification

Anthony N. Maluccio

In response to the increasing numbers of children who are placed in foster family care or residential settings, there has been considerable emphasis over the past two decades on programs that facilitate the reunification of children in out-of-home care with their birth families. This emphasis also has been promoted by federal legislation, particularly the Adoption Assistance and Child Welfare Act of 1980 (PL 96–272) and the Adoption and Safe Families Act of 1996 (PL 105–89).

Federal legislation and state laws have encouraged the return of children in placement to their own homes as soon as possible—as long as such return can be safely accomplished. Such legislation is consistent with philosophical perspectives and research findings regarding the value of the birth family in the development and functioning of children. Family reunification has been defined as "the planned process of reconnecting children in out-of-home care with their families" to help them achieve and maintain that reconnection at an optimal level [Warsh et al. 1994: 3]. In essence, reunification should be viewed along a continuum, with outcomes ranging from full reentry into the family system, to partial reentry, to visiting or other occasional contact.

Although there is wide acceptance of the importance of family reunification, it has been difficult to accomplish in the reality of practice. In addition to the challenges posed by diminishing resources for helping families, there has been, in recent years, a substantial increase in the number of children coming to the attention of child welfare authorities as a result of societal problems such as unemployment, poverty, family violence, substance abuse, and homelessness. Many of these children are eventually placed in foster care and their return to their families of origin is delayed or becomes problematic, particularly when the functioning and situations of their parents remain unchanged or do not sufficiently improve.

What Works in Family Reunification Programs

Research findings from recent outcome studies have a number of implications for policy and practice.

- *Intensive time-limited services.* Relatively brief but intensive, family-centered services positively affect reunification rates. As shown in two studies of children placed by public agencies in Utah (See Figure 1), 96.5% of children in a treatment group receiving intensive services were reunited within 90 days compared to 32.1% of children receiving routine agency services. At the end of one year following the initial 90-day period, 75.4% of the children receiving intensive services were reunited compared to 49% of children receiving regular services [Fraser et al. 1996; Walton et al. 1993].

  These studies found that especially valuable strategies were strong client-worker alliances, skill training programs, services to meet the concrete needs of family members, and services to enhance the family's social supports from relatives and neighbors. Evaluation of another program using comparable approaches showed that 33 of 42 children (79%) were reunited within 12 to 16 weeks, and that 91% of the reunited children were still living with their families at the one-year follow-up [Gillespie et al. 1995].

- *Services for parents.* Successful reunification is facilitated by strategies for building parent-worker relationships, behavioral interventions such as training parents in stress relief techniques, and provision of concrete services. Of crucial importance is transportation for parents and their children—once they are reunited—to medical and other appointments [Lewis et al. 1995].

Figure 1: Intensive Services Increased Family Reunification

Children in Out-of-Home Care

90 days — **Reunification Service**

Percent of Children Reunified with Family within 90 Days

FIRS Treatment Group
N = 57

FIRS Intensive Services

- Average caseload of six families/worker
- Home visits at least three times per week as part of an initial goal of reunification.
- In-home services heavily focused on: building collaborative, supportive relationships with parents; strengthening family member's communication and problem-solving skills; addressing concrete needs for food, housing, employment, and health; and providing in-home support during the reconnecting process.

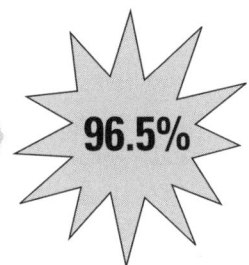

96.5%

Control Group
N = 53

Routine Agency Services

- Average caseload of 22 families/worker.
- Home visits at least once per month to ensure a stable placement and normal pattern of growth.
- Reunification services as part of an overall out-of-home care plan, which assists families in obtaining necessary resources, such as mental health counseling and parenting skills training concrete.

32.1%

Note: Intensive services increased the percent of children in out-of-home care who were reunified with their families. One hundred-ten children were randomly assigned to experimental (FRS) and control groups (routine agency services). Families were followed for 445 days after the onset of services. The number of children who were fully reunified with their families was determined. Data was obtained from caseworkers and agency databases.

SOURCES:

Fraser, M., Walton, E., Lewis, R.E., Pecora, P. & Walton, W.K. (1996). An experiment in family reunification: Correlates of outcomes at one-year follow-up. *Children and Youth Services Review, 18,* 335–362.

Walton, E., Fraser, M., Lewis, R., Pecora, P. & Walton, W.K. (1993). In-home family-focused reunification: An experimental study. *Child Welfare, 72,* 473–487.

- *Maintaining continuity between children and parents during placement.* Consistent parent-child visiting while the child is in foster care is the heart of reunification as it promotes successful reunion of children with their families [Hess & Proch 1988]. Successful reunification is associated with maternal visiting (in 54% of the cases) and paternal visiting (in 61% of the cases) at the level recommended by the court [Davis et al. 1996].

- *Considering racial and ethnic dimensions.* There is a relationship between race and ethnicity and reunification. In particular, "African American children are far less likely than Caucasian children to be reunified with their families (41% versus 58%)" [Barth 1997: 289, 294]. Such findings suggest the need for aggressive outreach in providing reunification services for children of color.

- *Improving children's psychosocial functioning.* Children in foster care with emotional and behavioral problems are significantly less likely to be reunited with their families, as demonstrated in studies using the Achenbach Child Behavior Checklist and other standardized measures [Landsverk et al. 1996]. It is, therefore, essential to provide mental health services to children prior to reunification and "to assist parents in addressing behavioral problem challenges in children when reunified" [Landsverk et al. 1996: 448].

- *Availability of adequate housing and income.* There is a moderate correlation between the success of reunification efforts and the adequacy of the family's housing and income [Jones 1998]. In a study of 445 children from 245 families who were reunited through a county child welfare agency in California, 156 children were re-referred to the agency following reunification and 61 returned to foster care. Poverty and inadequate housing were most instrumental in placing children at risk of return to out-of-home care [Jones 1998].

- *Involving the extended family in the reunification process.* A qualitative study of family group decision-making in several child welfare agencies showed that the inclusion of kin in making permanent plans for the child contributed to successful reunification [Burford et al. 1997]. Especially constructive was the involvement of relatives and informal helpers in the decision-making process and in working with the birth parents.

Conclusion

There are important service delivery issues that must be addressed to advance the knowledge base as well as determine the cost-effectiveness of family reunification services, an area that thus far has received limited research attention. These issues include the resolution of the tension between family preservation values and the imperatives of child protection; guidelines to assess the risk of returning children to their families versus the risk of prolonging their stay in out-of-home care; establishing the minimum level of care and "good enough" parenting that are necessary for family reunification; and determining where to draw the line between providing continuing support to reunited families and perpetuating their dependence [Maluccio et al. 1996].

In the meantime, it is apparent that it can be cost-effective as well as humane to support practitioners in efforts to create and use opportunities to work with families during foster care placement; provide supports to parents before and after reunification; and encourage and facilitate child-family visiting throughout placement. With proper supports to the child and caregivers, kinship care also can be an effective strategy when birth parents are not available or competent [Hegar & Scannapieco 1999]. Above all it should be stressed that, as a form of preserving families, reunification embodies conviction about the role of the biological family as the preferred child-rearing unit; the potential of most families to care for their own children, if properly assisted; and the value of involving, as appropriate, any and all members of the extended family.

References

Barth, R. P. (1997). Effects of age and race on the odds of adoption versus remaining in long-term out-of-home care. *Child Welfare, 76*, 285–308.

Burford, G., Pennell, J., MacLeod, S., Campbell, S., & Lyall, G. (1997). Reunification as an extended family matter. *Community Alternatives: The International Journal of Family Care, 9*(2), 33–55.

Davis, I., Landsverk, J., Newton, R., & Ganger, W. (1996). Parental visiting and foster care reunification. *Children and Youth Services Review, 18*(4/5), 363–382.

Fraser, M., Walton, E., Lewis, R. E., Pecora, P., & Walton, W. K. (1996). An experiment in family reunification correlates of outcomes at one-year follow-up. *Children and Youth Services Review, 18*(4/5), 335–362.

Gillespie, J. M., Byrne, B., & Workman, L. J. (1995). An intensive reunification program for children in foster care. *Child and Adolescent Social Work Journal, 12*(3), 213–228.

Hegar, R. L. & Scannapieco, M. (1999). *Kinship foster care—Policy, practice, and research.* New York: Oxford University Press.

Hess, P. M. & Proch, K. O. (1988). *Family visiting in out-of-home care.* Washington, DC: Child Welfare League of America.

Jones, L. (1998). The social and family correlates of successful reunification of children in foster care. *Children and Youth Services Review, 20*(4), 305–323.

Landsverk, J., Davis, I., Ganger, W., Newton, R., & Johnson, I. (1996). Impact of child psychosocial functioning on reunification from out-of-home placement. *Children and Youth Services Review, 18*(4/5), 447–462.

Lewis, R., Walton, E., & Fraser, M. W. (1995). Examining family reunification services: A process analysis of a successful experiment. *Research on Social Work Practice, 5*(3), 259–282.

Maluccio, A. N., Pine, B. A., & Warsh, R. (1996). Incorporating content on family reunification into the social work curriculum. *Journal of Social Work Education, 32*(3), 363–373.

Walton, E., Fraser, M., Lewis, R., Pecora, P., & Walton, W. K. (1993). In-home family focused reunification: An experimental study. *Child Welfare, 72,* 473–487.

Warsh, R., Maluccio, A. N., & Pine, B. A. (1994). Teaching family reunification: A sourcebook. Washington, DC: Child Welfare League of America.

What Works in Family Reunification

Study Authors	Survey Sample	Research Design/Outcome Measure	Findings
Fraser, M.W., Walton, E., Lewis, R.E., Pecora, P.J. & Walton, W.K. (1996). An experiment in family reunification: Correlates of outcomes at one-year follow-up. *Children and Youth Services Review, 18*(4/5), 335–361.	• 100 children placed in foster care in the Utah state agency • The families of 57 children received intensive time-limited services compared to 53 children whose families received routine reunification services	• Data were obtained from caregivers, caseworkers, and the agency's data base. • Outcome measured was return to the birth family.	• 55 of the 57 children receiving intensive services returned to their homes within 90 days. • 17 of the 53 children receiving routine agency services returned to their homes within 90 days.
Gillespie, J.M., Byrne, B. & Workman, L.J. (1995). An intensive reunification program for children in foster care. *Child and Adolescent Social Work Journal, 12*(3), 213–228.	• 42 children in state foster care and their birth families	• Data obtained from caseworkers and case records. • Outcome measured was reunification during project participation	• 33 of the 42 children (79%) were reunified within 12 to 16 weeks. • 28 of reunited children (91%) were still living with their families at one-year follow-up.
Jones, L. (1998). The social and family correlates of successful reunification of children in foster care. *Children and Youth Services Review, 20*(4), 305–323.	• 445 children from 245 families placed in foster care through a county child welfare agency in California and reunited with their families	• Data obtained primarily through case files, court documents, and agency records • Cases were followed during foster care placement and for nine months following reunification with their parents. • Outcome measured in terms of success of the reunification with birth family.	• Of the 445 children in the sample, 156 were re-referred to the agency following reunification and 61 returned to foster care. • Poverty and especially inadequate housing were most instrumental in placing children at risk of return to out-of-home care.

17

What Works in Parent-Child Visiting Programs

Robin Warsh and Barbara Pine

Visitation is at the center of all plans to reunify children with their families. In fact, parent-child visiting can be thought of as the laboratory in which children and their parents learn to be together again. Research supports the importance of contact in maintaining children's psychological health. One study of adolescent boys in a state correctional school, for example, showed that only 29% of adolescents whose frequency of visits with their parents was above the median were cited for major misconduct compared to 61% of the less frequently visited youths [Borgman 1985] (See Figure 1).

Moreover, 70% of the adolescents who committed a major infraction were youth whose assessments showed that their attachment to their families was above the median but whose frequency of visits from their families was below the median [Borgman 1985]. Research demonstrates visiting benefits children by:

- Reassuring them that their parents want to see them;
- Permitting them to experience and work through feelings stirred by the separation from their parents, thus allowing developmental gains; and
- Helping them maintain family ties while providing opportunities for family members to learn and practice new behaviors and styles of communicating [Hess & Proch 1988].

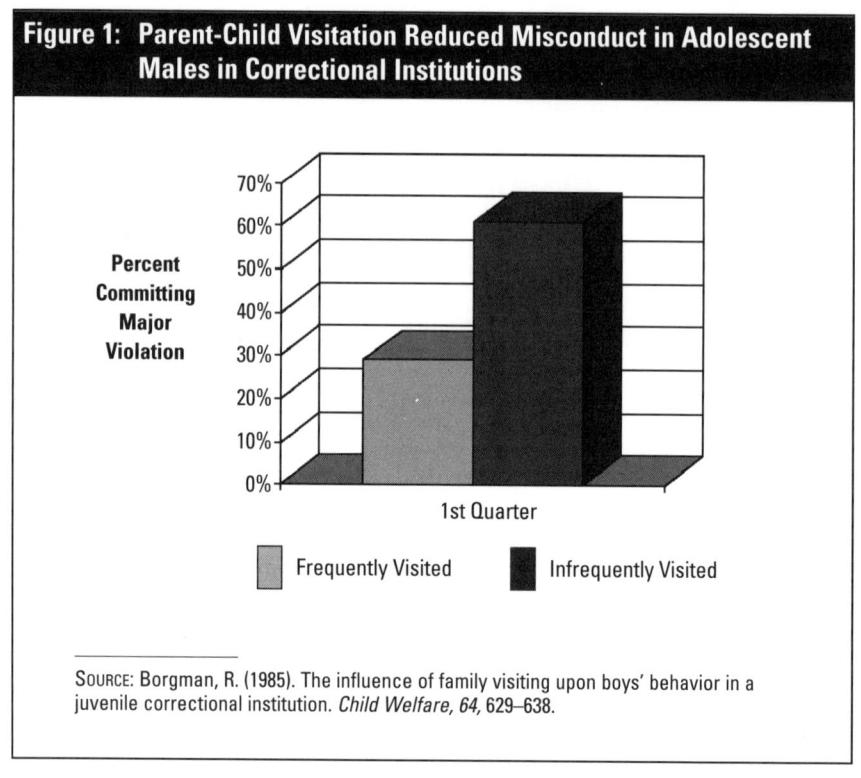

Figure 1: Parent-Child Visitation Reduced Misconduct in Adolescent Males in Correctional Institutions

Percent Committing Major Violation

1st Quarter

Frequently Visited   Infrequently Visited

SOURCE: Borgman, R. (1985). The influence of family visiting upon boys' behavior in a juvenile correctional institution. *Child Welfare, 64,* 629–638.

Conditions that Promote Positive Visiting

There is much that social workers, foster parents and agencies can do to support positive parent-child visiting. Key elements of a successful visiting program include:

- *Close geographic proximity.* Children should be placed near their parents and other significant family members in order to facilitate visits. In cases involving child sexual abuse, one study indicated that when the mother visited as recommended, the child was approximately 10 times more likely to be reunified [Davis et al. 1996]. Siblings also should be placed together unless otherwise indicated [Hess & Proch 1988]. Research has shown that nearly 90% of children and young people in care return home, albeit at different times and through various routes [Bullock et al. 1993].

Thus, continuity of sibling relationships is especially important as they are typically lifelong.

- *Training staff and foster parents in planning and carrying out positive visits.* Social workers should adequately prepare children, families, and foster parents for visits and give them opportunities to work through their reactions to visits. Work with foster parents is particularly important. Gean, Gillmore, and Dowler [1985] found that when foster parents were opposed to or expressed significant anxiety about visiting, children had the greatest number of anxiety symptoms. Foster parents should be encouraged to allow family visits in the foster home, unless otherwise indicated. In addition, visiting environments should make use, whenever possible, of natural settings, such as parks, zoos, and children's museums.

- *Formal visitation plans.* Agencies should require written visiting plans that specify visit purposes, frequency, length, location, supervision, participants, supportive services, and planned activities. Clear plans are especially important because research shows that when there is no formal schedule, parents do not visit and when there is a visiting schedule, parents keep to it, especially if they were involved in its development. One study showed that approximately 60% of the mothers who had a clear plan to visit monthly did so, and over 68% of the mothers who were scheduled to visit more often than once a month increased their visits accordingly [Proch & Howard 1986].

- *Purposeful Visiting.* In addition to the reassurances provided to children and the opportunities for children and parents to learn and practice new skills visiting also allows for assessment—the identification of the needs of children and parents—and documentation, so that parents can be provided with feedback regarding their progress [Hess & Proch 1993]. Visiting can encompass a very wide range of contacts between children and parents: preparing and eating a meal, going for haircuts together, shopping for clothing, keeping medical appointments together, attending school conferences, and doing household tasks. It is essential that social workers and foster parents work with birth parents to plan visiting activities that meet two criteria: (1) the proposed activity helps children and parents learn to be together again, and (2) the activity maximizes opportunities for parents to identify and respond to their child's needs. The aim is to link the choice of the visiting activity to the achievement of case goals. If, for example, the goal for parents is to set limits and teach their children right from wrong without hurting them physically or with words, the visit might involve the parents taking the child to a sandbox, where there will be opportunities to learn and practice effective discipline approaches.

- *Gradual visitation intensity.* Another key element of a successful visiting program is the arrangement of visits along a continuum of increasingly stressful situations, such as, for example, from playing to difficulty at bedtimes. This strategy helps families gradually achieve competence in such areas as limit-setting, teaching children right from wrong, and effective discipline approaches. Children should only return home after they have had safe, unsupervised visits in their own homes, including overnight visits and visits lasting several days or more over an appropriate period of time [Warsh et al. 1996]. Through flextime or compensatory time for workers, agencies can assure that visits occur when families can schedule them. Agencies also should provide financial assistance for visit-related expenses such as transportation and food for foster and birth families.

Cost-Effectiveness

There is no information to date on the cost-effectiveness of parent-child visitation programs. If parent-child visiting contributes to reunification, there will be a reduction in the money spent on foster care and other out-of-home placements. Additionally, research suggests that, regardless of whether reunification is achieved, positive visiting is associated with children's positive psychological health [Borgman 1985], thus avoiding expenses that result from psychological problems.

Conclusion

Agencies should offer quality visiting services that promote a child's timely return home or make possible a conclusion that the child cannot return to full-time care in the family. Even in cases in which the family cannot care for the child fully, efforts should be made to teach parents how to relate at least in part to their children. This goal is especially important for adolescents who move into independent living situations because research has shown that many of these young people resume contacts with their parents upon discharge from care [Fanshel et al. 1990].

Child and family visiting can be time-consuming and frustrating. It is, however, a highly complex child welfare strategy that requires a set of skills and resources and is a key to safe and lasting reunifications. Research is needed to understand the cost-benefits of child-family visiting. Even in the absence of such research, it is essential that agencies, staff, and foster parents be trained to enable families to use visiting as a laboratory in which children and their parents can learn to be together again.

References

Borgman, R. (1985). The influence of family visiting upon boys' behavior in a juvenile correctional institution. *Child Welfare, 64,* 629–638.

Bullock, R., Little, M., & Millham, S. (1993). *Going home: The return of children separated from their families.* Dartmouth: Aldershot.

Davis, I. P., Landsverk, J., Newton, R., & Ganger, W. (1996). Parental visiting and foster care reunification. *Children and Youth Services Review, 18*(4/5), 363–382.

Fanshel, D., Finch, S. J., & Grundy, J. F. (1990). *Foster children in a life course perspective.* New York: Columbia University Press.

Gean, M. P., Gillmore, J. L., & Dowler, J. K. (1985). Infants and toddlers in supervised custody: A pilot study of visitation. *Journal of the American Academy of Child Psychiatry, 24*(5), 608–612.

Hess, P. M. & Proch, K. O. (1988). *Family visiting in out-of-home care: A guide to practice.* Washington, DC: Child Welfare League of America.

Hess, P. M. & Proch, K. O. (1993). Visiting: The heart of reunification. In B. Pine, R. Warsh, & A. N. Maluccio (Eds.), *Together again: Family reunification in foster care* (pp. 119–139). Washington, DC: Child Welfare League of America.

Proch, K. & Howard, J. (1986). Parental visiting of children in foster care: A study of casework practice. *Social Work, 31*(3), 178–181.

Warsh, R., Pine, B. A., & Maluccio, A. N. (1996). *Reconnecting families: A guide to strengthening family reunification services.* Washington, DC: Child Welfare League of America.

What Works in Parent-Child Visiting Programs

Study Authors	Survey Sample	Research Design/Outcome Measure	Findings
Borgman, R. (1985). The influence of family visiting upon boys' behavior in a juvenile correctional institution. *Child Welfare, 64*(6), 629–638.	• 47 adjudicated delinquent boys, ages 13–16, who had committed at least one criminal offense • Sample drawn from a state correctional school in a southeastern state of youth who had come from counties that were largely rural or that contained only one small city	• Data collected from record review of visits; infractions; length of time child spent in custody to earn release and; psychological evaluations • Outcome measured was number of misconduct events and other violations.	• 29% of those frequently visited committed violations; 61% of the less frequently visited did so. • 21% of those frequently visited, compared to 48% of those less frequently visited, ran away at least once. • 70% of those whose evaluations showed significant family attachment committed violations when visit frequency was below median.
Proch, K. & Howard, J. (1986). Parental visiting of children in foster care: A study of casework practice. *Social Work, 31*(3), 178–181.	• 256 children in foster family care under the age of 13: 56% were Caucasians; 44% African American; less than 5% were Hispanic • Sample drawn from nine randomly selected field offices of a statewide public child welfare agency in Illinois	• Data collected from record review of the extent to which visiting plans were included in the case plan, the specifications of visiting plan, and the relationship between visiting plans and actual visiting patterns.	• Despite agency policy mandating a visiting plan when reunification is the goal, no plans existed in approximately 30% of the cases. • In almost 52% of the cases in which there were no regularly scheduled visits, the mother did not visit during the year prior to the time data were collected. • Approximately 60% of the mothers who were scheduled to visit monthly did so; over 68% of the mothers scheduled to visit more often than monthly did so.

18

What Works in Residential Child Care and Treatment: Partnerships With Families

James K. Whittaker

There has long been recognition of the importance of partnerships with families for children in out-of-home group care [Whittaker & Trieschman 1972; Maluccio & Marlow 1972; Finkelstein 1974; Whittaker 1979, 1997]. The cumulative findings of a number of outcome studies dating back to the early 1960s seem to point to the critical role that familial and community support factors play in determining post placement adjustment of children returning from residential care [Allerhand et al. 1966; Jenson & Whittaker 1987; Taylor & Alpert 1973; Wells et al. 1991]. Whittaker and Pfeiffer [1994], Pecora, Whittaker and Maluccio [1992], and Curry [1991] provide reviews of the findings of this literature as well as some of the common weaknesses of residential outcome studies.

Since 1990, fortunately, the group care practice literature focused on building family-agency partnerships for children in out-of-home care has burgeoned (See Appendix). This literature recognizes that partnerships with special populations and cultural variations are important. Among residential populations that may require customization of family work are children orphaned by AIDS [Levine et al. 1998] and youth who are dual-diagnosed and who may be involved with recovery efforts [Whittaker & Pfeiffer 1994]. At the same time, Braziel [1996], in an overview of family focused practice innovations, notes that families represent a spectrum of cultural and ethnic diversity and working effectively with them requires a solid grounding in cultural competence and family practice techniques—a point underscored by the work of Leigh [1998].

Emergent Practice and Research Challenges

Enthusiasm for family-agency partnerships for children and youth in residential group care must be tempered by the inconclusive nature of the evidence regarding residential treatment itself. As a recent report from the U.S. General Accounting Office (GAO) [1994] noted, not enough is known about residential care programs to provide a clear picture of which kind of treatment approach works best or the effectiveness of treatment over the long-term. The GAO's examination of programs nominated as exemplary, however, found certain attributes to be most frequently associated with successful residential care: family involvement; participation of a caring adult; planning for post-program life; post-program support; skills teaching; service coordination; development of individual treatment plans; positive peer influence; enforcement of a strict code of discipline; self-esteem building; and provision of a family-like atmosphere.

As residential programs move forward to adopt and adapt family-focused practice innovations, these efforts must be accompanied by rigorous evaluations to assess the relationship between these practices and the ultimate outcomes of community adjustment and integration for youth returning from care. Researchers and practitioners will face critical challenges in providing empirical validation for family-agency partnerships, including:

- *Developing family practice protocols.* At present, no clear consensus exists in the field of residential care with respect to the locus of family engagement (in-home, agency- or community-based); the focus of the engagement with families (family treatment, counseling, education); the format for family involvement (telephone contact or face-to-face, group, or individual), the knowledge and skills required of the family worker; and the sequencing of the family-focused interventions (such as the advantages and disadvantages of front-loading and back-loading family involvement for youth in care). The ability to train families in these practices also must be further specified and empirically validated if the field is to move beyond simply enumerating the values and principles of a family-focused approach.

- *Rapid assessment and brief intervention models for family work.* The increasing influence of managed care with its emphasis on shorter-term residential programming highlights the need for adaptation of assessment and intervention protocols to meet shorter time frames. Such time pressures underscore the point made by some commentators regarding the importance of constructing a seamless path of family involvement—beginning with pre-placement and extending through placement into aftercare activity [Jenson & Whittaker 1987].

- *Focus on outcomes.* Although the existing corpus of residential outcome research leads inevitably to work on improving agency-family partnerships, the extent to which increasing familial support improves and enhances youth outcomes has not been documented. The growing trend toward outcome-based contracting emphasizes the need for a better understanding of the mechanisms by which a supportive and well-supported family buffer the adverse effects of the otherwise stark community environments to which youth characteristically return after residential placement.

Planning for the Youth's Return to the Community After Completing the Residential Program

Consistent with other recent reviews of residential care research, the GAO report [1994] identified planning for the youth's return to the community after completing the program as crucial to successful outcomes in residential care. In their review of a number of residential outcomes studies, Pecora, Whittaker and Maluccio [1992] found that regardless of a youth's status at discharge, the quality of supports available in the post-discharge environment appeared to be associated with subsequent community adjustment. They also found that youth with supportive community networks were more likely to maintain their treatment gains than those who lacked such supports. They noted that contact and involvement with family appeared to be positively correlated with post-placement success. Earlier, Whittaker and Pecora [1984] pointed out that gains for youth while in residential care were not maintained if supports were not in place when the child returned home.

Cost-Effectiveness

As noted Chapter 36, residential care is one of the costliest child welfare services available. A study of children with serious emotional disturbances who had been placed in residential treatment facilities for educational purposes reported the average monthly cost per child to be $6,316 [Hoagwood & Cunningham 1992]. Although further research on cost-effectiveness is needed, it is logical to assume that youth who receive effective residential care have more favorable outcomes when they enter adulthood than youth who receive no services at all.

Conclusion

Although no clear cut evidence exists favoring a particular family engagement strategy, there is sufficient evidence in the corpus of residential research to favor increased emphasis on family-agency partnerships before, during, and following treatment placement. Planning for the youth's return to the community after discharge from residential care is also critical to successful outcomes for these youth. Future research should focus on what is meant by "family engagement" in residential care and treatment and which engagement strategies work best and lend themselves to training efforts targeted toward parents.

Appendix

Building Family Partnerships: Practice Resources for Children in Residential Group Care

Building on existing research, a range of innovative projects has been initiated in recent years—all of which expand our knowledge of effective familial engagement for children in residential care. A recent compilation by the Child Welfare League of America [Braziel 1996] provides an excellent overview of family-focused practice innovations in residential child care. These range from overarching conceptual and value frameworks [Ainsworth et al. 1996; Mallon 1996] to specific programmatic examples and training resources for increasing family involvement and overcoming barriers to family partnership [Braziel 1996].

A number of individual agencies have provided key leadership in developing specific family involvement strategies and fostering interagency collaboration around the development of training resources. Some projects reflect direct residential family engagement strategies, while others offer innovative approaches to family involvement that potentially have rich application to the residential sector. Among these are Hathaway Children's Service, Highland Park Resource Center in Sylmar, California; Eastfield Ming Quong in San Jose, California; The Los Angeles Children's Bureau Project Learn; and the William Roper Hull Family Initiative Program in Calgary, Alberta. At a 1995 national symposium on "moving from child-centered to family-focused care"—sponsored by Boysville of Michigan in conjunction with the Albert E. Trieschman Center's "Finding Better Ways" conference in Cambridge, Massachusetts [1995]—participants received a resource notebook containing profiles of these programs and others. In addition, Boysville has developed an extensive array of family focused resources, including assessment and evaluation protocols oriented to an agencywide practice focused information system.

In recent years, perhaps the most ambitious multiagency effort has been the Carolinas Project sponsored by the Albert E. Trieschman Center and The Walker School in Needham, Massachusetts, and funded by the Duke Endowment. This project has provided extensive training to clusters of agencies in North and South Carolina on improving family outreach and enhancing the organizational climate for effective family work.

Two additional national resources worthy of note are the extensive materials developed at Boston College's Graduate School of Social Work in a series of related family reunification research and demonstration projects, and Father Flanagan's Boys Home (Boys Town) in Nebraska, which has developed a wide range of family-focused training resources for youth in residential care as well as therapeutic foster care, family preservation services, and parent training. The Boy's Town National Training Center also provides extensive technical assistance on family focused work to a wide range of agency programs.

References

Ainsworth, F., Maluccio, A. N., & Small, R. W. (1996). A framework for family centered group care practice: Guiding principles and practice applications. In D. J. Braziel (Ed.), *Family-focused practice in out-of-home care* (pp. 35–45). Washington, DC: Child Welfare League of America.

Allerhand, M. E., Weber, G., & Haug, M. (1966). *Adaptation and adaptability: The Bellefaire follow-up study.* Washington, DC: Child Welfare League of America.

Braziel, D. J. (Ed.) (1996). *Family-focused practice in out-of-home care.* Washington, DC: Child Welfare League of America.

Curry, J. (1991). Outcome research on residential treatment: Implications and suggested directions. *American Journal of Orthopsychiatry, 61,* 348–358.

Finkelstein, N. E. (1974). Family participation in residential treatment. *Child Welfare, 53*(9), 570–576.

Hoagwood, K. & Cunningham, M. (1992). Outcomes of children with emotional disturbance in residential treatment for educational purposes. *Journal of Child and Family Studies, 1*(2), 129–140.

Jenson, J. & Whittaker, J. K. (1987). Parental involvement in children's residential treatment: From pre-placement to aftercare. *Children and Youth Services Review, 9*(2), 81–100.

Leigh, J. W. (1998). *Communicating for cultural competence.* New York: Allyn & Bacon.

Levine, C., Brandt, A. & Whittaker, J. K. (1998). *Staying together, living apart: New perspectives on youth group living from the AIDS epidemic.* New York: The Orphan Project.

Mallon, G. P. (1996). Toward a family-centered approach to out-of-home child welfare service: Theories, models & suggestions. In D. J. Braziel (Ed.), *Family-focused practice in out-of-home care* (pp. 45–59). Washington, DC: Child Welfare League of America.

Maluccio, A. N. & Marlow, W. D. (1972). Residential treatment of emotionally disturbed children: A review of the literature. *Social Service Review, 46*(2), 230–251.

Pecora, P. J., Whittaker, J. K., & Maluccio, A. N. (1992). *The child welfare challenge: Policy, practice and research.* New York: Aldine de Gruyter.

Taylor, D. A. & Alpert, S. W. (1973). *Continuity and support following residential treatment.* Washington, DC: Child Welfare League of America.

U.S. General Accounting Office (1994). *GAO Report: Residential Care* (B–249960) Washington, DC: U.S. Government Printing Office.

Wells, K., Wyatt, E., & Hobfoll, S. (1991). Factors associated with adaptation of youth discharged from residential treatment. *Children and Youth Services Review, 13*(3), 199–217.

Whittaker, J. K. (1979/1997). *Caring for Troubled Children: Residential Treatment in a Community Context.* New York: Aldine de Gruyter.

Whittaker, J. K. & Pecora, P. J. (1984). A research agenda for residential care. In T. Philpot (Ed.), *Group care practice: The challenge of the next decade.* Surrey, UK: Community Care/Business Press International.

Whittaker, J. K. & Trieschman, E. T. (Eds.). (1972). *Children away from home: A sourcebook of residential treatment.* Chicago: Aldine.

Whittaker, J. K. & Pfeiffer, S. I. (1994). Research priorities for residential group child care. *Child Welfare, 73*(5), 583–601.

What Works in Residential Child Care and Treatment

Study Authors	Survey Sample	Research Design/Outcome Measure	Findings
Wells, K., Wyatt, E. & Hobfoll, S. (1991). Factors associated with adaptation of youths discharged from residential treatment. *Children and Youth Services Review, 13*(3) 199–217.	• 50 male and female youths who had been in residential treatment at an urban multiservice mental health agency for at least six months • Youths selected from a total pool of 89 who had been discharged for at least 12 months but less than 36 months and who were 13–18 years old at time of data collection (July 1985–February 1988)	• Descriptive follow-up study. Data collected from case records and from structured follow-up interview which included four standardized scales. • Measures included post adaptation discharge; self- esteem; mastery; absence of psychopathology; role fulfillment; antisocial behavior; substance abuse; social support; stress; and residential stability. • Multiple regression analyses used to determine combined and independent effects of predictor variables on "adaptation."	• "Our data confirm what many practitioners suspect: former adolescent residents of long-term residential treatment programs who enjoy little or no family support, who experience high stress and who have little residential stability after placement are unlikely to adapt well after discharge" (1991: 213). • Authors urge further study of particular patterns of social support and their impact on youth outcomes, and the reconceptualization of residential treatment as a "family support system."

Reference	Method	Findings
U.S. General Accounting Office. (1994). *GAO Report: Residential Care* (B–249960). Washington, DC: U.S. Government Printing Office.	• Survey of 29 residential youth service programs of which 18 were selected for more intensive study, including on-site visits • Program surveys augmented with key informant (expert) interviews and literature reviews	• Telephone and on-site surveys of residential youth service programs nominated by program officials and other experts as showing some documented measures of effectiveness. • Key questions attempted to discern program characteristics identified by programs as critical to their success.	• Program elements most frequently judged as important to successful treatment included: individual treatment plans; participation of a caring adult; self-esteem building; planning for post-program life; skills teaching; service coordination; family involvement; positive peer influence; enforcement of a strict code of discipline; post-program support; and a family-like atmosphere. • Study otherwise noted low level of consensus on efficacious of treatment and little evidence of controlled follow-up research.
Taylor, D. A. & Alpert, S.W. (1973). *Continuity and support following residential treatment*. New York: Child Welfare League of America.	• Early follow-up study of children participating at least six months in a residential treatment program • 75 of 186 children completed the study, limiting generalizability	• Primary focus on the role of environmental supports and the continuity of experience and relationships as they impact children in residential care. • Study developed a standardized measure of community adaptation, the Community Adaptation Schedule (CAS).	• "This study suggested that adaptation after discharge was related to the child's perception of available support from significant others and to continuity, defined as the degree to which the child lived continuously with his or her parents after discharge" (Curry 1991: 351). • This study suggested the importance of early engagement of families in the residential treatment process.

19

What Works in Employment Programs for Youth in Out-of-Home Care

Nan Dale

A dolescents leaving the foster care system—especially those from group care settings—face many challenges in their transition to adulthood and independence. Most are poor and from ethnic minority backgrounds and have serious emotional and behavioral problems that led to their placement. The odds of becoming self-sufficient and productive adults are not in their favor. Employment programs for youth are needed for older youth in residential group care. Youngsters who age out of the system may be helped by youth development programs that offer long-term interventions, including work experience, counseling, and mentoring.

Findings from Studies of Youth Employment Programs

Findings from studies of youth employment programs over the last three decades have identified four key elements to success [see Kazis & Kopp 1997; Walker 1997]:

1. *School completion.* A crucial step in improving the employability of disadvantaged youth is high school completion. Labor economists believe that joblessness among inner city youth is, in part, the result of a mismatch. Employers' needs for a skilled labor force cannot be met when there is a growing pool of unskilled youth who

have dropped out of school and lack even basic educational skills [Holzer 1996].

2. *High-intensity programs* that provide residential and educational components over an extended time period. Providing short-term skills training is not enough to raise youth employment or earnings over the long run but intensive programs can have marked success. Job Corps is considered one of the most intensive and successful federal employment initiatives ever implemented. Participating youth receive 12 months of employment and supportive services while living in Job Corps housing. One study followed approximately 5,000 Job Corps youth for four years after program completion and found that these youth, compared to nonparticipants, had higher earnings, higher educational attainment, less reliance on public assistance, and fewer felony arrests [Maller 1982].

3. *Work experience.* Disadvantaged youth want to work and will do so if given the opportunity. Manpower Demonstration Research Corporation studies of youth employment programs conducted in the 1980s suggest that work experience during high school can have positive effects on later employability, particularly for disadvantaged youth. For example, Farkas [1984] found that African American youth who participated in the Youth Incentive Entitlement Pilot Program (YIEPP)—(a program which guarantees disadvantaged youth full-time summer jobs and part-time school-year jobs if they agree to stay in school)—had significantly higher earnings in the post-program period than youth in the comparison groups. High participation rates in the program confirmed that unemployed youth will work if given the chance.

4. *The presence of a stable, caring adult* in the young person's life. Walker [1997: 4], summarizing the body of evidence on the effectiveness of youth employment programs, concludes that young people consistently emphasize "one adult who cared and helped" as the single most positive factor. Research on childhood resilience and adolescent development underscores this point [see Garmazy 1991; Rutter 1987].

Employment Programs for Youth in Out-of-Home Care: The WAY Program

One program found to be effective in working with youth in residential group care is the Children's Village Work Appreciation for Youth (WAY) Scholarship Program. Started in 1984, WAY has been adapted for community-based youth development programs and replicated in several sites spanning three states.

WAY is a long-term intervention that offers sequential work experience, individualized counseling, work ethics training, tutoring, financial incentives for saving, and, perhaps most significantly, a long-term (five-year) mentoring commitment to participants. It meets and exceeds all of the federal and state independent living programming expectations.

WAY is unique in that it starts earlier and lasts longer than other youth employment programs. It targets the highest-risk youth in the New York child welfare system—youth in residential treatment centers—and provides mentoring by professionals for up to five years after youth leave treatment. The average age of participants is 14 at the time of enrollment and the program "sticks with" youth post-discharge until they are 19 or 21 years old.

WAY targets adolescents with histories of abuse, neglect, psychiatric hospitalization, juvenile delinquency, parental substance abuse, and other challenges deemed by New York City's Department of Social Services as too severe to live in foster homes or other community-based settings. Most youth come from low-income families and require special education–two additional factors that place them at risk for negative outcomes.

There is both an in-care component (WAY Works) and an aftercare component (WAY Scholarship). Each year, a group of 15 to 20 boys is inducted into the WAY Scholarship Program. At present there are 265 WAY scholars in the 14 cohorts in the history of the program. Seventy-five percent of participants (115 of 155 boys) in the first 10 cohorts completed at least two-and-a-half years of the five-year program, and 110 boys in cohorts 11 through 14 are currently receiving services in the program.

Effectiveness of the WAY Program

The effectiveness of the WAY Program has been examined and found to be effective in several areas.

- *Participation in WAY Scholarship is associated with high rates of school completion.* The boys who completed at least two-and-a-half-years of the five-year WAY Scholarship Program (the first six cohorts) evidenced high educational achievement rates. Eighty percent had graduated high school, were still in school, or had earned a GED by the end of the program. By age 21, 51% of those who had graduated from high school or earned a GED had gone on to college. These numbers compare favorably to citywide and national graduation rates and exceed educational achievement rates for youth who exit foster care without such services. One study, for example, found that only 71% of youth who had been discharged from group foster care had graduated by 23 to 26 years of age [Festinger 1973]. School achievement rates for WAY youth are also higher than rates for Hispanic youth nationally (63%), Hispanic and African American youth in New York City (54% and 68%, respectively), New York City youth in special education (62%) [Board of Education of the City of New York 1996], and youth living below the poverty level (53%) [Westat 1991].

- *Youth formerly in foster care need more than four years to complete high school.* It took more than four years for many WAY scholars to obtain their high school diploma or GED. A cohort required between seven and eight years to reach its "final" school completion rate—the point at which the additional likelihood of school completion was low. This prolonged time in school is not surprising given the remediation most participants needed to make up for significant academic and attendance problems.

- *WAY provided youth with work opportunities.* WAY scholars gained work experience in the program despite the fact that the program offers no job placement services. Over three-quarters of WAY scholars held one or more jobs during four of their five program years.

- *WAY youth had low rates of criminality.* WAY scholars are from populations that tend to be at high-risk for criminal activity and are more likely to be viewed as suspects by police officers because they are minorities [Kennedy 1992]. Indeed, many had early encounters with the law and had been placed in residential treatment as a result of delinquent or violent behaviors. The question has been whether WAY scholars are able to avoid encounters with the criminal justice system. A search for criminal records of 93 WAY youth over age 21 was conducted. Only 12 WAY scholars (13%) were arrested, convicted, and sentenced to state prison, a finding considered impressive in light of their high-risk for criminality. Fanshel [1992: 55] notes that "foster children are probably among the most disadvantaged among the larger group of children in the United States who have been deprived of the basic essentials of normal childhood," particularly given their chronic exposure to unusual degrees of family violence, abuse, and neglect. Fanshel concludes that youngsters from such families are a major potential source of tomorrow's criminals.

Cost-Effectiveness

The average cost per participant in WAY Scholarship is $3,000 per year or $9.00 a day per child. This cost is extremely small in light of the costs associated with alternative outcomes that might be expected for many of these young people. Costs for WAY Works are covered by Independent Living (ILP) funds. In some states, ILP funds may be used for aftercare, but ILP funds are not available for this purpose in New York. WAY Scholarship Program expenses are primarily the salaries of full-time WAY Scholarship counselors ($30,000 annually) who each work with 20 youths.

Conclusion

Over the last three decades of studying youth employment programs, school completion has been determined to be a crucial step in improving employability of disadvantaged youths. Further, providing individualized, long-term services is more likely to result in a successful outcome rather than short-term skills training alone. The presence of a stable, caring adult in a young person's life over an extended period of time appears to make the difference between success and failure for the many disadvantaged youth who wish to remain in school and who will work if given the support and opportunity to do so. The WAY Program puts this knowledge into practice and has had significant success with disadvantaged youth.

References

Board of Education of the City of New York. (1996). *The class of 1993.* New York: Board of Education.

Fanshel, D. (1992). Foster care as a two-tiered system. *Children and Youth Services Review, 14,* 49–60.

Farkas, G. (1984). *Post-program impacts of the Youth Incentive Entitlement Pilot Projects.* New York: Manpower Demonstration Research Corporation.

Festinger, T. (1973). *No one ever asked us . . . A postscript to foster care.* NY: Columbia University Press.

Garmazy, N. (1991). Resilience in children's adaptation to negative life events and stressed environments. *Pediatric Annals, 20,* 459–466.

Holzer, H. (1996). *What employers want: Job prospects for less-educated workers.* New York: Russell Sage Foundation.

Kazis, R. & Kopp, H. (1997). *Both sides now: New directions in promoting work and learning for disadvantaged youth. A report to the Annie E. Casey Foundation.* Boston: Jobs for the Future.

Kennedy, R. (1992). *Race, crime, and the law.* New York: Pantheon Books.

Maller, C. (1982). *Third follow-up report of the evaluation of the economic impact of the Job Corps program.* Plainsboro, NJ: Mathmatica Policy Research.

Rutter, M. (1987). Psychosocial resilience and protective mechanisms. *American Journal of Orthopsychiatry, 57,* 316–331.

Walker, G. (1997). *Out of school and unemployed: Principles for more effective policy and program.* Philadelphia, PA: Public/Private Ventures.

Westat. (1991). *A national evaluation of Title IV-E foster care independent living programs for youth.* Rockville, MD: Westat.

What Works in Employment Programs for Youth in Out-of-Home Care

Study Authors	Survey Sample	Research Design/Outcome Measure	Findings
Festinger, T. (1983). *No one ever asked us...A postscript to foster care.* New York: Columbia University Press.	• 394 youths discharged from New York City foster care as 18–21 year olds in 1975 • 277 were interviewed • Youths were 23–26 years old at time of study	• Data collected from individual interviews; conducted in-person and by telephone. • Outcome measures included educational attainment, employment, and adult functioning.	• 71% of the youth who had been discharged from group foster care had graduated from high school at the time of the interview.
Maller, C. (1982). *Third follow-up report of the evaluation of the economic impact of the Job Corps program.* Plainsboro, NJ: Mathmatica Policy Research.	• Over 5,000 youths who completed the program in the early 1980s • Demographically matched comparison group	• Surveys and official records were collected four years after program completion. • Earnings, educational attainment and criminality were outcomes of interest.	• Four years after program completion, Job Corps participants earned on average $1,300 more each year than comparison youths. • One-fourth of Job Corps youth had graduated from high school or GED programs, compared to only 5% of the comparison youths.
Farkas, G. (1984). *Post program impacts of the Youth Incentive Entitlement pilot projects.* New York: Manpower Demonstration Research Corporation.	• 3765 disadvantaged youths 15–16 years old who had completed all waves of data collection	• In-person or telephone surveys of youth were conducted along with surveys of youths in comparison sites with no YIEPP program in place.	• The earning effects for the post-program follow-up period was $10.48 per week, translating into $500–$550 annually.

20

What Works in Independent Living Preparation for Youth in Out-of-Home Care

Kimberly A. Nollan

The disruptions and traumas often suffered by youth in out-of-home care may result in delays or interruptions in the development of life skills needed for successful transition from out-of-home care to independent living.[1] The findings of several outcome studies indicate that youth placed in foster care do not do as well as their peers in the general population in rates of high school completion [Barth 1990; Cook et al. 1991; Cook 1994; Festinger 1983; Jones & Moses 1984; Zimmerman 1982] and employment [Cook et al. 1989; Cook 1994; Triseliotis & Russell 1984]. They also have higher incidences of homelessness [Susser et al. 1991]. This information, however, should be viewed with some caution, as many of the studies did not take into consideration differences resulting from child maltreatment, family poverty, neighborhood conditions, and other factors [Polowy et al. 1986; Cook et. al 1989; Ryan et al. 1988].

Strategies for Preparing Youth for Self-Sufficiency

There are four strategies that are effective in preparing youth for self-sufficiency: (1) systematic skills assessment, (2) independent living skills training, (3) involving caregivers as teachers, and (4) developing community connections. Although the research data supporting these strategies are scant, findings in support of the effectiveness of these strategies are cited when available. It is imperative that programs providing independent living services evaluate their effectiveness to further the knowledge base in this area.

Systematic Skills Assessment

One study of youth in foster care found that, depending on the skills tested, between one-fifth to one-third of the youth were in serious need of specialized services, independent living planning, follow-up, and/or aftercare [Hahn 1994]. Based on these findings, the researcher recommended systematic skills assessments to document the competency levels of youth. This recommendation is supported by P.L. 99–272, the Federal Independent Living Initiative, which requires all youth age 16 and older to be assessed for their readiness to live on their own. Furthermore, the John H. Chafee Foster Care Independence Act of 1999 requires that outcome measures be developed to assess state performance in areas such as educational attainment, employment and homelessness.

Systematic skills assessment helps in the development of a specific plan based on a comprehensive evaluation of the youth's strengths and deficits, involves foster parents and youth in the process, and teaches caregivers to recognize tangible and intangible essential life skills and become more adept at teaching them. Further, assessment information gathered in this manner helps independent living programs meet the requirement of the Act that youth directly participate in the design of their program activities.

Youth are best prepared for independent living when a set of services is targeted to meet specific goals [Cook 1994]. One pilot program, for example, found that a focused life skills assessment linked with targeted services based on the assessment increased youth's life skills scores after one year of services [Nollan et al. 1999]. There are a variety of instruments designed to measure life skills. The Ansell-Casey Life Skills Assessment is one tool that caregivers, youths, and service providers can use to identify and measure tangible and intangible life skills in 15 areas, including emotional well-being, self-awareness, decision-making, work and study skills, and housing and money management [Nollan et al. 1997].

Independent Living Skills Training

The second strategy in preparing youth for self-sufficiency is focused skills training. Training is recommended to better prepare youth for adulthood [English et al. 1994] and is encouraged by P.L. 99–272. There is a positive relationship between skills training and youth's ability to maintain a job, obtain health care, function so as not to be a cost to the community, and overall satisfaction with life, particularly when training addresses the skill areas of money management, credit, consumer skills, education, and employment [Cook 1994]. Positive effects have been found from training in specific skill areas. For instance, money management and budgeting training have been found to be significant predictors of high school completion; consumer skills and employment training are associated with a youth's ability to avoid becoming a cost to the community; consumer skill training is a predictor of a youth's decision to delay parenting; and education training is a predictor of the ability to maintain a job for more than one year [Cook 1994]. When the five core skill areas of budgeting, obtaining credit, consumer skills, education, and employment are considered together, they are significant predictors of multiple positive outcomes (maintaining a job for more than one year, not being a cost to the community, ability to access health care, and general life satisfaction) [Cook 1994]. Training in more skill areas results in larger effects [Cook 1994].

Involving Caregivers as Teachers

A caregiver or other significant adult in the youth's life can offer skills training formally as part of an independent living program and informally. One study found that closeness and identification with the foster parent while the youth was in care was significantly related to greater social and academic progress and improvement in emotional and behavior problems [Palmer 1976]. Because of the contact and closeness, the relationship between the youth and foster parent is a natural place for independent living skills training to occur. Studies also have found that youth tend to remain in contact with their foster parents after leaving care [Barth 1990; English, et al. 1994; Festinger 1983; Jones & Moses 1984].

There are a variety of advantages of using caregivers as the primary teachers of independent living skills for youth:

- The foster home most closely replicates the environment where most children and youth learn these tasks.
- Foster parents are available and have time to offer individualized learning experiences and, when necessary, coordinate their instructional plan with that of a youth's special education teacher.

- Foster parents can coach and model appropriate behaviors in real situations; skills can be taught incrementally and tailored to the youth's unique strengths and needs; skills can be practiced in a safe environment; and progress can be regularly reinforced [Ryan et al. 1988].

In order for caregivers to be effective teachers of life skills, however, they must be cognizant of the range of life skills that promote independence in young people; understand how a young person acquires life skills and other competencies and what behaviors can be expected from youth at different developmental stages; and receive training in how to teach independent living skills [Wolf et al. 1998].

Caregivers can become effective teachers of life skills through the use of life skills assessments and training in how to use assessment information.

Developing Community Connections

The final strategy for preparing youth to live on their own is ensuring their connections to birth family and other community contacts. These associations are important because some youth turn to their birth families for social and other support once they leave out-of-home care [Jones & Moses 1984; Zimmerman 1982]. One study found that youth most often name relatives as the persons who did the most to encourage them to develop work skills [English et al. 1994]. On the other hand, another study found that most youth (45.5%) did not have a strong identification with their birth families [Palmer 1976]. This finding suggests that special attention needs to be placed on developing relationships between youth and birth family members and resolving birth family issues.

In addition to connections with birth family, it is important for youth to develop other community connections. Community connections are helpful in replacing youth's reliance on the agency for help, and connections and relationships with individuals in the community can help youth address and resolve feelings of grief, loss, and rejection—an important task for youth to accomplish prior to living on their own [Mauzerall 1983; Mech 1994; Ryan et al. 1988]. Community contacts also are important in establishing workplace connections, which provide access to jobs and support in job retention.

Conclusion

Implicit in federal policy that views self-sufficiency as lack of dependence on public assistance is the expectation that youth will become self-reliant and less dependent on others. Most youth in the U.S. are not expected to be self-reliant as abruptly or as soon as are youth in out-of-home care. Better preparation of youth for self-sufficient living while they are still in care is essential. To ensure that appropriate independent living training is provided, it is critical to assess youth skill levels and determine appropriate goals and areas for growth that can guide individual and program planning and make it possible to document outcomes of service. Foster parent training should focus on preparing youth to successfully assume their places as adults in the community. Training foster parents to prepare youth for independence readies them to be independent living skills teachers and is required by the recent federal legislation.

Another important aspect of independent living skills preparation addresses separation and loss issues through connecting youth with birth family and the community. There is a high likelihood of birth family contact after a youth leaves care. Reconnecting with birth family members should be a part of independent living programs and, more generally, a part of the services to youth while they are in out-of-home care. Community connections are helpful in transitioning the youth from reliance on the agency and are critical to securing and maintaining employment.

Note

1. National legislation (P.L. 99-272) refers to independent living as the ability to provide economically for oneself. To be consistent, the terms "independent living" or "self-sufficiency" are used in this chapter interchangeably. It is recognized, however, that no one truly lives "independently," and that "interdependent living" is a more accurate description of a person's state of living on their own.

References

Barth, R. (1990). On their own: The experiences of youth after foster care. *Child and Adolescent Social Work Journal, 7*(5), 419–446.

Cook, R., McLean, J. L., & Ansell, D. I. (1989). *A national evaluation of Title IV-E foster care independent living programs for youth, Phase 1* (Final Report for Contract No. 105-87-1608). Rockville, MD: Westat, Inc.

Cook, R., Fleishman, E., & Grimes, V. (1991). *A national evaluation of Title IV-E foster care independent living programs for youth, Phase 2* (Final Report for Contract No. 105–87–1608). Rockville, MD: Westat, Inc.

Cook, R. J. (1994). Are we helping foster care youth prepare for their future? *Children and Youth Services Review, 16*(3/4), 213–229.

English, D. J., Kouidou-Giles, S., & Plocke, M. (1994). Readiness for independence: A study of youth in foster care. *Children and Youth Services Review, 16*, 1–5.

Festinger, T. (1983). *No one ever asked us: A postscript to foster care.* New York: Columbia University.

Hahn, A. (1994). The use of assessment procedures in foster care to evaluate readiness for independent living. *Children and Youth Services Review, 16*(3/4), 171–179.

Jones, M. & Moses, B. (1984). *West Virginia's former foster children: Their experiences in care and their lives as young adults.* Washington, DC: Child Welfare League of America, Inc.

Mauzerall, H. A. (1983). Emancipation from foster care: The independent living project. *Child Welfare, 62*, 47–53.

Mech, E. V. (1994). Preparing foster youth for adulthood: A knowledge-building perspective. *Children and Youth Services Review, 16*(3/4), 141–145.

Nollan, K. A., Austin, J. I., Choca, M., Pesce, M., & Stern, E. (1999). *Tucson Division Self-Sufficiency Initiative Summary 1996–1997.* Seattle, WA: The Casey Family Program.

Nollan, K. A., Downs, A. C., Pecora, P. J., Ansell, D., Wolf, M., Lamont, E., Horn, M., & Martine, L. (1997). *Ansell-Casey life skills assessment manual: Version 2.0.* Seattle, WA: The Casey Family Program.

Palmer, S. E. (1976). *Children in long-term care: Their experience and progress.* Unnamed city, Canada: Family and Children's Services of London and Middlesex.

Polowy, M., Wasson, D., & Wolf, M. (1986). *Fosterparentscope.* Buffalo: New York State Child Welfare Training Institute.

Ryan, P., McFadden, E. J., Rice, D., & Warren, B. L. (1988). The role of foster parents in helping young people develop emancipation skills. *Child Welfare, 67*(6), 563–572.

Susser, E., Lin, S., Conover, S., & Struening, E. (1991). Childhood antecedents of homelessness in psychiatric patients. *American Journal of Psychiatry, 148*(8), 1026–1030.

Triseliotis, J. & Russell, J. (1984). *Hard to place: The outcome of adoption and residential care.* London: Heinemann Educational Books.

Wolf, M., Copeland, W., & Nollan, K.A. (1998). All in a day's work: Resources for teaching life skills. *Journal of Child and Youth Care, 12*(4), 1–10.

Zimmerman, R. B. (1982). Foster care in retrospect. *Tulane Studies in Social Welfare, 14,* 1–119.

What Works in Independent Living Preparation

Study Authors	Survey Sample	Research Design/Outcome Measure	Findings
Cook, R. J. (1994). Are we helping foster care youth prepare for their future? *Children and Youth Services Review,* 16(3/4), 213–229.	• Probability sample of youth 16 and older discharged from foster care • 1,644 adolescents discharged from foster care between January 1987 and July 1988 • 57% female, 61% Caucasian, 47% disabled	• Data collected from case record reviews and interviews (n = 810) approximately 2.5–4 years post-discharge. • Outcomes measured were status of youth after discharge (education, parenthood, public assistance, economic self-sufficiency, housing, drug/alcohol use, health care, support networks).	• 54% completed high school. • 60% had given birth to at least one child. • 30% were public assistance recipients. • 49% held jobs. • 86% had at least one person in their lives who provided a strong, close relationship. • 60% reported having a strong emotional support network. • 50% reported ever taking drugs. • 33% lived in five or more different places; 25% had experienced at least one night of homelessness. • 30% reported difficulties obtaining health care. • Skills training in targeted areas were associated with better outcomes in related areas. • Skills training in budgeting, obtaining credit, consumer skills, education, and employment were predictive of maintaining a job for more than one year, not being a cost to the community, accessing health care, and general satisfaction with life. • Training in more skills areas was associated with better outcomes.

Citation	Sample	Methods	Findings
Festinger, T. (1983). *No one ever asked us: A postscript to foster care.* New York: Columbia University Press.	• 277 young adults (ages 22–26) who had been discharged from foster care in the New York metropolitan area in 1975; had been in care for at least the preceding five years; and who were 18–21 years old at discharge	• In-person and telephone interviews and case records • Outcomes measured: well-being, family life and relationships, personal problems, social support, educational achievement, employment, finances, health, drug/alcohol use, criminal behavior, use of formal help providers, and perceptions of foster experience.	• 24% completed less than high school, 37% completed high school, 34% completed some college, and 5% completed college. • 75% males and 55% females were employed at follow-up. • 34% of females and 10% of males received public assistance. • 37% had children. • 48% reported contact with birth mother, father or other relatives and 23% had contact with siblings.
Jones, M. A. & Moses, B. (1984). *West Virginia's former foster children: Their experiences in care and their lives as young adults.* New York: Child Welfare League of America.	• 328 young adults (ages 19–28) who had received foster care in West Virginia for at least one year and who were at least 19 years of age on 1/1/84	• Personal and telephone interviews • Outcomes measured: living arrangements, employment/finances, social support, family life and relationship, evaluation of care received, education, health, legal history, alcohol/drug usage, and life satisfaction.	• 27% reported having a child. • 63% graduated from high school or a high school equivalency program. • 33% were employed. • 16% received some form of public assistance and about half had received some form of public assistance at some time. • 47% reported having been picked up or arrested by the police. • 20% reported health problems. • 81% indicated happiness and optimism about the future.

What Works in Independent Living Preparation (*continued*)

Study Authors	Survey Sample	Research Design/Outcome Measure	Findings
Zimmerman, R. B. (1982). Foster care in retrospect. *Tulane Studies in Social Welfare, 14*, 1–119.	• 109 former foster children (ages 19–29) in New Orleans who entered from 1951–1969, had been in a foster home for at least a year, and had not been adopted	• Data collected via interviews. • Outcomes measured included: educational achievement, financial status, life satisfaction, family life and relationships, social support, views regarding foster experience, employment, health, history of mental illness or antisocial behavior, leisure time, and satisfaction with life.	• 25% received public assistance. • 65% were employed. • 39% completed high school or equivalent. • 46% had children • 38% had married and 30% of those marriages ended in divorce or separation. • 47% reported chronic health problems. • 18% had been convicted of a criminal offense. • 50% who reported no current pattern of kinship association were rated as not functioning adequately.

21

What Works in Aftercare

Edmund V. Mech

A ftercare is defined by Irvine [1988: 91] as a "system of services and resources for youth 16 to 21 years of age who have been discharged from a foster home setting and currently live in an independent arrangement." Youth in foster care consistently identify the period after discharge from placement as a critical point in their lives. In Festinger's study of youth who aged-out of placement [1983], nearly 75% reported a lack of usable knowledge about employment, job training, or career planning.

Public Law 99–272, codified in Title IV-E of the Social Security Act, provides states with funds to assist youth in out-of-home placement to prepare for independent living. Policies vary, however, with respect to the range of services that are made available to young people who exit foster care. Although there is agreement about the need for aftercare services, little consensus exists as to what should be provided or for how long. Aftercare is probably the weakest component in independent living programs. It is common knowledge that most young people are unable to be fully self-supporting at age 18, yet legislative policy and judicial decision-making persists in adhering to an arbitrary age-criterion for independence. A multistate study of emancipated youth from foster care found that at age 18, fewer than 1 in 10 youth are able to attain economic self-sufficiency, and by age 21, fewer than 20% are able to live without aid from means-tested programs or help from family, relatives, or friends [Mech & Fung 1998].

Linkages With Familial and Nonagency Community Support Systems

Successful aftercare depends on replacing agency services with a "natural system"—that is, nonagency resources. Families, relatives, significant others, friends, church groups, employers, and mentors can be critical in forming a community support network. Whenever possible, youth should be helped to connect or reconnect with birth families and relatives and to utilize resources offered by former foster families and guardians. Courtney and Barth [1996] recommend that independent living programs devote attention to maintaining the family ties of youth in placement. Evidence suggests that using natural systems and community resources are important in helping youth in foster care to achieve a successful transition to community life [Jenson et al. 1986].

Jensen and colleagues [1986] cite several investigations on the effectiveness of social and natural systems support in adolescent aftercare. Based on a cumulative sample of more than 1,700 cases, they found positive results for adolescents described as anti-social, disturbed, pre-delinquent, and juvenile offenders. The authors [1986: 343] conclude, "There is sufficient evidence to suggest that social support strategies are beneficial to youths during community reintegration. Greater coordination is needed between residential facilities and community-based agencies" [Doherty 1975; Feldman et al. 1983; Kirigin et al. 1982; Montgomery et al. 1978; Smith et al. 1972; and Wall et al. 1981].

Workplace Connections with Public and Private Sector Employers

It is difficult to envision positive economic outcomes for youth in independent living programs without connections in the world of work. A multistate study conducted by the University of Illinois obtained employment outcomes at age 21 for a sample of 410 emancipated youth from foster care [Mech & Fung 1998]. Only 52% of the youth reported being employed. When employment status was classified as either full-time or part-time, only 29% were in a full-time job (See Figure 1). With respect to income, approximately 90% of the youth reported making

$10,000 or less per year through jobs in the "low skill" category. Youth reported working as dishwashers, laborers, waitpersons, custodians, and file clerks. The average wasge was about $5 per hour. Of the youth in the age 21 follow-up, fewer than 10% reported income in excess of $10,000 per year.

Intensive Skill and Vocational Training Provided by and Within Work-Relevant Settings

Youth in placement typically receive an orientation to employment through classes on independent living. Classroom training may be beneficial but does not appear to successfully help youth to acquire practical

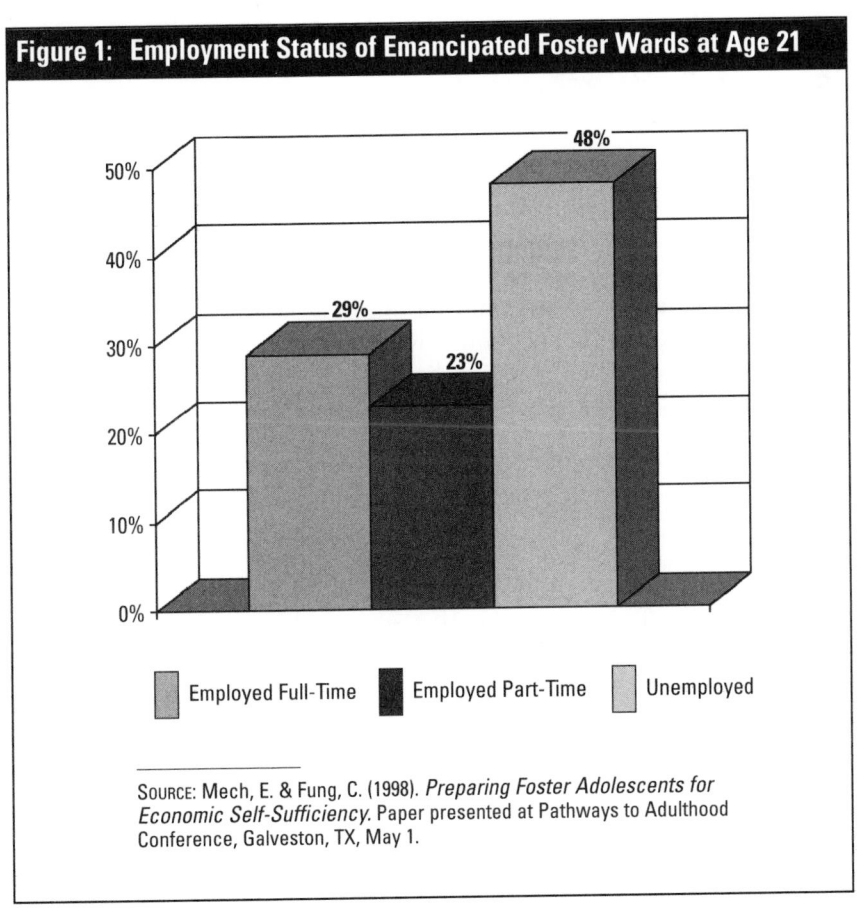

Figure 1: Employment Status of Emancipated Foster Wards at Age 21

Employed Full-Time — Employed Part-Time — Unemployed

Source: Mech, E. & Fung, C. (1998). *Preparing Foster Adolescents for Economic Self-Sufficiency.* Paper presented at Pathways to Adulthood Conference, Galveston, TX, May 1.

vocational skills. Current evidence with difficult-to-reach youth indicates that employment training needs to be more intensive than is provided by classroom work and should be given by persons from business, industry, or other work-relevant settings [U.S. Congress 1995]. The Center for Employment and Training (CET) in San Jose, California, is a case in point [National Youth Employment Coalition 1998]. CET youth receive four to six months of vocational skills training. Classes are taught by instructors from business and industry, and training is supplemented by job placement assistance. Earnings for the experimental group over the first four years was 33% higher than for the control youth. Table 1 summarizes additional job preparation programs judged to be successful by the National Youth Employment Coalition [1998]. Evidence of success includes a high percentage of job placement, high rates of GED and high school completion, and enrollment in post-secondary education.

Transitional Apartment Experience

Apartments are cost-effective settings for preparing youth for independent living. The apartment model simulates real-world situations and offers youth opportunities on a daily basis to apply life-skills knowledge. Youth are responsible for purchasing food, planning and preparing meals, obtaining employment, holding a job, getting to school or work on time, living within a budget, and paying bills. A 10-year review of the Lighthouse Services Independent Living Program details how and why the apartment model works [Kroner 1992, 1999]. Success is related to the following characteristics of transitional apartment programs:

- Youth have some measure of control over their lives;
- Youth can develop a self-reliant life-style;
- Youth are exposed to the expectations of landlords and learn what is required; for successful apartment and community living;
- Youth can live in a location that is accessible to school, workplace, and support resources; and
- Youth learn to act on behalf of themselves and are accountable for the consequences of their actions.

Kroner's view of the value of an apartment experience is summarized best by his conclusion, "All the classes and training in the world do not

Table 1. Youth Employment Initiatives Judged to Be Effective and Indicative of "Best Practices"

"Best Practices" Program	Location	Population Served	Evidence of Success
• Academy for Career Excellence	New York, New York	Low-income out-of school, ages 16–25	68% placed in career-type employment
• Career Link Academy	Seattle, Washington	Out-of-School, ages 16–19	GED rate of 90% Placement in employment
• Manufacturing Technology Partnership	Flint, Michigan	Age 16 and in Junior Year of High School	94% passed United Auto Workers/General Motors Apprenticeship Test
• Moving Up Career Advancement Program	Vocational Foundation, New York	Out-of-school, ages 17–24, 85% dropouts	72% placed in jobs following program completion
• Youth Build McLean County	Bloomington, Illinois	High School dropouts, ages 16–24	67% obtained GED 94% had average wage of $8.92 per hour with benefits
• Educational Methodologies for Youth Employment	San Jose, California	Six school districts six alternative high schools six private secondary schools. 12 major career occupations.	75% retention/completion 65% completers had a positive job placement outcomes
• Community Youth Corps	Norwalk, California (Los Angeles area)	At-risk, ages 16–21 High School dropouts. Group Served: 85% gang members. 64% parenting teens.	47% completed GED and met Youth Employment Competencies 67% placed in full-time unsubsidized employment

SOURCE: National Youth Employment Coalition PEPNET 98. (1998). *Lessons from 43 effective youth employment initiatives.* Washington, DC: National Youth Employment Coalition.

have the impact of a month living alone in an apartment" [1999: 18]. Based on current evidence, transitional apartments should be utilized in preparing youth in foster care for independence [Mech et al. 1994].

Specialized Independent Living Foster Homes

The aim of the specialized independent living foster home model is to provide opportunities for youth to make financial decisions and to learn from mistakes while living with a foster family that provides a safety-net. Specifically, this approach teaches financial responsibility with emphasis on budgeting and money management. An evaluation of one such program in New York State found promising interim results [Colca & Colca 1996]. The study found that of the youth served, 90% demonstrated improvement in money management skills, and the majority improved decision-making with respect to daily living skills, including living on a limited budget and building a savings account.

Cost-Effectiveness

Although no studies have reported specific figures, transitional living apartments appear to be cost-effective settings for preparing youth for independent living. Money spent in successful preparation for independent living is likely to save future dollars that might otherwise be spent on adult governmental subsidies.

Conclusion

Aftercare is the weakest aspect of most independent living programs. A state-by-state survey of statutes and regulations relative to aftercare services for adolescents in foster care estimated that 70% of the states lack provision for extending services to youth who emancipate from placement [Tobis 1989]. Evidence suggests that what works includes apartment settings which are believed to be cost-effective and can produce positive results. Specialized independent living foster homes have promise, but additional evidence is needed with respect to outcomes. World of work connections can be enhanced by providing intensive skill and vocational training using instructors from business and industry. Because youth who emancipate from placement usually need help in forming a support network, the process of replacing agency services with natural system resources is particularly important.

In 1999, the U.S. Congress addressed the need to strengthen aftercare services for emancipated foster youth. Section 477 of the Social Security Act was amended to extend "financial, housing, counseling, employment, education, and other appropriate support and services to former foster care recipients between 18 and 21 years of age." The newly enacted John H. Chafee Foster Care Independence Program provides states with authorization and resources to expand and strengthen aftercare services. It is now the responsibility of state child welfare services to meet this challenge.

References

Colca, L. & Colca, C (1996). Transitional independent-living foster homes: A step toward independence. *Children Today, 24*, 7–11.

Courtney, M. & Barth, R. P. (1996). Pathways of older adolescents out of foster care: Implications for independent living services. *Social Work, 3*, 74–83.

Doherty, G. (1975). Basic life-skills and parent effectiveness training with the mothers of acting-out adolescents. *Journal of Clinical Child Psychology, 31*, 3–6.

Feldman, R. A., Caplinger, T. E., & Wodarski, J. S. (1983). *The St. Louis conundrum: The effective treatment of antisocial youths.* Englewood Cliffs, NJ: Prentice-Hall.

Festinger, T. (1983). *No one ever asked us . . . A postscript to foster care.* New York: Columbia University Press.

Irvine, J. (1988). Aftercare services. In E. V. Mech (Ed.), *Independent-living services for at-risk adolescents* (pp. 91–98). Washington, DC: Child Welfare League of America.

Jenson, J., Hawkins, D., & Catalona, R. (1986). Social support in aftercare services for troubled youth. *Children and Youth Services Review, 8*, 323–347.

Kirigin, K. A., Braukmann, C. J., Atwater, J. D., & Wolf, W. M. (1982). An evaluation of teaching-family group homes for juvenile offenders. *Journal of Applied Behavior Analysis, 15*, 1–16.

Kroner, M. (1999). *Housing options for independent living programs.* Washington, DC: Child Welfare League of America Press.

Kroner, M. (1992). Independent-living: Mapping out the territory. *Children's Voice, 2*, 16–17, 29.

Montgomery, P. A. & Van Fleet, D. S. (1978). Evaluation of behavioral and academic changes through the Re-Ed process. *Behavioral Disorders, 3,* 136–146.

Mech, E., & Fung, C. (1998). Preparing foster adolescents for economic self-sufficiency. Paper presented at *Pathways to Adulthood Conference. Transitional Living/Independent Living,* Galveston, TX, May 1.

Mech, E., Ludy-Dobson, C., & Hulseman, F. (1994). Life-skills knowledge: A survey of foster adolescents in three placement settings. *Children and Youth Services Review, 16,* 181–200.

National Youth Employment Coalition PEPNET 98: (1998). *Lessons from 43 effective youth employment initiatives.* Washington, DC: National Youth Employment Coalition.

Smith, D., Farrant, M. & Marchant, M. (1972). *The Wincroft Youth Project: Social-work programme in a slum area.* London: Travistock.

Tobis, D. (1989). *Services to youth after leaving foster care: Survey of state laws, regulations, and programs.* New York: Welfare Research, Inc., The Legal Action Center for the Homeless, Metropolitan Studies Program, New York University.

U.S. Congress, Office of Technology Assessment. (1995). *Learning to work: Making the transition from school to work.* OTA-EHR-637. Washington, DC: U.S. Government Printing Office.

U.S. Department of Labor (1995). *What is working (and what's not): A summary of research on the economic impacts of employment and training programs.* Washington, DC: U.S. Department of Labor.

Wall, J., Hawkins, J. D., Lishner, D., & Fraser M. (1981). *Juvenile delinquency prevention: A compendium of thirty-six program models.* Washington, DC: U.S. Government Printing Office.

What Works in Aftercare Services for Independent Living Programs

Study Authors	Survey Sample	Research Design/Outcome Measure	Findings
Colca, L. & Colca, C. (1996). Transitional independent living foster homes: A step toward independence. *Children Today, 24,* 7–11.	• Youth in transitional independent living foster homes in New York State	• Tested a transitional foster home model to prepare youth for independent living.	• A high percentage demonstrated improvements in daily living skills. • Of the youth served, 90% demonstrated improvement in money management skills. • The majority improved decision-making with respect to daily living skills, including learning to live on a limited budget and build a savings account.
Festinger, T. (1983). *No one ever asked us . . . A postscript to foster care.* New York: Columbia University Press.	• Several hundred youth who emancipated from placement	• Conducted a follow-up study	• 75% reported a lack of usable knowledge about employment, job training, or career planning.
Kroner, M. (1992). Independent Living: Mapping out the territory. *Children's Voice, 2,* 16–17, 29.	10-year review of the Lighthouse Services Independent Living Program	• Details how and why the apartment model works to prepare youth for independence	• Apartment settings are cost-effective. •Best results are obtained with scattered-site placements.

(continued next page)

What Works in Aftercare Services for Independent Living Programs (continued)

Study Authors	Survey Sample	Research Design/Outcome Measure	Findings
Mech, E. & Fung, C. (1998). *Preparing foster Adolescents for economic self-sufficiency.* Paper presented at Pathways to Adulthood Conference, Galveston, TX, May 1.	• A multistate study of emancipated foster wards	• Analyzes effectiveness of three placement options in preparing foster adolescents for independence	• Found that 1 in 10 foster youth were able to attain economic self-sufficiency. • By age 21, fewer than 20% were able to live without aid from means-tested programs or help from family, relatives, or friends. • Youth with transitional apartment experience were more successful than youth discharged without an apartment placement.
Tobis, D. (1989). *Services to youth after leaving foster care: Survey of state laws.* New York: Metropolitan Studies Program, New York University.	• State-by-state survey of statutes and regulations relative to aftercare services for foster adolescents	• Analysis of state statutes and regulations pertaining to aftercare services for youth who emancipate from placement	• 70% of the states failed to offer post-discharge services to youth who emancipate from placement.

Section IV

Adoption Services

22

What Works in Permanency Planning: Adoption

Richard P. Barth

A dopted children are finding success in many venues. A former president (Gerald Ford), a talented newscaster (Faith Daniels), and a microcomputing original (Steve Jobs) are all renowned adoptees. Given that adoption is, on the whole, a very successful experience for most children [Barth 1997], the question remaining is what makes adoption more or less successful? The answer to this question relies on bits and pieces of evidence, as there has been little direct research on this question.

Adoption has many faces—the best known are: independent adoption of children (most often infants) who are placed without the prior review of agencies; agency adoption of children from foster care (although some agency adoptions are of infants relinquished directly to the agency); and international adoption. There are few data comparing the success of these approaches to adoption, although Meezan, Katz, and Russo [1978] found no significant difference in a variety of procedures and outcomes between independent and agency adoption of infants. Families that adopted through private agencies did, however, report more satisfaction with the accuracy of the information they received than those who adopted through public agencies.

Findings on Adoption Outcomes

Research on adoption outcomes indicate overall favorable outcomes.

- In general, adoptions are highly successful. Berry and colleagues [1996] found that families who adopted were highly satisfied and would recommend the adoption agency or program they had used. In a study comparing adoptions of drug-exposed and non-drug exposed children at eight years post-adoption, about 95% of parents reported being "somewhat" to "very satisfied" with how affectionate or tender their child was and 97% reported feeling "somewhat" to "very close" to their child [Barth & Brooks 1999]. Although only 66% indicated that they were "very satisfied" with the adoption, more than 90% indicated that if they had it to do over, they would adopt again.

- Low adoption disruption rates also reflect the general success of adoptions. Three federally funded studies completed in the late 1980s used different methods and samples, but consistently found a disruption rate for children with special needs between 10% and 14% [Barth & Berry 1988; Partridge et al. 1986; Urban Systems Research and Engineering, Inc. (URSE) 1985]. Each study relied on existing agency data for the overall disruption rates. The duration of time since finalization of the adoption varied by child and, in the case of the URSE study, by state. Disruption rates were computed using cases in which children had been adopted no more than five years earlier. As a result, none of the estimates are as high as they would be if the studies had followed adopted children to the age of majority.

Although there has been little support for adoption disruption research in the last decade, one important additional study was done by Goerge, Howard, and Yu [1996]. That study used classic definitions of disruption—adoption breakdown after placement—and dissolution—adoption breakdown after legal finalization. The study followed 4,840 children in foster care who exited to adoption between 1976 and 1994 to determine whether they returned to foster care. Among those children, 12.1% of children placed with adoptive families subsequently experienced a disruption. An additional 4.2% of children whose adoptions had been legally finalized returned to the child welfare agency (that is, the adoptions ended in dissolution). The authors concluded that since the passage of PL 96–272, the Adoption Assistance and Child Welfare Act of 1980 (AACWA), the number of children with special needs who were adopted has increased but "the percentage of failures from adoptions and adoptive placements has declined" [1996: 6]. Indeed, the proportion of adoptions that were disrupted declined from 21.1% prior to AACWA to 9.9% after permanency planning was implemented, although adoption dissolution rates remained unchanged (See figure 1). Overall, statistics indicate that adoption disruption rates are far lower than the rate of disruptions of guardianships or long-term foster care placements [Berrick et al. 1998].

Age is the greatest challenge to adoption stability, as adoption disruption and satisfaction rates vary with the age of children at the time of

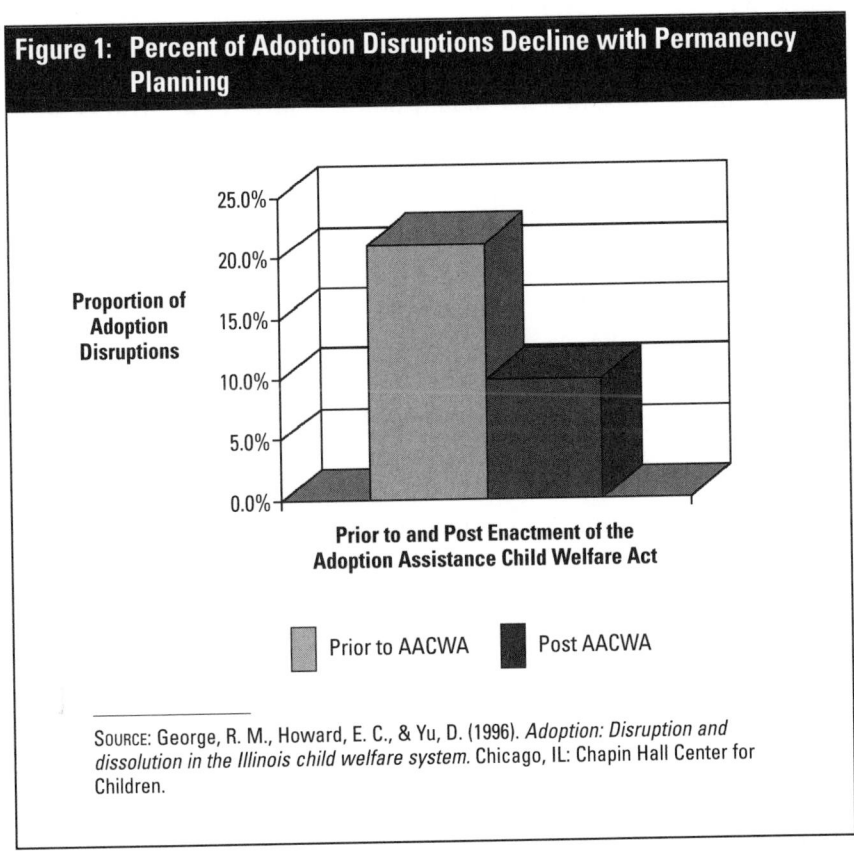

Figure 1: Percent of Adoption Disruptions Decline with Permanency Planning

SOURCE: George, R. M., Howard, E. C., & Yu, D. (1996). *Adoption: Disruption and dissolution in the Illinois child welfare system.* Chicago, IL: Chapin Hall Center for Children.

adoption [Barth & Berry 1988]. As a result, moving children into adoption quickly after it is determined that they cannot return home is critical to the success of adoptions.

Adoption of children with fetal alcohol exposure appears to be particularly challenging. Cadoret and Riggins-Caspar [in press], for example, found that children with a history of prenatal alcohol exposure had a higher likelihood of having multiple psychiatric symptoms as adults, although the adults in their study had been raised in families in which difficulties ranged from parent-child conflict to divorce. On the other hand, there is more evidence of success in adopting drug-exposed children—at least in the first eight years [Brooks & Barth 1999]—although at this age, children have not yet reached a point when longer-term outcomes are more predictable. Supportive educational services—particularly special education and private school education—seem to be contributors to success in the adoption of these children as well as adoption in general [Barth & Berry 1988; Nelson 1985; Walsh 1991].

The success of adoptions should be thought of in a broad context. There are few studies that have systematically compared children who are adopted and those who remain at home, but studies that have made such comparisons [Dumaret 1985] show that children who are adopted fare very well over time. This important public policy comparison shows that adoption is generally beneficial for children. Policymakers and practitioners should, as a result, operate open and flexible adoption programs that encourage the breaking of antiquated barriers to adoption.

Actions that Increase the Success of Adoptions

Adoption is likely to be most successful when adoption agencies:

- Take an open approach to matching children and parents [Barth & Berry 1988];

- Provide accurate information—preferably in a group format—for families before they accept children into their homes [Barth & Berry 1988];

- Assist families to obtain early compensatory education services for their children [Barth & Berry 1988];

- Help adoptive families develop expectations so they are not wildly beyond what their adopted children can meet [Brodzinski et al. 1998];

- Identify children who will not return home from foster care so that they can be placed with adoptive families at an early age [Barth & Berry 1988]; and

- Offer flexible, longer-term post adoptive services [Howard & Smith 1995].

There are several other strategies that appear to increase the success of adoptions. Although there is little research about pre-placement activities that increase the success of adoptions, group—as opposed to individual—home studies appear to be helpful [Barth & Berry 1988]. Similarly, adoptive families seem to benefit from early contact with self-help groups or other adoptive parents who can later provide respite and support [Nelson 1985]. There has been some interest in the use of family-focused adoption preservation services. Although brief, intensive family preservation services models do not routinely fit the needs of adoptive families [Barth 1995; Howard & Smith 1995], a less time-limited family-focused approach seems suitable [Barth 1995; Howard & Smith 1995; Prew et al. 1990]. An evaluation of Illinois' adoption preservation program which incorporated family-focused services showed that 88% of referred families were still intact at the end of treatment [Howard & Smith 1995]. In Oregon's Post-Adoption Family Therapy Project, only 8% of adoptive families disrupted by the end of the service period [Prew et al. 1990]. There were no comparison groups for these studies.

Finally, successful adoption practice requires that practitioners and families be realistic about what adoption offers. When social workers overpromise the impact of adoption in improving the outcomes for children, more harm than good is done [Nelson 1985]. Studies have begun to compare adopted children and biological children, and they show that children who are adopted do not fare as well as biological children in the same families. Using different samples and methods, Feigelman [1997] and Brooks and Barth [1999] found that adopted children have, on average, more problems in early adulthood than children who are not adopted. These data suggest that young adopted adults may not have all the strengths that parents expect from their biological children. Being aware that adopted children may experience more problems in adolescence and early adulthood than biological children can help adoptive parents develop reasonable expectations—a critical component of successful adoptions [Brodzinsky et al. 1998].

Cost-Effectiveness

Although a precise cost-accounting related to finalizing and supporting an adoption has not been done, adoptions appear to be cost-effective because expenditures on subsidies are considerably lower than they are for foster care, and adoptive families contribute substantial resources on behalf of their adopted children (Alexander this volume; Barth 1997]. One estimate of the value of adoption for an eight-year-old who would otherwise remain in foster care until emancipation is more than $500,000 [Barth & Berry 1988]. Adoption, however, also offers many nonmonetized benefits for the child, family, and community.

Conclusion

Research shows that adoption is generally beneficial for children. Low adoption disruption rates reflect the general success of adoptions. Families who enter adoption must be sensitive to the individual needs of children. Age is the greatest challenge, as adoption disruption and satisfaction rates vary with the age of children at the time of adoption. Moving children into adoption quickly after it is determined that they cannot return home is critical to the success of adoptions. In addition, agencies can increase the odds of successful adoptions by taking an open approach to matching children and parents; providing families with accurate, realistic information; assisting families in getting early, compensatory education services; and offering flexible, longer-term post-adoption services. Adoption involves a profound public-private partnership between public agencies and families, and efforts to support a child's success in a family are most often richly rewarding for all involved.

References

Barth, R. P. (1995). Adoption services. In *Encyclopedia of Social Work*. Washington, DC: National Association of Social Workers.

Barth, R. P. (1997). The costs and benefits of adoption. In R. Avery & D. Mont (Eds.), *Public adoption policy* (pp. 171–204). New York: Auburn House.

Barth R. P. & Berry, M. (1988). *Adoption and disruption: Rates, risks and resources.* New York: Aldine.

Barth, R. P. & Brooks, D. (2000). Outcomes for drug-exposed children eight years postadoption. In R. P. Barth, M. Freundlich, & D. Brodzinsky (Eds.), *Adoption and prenatal drug and alcohol exposure* (pp. 23–58). Washington, DC: CWLA Press.

Berrick, J. D., Needell, B., Barth, R. P., & Jonson-Reid, M. (1998). *The tender years: Toward developmentally-sensitive child welfare services.* New York: Oxford.

Berry, M., Barth, R. P., & Needell, B. (1996). Preparation, support, and satisfaction of adoptive families in agency and independent adoptions. *Child and Adolescent Social Work Journal, 13,* 157–183.

Brodzinsky, D. W., Smith, D. M., & Brodzinsky, A. (1998). *Children's adjustment to adoption.* Thousand Oaks, CA: Sage.

Brooks, D. & Barth, R. P. (1999). Adult transracial and inracial adoptees: Effects of race, gender, adoptive family structure, and placement history on adjustment outcomes. *American Journal of Orthopsychiatry, 69,* 87–99.

Cadoret, R. J. & Riggins-Caspars, K. (2000). Fetal alcohol exposure and adult psychopathology: Evidence from an adoptive study. In R. P. Barth, M. Freundlich, & D. Brodzinsky (Eds.), *Adoption and prenatal alcohol and drug exposure* (pp. 83–113). Washington, DC: CWLA Press.

Dumaret, A. (1985). IQ, scholastic performance, and behavior of siblings raised in contrasting environments. *Child Psychology, 26,* 553–580.

Feigelman, W. (1997). Adopted adults: Comparisons with persons raised in conventional families. *Marriage and Family Review, 25*(3–4), 199–223.

Goerge, R. M., Howard, E. C., & Yu, D. (1996). *Adoption: Disruption and dissolution in the Illinois child welfare system.* Chicago: Chapin Hall Center for Children.

Howard, J. A. & Smith, S. L. (1995). *Adoption preservation in Illinois: Results of a four-year study.* Normal: Illinois State University School of Social Work.

Meezan, W., Katz, S., & Russo, E. M. (1978). *Adoptions without agencies: A study of independent adoptions.* New York: Child Welfare League of America.

Nelson, K. A. (1985). *On the frontier on adoption.* New York: Child Welfare League of America.

Partridge, S., Hornby, H., & McDonald, T. (1986). *Legacies of loss—visions of gain: An inside look at adoption disruption.* Portland: University of South Maine.

Prew, C., Suter, S., & Carrington, J. (1990). *Post-Adoption Family Therapy.* Salem, OR: Children's Services Division.

Urban Systems Research and Engineering, Inc. (1985). *Evaluation of state activities with regard to adoption disruption.* Washington, DC: Author.

Walsh, J. A. (1991). *After adoption parent survey.* Champaign: Illinois Department of Children and Family Services.

What Works in Adoption

Study Authors	Survey Sample	Research Design/ Outcome Measure	Findings
Barth, R. P. & Berry, M. (1988). *Adoption and disruption: Rates, risks, and responses.* New York: Aldine de Gruyter.	• 927 children adopted at age 3 or older followed with administrative data to determine whether or not disruption occurred (120 families were also interviewed) • Sample drawn from adoptive placements between 1980 and 1984	• Behavior problems were assessed using the Child Behavior Checklist. • Outcome measures: whether disruption had occurred or been considered and parental satisfaction.	• Approximately 10% of the adoptions in the sample were disrupted. • Families were highly satisfied with their adoptions and even those that experienced disruptions often reported that they would be willing to adopt again. • Age at the time of adoptive placement was strongly associated with the likelihood of disruption.
Dumaret, A. (1985). IQ, scholastic performance and behavior of siblings raised in contrasting environments. *Child Psychology, 26,* 553–580.	• 102 progeny of 28 mothers were followed to approximately age 10 • Group A: 35 children were adopted early into privileged environments; Group B: 46 biological mother raised their children in disadvantaged environments; and Group C: 21 children were raised in institutions or foster homes	• IQ, scholastic aptitude, and behavior were assessed.	• WISC Full Scale IQ scores were 109, 93, and 82 for Groups A, B, and C, respectively. • Overall, in primary and secondary school, the percentages of school failure were 17.1%, 66.6%, and 100% for Groups A, B, and C, respectively. • The proportion of behavior problem scores (23%) of adopted (A) children was higher for their SES-matched classmates (15%) but somewhat lower than those for the biological home-reared children (33%).

(continued next page)

What Works in Adoption (continued)

Study Authors	Survey Sample	Research Design/ Outcome Measure	Findings
Brooks, D. & Barth, R. P. (1999). Adult transracial and inracial adoptees: Effects of race, gender, adoptive family structure, and placement history on adjustment outcomes. *American Journal of Orthopsychiatry, 69*, 87–99.	• 224 inracial and transracial adoptees were recontacted after 17 years—almost all adopting parents were Caucasian. • Children in the study were Asian females (94), Asian males (54), Caucasian males (22), Caucasian females (19), African American males (20), and African American females (19).	• Parents reported on the outcomes for their children using the Global Assessment Scale and other indicators of involvement with specific services (such as corrections) and educational and employment institutions, and the existence of certain problems (such as substance abuse). • Parental satisfaction was also assessed.	• Ethno-racial background of the child nearly doubled the odds of having good adjustment for Asian adoptees and halved the odds for Caucasian adoptees. • Being male increased the odds of problems 1.5 times. • Adopted children who had only birth siblings (that is they were not only children or were not adopted along with other children) had increased odds of poor adjustment. • Satisfaction with parenting was lowest during teenage years but bounced back to much higher levels by the time their children were in their 20s.

23

What Works in Special Needs Adoption

Noelle Gallant

The adoption of children with special needs involves children with a variety of characteristics which make them more challenging to place and the adoptions more challenging to maintain. These characteristics include minority ethnic status, physical or developmental disabilities, older age, emotional and behavioral problems, and membership in a sibling group. Approximately 20,000 to 25,000 children with special needs have been adopted each year [Tatara 1993], a number that increased to 31,000 in 1997 [U.S. Department of Health and Human Services 1999], and the majority of these adoptions have positive outcomes. Approximately 10% –15% of the adoptions, however, end in disruption, which is defined as the termination of the adoptive placement before legal finalization [Rosenthal 1993].

Factors Related to Outcomes in Special Needs Adoption

For the past three decades, researchers have investigated the factors which contribute to the outcomes of special needs adoption. Studies have focused on the causes of disruption and the factors associated with the quality of family functioning after the adoption. Although the studies often have yielded contradictory findings, some clear patterns have emerged. There are three sets of factors which can contribute to successful outcomes in special needs adoption: (1) child characteristics, (2) family characteristics, and (3) service provision characteristics.

Child Characteristics

There are several child-related factors that are related to outcomes in special needs adoption:

- The older the adoptive child with special needs at placement, the greater the risk of disruption [Barth & Berry 1988; Rosenthal 1993].

- Emotional and behavioral problems—such as physical aggression, disobedience at school, stealing, cruelty and meanness to others— contribute to adoption failures. Developmental and physical disabilities, however, are unrelated to disruption [Barth & Berry 1988; Barth & Berry 1991; Rosenthal 1993].

- A past history of physical or sexual abuse also may increase the risk of disruption [Barth & Berry 1991; Rosenthal 1993].

- A child's gender and race/ethnicity have not been found to be significant factors in adoption disruption [Rosenthal 1993].

Family Characteristics

Research suggests that disruption is less likely when the adoptive parents have been married for longer periods of time; the husband is self-employed, employed as a professional, or a high-level manager; and the couple adopted for reasons other than a history of miscarriage [Westhues & Cohen 1990]. Adoptions are more likely to disrupt when parental expectations of the child are too high [Berry 1997], and conversely, adoptions are more successful when adoptive parents have flexible expectations of their adopted children, including their children's academic achievement [Westhues & Cohen 1990]. Successful adoptions are also associated with nurturing parents and an involved father [Westhues & Cohen 1990]. Disruption has been found to be related to rigid family rules—as opposed to appropriate rules or an inconsistent or chaotic environment [Rosenthal et al. 1988].

Foster parent adoptions consistently have been demonstrated to be related to positive adoption outcomes. One study found that foster parent adoptions represented 41% of the intact adoptive placements and 22% of the disrupted adoptions [Rosenthal et al. 1988].

Service Characteristics

There is a higher risk of adoption disruption for children who have had multiple placements, experienced a time lag between being freed for adoption and being placed with an adoptive family, or who have been served by different social workers at various points in their adoptions [Westhues & Cohen 1990]. Multiple-agency involvement also has been identified as a risk factor for disruption [Westhues & Cohen 1990]. In one study, 67% of adoptive placements that had been supervised by the county agency with initial custody of the children remained intact, while only 48% of disrupted adoptions had had single-agency supervision [Rosenthal et al. 1988]. In this study, researchers found that 6% of in-county adoptions and 13% of out-of-county adoptions ended in disruption [Rosenthal et al. 1988]. Lack of adequate background information has also contributed to disrupted special needs adoptions [Groze 1996]. According to Berry [1997], disruption is associated with parental surprise in learning about an adoptive child's history of sexual abuse or behavior or emotional problems and their difficulties coping with these issues.

The provision of agency services is related to a reduced risk of adoption disruption [McDonald et al. 1991]. The mere provision of services such as counseling, support groups, and home visits, however, is not enough. The length of time the services are provided both pre- and postplacement is critical [McDonald et al. 1991].

Adoptive Family Functioning Postplacement

In general, the same factors that predict an outcome of stability or disruption in adoption also predict parental satisfaction or dissatisfaction with the adoptive experience [Rosenthal 1993].

Researchers have explored the relationship between child and adoptive family characteristics and family functioning after the adoptive placement [Erich & Leung 1998]. Higher family functioning has been associated with:

- *More children in the home*—which increases the likelihood that children with special needs have healthy and appropriate models of behavior. Families with several children may have greater tolerance for stress and change.
- *Participation in religious activities*—which suggests that both spiritual and social support is present in these families.
- *Less-educated fathers*—which is associated with a higher level of paternal presence in the home because of fewer educational and/ or vocational responsibilities and a greater potential for family cohesiveness and children's ability to participate in family decision-making activities.

Rosenthal and Groze [1994] examined postplacement family functioning and found that more favorable outcomes were associated with several factors: a child's entry into the home at a younger age; lower adoptive parent education level; minority status, with better outcomes for inracial placements of minority children and transracial placements than for inracial placements of Caucasian children; lower family income; foster parent status; and the disability of the adopted child. Groze [1996] found little difference between outcomes for siblings placed together and apart, irrespective of any history of physical or sexual abuse. The presence of social support, however, was strongly related to positive family functioning (See figure 1).

Groze [1996] found that important sources of social support for adoptive families were: work/school, other family, household assistance, agencies or other formal service providers, neighbors, other friends, and organizations (clubs and churches).

Conclusion

Research has provided valuable information to aid both professionals and potential adoptive families. To best promote positive outcomes, each adopted child with special needs and each potential adoptive family need to be assessed individually to determine how their personalities and characteristics may complement one another or cause conflict [Berry 1997]. Information about the child's history should be shared freely with the potential adoptive family. Training for parents should include appropriate and flexible disciplinary techniques and assistance in understanding

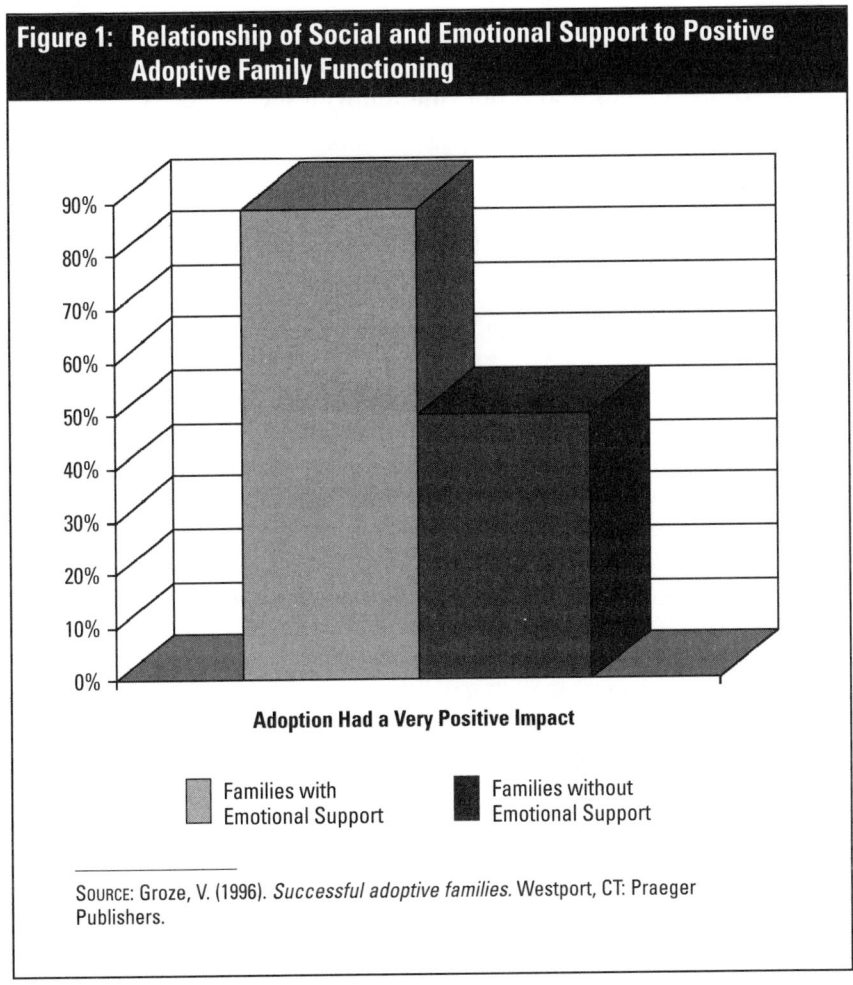

Figure 1: Relationship of Social and Emotional Support to Positive Adoptive Family Functioning

SOURCE: Groze, V. (1996). *Successful adoptive families.* Westport, CT: Praeger Publishers.

expectations for children with special needs. Social workers should assess the level of social support available to adoptive families and be prepared to enhance the families' support, if needed. Given the availability of adoption subsidies, families with limited incomes should not be considered less desirable adoptive parents.

Research has consistently demonstrated that most special needs adoptions work well and result in positive outcomes for adoptive children and families. As the number of special needs adoptions increases in this country, however, it will become increasingly important to identify the factors that make these adoptions work. Research should focus on the service needs of families who adopt children with special needs.

References

Barth, R. & Berry, M. (1988). *Adoption and disruption: Rates, risks and responses.* New York: Aldine de Gruyter.

Barth, R. P. & Berry, M.(1991). Preventing adoption disruption. *Prevention in Human Services, 9*(1), 205–222.

Berry, M. (1997). Adoption Disruption. In R. Avery (Ed.), *Adoption Policy and Special Needs Children.* Westport, CT: Greenwood Publishing Group, Inc.

Erich, S. & Leung, P. (1998). Factors contributing to family functioning of adoptive children with special needs: A long-term outcome analysis. *Children and Youth Services Review 20*(1/2), 135–150.

Groze, V. (1996). *Successful Adoptive Families.* Westport, CT: Praeger Publishers.

McDonald, T., Lieberman, A. Portridge, S., & Hornby, H. (1991). Assessing the role of agency services in reducing adoption disruptions. *Children and Youth Services 13,* 425–438.

Rosenthal, J. (1993). Outcomes of Adoption of Children with Special Needs. *The Future of Children 3*(1), 77–89.

Rosenthal, J. & Groze, V. (1994). A longitudinal study of special-needs adoptive families, *Child Welfare, 73,* 689–706.

Rosenthal, J., Schmidt, D., & Connor, J. (1988). Predictors of special needs adoption disruption: An exploratory study. *Children and Youth Services Review 10,* 101–117.

Tatara, T. (1993). *Voluntary Cooperative Information System (VCIS), Characteristics of children in substitute and adoptive care (Based on FY82 through FY90 Data).* Washington, DC: American Public Welfare Association.

U.S. Department of Health and Human Services. (1999). AFCARS Data. Online: www.acf.dhhs.gov/programs/cb.

Westhues, A. & Cohen, J. (1990). Preventing disruption of special needs adoptions. *Children Welfare, 69,* 141–155.

What Works in Special Needs Adoption

Study Authors	Survey Sample	Research Design/Outcome Measure	Findings
Rosenthal, J., Schmidt, D. & Conner, J. (1988). Predictors of special needs adoption disruption: An exploratory study. *Children and Youth Services Review (10)*, 101–117.	• 57 children from Colorado age 3 to 16 who sustained a total of 62 adoption disruptions or dissolutions between 1981 and 1984 • 391 adoptive placements made by the Oklahoma Department of Human Services between January 1982 and September 1985	• Data on child and family characteristics were obtained from a 25-page questionnaire completed by adoption social workers. • Matched pairs design was used to compare characteristics of disrupted placements with those of intact placements.	• Behavioral and emotional problems are related to the outcome of adoption. • Foster parent adoption reduces the risk of disruption. • The income of adoptive parents is negatively associated with intact adoptions. • Capacity of adoptive parents to deal with emotionally nonresponsive child, acting out behavior, and withdrawn behavior is associated with intact adoptions. • Rigid rule structures are associated with disrupted adoptions. • 67% of intact placements had been supervised by the county agency with initial custody of the children remained intact; 48% of disrupted adoptions had had single agency supervision. • 6% of in-county adoptions and 13% of out-of-county adoptions ended in disruption.

(continued next page)

What Works in Special Needs Adoption (*continued*)

Study Authors	Survey Sample	Research Design/Outcome Measure	Findings
Westhues, A. & Cohen, J. (1990). Preventing disruption of special needs adoptions. *Child Welfare, 69*(2), 141–155.	• Families from five Children's Aid Societies in Southern Ontario who had had a special-needs child placed with them between January 1984 and September 1985 • Final sample size was 58 families who had adopted 79 children	• Data were collected on the independent variable of family functioning using the Family Assessment Measure. • Data on the placement outcome were gathered one year after placement.	• Fathers in the disrupted group were more likely to report functioning as average in their family functioning, with respect to their own functioning, and with respect to the functioning of their wives. • Fathers in the sustainer group were likely to report functioning as being toward the strength area of the average range. • Wives who scored their husbands positively on values and norms were more likely to have sustained adoptions. • Families who sustained placements were likely to have been married longer and have a husband who was self-employed, a professional, or in a high-level management position.
Rosenthal, J., & Groze, V. (1994). A longitudinal study of special-needs adoptive families. *Child Welfare, 73*(6), 689–706.	• Adoptive families from Oklahoma (n = 89), Iowa (n = 88) and Illinois (125), resulting in a combined sample of 302 cases	• Longitudinal study examining changes in child and family functioning, parent-child relationships, school performance, child behavior, and perceived impact of adoption on the family, using a mailed survey of adoptive families. • The survey was administered twice, approximately four years apart. • The Child Behavior Checklist (CBCL) and the Family Adaptability and Cohesion Scale (FACES) were part of the survey.	• Lower-income, less-educated and minority families are more likely to experience positive outcomes. • At the first administration, 50% of the families reported that the adoption had a very positive impact upon the family; at the second administration, 43% of the families gave this response. • Responses to the CBCL indicated that the behavioral problems of children tend to persist over time and that adolescence is often a particularly difficult time for these children.

24

What Works in Open Adoption

Harold D. Grotevant

Open adoption refers to a continuum of degrees of contact and communication between members of an adopted child's birth family and adoptive family.

At one end of the spectrum, there is no contact, and information shared between parties is general (such as nationality or height) and nonidentifying. These are typically called confidential or closed adoptions.

Further on the spectrum are mediated or semiopen adoptions, in which birth family and adoptive family members communicate with one another, using a third party as go-between. The go-between role is typically played by an adoption agency staff member or an attorney who transmits communications from one party to another, preserving their anonymity. Meetings and phone calls between the parties do not typically take place in mediated adoptions; if they do, participants do not know each other's full name or address.

At the other end of the spectrum are fully disclosed adoptions, which involve direct contact between at least some birth family and some adoptive family members. Fully disclosed adoptions are often referred to as "open adoptions," although use of this term varies among practitioners and researchers. Even though fully disclosed adoptions involve direct contact and communication, the extensiveness of contact may vary from infrequent (every few years) to very frequent (several times a month).

The contact could include a combination of visits, phone calls, or exchanges of letters. The contact may only involve certain members of the families and, specifically, may or may not include the adopted child.

Favorable Outcomes: The Impact of Open Adoption

Open adoptions did not become commonplace in the U.S. until the mid-to-late 1980s. Critics made a number of predictions:

- Adopted children would be confused about who their "real parents" were, and consequently, would suffer in terms of identity development and self-esteem;

- Adoptive parents would fear constant intrusion by birth parents, would feel a lack of entitlement to serve as the child's "full parents," and would have a poorer relationship with their child; and

- Birth mothers would not be able to put the loss involved in their adoption behind them and get on with their lives, as contact with the child would prevent them from dealing with their ever-present grief.

The consequences of open adoption have been examined in several research studies. In addition, advocates for and against open adoption have written books and articles, typically presenting case studies as evidence (Lindsay 1987; Silber & Dorner 1990; Smith 1997). Although many of the studies are based on small convenience samples and rely on non-standard interviews and questionnaires, a consistent picture has begun to emerge from this literature.

Adopted Children

Only one study has assessed adopted children [Grotevant & McRoy 1997, 1998], and this study is now following the children as they move through adolescence. When the children were in their elementary school years, no differences emerged by level of openness on various aspects of socioemotional development or self-esteem. Within the group of mediated and fully disclosed adoptions, however, higher degrees of collaboration in the relationships between the adoptive parents and birth family predicted more positive socioemotional development [Grotevant et al. 1999]. Openness levels were also not predictive of children's curiosity about their birth parents. All children were curious, but they were found to be curious about different things—depending on their level of contact with their birth parent(s). Children in fully disclosed adoptions had a more cognitively sophisticated understanding of adoption than children in confidential or mediated adoptions, probably because the contact with birth family members stimulated more thinking about the topic.

Adoptive Parents

Research has found that adoptive parents in fully disclosed adoptions show greater empathy toward their children and the birth mother, have greater communication about adoption with their child, and acknowledge to a greater extent the special status of being an adoptive family [Grotevant et al. 1994]. Higher levels of contact were associated with greater comfort with contact [Berry 1993; Gross 1993]. Dissatisfaction with the frequency of contact typically involved adoptive parents wanting more rather than less contact with the birth family [Grotevant et al. 1994]. Parents in open adoptions also experienced lower levels of fear that the birth mother would attempt to reclaim her child, when compared to parents in confidential or mediated adoptions [Belbas 1987; Grotevant et al. 1994]. Adoptive parents felt that openness enhanced their feelings of entitlement [Iwanek 1987; Siegel 1993] and brought with it feelings of satisfaction [Etter 1993; Gross 1993]. Figure 1 shows the adoptive parents' levels of satisfaction with birth mother contact [Gross 1993].

Birth mothers

Research has found that birth mothers who had contact with the adoptive family through either ongoing mediated or fully disclosed adoptions showed better resolution of grief than did birth mothers who never had contact with the adoptive family or whose contact had stopped [Christian et al. 1997].

Conflicting Evidence

In general, the research reviewed here is quite consistent, with a few exceptions. In one study [Smith 1991], prospective adoptive parents were asked—before a child was placed with them—their preferences among confidential, semiopen, and open adoption. Of these perspective

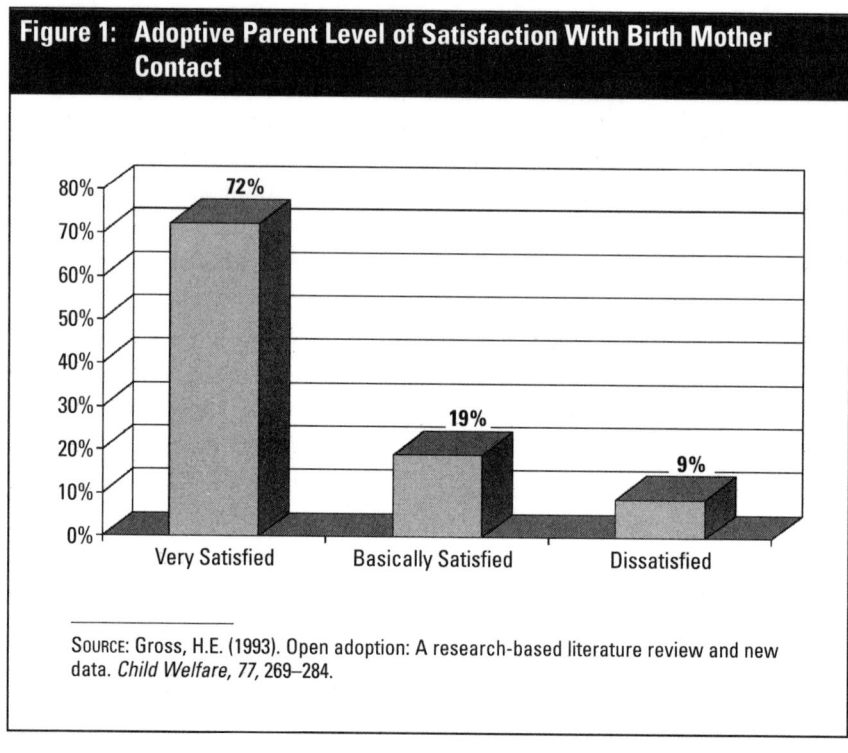

Figure 1: Adoptive Parent Level of Satisfaction With Birth Mother Contact

SOURCE: Gross, H.E. (1993). Open adoption: A research-based literature review and new data. *Child Welfare, 77,* 269–284.

adoptive parents, 75% chose confidential, 25% chose semiopen, and none chose open adoptions [Smith 1991]. This study, however, involved only agencies whose philosophies did not advocate openness. In contrast to the several studies that found differences in life satisfaction or perceived control confidential and open adoptions, Silverstein and Demick [1994] found no differences between families with different levels of openness. In a study of open and confidential adoptions [Blanton & Deschner 1990], birth mothers in open adoptions felt more isolation and despair.

Cost-Effectiveness

Conclusions about cost-effectiveness of open adoptions can only be drawn tentatively as no studies have directly examined this question. Open adoptions have allowed some private agencies to stay in business when other agencies have had to close because client demand for openness (especially from birth mothers) is strong. From an agency staffing perspective, fully disclosed adoptions may be less costly in the long run than mediated adoptions, because contact between adoptive parent(s) and birth parent(s) is left directly to the parties themselves. There may be increased need, however, for post-adoption counseling. With mediated adoptions, agency staff must deal with the flow of letters, pictures, and gifts that must to be transmitted from one party to the other. Thus, it is problematic that this form of adoption produces increasing demands on social service providers in an era of generally shrinking resources [Henney et al. 1998].

Conclusion

No single adoption arrangement is best for everyone. Each type of adoption presents distinctive challenges and opportunities. Open adoption can work well for those adoptive parents and birth parents who want to establish a fully disclosed adoption.

The complexity of relationships in open adoptions demands ongoing management of family boundaries and the commitment of the parties to continue working on their relationships toward mutual satisfaction. Such management requires communication, flexibility, commitment to the process, respect for the parties involved, and a primary commitment to meeting the child's needs. If these conditions are not present, the participants may want to consider other arrangements. Further, what may be best for one party in the adoption triad at one point in time may not be best for other parties, since parties' needs for more or less openness may change over time and may not always occur in synchrony among triad members [Grotevant & McRoy 1998].

Relatively more is known about openness outcomes for adoptive parents and birth parents than for adopted children, and only longitudinal research tracking children's developmental histories can shed light on this important question.

References

Belbas, N. (1987). Staying in touch: Empathy in open adoptions. *Smith College Studies in Social Work, 57,* 184–198.

Berry, M. (1993). Adoptive parents' perceptions of, and comfort with, open adoption. *Child Welfare, 77,* 231–253.

Blanton, T. L. & Deschner, J. (1990). Biological mother's grief: The postadop-tive experience in open versus confidential adoption. *Child Welfare, 69,* 525–535.

Christian, C. L., McRoy, R. G., Grotevant, H. D., & Bryant, C. (1997). Grief resolution of birthmothers in confidential, time-limited mediated, ongoing mediated, and fully disclosed adoptions. *Adoption Quarterly, 1*(2), 35–58.

Etter, J. (1993). Levels of cooperation and satisfaction in 56 open adoptions. *Child Welfare, 72,* 257–267.

Gross, H. E. (1993). Open adoption: A research-based literature review and new data. *Child Welfare, 77,* 269–284.

Grotevant, H. D. & McRoy, R. G. (1997). The Minnesota/Texas Adoption Research Project: Implications of openness in adoption for development and relationships. *Applied Developmental Science, 1,* 168–186.

Grotevant, H. D. & McRoy, R. G. (1998). *Openness in adoption: Exploring family connections.* Thousand Oaks, CA: Sage.

Grotevant, H. D., McRoy, R. G., Elde, C. L., & Fravel, D. L. (1994). Adoptive family system dynamics: Variations by level of openness in adoption. *Family Process, 33,* 125–146.

Grotevant, H. D., Ross, N. M., Marchel, M. A., & McRoy, R. G. (1999). Adaptive behavior in adopted children: Predictors from early risk, collabora-tion in relationships within the adoptive kinship network, and openness arrangements. *Journal of Adolescent Research, 14,* 231–247.

Henney, S. M., Onken, S., McRoy, R. G., & Grotevant, H. D. (1998). Changing agency practices toward openness in adoption. *Adoption Quarterly, 1*(3), 45–76.

Iwanek, M. (1987). *A study of open adoption placements.* Petone, New Zealand: Iwanek.

Lindsay, J. W. (1987). *Open adoption: A caring option.* Buena Park, CA: Morning Glory Press.

Siegel, D. H. (1993). Open adoption of infants: Adoptive parents' perceptions of advantages and disadvantages. *Social Work, 38*(1), 15–23.

Silber, K. & Dorner, P. M. (1990). *Children of open adoptions.* San Antonio, TX: Corona Publishing Co.

Silverstein, D. R. & Demick, J. (1994). Toward an organizational-relational model of open adoption. *Family Process, 33,* 111–124.

Smith, J. (1991). *Attitudes of prospective adoptive parents towards agency adoption practices, particularly open adoption.* Paper presented at the meeting of the National Committee for Adoption, Washington, DC.

Smith, J. (1997). *The realities of adoption.* Lanham, MD: Madison Books.

What Works in Open Adoption

Study Authors	Survey Sample	Research Design/Outcome Measure	Findings
Blanton, T. L. & Deschner, J. (1990). Biological mothers' grief: The postadoptive experience in open versus confidential adoption. *Child Welfare, 69*(6), 525–535.	• 59 birth mothers: 18 in open adoptions, 41 in confidential adoptions • Openness category determined by whether there was a meeting at placement	• Questionnaire (demographics, attitudes about and experience with adoption, Grief Experience Inventory) • Surveys mailed to former clients of four adoption agencies	• Birth mothers in open adoptions felt more isolation, more despair, had more difficulty with physical functions, and felt more dependency.
Berry, M. (1993). Adoptive parents' perceptions of, and comfort with, open adoption. *Child Welfare, 77*(3), 231–253.	• 1,268 adoptive parents in California; compared confidential and open adoptions	• Mailed survey • Focus on adoptive parents' perceptions of openness, comfort with openness, and satisfaction with adoption	• Higher levels of direct contact were associated with greater comfort with contact. • Key predictors of openness were adoptive parents' plans for contact, absence of history of child maltreatment, birth mother's level of education, direct contact, adoptive mother's older age, and adoptive parents having talked with birth mother prior to placement.
Gross, H.E. (1993). Open adoption: A research-based literature review and new data. *Child Welfare, 77*(3), 269–284.	• Interviews with 32 adoptive parents and 16 associated birth mothers • Questionnaires to 75 adoptive parents • All recruited from a private adoption agency	• Interviews and questionnaires • Focus on satisfaction with openness	• In the interview sample, 72% of adoptive parents were "very satisfied" with contact with birth mothers; 19% were "basically satisfied" but had some reservations; two families were dissatisfied and had ceased contact. 15 of the 16 birth mothers were satisfied with contact. • In the questionnaire sample, there was an association between higher degrees of satisfaction and more frequent contact. "Best" aspects of openness involved adoptive parent comfort in knowing that they and their child would have access to information and personal contact with birth family members that they might want or need. "Worst" aspects of openness were "none" and arranging the logistics of visits.

(continued next page)

What Works in Open Adoption (*continued*)

Study Authors	Survey Sample	Research Design/Outcome Measure	Findings
Siegel, D.H. (1993). Open adoption of infants: Adoptive parents' perceptions of advantages and disadvantages. *Social Work, 38* (1), 15–23.	• 21 adoptive couples • Snowball sample	• Interviews administered at home • Focus on perceptions of openness—advantages and disadvantages	• Perceived advantages of openness: were able to adopt faster, felt some control over how they would deal with birth mother, liked knowing things about birth parents, felt openness helped decrease fantasies and enhanced entitlement, and felt relationship was "more natural." Adoptive parents also felt there were advantages for adopted children and birth mothers, although only adoptive parents were interviewed. • Perceived disadvantages: uncertainty about long-term effects on children, lack of social norms, emotional demands of relationship with birth mother, and fear of rejection by birth mother. Overall, no regrets about openness; advantages seen as outweighing disadvantages.
Grotevant, H.D. & McRoy, R.G. (1997). The Minnesota/Texas Adoption Research Project: Implications of openness in adoption for development and relationships. *Applied Developmental Science, 1,* 168–186.; Grotevant, H.D. & McRoy, R.G. (1998). *Openness in adoption: Exploring family connections.* Thousand Oaks, CA: Sage.	• 190 adoptive families (190 mothers, 190 fathers, 171 children; 169 birth mothers (total N = 720) • Three primary types of adoption: confidential, mediated, fully disclosed	• Adoptive parents interviewed in the homes across the U.S.; birth mothers interviewed by phone or at home. • Child outcomes: understanding of adoption, self-esteem, socioemotional adjustment, and curiosity about birth parents. • Adoptive parent outcomes: empathy, communication, acknowledgment of difference, entitlement, and fear of reclaiming. • Birth mother outcomes: grief resolution, career identity, intimacy, adoption adjustment, self-esteem, and psychological symptoms.	• Adopted child: No difference by openness on self-esteem, curiosity, or socioemotional adjustment; children in fully disclosed adoptions had higher levels of cognitive understanding of adoption. • Adoptive parents: parents in fully disclosed adoption show higher levels of empathy, acknowledgment of difference, and communication, and lower levels of fear of reclaiming. • Birth mothers: birth mothers in fully disclosed adoptions showed higher levels of grief resolution; no differences by openness on self-esteem or psychological symptoms.

25

What Works in Transracial Adoption

William Feigelman

Though transracial adoptions have a nearly 50-year history, they still remain a controversial subject in American social service practice. In the absence of systematic data gathering by governmental agencies, no one knows how many of these adoptions occur annually, though it is known that they comprise a small fraction of the total number of adoptions [Bachrach et al. 1990]. Judging from a variety of available data sources, a figure of 5,000 would be a close approximation of their annual frequency.

Evidence suggests that prior to World War II, the adoption of minority children, whether by Caucasians or by non-Caucasians, represented an extremely rare and uncommon event in America. Only after World War II—with the pronatalist and profamily mood that followed the War—did interest in these adoptions surge and begin to include the placement of many so-called "nonadoptable" children—older and minority children and children with disabilities [Carp 1998]. World War II also triggered the expansion of transracial adoptions in efforts to find homes for several thousand war-orphaned Japanese children. Transracial adoptions drastically expanded in the aftermath of the Korean War and again during and after the war in Vietnam. Warfare led to the establishment of various humanitarian enterprises, located principally in Asia, committed to helping dislocated children find adoptive homes [Silverman 1993]. Thus, the history of transracial adoption is primarily a history of intercountry adoptions.

In the early 1960s, not long after transracial adoption was employed as a solution for war-ravaged children in other lands, American social service professionals began to see this type of adoption as an answer for homeless children in the United States who were casualties of family poverty, parental illness, substance abuse, and other family dislocating events. Native American children, underclass, and ghetto-resident children also became recipients of relief efforts that included transracial placements. The first major objection to transracial adoption emerged in the early 1970s when the National Association of Black Social Workers (NABSW) opposed transracial placement as a form of cultural genocide [Simon & Altstein 1977]. Critics of transracial adoption claim that children subjected to this experience will become confused about their ethnic self-identities; will not find acceptance either in their original birth culture group or in the Caucasian American majority; and will identify with the majority culture and will not develop any sense of membership or belonging to their racial or ethnic group of birth. Thus far, the research on transracial adoptive placements has not yielded any systematic evidence supporting critics' claims of confused self-identities, except for a few isolated cases. Yet, despite their mostly successful outcomes, the criticisms of transracial adoption have effectively stopped the adoptions of Native American children by Caucasians (common in the early 1970s) and have effectively minimized the adoptions of homeless African American children, obliging many to spend most of their childhood years in a variety of foster homes.

Research Evidence

The research on transracial adoption can be roughly divided into three parts: (1) research on younger children, (2) research on older children and early adolescents, and (3) research on young adult transracial adoptees. Early childhood research consistently shows transracial adoptees to be well-adapted when compared with their inracially adopted peers and with comparable biological offspring [Fanshel 1972; Grow & Shapiro 1974; Ladner 1977; Feigelman & Silverman 1983; Simon & Alstein 1977]. Most of this research does not allow any firm conclusions about racial self-identity given the youth of respondents.

Late childhood and early adolescent studies also show comparable adaptations between transracial adoptees and their inracially adopted peers (comparing African American children adopted by Caucasian parents to

African American children adopted by African American parents; also comparing Latino, Asian, and African American children adopted by Caucasian parents to Caucasian children adopted inracially) [Kim 1976; McRoy & Zurcher 1983; Shireman & Johnson 1988]. Some of the studies also show that transracially adopted Latino and Asian children are more likely to relinquish their self-identifications to their birth cultures than may be the case for African American transracial adoptees [Feigelman & Silverman 1983; Simon et al. 1994]. None of these studies uncovered problematical adaptations as a result of a child's closer affiliations to the Anglo-Caucasian American majority [Silverman & Feigelman 1990].

Relatively few studies have been completed among the most intriguing research subset—young adult transracial adoptees. Available evidence, which presents some methodological shortcomings, suggests these older transracial adoptees are no less well-adapted than their inracially adopted counterparts [Feigelman in press]. For example, in one of the young adult studies [Feigelman in press], it was noted that about one-fourth of all Caucasian parents who adopted Caucasian children reported that their children had three or more problems in the following areas: running away from home, requiring counseling for emotional problems, having drug or alcohol problems, being arrested, or being expelled from school. This finding compared to 32% of Caucasian parents of African American children, 19% of Caucasian parents of Asian children, and 16% of Caucasian parents adopting Latino children. These differences did not approach statistical significance. In most other adjustment comparisons made among these four subgroups, the evidence showed comparability among the three transracial subgroups and the inracially adopted Caucasian controls [Feigelman in press; Simon et al. 1994; Vroegh 1992]. The evidence thus offers consistency on the value of transracial placement as a useful resource for minority children who have no immediate same-race placement opportunities and who would otherwise languish in a variety of foster care placements.

What Works Best With Transracial Adoptions

There are several factors that facilitate favorable outcomes for transracial adoptions:

- *Placements are made when children are younger.* At least four studies document the value of early placement—before age 2 [Fanshel

1972; Feigelman & Silverman 1983; Grow & Shapiro 1974; Kim 1976]. In the younger child adoption study by Feigelman and Silverman [1983], for example, it was found that slightly more than half of the adoptive parents whose children were adopted before age 2 reported "some" or "many" adjustment problems among their children, whereas four-fifths of parents who adopted children at older ages reported similar levels of problem behaviors among their adopted children.

- *When adoptive parents respect, acknowledge and cultivate their child's affiliation with his or her birth culture.* The importance of adoptive parents' attitudes about and behaviors in relation to their child's birth culture has been substantiated in almost every transracial adoption study done to date [Feigelman & Silverman 1983; Ladner 1977; Simon & Altstein 1981, 1987; McRoy & Zurcher 1983]. In the Feigelman and Silverman study [1983], for example, it was found that when parents occasionally or often read materials about African American culture to their African American adopted children, 73% of their children identified themselves as African American, and that when parents rarely, if ever, read to their child about their culture, only 38% of their children identified themselves as African American. The same study also found that when parents often or occasionally talked to their children about being African American, 75% of their children identified themselves as being African American compared with only 33% who did so when their parents rarely had such discussions with them.

- *When families live in integrated neighborhoods.* Integrated neighborhoods have been found to be particularly important for African American transracial adoptees because they enhance opportunities for children to make ties with others belonging to their group and minimize instances of racial stigmatization. This finding, too, has been substantiated in all studies, especially those following transracial adoptees into early adulthood [Feigelman in press; Simon et al. 1994; Vroegh 1992]. In one study [Feigelman in press], half of the parents residing in racially segregated Caucasian neighborhoods reported that their children felt uncomfortable about their appearance compared to only about one-fourth of parents who resided in racially mixed locations.

Cost-Effectiveness

From a cost-benefit standpoint, transracial adoption represents a far more economical alternative to the higher costs for case management and long-term foster care. Even when adoptive parents receive subsidies, as is sometimes the case in the adoption of hard-to-place children, these costs are likely to be far less than the costs incurred when individuals deprived of family memberships become dysfunctional adults, welfare recipients, prison inmates, drug offenders, or chronically mentally ill.

Conclusion

Overall, available evidence suggests that transracial placement produces positive results among children who are adopted into majority homes. Arguments made by some of its critics, claiming that transracial adoptees may be lost to their birth cultures, cannot be wholly discounted. The research on transracial adoption suggests that it works best when the placement is made when children are younger; adoptive parents respect, acknowledge, and cultivate their child's affiliation with his or her birth culture; and when families live in integrated neighborhoods.

References

Bachrach, C. A., Adams, P. F., Sambrano, S., & London, K. A. (1990). *Adoption in the 1980's, Advance data from vital and health statistics, number 181.* Hyattsville, MD.: National Center of Health Statistics.

Carp, E. W. (1998). *Family matters, secrecy and disclosure in the history of adoption.* Cambridge, MA: Harvard University Press.

Fanshel, D. (1972). *Far from the reservation: The transracial adoption of American Indian children.* Metuchen, NJ: The Scarecrow Press.

Feigelman, W. & Silverman, A. R. (1983). *Chosen children: New patterns of adoptive relationships.* New York: Praeger.

Feigelman, W. (in press). Adjustments of transracially and inracially adopted young adults. *Child and Adolescent Social Work Journal.*

Grow, L. & Shapiro, D. (1974). *Black children—white parents: A study of transracial adoption.* New York: Child Welfare League of America.

Kim, D. S. (1976). *Intercountry adoptions: A study of self concept of adolescent Korean children who were adopted by American families.* Unpublished Ph.D. dissertation, University of Chicago, Illinois.

Ladner, J. (1977). *Mixed families.* Garden City, NY: Doubleday Anchor.

McRoy, R. & Zurcher, L. A. (1983). *Transracial and inracial adoptees.* Springfield, IL: C.C. Thomas.

Shireman, J. & Johnson, P. (1988). *Growing up adopted.* Chicago: Chicago Child Care Society.

Silverman, A. R. & Feigelman, W. (1990). Adjustment in interracial adoptees: An overview. In D. Brodzinsky and M. Schechter (Eds.), *The psychology of adoption* (pp. 187–200). New York: Oxford University Press.

Silverman, A. R. (1993). Outcomes of transracial adoption. *The Future of Children, 3*(1), 104–118.

Simon, R. J. & Altstein, H. (1977). *Transracial adoption.* New York: John Wiley.

Simon, R. J., Altstein, H., & Melli, M. S. (1994). *The case for transracial adoption.* Washington, DC: American University Press.

Simon, R. J. & Altstein, H. (1987). *Transracial adoptees and their families.* New York: Praeger.

Simon, R. J. & Altstein, H. (1981). *Transracial adoption: A followup.* Lexington, MA: Lexington Books.

Vroegh, K. (1992, April). *Transracial adoption: How it is 17 years later.* Unpublished report. Chicago: Chicago Child Care Society.

What Works in Transracial Adoption

Study Authors	Survey Sample	Research Design/Outcome Measure	Findings
Simon, R. J. & Altstein, H. (1977). *Transracial adoption*. New York: John Wiley. Simon, R. J. & Altstein, H. (1981). *Transracial adoption: A follow up*. Lexington, MA: Lexington Books. Simon, R. J. & Altstein, H. (1987). *Transracial adoption & their families*. New York: Praeger. Simon, R. J., Altstein, H. & Melli, M.S. (1994). *The case for transracial adoption*. Washington, DC: American University Press.	• 204 Caucasian families from five mid-western cities • 366 children, of whom 157 were transracial adoptees (African American, Asian & Mexican), 166 Caucasian birth children, and 42 Caucasian in-race adoptees	• Original study began in 1971, with follow-ups in 1978, 1983–84 and 1990–91. • Comparisons were made between transracial adoptees and Caucasian inracially adopted and birth children.	• Positive results shown by parents and children at each follow-up point. Researchers tracked children from early childhood into their twenties, though only 98 children from the original sample were tracked at final follow-up.
Feigelman, W. & Silverman, A. R. (1983). *Chosen children: New patterns of adoptive relationships.* New York: Praeger. Feigelman, W. (in press). Adjustments of transracially and inracially adopted young adults. *Child and Adolescent Social Work Journal*, 17, (3)	• 717 Caucasian families from a national sample of adoptive families • 546 transracially adopted children (African American, Asian & mostly Colombian children) compared with 96 inracially adopted Caucasians	• Based primarily upon parental judgments, this original study began in 1975; respondents were followed up twice—once in 1981 and again in 1993. • All information collected about adopted children's behavior was obtained from their parents.	• Positive results obtained at each follow-up point, extending until, on average, adoptees reached age 23.

(continued next page)

What Works in Transracial Adoption (*continued*)

Study Authors	Survey Sample	Research Design/Outcome Measure	Findings
McRoy, R. & Zurcher, L. A. (1983). *Transracial and inracial adoptees.* Springfield, IL: Charles Thomas.	• 60 families from southern, midwestern and southwestern locations: 30 Caucasians who had adopted African American children were compared with 30 African American parents who had adopted African American children	• Both parents and children were interviewed and children were studied at approximately age 14. • An extensive battery of psychological tests were administered to the adoptees in this study.	• Favorable adaptations noted among the transracially adopted children when compared to the inracially adopted African Americans. • 60% of transracial adoptive parents lived in primarily Caucasian communities, putting their adopted children in disadvantaged positions to interact readily with same race peers.
Shireman, J. & Johnson, P. (1988). *Growing up adopted.* Chicago: Chicago Child Care Society. Vroegh, K. (1992). *Transracial adoption: How it is 17 years later.* Unpublished report. Chicago: Chicago Child Care Society.	• 87 Chicago families who had adopted children in 1970–1972 • Comparisons between 42 African-American children transracially adopted and 45 African American children placed inracially in African American two-parent homes	• Both parents and children were interviewed at four year intervals, when children were approximately 4, 8, 13, and 21 years old.	• Parents and children were highly satisfied with their adoptions at all data collection points. • Transracially adopted children had good relations with siblings and high self-esteem and showed overall comparability to their inracially adopted African American peers.

26

What Works in Intercountry Adoption

Isaac V. Gusukuma and Ruth G. McRoy

Throughout history, most children have been adopted by relatives, childless couples, and families who lived in the same community, geographic area, or country [Kim 1978]. In traditional adoptions, the adopted child and adoptive families share similar ethnic, social, and cultural backgrounds. Recently, traditional adoption practices have changed as a result of a significant increase of intercountry adoptions. Between 1975 and 1995, the number of intercountry adoptions increased from 5,000 to more than 9,600 children adopted annually from other countries by United States families [U.S. Immigration and Naturalization Services 1997]. In 1997, the U.S. State Department reported that more than 13,600 orphaned children were issued immigrant visas. The top 20 source countries of children in 1997, as reported by the U.S. State Department [1999], are listed in Table 1.

Proponents of intercountry adoptions emphasize that adoption of a child from another country is a direct humanitarian service provided by the family to the child [Adams & Kim 1971]. Furthermore, the adoption of a child into a permanent home, even if the home is in another country, is more desirable for a child than placement in an institution such as an orphanage or another system of child care. Intercountry adoption is endorsed by groups such as the North American Council on Adoptable Children

Table 1. Top 20 Source Countries for Intercountry Adoptions, 1998

Source Country	Number of Children
Russia	4,491
China	4,206
S. Korea	1,829
Guatemala	911
Vietnam	603
India	478
Romania	406
Colombia	351
Cambodia	249
Philippines	200
Ukraine	180
Mexico	168
Bulgaria	151
Dominican Republic	140
Haiti	121
Brazil	103
Ethiopia	96
Thailand	84
Poland	77
Latvia	76

SOURCE: U.S. State Department Bureau of Consular Affairs
http://travel.state.gov/index.html

(NACAC), representing more than 400 child advocacy organizations in the United States and Canada, and the National Committee on Adoption, an organization representing 145 nonprofit adoption agencies [Silverman & Feigelman 1990]. Child welfare social workers and other child care professionals historically have been concerned about and involved in the adoption process. These professionals have focused on helping adopted children and their families make a healthy adjustment to a new environment and a new family relationship. The central issue in intercountry adoption is whether the fundamental needs of adopted children can be better served in the new social and family environment [Kim 1978].

The Benefits of Intercountry Adoption

Research studies have documented several advantages to intercountry adoptions:

Parental Benefits

The overwhelming majority of parents who adopt internationally report that they and their child benefited from and adjusted well to the adoption [Westhues & Cohen 1997; Groze & Ileana 1996; Alstein et al. 1991]. Most report that they overcame health or other adjustment problems as they and their children learned to adjust to the new family and home environment. Although the long-term adjustment of intercountry adoptive families and their children is unclear because of a lack of longitudinal family studies, all indicators are that the majority of internationally adopted children and their families do very well in the new family environment. Parental benefits of intercountry adoptions include:

- *Adoptive parents have an opportunity to parent through intercountry adoptions and provide for the needs of a child.* For parents who may have previously dealt with infertility, intercountry adoption is an opportunity to parent a child who would not otherwise have been available to them. Other intercountry adoptive parents have biological children or other adopted children and are able to add to their families through intercountry adoption. The adoption of a child from another country may be viewed as an opportunity to provide a home to a child in need.

- *Intercountry adoptions provide an opportunity for single parenthood.* Historically, many U.S. adoption agencies did not place children with single adults. However, in recent years, this practice has changed as the number of children with special needs requiring an adoptive placement has escalated, and adoption agencies have recognized the growing number of single adults in the United States who are interested in parenting. Intercountry adoption has become an opportunity for a single adult to parent a child. A recent study of intercountry adoptions noted that 24 of 153 intercountry adoptive families were single, never married adoptive parents [Gusukuma 1997]. Many countries—including Brazil, El Salvador, Honduras, Peru, Bolivia, and China—place children with single adults, although policies in other countries regarding the adoption of children by single adults are constantly changing. Single adoptive parents are a growing phenomenon, but their experiences, their adjustment, and the needs of these adoptive families have not been extensively studied.

- *Parents benefit from preparation in understanding the issues of transethnic adoptions.* Current adoption practice emphasizes the importance of preparing families to understand and recognize the importance of the child's cultural identity. Intercountry adoptive families are faced with the challenge of raising a child who may not look like their parents, immediate and extended family members, or others in their community, but studies suggest that adoptive parents appear to feel a sense of security in their ability to provide for the needs of their child. In a study of adult adoptees born in other countries and their parents in northeastern United States, adoptees were found to be well-adapted and did not feel that their differing ethnicity from that of their parents had been a major factor in their lives [Alstein et al. 1994]. Most of the adoptive parents in the study emphasized the importance of maintaining their adopted children's cultural awareness.

- *Parents and children benefit from adoption support groups.* Adoptive family support groups provide adoptive parents and children an opportunity to identify and share common experiences. Adoption support group activities include parenting discussions, social gatherings, cultural programs, and opportunities to share experiences common to intercountry adoptive families. Recently, intercountry adoption agencies and programs have begun to sponsor cultural camps and tours to children's countries of origin for older adopted children and adoptive parents. Adoptive parents with younger children tend to be more involved with adoption support groups with family participation declining as children get older [Gusukuma 1997]. The Internet, however, provides many adoptive families access to information and support. Sites such as Internet Resources for Adoption [http://fwcc.org/internetsources.html 1999] provide links to sites with helpful general information about adoption, particularly the adoption of Asian children.

Choosing Intercountry Adoption

Studies of intercountry adoption find that adoptive parents seek the adoption of a child from another country for a range of reasons [Altstein & Simon 1991; Bagley et al. 1993; Silverman & Feigelman 1990]. Although adoptive parents identify many reasons for adopting a child from another country, a recent study of intercountry adoptions [Gusukuma 1997] identified the following major reasons for adopting a child from another country:

- *Infertility.* In studies of both intercountry and intracountry adoptive parents, the major reason for seeking the adoption of a child has been found to be infertility of one or both parents [Daly 1991; Gusukuma 1997; Tizard 1991]. Intercountry adoptive parents reported receiving infertility treatments for up to 12 years [Gusukuma 1997].

- *Familiarity with a world region.* The decision to adopt a child from another country was, in some cases, partly based on one of the adoptive parent's previous experience with or knowledge of a country or world region [Gusukuma 1997]. A parent who traveled to China on a vacation, for example, may be more likely to adopt a child from Asia.

- *Availability of children.* Parents note that intercountry adoption may involve a shorter wait for a child than intracountry adoptions. Single parents, in particular, note that although adoption is difficult, certain countries are more accepting of single adoptive parents.

- *Concern with in-country adoptions.* Intercountry adoptive parents express concerns about the media and legal controversies surrounding adoption in the United States. Adoptive parents expressed concern and a sense of nervousness about "birth mothers changing their minds" and "the courts returning children to parents who had earlier placed them for adoption" [Gusukuma 1999: 196].

Families make the decision to adopt a child from another country in different ways. The decision to adopt a child from another country requires an emotional, psychological, physical, and financial investment on the part of the adoptive parents.

Intercountry adoptive parents may make significant financial investments in adoption. In a recent study the average cost of an intercountry adoption was more than $17,000 compared to an average cost of $14,500 for an intracountry adoption [Gusukuma 1997]. Intercountry adoptions involve a wide range of fees, including agency fees and fees for copying documents (birth, marriage, divorce and death certificates). Additional costs involve travel, transportation, and room and board in the child's country of origin while processing the adoption. Some adoptive parents obtain loans and financing to meet the financial requirements, and other parents use savings and investment resources [Gusukuma 1997].

Intercountry adoptive parents invest time in their adoptions. Countries have different requirements for adoptive parents. One country may require a stay of four or five days to process the adoption, and another country may require a stay of weeks or months. As a consequence, parents may face time away from home, family, job, and, for many adoptive parents, time away from other children at home.

Intercountry adoptive parents invest in the health of their children. Intercountry adoptive parents may adopt children who have mild developmental delays, suffer from the effects of malnourishment, or have health problems such as mild infections, scabies, or a cold at the time of the adoption. Experienced adoptive parents advise consulting a pediatrician prior to the adoption and advising the physician of their adopted child's country of origin. The pediatrician may then become familiar with the child's potential exposure to common parasites and diseases prior to the child's arrival in the United States. Adoptive parents also express concern about the limited medical history that is available for their children. A child's medical records may be vague and incomplete, or translations may be inaccurate. Intercountry adoptive parents note the importance of timely, complete, and periodic medical evaluations for their children.

Concerns about Intercountry Adoption

The desirability, benefits, and effects of intercountry adoption for the adopted child and adoptive family have been debated by child care professionals and others in the field of adoption [Kim 1977]. Some have argued that intercountry adopted children will be isolated from their culture and ethnicity [Joe 1978; Bagley & Young 1980], and children adopted from other countries will lose their cultural roots, resulting in a confused identity [Tizard 1991]. Critics of intercountry adoption have charged that adopters from the West travel to poorer countries in the wake of war, earthquake, famine, and disaster and adopt healthy children, leaving older or disabled children in institutional care in their countries of origin [Melone 1976]. Others note that the practice of intercountry adoptions means needy American children are passed over in favor of the adoption of healthier infants in other countries [Joe 1978]. Though the debate about intercountry adoptions may continue in the future, the greater majority of current studies of intercountry adoptive families note the overall success, stability and positive adjustment of the children and their families.

Conclusion

American families are adopting a significant number of children from other countries, and additional research assessing the long-term adjustment of intercountry adoptive parents and their children is needed. For prospective adoptive parents, intercountry adoption is an option. Each adoptive parent or couple will have personal reasons that guide the decision to adopt a child from another country. Although the investment in an intercountry adoption is great, so are its benefits. Adoption agencies and their policies play a key role in the intercountry placement of a child. The placement of a child with an adoptive family indicates that the agency has made a considered judgment that the family will best serve the interests of the child and is preferable to other available options. Adoptive parents who choose intercountry adoption can provide opportunities for a child that, given the circumstances, may not have been otherwise available.

References

Adams, J. E. & Kim, H. B. (1971). A fresh look at intercountry adoptions. *Children, 18,* 214–217.

Alstein, H., Coster, M., First-Hartling, M., Ford, C., Glascoe, B., Hairston, S., Kasoff, J., & Wellborn-Grier, A. (1994). Clinical observations of adult intercountry adoptees and their adoptive parents. *Child Welfare, 73,* 261–269.

Alstein, H. & Simon, R. (Eds.). (1991). *Intercountry adoption: A multinational perspective.* New York: Praeger.

Bagley, C. & Young, L. (1979). The identity, adjustment and achievement of transracially adopted children: A review and empirical report. In G. K. Verma & C. Bagley (Eds.), *Race, education, and identity* (pp. 192–219). New York: MacMillan Press.

Bagley, C. & Young, L. (1980). The long-term adjustment and identity of a sample of inter-country adopted children. *International Social Work, 23*(3), 16–22.

Bagley, C., Young, L., & Scully, A. (1993). *International and transracial adoptions: A mental health perspective.* Brookfield, VT: Ashgate Publishing Company.

Child Welfare League of America. (1988). *Standards for Adoption Services* (rev.). New York: Child Welfare League of America.

Daly, K. (1991). Infertility resolution and adoption readiness. *Families in Society: The Journal of Contemporary Human Services, 71*(8), 483–492.

Groze, V. & Ileana, D. (1996). A follow-up study of adopted children from Romania. *Child and Adolescent Social Work Journal, 13*(6), 541–65.

Gusukuma, I. (1997). *Intercountry adoptions: The experiences and adjustments of families adopting children from Latin America, China, and the United States.* Unpublished doctoral dissertation. Austin, TX: University of Texas at Austin.

Joe, B. (1978). In defense of inter-country adoption. *Social Service Review, 52,* 1–20.

Kim, D. S. (1977). How they fared in American homes: A follow-up study of adopted Korean children in the U.S. *Children Today, 6*(2), 2–6.

Kim, D. S. (1978). Issues in transracial and transcultural adoption. *Social Casework, 59,* 477–486.

Melone, T. (1976). Adoption and crisis in the third world. *International Child Welfare Review, 28,* 20–25.

Silverman, A. R. & Feigelman, W. (1990). Adjustment in interracial adoptees: An overview. In D. M. Brodzinsky & M. D. Schechter (Eds.), *The Psychology of Adoption* (pp.187–200). New York: Oxford University Press.

Tizard, B. (1991). Intercountry adoption: A review of the evidence. *Journal of Child Psychology and Psychiatry, 32*(5), 743–756.

U.S. Immigration and Naturalization Service. (1997). *Statistical Yearbook of the Immigration and Naturalization Service.* Washington, D C: U.S. Government Printing Office.

U.S. State Department. (1999). *Immigrant visas issued to orphans coming to the U.S.* Online: http://209.67.208.64/orphan_numbers.html

U.S. State Department. (1999). *Immigrant visas issued to orphans coming to the U.S.: Top countries of origin.* Bureau of Consular Affairs. Online: http://travel.state.gov/orphan_numbers.html

Westhues, A. & Cohen, J. (1997). A comparison of the adjustment of adolescent and young adult intercountry adoptees and their siblings. *International Journal of Behavioral Development, 20*(1), 47–65.

What Works in Intercountry Adoption

Study Authors	Survey Sample	Research Design/Outcome Measure	Findings
Westhues, A. & Cohen, J. (1997). A comparison of the adjustment of adolescent and young adult inter-country adoptees and their siblings. *International Journal of Behavioral Development, 20* (1), 47–65.	• 86 adolescent inter-country adoptees of both sexes and 33 of their adolescent siblings in Canada • 49 young adult adoptees of both sexes and 65 of their young adult siblings in Canada	• Data collected through interviews with adoptive parents, adoptees, and siblings of adoptees • Study measured six areas of adjustment for intercountry adoptees: family integration, self-esteem, peer relations, comfort with ethnic or racial background, and school performance.	• Data demonstrated that intercountry adoptees adjusted well to life in Canada. • Differences were found in adjustment between inter-country adoptees and their siblings, with siblings, on average, showing more positive adjustment. • No significant gender differences were found.
Boer, F., Versulius-den Bieman, M. & Verhulst, F. (1994). International adoption of children with siblings: Behavioral outcomes. *American Journal of Orthopsychiatric Association 64* (2), 252–62.	• 399 internationally adopted children in the Netherlands placed with their siblings • Comparison to 1,749 children placed alone	• Parents completed Child Behavior Checklist to measure children's competencies and behavioral-emotional problems. • Parents also provided additional written comments on the same topics.	• Children adopted with siblings tended to be older at the time of placement. • Children adopted with siblings tended to be healthier and showed fewer behavior problems than children adopted alone.
Groze, V. & Ileana, D. (1996). A follow-up study of adopted children from Romania. *Child and Adolescent Social Work Journal, 136*), 541–65.	• Adoptive parents, mostly adoptive mothers (87%), of 200 male and 262 female Romanian adoptees • Sample taken from Adoptive Families of America's list of visas issued to children from Romania between 1990 and 1993	• Adoptive parents completed a questionnaire that probed the adopted children's history and development and the family's activities, stability, and social and medical resources and needs.	• Most of the children were developmentally appropriate. • Parents reported good parent-child relations. • Few of the children had behavioral problems and those with problems tended to come from institutions. • The adoptions are very stable.

Citation	Sample	Methods	Findings
Alstein, H., Coster, M., First-Harting, M., Ford, C., Glascoe, B., Hairston, S., Kasoff, J. & Wellborn-Grier, A. (1994). Clinical observations of adult intercountry adoptees and their adoptive parents. *Child Welfare, 73*(3), 261–269.	• 29 adoptees born in other countries and their adoptive parents in the northeastern United States (26 female and three males) • 23 sets of parents • Average age of adoptees was 22 • All participants were Asian with 90% from Korea	• Questionnaire was used to gauge the psychosocial adjustment of adoptees and their relationship with their parents, siblings, and extended families • School performance, friendship patterns, social activities, future ambitions, and community and religious involvement were measured.	• Most adoptees lived in Caucasian neighborhoods, had Caucasian best friends, and dated Caucasians. • 79% of adoptees reported some awareness of their cultural background. • 38% of adoptees said they attended church at least once a month. • Familial problems usually were not related to adoption. • Most adoptees were well-adapted and did not feel that their differing ethnicity from that of their parents had been a major factor in their lives. • Many parents emphasized the importance of their children maintaining awareness of their country of birth and its culture.
Trolley, B., Wallin, J. & Hansen, J. (1995). International adoptions: Issues of acknowledgement of adoption and birth culture. *Child and Adolescent Social Work Journal, 12*(6), 465–79.	• 34 families who internationally adopted children with an average parental age of 39 • All of the parents were married and Caucasian • 54.5% of the children were Asian, 17.5% Latin, and 15% Caucasian. • The average age of the children was 4 years old.	• Questionnaires used were Kirk's "Attitudes Toward Adoption" to measure parental feelings about the adoption process and the way adoption was discussed with the adoptive child; Trolley's "Culture Form" was used to assess the parents' perception of the relevance of introducing information to adoptive children about their cultural backgrounds.	• Parents discussed the child's birth culture with their children. • 100% of parents revealed the adoption to the child before age 5. • 86% of parents felt that birth culture was relevant to their child's identity and 90.5% of parents were concerned that their child might worry about his or her background.

(continued next page)

What Works in Intercountry Adoption (*continued*)

Study Authors	Survey Sample	Research Design/Outcome Measure	Findings
Friedlander, M. (1999). Ethnic identity development of internationally adopted children and adolescents: Implications for therapists. *Journal of Marital and Family Therapy, 25*(1), 43–60.	• One 13-year-old male adoptee and his parents; adoptee of Brazilian, Portuguese and African descent; parents were Caucasian Americans	• Case study describing family's interaction with therapist. • Adopted child was experiencing difficulties at school with his peers and frequently had arguments with and disobeyed parents.	• Therapists should consider familial and marital problems not related to adoption during counseling. • Therapist should caution adoptive parents of the difficulty experienced by some intercountry and transracial adoptees because of their racial and ethnic background. • Adoptive parents should be well-informed and educated about problems that may arise in transethnic adoptions.
Verlhurst, F. & Versulius-Den Bieman. (1995). Developmental course of problem behaviors in adolescent adoptees. *Journal of the American Academy of Child and Adolescent Psychiatry, 34*(2), 151–159.	• 1,538 intercountry adoptees in the Netherlands age 11–14 at initial assessment and ages 14 to 17 at follow-up	• Child Behavior Check List (CBCL) was used to determine the three-year developmental course of problem behaviors and competencies in intercountry adoptees during adolescence and the role of ethnicity and environment in influencing developmental problems.	• Follow-up study showed an increase in problem behaviors and a decrease in competencies, particularly in CBCL Withdrawn and Delinquency scales. • No conclusions could be made that related specific adoption issues (such as age or medical condition at time of placement, ethnic background, or early neglect or abuse) as the cause of increased problems. • Other factors pertaining to adolescent development and adoption-specific factors were cited as interacting negatively to increase problems for adoptees in comparison to general population.

Verlhurst, F., & Versulius-Den Bieman. (1995). Self-reported and parent reported problems in international adoptees. *Journal of Child Psychology and Psychiatry, 36*(8), 1411–28.	• 1,538 intercountry adoptees ages 14 to 18 in the Netherlands • 513 adolescents from a sample of the general population in the Netherlands	• Child Behavior Check List (CBCL) was used to determine problem behaviors and competencies in intercountry adoptees during adolescence. • CBCL also used to determine the role of ethnicity and environment in influencing developmental problems.	• Based on self-reports, 22% of adopted boys and 18% of adopted girls were regarded as deviant compared to 10% of participants from the general population. • Childhood deprivation was most often cited as a cause of problem behavior. • Other factors pertaining to adolescent development and adoption-specific factors were cited as interacting negatively to increase problems for adoptees in comparison to the general population.

27

What Works in Adoption Assistance

Gina Alexander

Public Law 96-272, the Adoption Assistance and Child Welfare Act of 1980, required states to establish adoption subsidy programs for children with special needs and provided federal matching dollars for adoption subsidies for eligible children. According to the North American Council on Adoptable Children [Wiedemeier et al. 1996], the program has grown from no federally funded adoption subsidies in 1980 to $267 million, supporting nearly 100,000 adopted children in 1996.

Most children in out-of-home care awaiting adoption have "special needs," which means they have characteristics that make them harder to place with adoptive families. Two-thirds of the children with "special needs" have medical problems, developmental delays and disabilities, and/or behavioral or psychological problems [U. S. Department of Health and Human Services 1997]. The median age of children who are legally free and awaiting adoption is about 9 years old, and over half of them are minorities.

The Impact of Adoption Assistance

Adoption assistance or adoption subsidy programs are effective tools in facilitating the adoption of children with special needs. The National Study of Adoption Assistance Impact and Outcomes [Sedlak & Broadhurst 1992] looked at the impact of adoption assistance programs on increasing the adoption of special needs children. The study used a nationally representative sample of 2,200 children who had been adopted between 1983 and 1987. The authors found that adoption assistance increased adoption opportunities for children in a number of respects.

- Adoption assistance removed the disadvantage associated with children's age, prior disability status, and need for ongoing treatment. Children with these characteristics frequently wait longer to be adopted. When adoption subsidy was available, the waiting time decreased.

- Adoption assistance eliminated the waiting time for children with negative background experiences. With subsidy, children who had been abused or neglected, multiple foster care placements, caretakers who abused alcohol or drugs, or displayed acting out or other behavior problems waited no longer for adoption than those without these background factors.

- Adoption assistance facilitated the adoption of children with previous disrupted adoptive placements. With assistance, children with a prior disrupted placement waited an additional 5.5 months to be placed with another adoptive family; without subsidy, they waited an additional 8.7 months. The difference in waiting time for children of color appeared greatly reduced when adoption assistance was given, although the reduction was not statistically significant.

- The provision of adoption assistance also appears to mitigate the risk for adoption disruption. In a study of adoption disruptions in northern California, Barth and Berry [1988] found that the higher disruption rate for older children was more profound in unsubsidized adoptions than for subsidized adoptions. "Among placements predicted to disrupt, somewhat more did disrupt when there was no subsidy" [Barth & Berry 1988: 203].

Problems in Administration

Although adoption assistance has been shown to be an effective tool in achieving permanency for children with special needs, states vary considerably in their policies regarding the children who are eligible to receive adoption assistance [Barth & Berry 1988; Sedlak & Broadhurst 1992; Gilles 1995; U.S. Department of Health and Human Services

1997]. Gilles [1995] conducted a multistate survey of adoption administrators, adoption workers, and adoptive families to assess the effectiveness of adoption assistance programs. Although the majority of respondents believed that adoption assistance programs facilitated adoption for waiting children, they identified a number of problems in the administration of the programs. The respondents reported:

- Despite the expansion of subsidized adoption, many children with special needs and their adoptive families remained unserved by adoption assistance programs. Thirteen percent of the adoptive families were never notified of their state's adoption assistance program, and 20% of the children identified as having special needs were placed without monthly subsidy payments.

- Children and families served by private agencies did not have equivalent access to adoption assistance benefits as those served by public agencies. Eighty-five percent of the families who adopted children with special needs through public agencies received monthly subsidy payments compared to only 65% of adoptive families of children with special needs who adopted through private agencies.

- The linkage of Title IV-E eligibility to Aid to Families with Dependent Children (AFDC) eligibility prevented many children with special needs from receiving adoption assistance. The linkage between IV-E eligibility and eligibility for AFDC was identified as the major impediment to comprehensive and equitable distribution of adoption assistance benefits nationwide.

- Inadequate adoption assistance training and programmatic understanding by front-line staff detrimentally impacted children with special needs and their adoptive families. Forty-one percent of the front-line workers who were interviewed had never received training in adoption assistance. Among the adoptive parents who were notified of their state's adoption assistance program, only 63% said they received information in a clear and understandable manner.

Additionally, the survey found a growing trend among adoption administrators to use adoptive family income and resources when determining program eligibility, potentially limiting the number of prospective adoptive families for children with special needs. Barth and Berry [1988] identified similar problems in administration. They found that the adoptive family's income often determined whether or not a placement was made with subsidy. Among those adoptions of children with special needs that were not subsidized, over half had been determined ineligible due to adoptive family income even though this practice is prohibited by federal law. Barth and Berry [1988] also found that children with greater needs did not have higher subsidies. Parents who experienced adoptive placements as more difficult also reported inadequate subsidies.

The Adoption and Safe Families Act of 1997 (P.L. 105–89) addresses some of the barriers to adoption associated with access to subsidy. The law expands adoption support services through continuing eligibility for adoption subsidy to children whose adoptions disrupt and through expanding of health care coverage for non-Title IV-E eligible adopted children with certain medical needs. Further research on this law will be needed to determine its impact in promoting permanency for children and reducing barriers to adoption.

Cost-Effectiveness

Cost-benefit analyses reveal that adoption assistance is a cost-effective alternative to out-of-home care [Gilles 1995; Sedlak & Broadhurst 1992; Office of Inspector General 1988; Barth and Berry 1988]. Sedlak and Broadhurst [1992], in a national study of the impact of adoption assistance programs, compared the financial and human costs to children placed with adoption assistance with the costs associated with children's remaining in out-of-home care until emancipation. The authors studied 40,700 children who were adopted between 1983 and 1987 and found:

- Eighty-four percent of the children freed for adoption had one or more characteristics that would have qualified them as children with special needs and, thus, eligible for adoption assistance. Only 63%, however, were adopted with subsidy. If adoption assistance had been given to all eligible children, the number of children adopted would have risen to 7,200 (a 16% increase).

- Table 1 shows the average monthly per-child administrative costs of foster care and adoption assistance. For each child receiving adoption assistance, $146 fewer were spent each month as measured in 1988 dollars. Adoption assistance represented a substantial savings over out-of-home care. Federal and state governments

Table 1. Administrative Costs for Foster Care and Adoption, 1988*

	Average Monthly Number of Children	Average Monthly Administrative Costs	Per-Child Average Administrative Costs
Foster Care	132,120	$27,576,975	$209
Adoption Assistance	34,849	$ 2,194,456	$ 63

SOURCE: Sedlak, A. & Broadhurst, D. (1992). *Study of adoption assistance impact and outcomes: Final report.* (Contract No. 105-89-1607, Westat, Inc.). Washington, DC: U.S. Department of Health and Human Services.

*The first column of figures reflects the average monthly number of children who were in the Title IV-E foster care program and the average monthly number of children who were in the adoption assistance program.

would save a total of $1.6 billion in administrative costs alone for the 40,700 children studied whose families received adoption assistance. The projected savings are based on a comparison of the costs of adoption assistance with the costs of continued foster care had the children remained in care until their emancipation at age 18.

In addition to substantial savings in administrative costs, assistance payments to adoptive families are less than maintenance payments for out-of-home care, which include room and board, clothing, and other expenses. A comparison between the costs to maintain children in family foster homes and the cost of adoption assistance is shown in Figure 1.

Sedlak and Broadhurst [1992] also found that out-of-home care is more costly than adoption in terms of the effect on the outcomes for the children themselves. The study used comparison information from a national study of children discharged from family foster care to develop predictions of the outcomes of the adopted child population and the outcomes that would have been expected for them had they not been adopted.

The outcomes of the adopted children were generally positive. These children were predicted to be comparable to, or better than, youth in the general population in a number of respects including having close relationships and having been married, educational level, use of alcohol and drugs, problems with the law, employment history, and satisfaction with life (See Table 2).

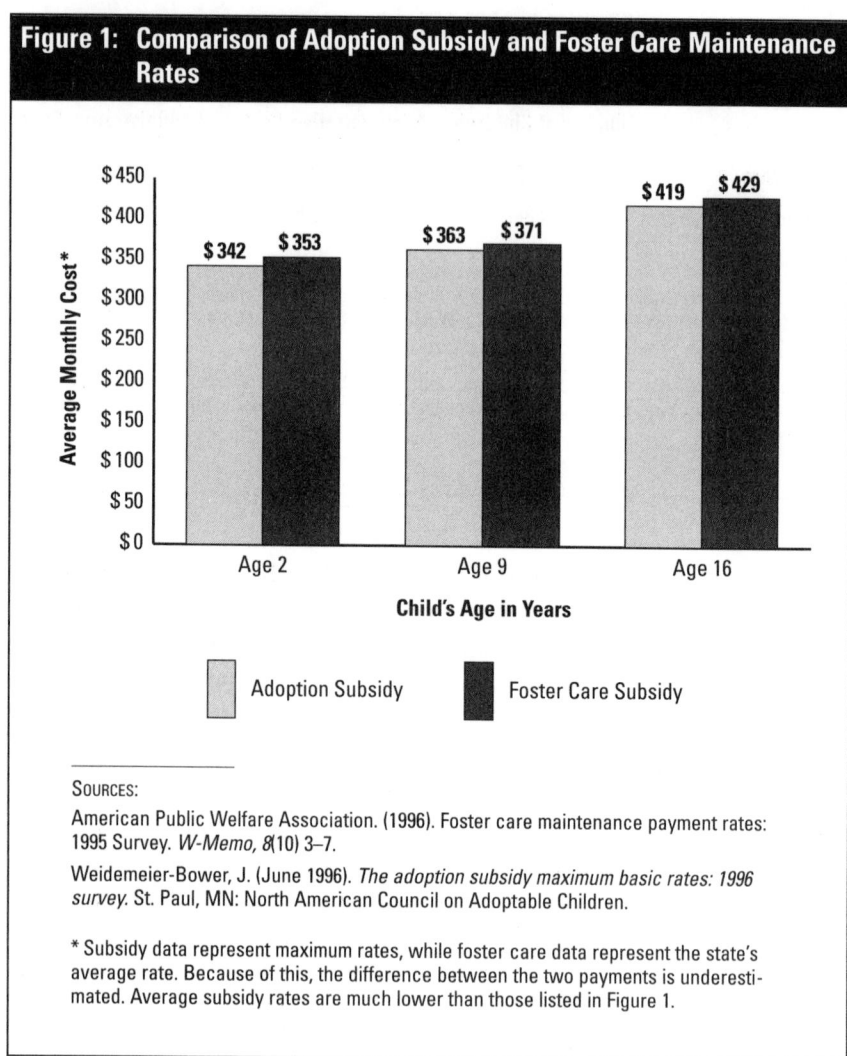

Figure 1: Comparison of Adoption Subsidy and Foster Care Maintenance Rates

Child's Age in Years

Average Monthly Cost*

Age 2: Adoption Subsidy $342, Foster Care Subsidy $353
Age 9: Adoption Subsidy $363, Foster Care Subsidy $371
Age 16: Adoption Subsidy $419, Foster Care Subsidy $429

Adoption Subsidy   Foster Care Subsidy

SOURCES:

American Public Welfare Association. (1996). Foster care maintenance payment rates: 1995 Survey. *W-Memo, 8*(10) 3–7.

Weidemeier-Bower, J. (June 1996). *The adoption subsidy maximum basic rates: 1996 survey.* St. Paul, MN: North American Council on Adoptable Children.

* Subsidy data represent maximum rates, while foster care data represent the state's average rate. Because of this, the difference between the two payments is underestimated. Average subsidy rates are much lower than those listed in Figure 1.

The outcomes for the children had they not been adopted substantially depended upon the stability of the children's family foster care placements. Continued foster care can be equivalent to adoption in terms of the children's eventual outcomes only when the stability of the foster home placement can be ensured. In the absence of this stability, continued family foster care will lead to less favorable outcomes.

Table 2. Outcomes Projected for Adopted Children When They Reach Young Adulthood

Outcomes at Ages 18–22 Years	Percent with the Outcomes
Would have any close relationship	85%
Would have ever married	30%
Would be a high school graduate	71%
Would have ever used illegal drugs	36%
Would have ever had alcohol to drink	75%
Would have had problems with the law	14%
Would have ever been employed	89%
Would be very satisfied with life	39%

SOURCE: Sedlak, A. & Broadhurst, D. (1992). *Study of adoption assistance impact and outcomes: Final report.* (Contract No. 105-89-1607, Westat, Inc.). Washington, DC: U.S. Department of Health and Human Services.

Conclusion

Adoption assistance programs promote permanency for children with special needs by increasing opportunities for adoption. Adoption assistance decreases the time that hard-to-place children wait to be adopted and appears to mitigate the risk for future adoption disruption. It is a cost-effective alternative to out-of-home care, both in financial and human terms. Despite the many positive aspects of adoption assistance programs, there continues to be great variability among the states in how these programs are administered. Consequently, many eligible, waiting children remain unserved by adoption assistance programs.

References

American Public Welfare Association, (1996). Foster care maintenance payment rates: 1995 survey. *W-Memo, 8*(10), 3–7.

Barth, R. P. & Berry, M. (1988). *Adoption and disruption: Rates, risks, and responses.* New York: Aldine de Gruyter.

Gilles, T. (1995). *Adoption assistance in America: A programmatic analysis fifteen years after federal implementation.* St. Paul, MN: North American Council on Adoptable Children.

Office of the Inspector General, Office of Analysis and Inspections. (1988). *Minority adoptions.* Washington, DC: Office of the Inspector General.

Sedlak, A. & Broadhurst, D. (1992). *Study of adoption assistance impact and outcomes: Final report.* (Contract No. 105-89-1607, Westat, Inc.). Washington, DC: U.S. Department of Health and Human Services.

U.S. Department of Health and Human Services. (1997). *Adoption 2002.* Washington, DC: Author.

Wiedemeier-Bower, J. (1996). *The adoption subsidy maximum basic rates: 1996 survey.* St. Paul, MN: North American Council on Adoptable Children.

Wiedemeier-Bower, J., Gilles, T., & Kroll, J. (1996). *User's guide to P.L. 96–272: A summarization and codification of administrative rulings.* St. Paul, MN: North American Council on Adoptable Children.

What Works in Adoption Assistance

Study Authors	Survey Sample	Research Design/Outcome Measure	Findings
Barth, R. & Berry, M. (1988). *Adoption and disruption: Rates, risks, and responses.* New York: Aldine de Gruyter.	• 927 children adopted at age 3 or older; 120 families were interviewed • Sample drawn from adoptive placements in 13 northern and central California counties between 1980 and 1984	• Data collected from record review and social worker and/or adoptive parent interviews. Of the 120 families interviewed, 61% received an adoption subsidy. • Outcome measured was adoption disruption.	• Approximately 10% of the adoptions in the sample disrupted. • 58% of predicted disruptions actually disrupted when there was an adoption subsidy, while 76% disrupted when there was no subsidy. • Inadequate subsidies were reported by parents experiencing placements as more difficult (r = 35, ρ < 002).
Gilles, T. (1995). *Adoption assistance in America: A programmatic analysis fifteen years after federal implementation.* St. Paul, MN: North American Council on Adoptable Children.	• 27 state adoption administrators, 140 front-line adoption workers, and 532 adoptive families from 20 states were interviewed. • Sample drawn from states that were the initial W.K. Kellog Foundation "Families for Kids" finalists	• Data collected via telephone interview and written survey instrument. • Study assessed the general effectiveness of adoption assistance programs in facilitating adoption of waiting children.	• 78% of the agency-facilitated adoptions finalized in the survey states were given adoption subsidy. • 13% of adoptive families were never notified of their state's adoption assistance program. • 20% of children with special needs were placed without subsidy payment and 43% of the families who adopted them received no reimbursement for nonrecurring adoption costs.

(continued next page)

What Works in Adoption Assistance *(continued)*

Study Authors	Survey Sample	Research Design/Outcome Measure	Findings
Sedlak, A. & Broadhurst, D. (1992). *Study of adoption assistance impact and outcomes: Final report.* (Contract No. 105-89-1607, Westat, Inc.). Washington, DC: U.S. Department of Health and Human Services.	• Nationally representative sample of 2,200 children adopted between 1983 and 1987, of which a subsample of 306 families were interviewed. • Sample drawn from public adoption agencies in 25 countries	• Data collected through analysis of case records and interviews with adoptive parents. • Study measured the impact of adoption assistance on placement of children with special needs and the outcomes of these children following adoptive placement.	• Adoption assistance removed the disadvantage associated with children's age, disability status, and need for ongoing treatment. • Adoption assistance eliminated the longer waiting times for children who had any of various negative background experiences. • Adoption assistance facilitated the adoption of children with previous disrupted adoptions. • Based on predictive models, adopted children were found to be comparable to, or better than, youth in the general population in respect to several outcomes where comparison data were available.

Section V

Child Care

28

What Works in Head Start

Elizabeth Schnur and Susan Belanger

H ead Start, perhaps the best-known and enduring legacy of the Great Society, began in the mid-1960s as a school readiness program. The hope was that a well-planned preschool intervention experience would allow young, economically disadvantaged children to begin school on an even level with their more economically privileged peers, and thereby promote equal access to achievement when the children entered public school. The program took a holistic approach to preschool intervention, focusing not just on traditional academic-readiness issues, such as letter recognition, but also on the child's social, emotional, and physical development. Importantly, Head Start was community-based—a quality it has always maintained—with the requirement of considerable community and parent input and parent participation.

Although the original Head Start program was designed as a summer program, it currently is a part-day, year-long program with many variations, such as extended day services. In 1995, the program began designating a small proportion of the national Head Start budget for an expansion to include infants and toddlers in an Early Head Start experience, seeking broadly to promote child development in multiple domains as well as family, staff, and community development.

Benefits of Head Start

Head Start has been the subject of voluminous research and evaluation since its inception, although the quality of this work has been extremely variable and frequently has used small, unrepresentative samples. In reviewing the program's impact and success, it is important to consider what it is reasonable to expect. As Edward Zigler, one of the designers and a tireless advocate for the program, has noted, "Overoptimism about the potential of Head Start began before the first centers opened their doors" [Zigler & Styfco 1994: 127].

There were two prevailing expectations at the program's inception. First, it was believed that the one-year Head Start experience would bring children to the level of more advantaged peers when they entered grade school. Second, Head Start was expected to "inoculate" children throughout development and have a continued, measurable impact on both cognitive and social outcomes when children became teens and young adults. Research repeatedly has demonstrated substantial increases in children's cognitive performance at the end of the Head Start experience and benefits to children's health and social development.

- *Children in Head Start had significant gains on measures of cognitive ability at one year post-Head Start.* Head Start participants appeared to produce significant one-year gains on some measures of cognitive ability. Children in Head Start gained significantly more than children not in preschool and children in "other" preschools on the Peabody Picture Vocabulary Test, which evaluates receptive vocabulary and provides a measure of IQ; the Caldwell Preschool Inventory, which evaluates sociocognitive skills; and the Motor Inhibition Test, which is not strictly a cognitive test and measures impulsivity [Lee et al. 1988]. These results suggest that Head Start was quite effective at reducing but not eliminating initial gaps between Head Start children and their more economically advantaged peers. Although the gap with respect to cognitive achievement between Head Start graduates and more advantaged peers narrowed as a result of the preschool experience, Head Start graduates have been found to remain behind more advantaged peers when they enter school [Hebbler

1985; Lee et al. 1988]. Moreover, with few exceptions [Schwein-hart et al. 1993], studies have failed to demonstrate long-lasting effects in any cognitive or social domain.

- *Children in Head Start had improved health care.* In 1985, for example, Head Start children received immunizations at a rate about 20% higher than the national average for poor children [Washington 1985].

- *Children in Head Start scored higher on measures of social competence than children who did not attend preschool.* In addition to cognitive gains, children who attended Head Start experienced gains in social competency as shown by their performance on the Caldwell Preschool Inventory [Lee et al. 1988].

Challenges of Head Start

Although it is possible to interpret the research findings as indicating that Head Start is a failure, a more accepted view is that the initial expectations for the program were hopelessly quixotic. Critical realities in the performance disparity between Head Start children and more advantaged peers following the Head Start experience are differences in the quality of the schools and environments that the children subsequently experience [Takanishi & DeLeo 1994; Lee et al. 1990] and continuing stressors associated with poverty and racism. Given these factors, it seems unwarranted to expect that, without continuing enrichment, Head Start would have a dramatic impact as children move beyond grade school.

The focus of past assessments of Head Start largely has been on cognitive issues, which, although extremely important, are only one aspect of the program. As Zigler and Styfco [1994] note, the impact of Head Start on social development, family health, parents, and community has received only minimal attention. It also is not clear how many of the new program variations, such as Early Head Start, will fare over time. More rigorous and extensive research is needed in order to answer many of these questions. The Head Start Bureau recently has put in place new and more rigorous Program Performance Measures [Head Start Research and Evaluation 1999]. It now is sponsoring a number of large-scale research projects focusing both on evaluation and basic research in developmental issues of children and families in poverty, including the Early Head Start Research and Evaluation Project. In summary, the findings from the research suggest the following:

- *Many criticisms of Head Start need to be reexamined.* Many past and some current criticisms of Head Start have arisen from unrealistic expectations such as the belief that one year in Head Start is sufficient to have a continued effect on a child's performance through high school. Criticisms have also arisen from research with small unrepresentative samples and loosely generalized evidence.

- *More rigorous research methods are needed to assess the effects of the Head Start experience.* Research findings in the past have failed to include differences in the quality of schools and the environments which children experience and the effects of continued poverty and violence which they encounter.

- *Assessments on the effects of Head Start need to expand beyond cognitive ability.* Cognitive ability is simply one aspect of Head Start enrichment. Head Start's impact on social competence, family health, parents, and community needs to receive attention.

- *New research promises to shed a more realistic light on the impact of Head Start.* The Head Start Bureau recently has established more rigorous performance and evaluation methods which should greatly add information to our understanding of the Head Start program.

Cost-Effectiveness

Without better data, it is difficult to address the question of cost-effectiveness. As information becomes available, it will be important to clarify which benefits of the program are critical to and appropriate for such an analysis. Increase in school-readiness skills in the cognitive domain will no doubt continue to be demonstrated by Head Start, particularly in an age in which programs such as Sesame Street are influenced by many of the principles upon which Head Start was founded. It is likely, however, that such advances may no longer reflect the most important contributions of the program. The focus on cognitive ability may continue with the Early Head Start program, given the findings from recent brain development research that suggest that very real and enduring cognitive benefits may accrue with earlier intervention. With respect to Head Start in general, however, advances in social development, health, and parent and community development may prove to be the most important, unique, and long-lasting benefits of the program. If benefits in these areas prove to be enduring, it seems that the relatively modest investment in preschool— or in the case of Early Head Start, pre-preschool—will more than be realized in making known the need for later costly educational, health, and social service interventions.

Conclusion

Head Start has been the subject of voluminous research and evaluation since its inception, although the quality of this work has been extremely variable and frequently has focused on small, unrepresentative samples. Research repeatedly has demonstrated substantial increases in children's cognitive performance at the end of the Head Start experience and benefits to children's health and social development. There are, however, differences in the quality of schools and environments for Head Start and non-Head Start children and continuing stressors associated with poverty and racism. As a result, it seems unwarranted to expect that, without continuing enrichment, the impact of Head Start would be dramatically demonstrated as children move beyond grade school.

References

Head Start Research and Evaluation Website. (1999).Head Start Research and Evaluation. Online: http://www.acf.dhhs.gov /programs/hsre.

Hebbeler, K. (1985). An old and a new question on the effects of early education for children from low-income families. *Educational Evaluation and Policy Analysis, 7,* 207–216.

Lee, V., Brooks-Gunn, J. & Schnur, E. (1988). Does Head Start work? A 1-year follow-up comparison of disadvantaged children attending Head Start, no preschool, and other preschool programs. *Development Psychology, 24,* 210–222.

Lee, V., Brooks-Gunn, J., Schnur, E., & Liaw, F. R. (1990). Are Head Start effects sustained? A longitudinal follow-up comparison of disadvantaged children attending Head Start, no preschool, and other preschool programs. *Child Development, 61*(2), 495–507.

Schweinhart, L. J., Barnes, H. V., & Weikart, D. P. with Barnett, W. S. & Epstein, A. S. (1993). *Significant benefits: The High/Scope Perry Preschool Study through Age 27.* (Monographs of the High/Scope Educational Research Foundation, 10). Ypsilanti, MI: High/Scope Press.

Takanishi, R. & DeLeon, P. (1994). A Head Start for the 21st Century. *American Psychologist, 49*(2), 120–122.

Washington, V. (1985). Head Start: How appropriate for minority families in the 1980s? *American Journal of Orthopsychiatry, 55*(4), 577–590.

Zigler, E. F. & Styfco, S. (1994). Head Start: Criticisms in a constructive context. *American Psychologist, 49*(2), 127–132.

What Works in Head Start

Study Authors	Survey Sample	Research Design/Outcome Measure	Findings
Lee, V.E., Brooks-Gunn, J., Schnur, E. & Liaw, F.R. (1990). Are Head Start effects sustained? A longitudinal follow-up comparison of disadvantaged children attending Head Start, no preschool and other preschool programs. *Child Development, 61,* 495–507.	• Children from original study sample (Analysis of ETS Head Start Longitudinal Data set—children aged 4 and 5 from Portland, Oregon, and Trenton, New Jersey, eligible for first grade in the fall of 1971) who remained in their communities and attended half-day public school kindergartens in 1970–1971 and first grade in 1971–1972	• Outcome measures tapped aspects of verbal achievement (Cooperative Primary Test), perceptual reasoning (Embedded Figures Test and Raven's Colored Progressive Matrices), and social competence (California Pre-School Competency Scale (CPSCS) and Schaeffer Classroom Behavior Inventory). • All measures were group administered to target classrooms by teachers.	• At the end of kindergarten, children with Head Start preschool experience scored higher on the CPSCS than those who did not attend pre-school. • Other effects, though not statistically significant, were favorable to Head Start. For example, on the CPT, the performance of Head Start children was better than both the scores of no preschool and the other groups.
Hebbeler, K. (1985). An old and new question on the effects of early education for children from low income families. *Educational Evaluation and Policy Analysis, 7,* 207–216.	• Three cohorts of children who attended a Head Start Program in Maryland in 1978–1979, 1974–1975 or 1970–1971 and who in 1983–1984 were in fourth, eighth, and 12th grades, respectively	• A long-term study of the effects of Head Start on educational achievement • Achievement was measured on the basis of pupil records (including test data), attendance, coursework, grades, and special education services.	• Results indicated that early childhood education has a positive impact on the long-term educational achievements of children from low-income families.

(continued next page)

What Works in Head Start (*continued*)

Study Authors	Survey Sample	Research Design/Outcome Measure	Findings
Lee, V., Brooks-Gunn, J. & Schnur, E. (1988). Does Head Start work? A 1-year follow-up comparison of disadvantaged children attending Head Start, no preschool and other preschool programs. *Developmental Psychology, 24,* 210–222.	• Analysis of ETS Head Start Longitudinal Study data comprised of 969 children ages 4 and 5 from Portland, Oregon and Trenton, New Jersey eligible for first grade in the fall of 1971	• Children were recruited in a door-to-door canvassing effort. • Tests were administered at two time points: (1) in the Spring of 1969 before possible entrance into a Head Start Program, and (2) at the end of a single year of preschool. • Outcomes were measured by the Peabody Picture Vocabulary test (PPVT), Caldwell Preschool Inventory (PI), the Motor Inhibition Test, and the 8-Block Toy Sort Test.	• Participants in Head Start appeared to make significant one-year gains on some measures of cognitive ability. • Children in Head Start made greater increases than children attending "other" preschools and children attending no preschool on: the PPVT which evaluates receptive vocabulary and provides a measure of IQ; the PI which measures aptitude and sociocognitive skills; and the Motor Inhibition Test which measures impulsivity. • These data suggest that Head Start was quite effective in closing the gap between children attending Head Start and their more economically advantaged peers.

29

What Works in Child Care

Martha G. Roditti

C hild care works through an ever increasing web of developmental services that encompasses a continuum of ages from infant/toddler care through school age care. Child care programs serve an array of families, and some serve maltreated children, developmentally and physically disabled children, and temporarily sick children. Parents choose child care in centers, family day care homes, and the homes of family members (See Figure 1). They use child care services offered by private nonprofits, governmental agencies, churches and synagogues, and for-profit corporations.

Research Findings on Child Care

Research on child care indicates the following:

- *There is general consensus that the better the quality of care the better the outcomes for young children* [Peisner-Feinberg et al. 1999; National Institute of Child Health and Human Development (NICHD) Early Child Care Research Network 1997; Frede 1995; Kagan & Cohen 1996; Young et al. 1997; Cost, Quality & Child Outcomes Study Team 1995; Galinsky et al. 1998]. The analysis of the national longitudinal study, *The Children of the Cost, Quality, and Outcomes Study Go to School,* found positive outcomes for

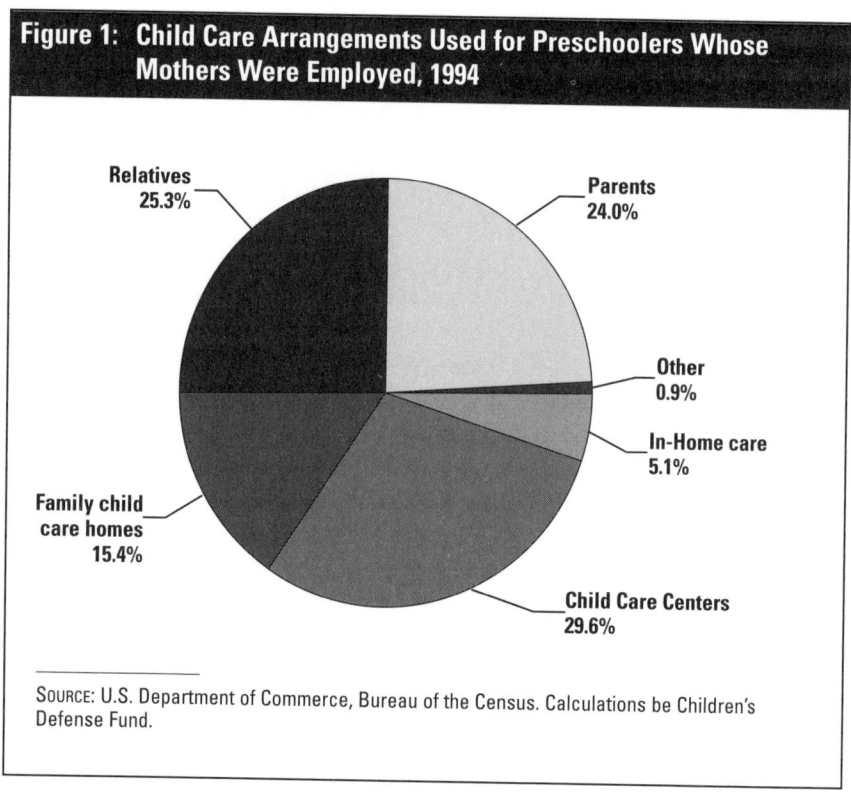

Figure 1: Child Care Arrangements Used for Preschoolers Whose Mothers Were Employed, 1994

Relatives
25.3%

Parents
24.0%

Other
0.9%

In-Home care
5.1%

Family child
care homes
15.4%

Child Care Centers
29.6%

SOURCE: U.S. Department of Commerce, Bureau of the Census. Calculations be Children's Defense Fund.

children who attended child care programs with higher-quality classroom practices. When children were followed from the pre-school years to the end of the second grade, the effects of quality child care on the children appear to be long-term and significant. These effects include better language and math skills, fewer behavior problems, and better relationships with peers.

Better-quality child care was even more strongly related to better math skills and fewer behavior problems when children had less highly educated mothers. In addition, the study found that children with closer teacher-child relationships in child care had better class-room social and thinking skills, language ability and math skills, and that these benefits also lasted through the second grade [Peisner-Feinberg et al. 1999; Peisner-Feinberg & Burchinal 1997].

- *Seamless child care has enabled parents on welfare to move to independence.* Child care is seamless when low-income parents move from one form of income to another without a disruption in the continuity of child care. An example of seamless child care is the use of subsidized child care funding for parents while they are in job training, as they begin employment, and then as they reach and sustain full employment as the child grows from infancy to school age [Ball and Stern 1993; U.S. General Accounting Office 1994; Minnesota State Department of Human Services 1996]. A U.S. General Accounting Office study of seamless child care efforts in California, Illinois, Massachusetts, Michigan, and Texas [1994] highlighted the fragmented nature of the child care system and the need for flexibility in spending federal dollars. El Paso County, Colorado, has developed a seamless child care system by combining programs in Temporary Assistance to Needy Families (TANF) and child welfare to enhance prevention and early intervention [Berns & Drake 1999].

- *Infant care is the most costly, least available, and most problematic of all care despite the fact that it has a significant effect on later child development.* Of the 225 infant child care rooms evaluated in one study, only 6% met the high-quality standard compared to 40% that met the poor quality standard [Cost, Quality & Child Outcomes Study Team 1995: 26]. These findings indicated that many infants were at risk during the hours they spent in centers because of unsanitary conditions for diapering and feeding, the absence of caring adults, and lack of stimulating toys.

- *Quality makes a difference in cognitive and language outcomes for young children. In the NICHD Study of Early Child Care* [1997], researchers found that the higher the quality of child care in the first three years of life, the greater the child's language abilities at 15, 24, and 36 months. Quality was defined as positive caregiving and measured in relation to provider-child interaction and language input in the form of verbal stimulation [Peth-Pierce 1997: 2]. The study found that when the quality of the child-caregiver interaction was taken into account, children in high-quality care for more than 10 hours per week performed better on cognitive and language tests. This study, however, emphasized that the "combination of family income, maternal vocabulary, home environment, and maternal stimulation were stronger predictors of children's cognitive development" than child care [Peth-Pierce 19972: 2].

- *Quality programs involve parents.* "Families are the first and foremost influence on a child's development" [Powell 1999: 53]. Early childhood programs that emphasize systematic inclusion of supportive relationships with parents appear to produce better outcomes for children than those with modest contact with parents [Powell 1999].

- *Middle-income families without access to government subsidies or added income are adversely effected by the availability of only the least expensive and often the worst forms of child care.* In a study analyzing two large data sets, The Profiles of Child Care Settings and the National Child Care Staffing Study, centers serving middle-income families had the poorest quality of care as measured by benefits and wages for child care staff, proportion of teachers with specialized and in-service training, activities for children, and teacher turnover [Phillips et al. 1994]. "Middle-class families may be at a particular disadvantage because they have neither the financial resources to purchase high-quality care nor access to public subsidies that, at least in the case of government intervention programs, appear to provide some assurance of quality" [Phillips et al. 1994: 489].

- *Inclusion of children with disabilities is an additional factor in quality child care.* Developmentally appropriate child care involves "being conscious of the ways in which children are the same, while being sensitive to the ways in which they are different" [Bananas 1999: 9]. Inclusion of children with disabilities requires new information that can enhance existing child care programs.

- *Consumer education is the key to providing quality child care.* Child Care Resource and Referral Programs offer parents consumer education about choosing child care and information about the types of child care programs in the parents' community, provider training, child care supply building, and child care availability data [Siegel 1997]. These programs are a significant source of social support for parents [Collins & Pancoast 1976; Powell 1987]. Information about child care is essential for effective parental monitoring of child care.

Poorly informed parents make poor consumers of child care. Parents' ability to choose high-quality child care from a range of available arrangements has an effect on their children.

Parents tend to overestimate the quality of the programs their children are attending, do not choose good care, and do not demand higher-quality care. In a recent study, parents were found to assign high scores to programs even though, by objective indicators, their children were in mediocre to poor programs [Cost, Quality & Child Outcomes Study Team 1995]. For example, in child care classrooms designated as poor quality by trained observers, 88% of parents rated the rooms as developmentally appropriate, 12% rated them as mediocre, and none rated the rooms as poor. The researchers offered the following explanations for the parents' failure to recognize poor-quality child care: parents may not have complete information about child care alternatives; they may be poorly informed about the child care their children receive; or they may not value the same characteristics of care as early childhood professionals [Cost, Quality & Child Outcomes Study Team 1995].

Parents can benefit from the personal attention of counselors in child care resource and referral programs who can assist them in choosing quality child care, exploring child care alternatives, identifying their child's needs, and obtaining information regarding subsidized child care or child care credits [Child Care Bureau 1998].

Cost-Effectiveness

There are strong indications that early childhood programs are affordable and that quality care is minimally more expensive than poor care. The *Cost, Quality, and Child Outcomes Study* [1995] found that better-quality services cost, on average, just 10% more than mediocre care. These findings suggest that modest investments, combined with reasonable regulation, could significantly improve the efficacy of early child care interventions [Cost, Quality & Child Outcomes Study Team 1995].

Conclusion

There is general consensus that the better the quality of child care, the better cognitive and language outcomes for young children. Consumer education is the key to providing quality child care. There are indications that parents tend to overestimate the quality of programs their children attend. Parents could benefit from the services of counselors in child care resource and referral agencies.

Child Care and its Benefits for Children and Their Families

Child care, due to its increasing use and importance to child well-being, can be seen as an emerging public utility. "Good quality child care is a collective good because, like public education in general, giving children a good start serves the interest of society as a whole. Society benefits if developmentally appropriate child care means reduced public expenditures on special education, health services, and the penal system and that children grow up to be productive adults. Those who benefit indirectly from child care must pay for the services in order to create the socially optimal amount of services" [Cost, Quality & Child Outcomes Study Team 1995: 17]. A national investment in quality child care would not only improve the developmental outcomes for children and society, but raise wages, improve the education of child care providers of all types, and tighten regulations.

Considerable information has been amassed about what constitutes quality child care. Early childhood educators, developmental psychologists, social workers, and researchers have developed clear standards concerning the learning and nurturing environments that work—what is most conducive to the socialization and development of young children, what is most helpful to families, and what is most effective for caregivers. As a result of this work, there are curricula that are effective for all levels of child care. This work has identified the types of teacher preparation and administrative organizational structures that are most instrumental in creating positive child outcomes and productive work environments.

Child care, when seen from the larger perspective, can be a significant source of social support to children and families. Families can obtain information about child development, receive counseling regarding their concerns about their children, and benefit from a concrete service that keeps their children safe, secure, and on a healthy developmental course [Powell 1987]. Maltreated children, their parents, and their caregivers benefit from the involvement of child care in the larger system of care that provides a multidisciplinary approach to services.

References

Ball, A. C. & Stern, L. M. (1993). Making seamless funding a reality in New York State. *Children Today, 22*(1), 28–31

Bananas. (1999). *Beyond barriers: Building inclusive services into your child care resource and referral organization.* Oakland, CA: Bananas, Inc.

Berns, D. A. & Drake B. J. (1999, March). Combining child welfare and welfare reform at a local level. *Policy & Practice of Public Human Services,* 26–34.

Child Care Bureau. (1998). *Reaching Parents with Child Care Consumer Education.* Washington, DC: Child Care Bureau, Administration for Children and Families, U.S. Department of health and Human Services, National Child Care Information Center. Online: www.acf.dhhs,gov/ccb/faq/consumer.htr

Children's Defense Fund. (1998). *The state of America's children: Yearbook 1998.* Washington, DC: Author.

Collins, A. H. & Pancoast, D. L. (1976). *Natural helping networks: A strategy for prevention.* Washington, DC: National Association of Social Workers.

Cost, Quality, & Child Outcomes Study Team. (1995). *Cost, Quality and Child Outcomes in Child Care Centers, Public Report.* Denver, CO: Denver Economics Department, University of Colorado at Denver.

Frede, E. C. (1995). The role of program quality in producing early childhood program benefits. *The future of children: Long-term outcomes of early childhood programs, 5*(3), 115–132.

Galinsky, E., O'Donnell, N. S., Beyea, B., & Boose, J. (1998). *The Florida child care quality improvement study.* New York: Families and Work Institute.

Kagan, S. L. & Cohen, N. E. (Eds.). (1996). *Reinventing early care and education.* San Francisco: Jossey-Bass Publishers.

Minnesota State Department of Human Services. (1996). *Seamless child care system: A report to the 1996 Minnesota legislature.* St. Paul, MN: Author.

NICHD Early Child Care Research Network. (1997). Child care in the first year of life. *Merrill-Palmer Quarterly, 43*(3), 340–360.

Peisner-Feinberg, E. S. & Burchinal, M. R. (1997). Relations between preschool children's child care experiences and concurrent development: The cost, quality and outcomes study. *Merrill-Palmer Quarterly, 43*(3), 451–477.

Peisner-Feinberg, E. S., Culkin, M. L., Howes, C., & Kagan, S. L. (1999). *The children of the Cost, Quality, and Outcomes Study go to school: Executive summary.* Online: www.fpg.unc.edu/~ncedl/pages/cqes.htm.

Peth-Pierce, R. (1997). *The NICHD Study of Early Child Care.* Washington, DC: Public Information and Communications Branch of the National Institute of Child Health and Human Development. Online: www.nih.gov/nichd/html/new/early-child/Early_Child_Care.htr.

Phillips, D. A., Voran, M., Kisker, E., Howes, C., & Whitebook, M. (1994). Child care for children in poverty: Opportunity or inequity? *Child Development, 65*(2), 472–492.

Powell, D. R. (1999). Early childhood development. In A. J. Reynolds, H. J. Walberg, & R. P. Weissberg (Eds.), *Promoting positive outcomes* (pp. 115–132). Washington DC: CWLA Press.

Powell, D. R. (1987). Day care as a family support system. In S. L. Kagan, B. W. Weissbourd, & E. R. Ziegler (Eds.), *America's family support programs* (115–132). New Haven, CT: Yale University Press.

Siegel, P. (1997). New directions for resource and referral agencies. In S. L. Kagan & B. T. Bowman (Eds.), *Leadership in early care and education* (pp. 129–136). Washington, DC: National Association for the Education of Young Children.

U.S. General Accounting Office. (1994). *Child care: Working poor and welfare recipients face service gaps.* Washington, DC: General Accounting Office, Health, Education, and Human Services Division.

Young, K. T., Marsland, K. W., & Zigler, E. (1997). The regulatory status of center-based infant and toddler child care. *American Journal of Orthopsychiatry, 67*(4), 535–544.

30

What Works in Center-Based Child Care

Martha G. Roditti

"Across all levels of maternal education and child gender and ethnicity, children's cognitive and social development are positively related to the quality of their child care experience" [Cost, Quality & Child Outcomes Study Team 1995: 29]. Children in high-quality, center-based, child care classrooms exhibit better cognitive skills, particularly in language development and premath, higher levels of socioemotional development, and better relationships with their teachers. Teachers in high-quality, center-based, child care programs relate more warmly to children and rate children higher in social skills than do teachers in lower-quality programs [Cost, Quality & Child Outcomes Study Team 1995]. Quality child care is also associated with positive parent-child relationships. A National Institute of Child Health and Human Development (NICHD) study found that, "quality child care modestly predicted greater involvement and sensitivity by the mother (at 15 and 36 months) and greater positive engagement of the child with the mother (at 36 months)" [Peth-Pierce 1997: 11]. Low-income parents using quality care had higher positive involvement with their children at 6 months after the initiation of child care services than those not using such care. Other factors, however, were found to affect the parent-child relationship. The study found that "a combination of family and home characteristics, including income, maternal education, two-parent family status, maternal separation anxiety, and maternal depression predicted the quality of mother-child interaction more than the children's experience in child care" [Peth-Pierce 1997: 11].

Quality Center-Based Child Care

Confirming earlier studies, recent studies in quality center-based child care programs for preschoolers, infants, and toddlers [Peisner-Feinberg et al. 1999; Galinsky et al. 1998; Cost, Quality & Child Outcomes Study Team 1995] report that quality center-based child care is most strongly associated with the following factors:

- *High staff-to-child ratios.* A high ratio of staff to children is the most significant factor affecting quality of child care for all age groups [Cost, Quality & Child Outcomes Study Team 1995]. Fewer children per staff member allows for greater opportunities for staff to have positive interactions with children. In one study, children's cognitive and emotional development improved over a four-year period when the teacher-to-child ratio was reduced from 1:6 to 1:4 for infants and from 1:8 to 1:6 for toddlers [Galinsky et. al. 1998]. Children showed enhanced language proficiency and improved behavior in the areas of aggression, anxiety, and hyperactivity, and there was greater teacher warmth, involvement, and sensitivity.

- *Well-trained and well-compensated staff.* Important characteristics that distinguish poor, mediocre, and high quality centers are teacher wages, education, and training [Cost, Quality & Child Outcomes Study Team 1995]. Centers that pay higher wages attract better-quality teaching staff. When teaching staff have no college education, a higher wage rate has been associated with higher quality. A one dollar hourly increase in wages for these staff brought about a significant increase in quality of care. Regardless of wage rates, centers with a greater proportion of teaching staff with a college degree were found to be of higher quality. When the teaching staff with college degrees increased from one-third to 100%, there was a significant increase in quality [Cost, Quality & Child Outcomes Study Team 1995].

- *Nonprofit status of child care programs.* Nonprofit child care centers consistently provide higher-quality care for children and higher wages for staff than for-profit centers [Cost, Quality & Child Outcomes Study Team 1995; Whitebook et al. 1989]. Nonprofit centers benefit from in-kind donations of time from staff, "foregone wages" (the difference between the wages that staff receive as child care workers and what they would receive in a comparable occupation), rent subsidies for facilities, volunteer services, and cash contributions. For-profit centers depend on parent fees, the economies of scale produced by owning larger numbers of centers, lower labor expenditures, and low wages [Cost, Quality & Child Outcomes Study Team 1995].

- *Experienced administrators.* Center directors' administrative experience was positively related to quality of care. Also of importance were the administrator's "years of education, age, prior experience in early childhood education, tenure at the center, as well as staff ratings of the administrator's organizational skills, curriculum leadership, community involvement, and early childhood education and professional community participation" [Cost, Quality & Child Outcomes Study Team 1995: 34.].

- *Positive child care environment.* The NICHD study found that better developmental outcomes were associated with safer, cleaner, more stimulating physical environments; small group sizes; and caregivers who interacted with the children and allowed them to talk and express their views [Peth-Pierce 1997].

Problems in Center-Based Child Care

Studies have documented several problems in center-based child care.

- *Although researchers and professionals have developed and tested quality standards and practices, many center-based programs are of poor quality.* The national study, Cost, Quality and Child Outcomes in Child Care Centers Study [1995], found that only 1 in 7 of the centers studied (14%) provided child care of a quality that promoted healthy development and learning. The majority of centers (86%) scored from poor to mediocre. Only 1 in 12 of the infants and toddlers (8%) in the 225 infant child care facilities spent their days in rooms of high quality.

- *Infant center-based care is generally of poor quality.* In a national analysis of infant and toddler care, Young, Marsland, and Zigler [1997] found that no state received an overall rating of "good" or "optimal" nor complied with recommended standards of quality for group composition, staff training, and programming. Two-thirds of the states' infant and toddler care received overall ratings of "poor" or "very poor." The satisfactory ratio of adult-to-child in infant and toddler care is 1:4 for infants and 1:5 for toddlers. As shown in Figure 1, the average national ratio is 1:8.5 for infants, and 1:10.5 for toddlers [Young et al. 1997].

- *Child care continues to be largely unregulated.* Licensing standards differ from state to state, and there is no national policy on the number of adults per children, the education of staff, or the size of child care groups. In the research reviewed, however, these

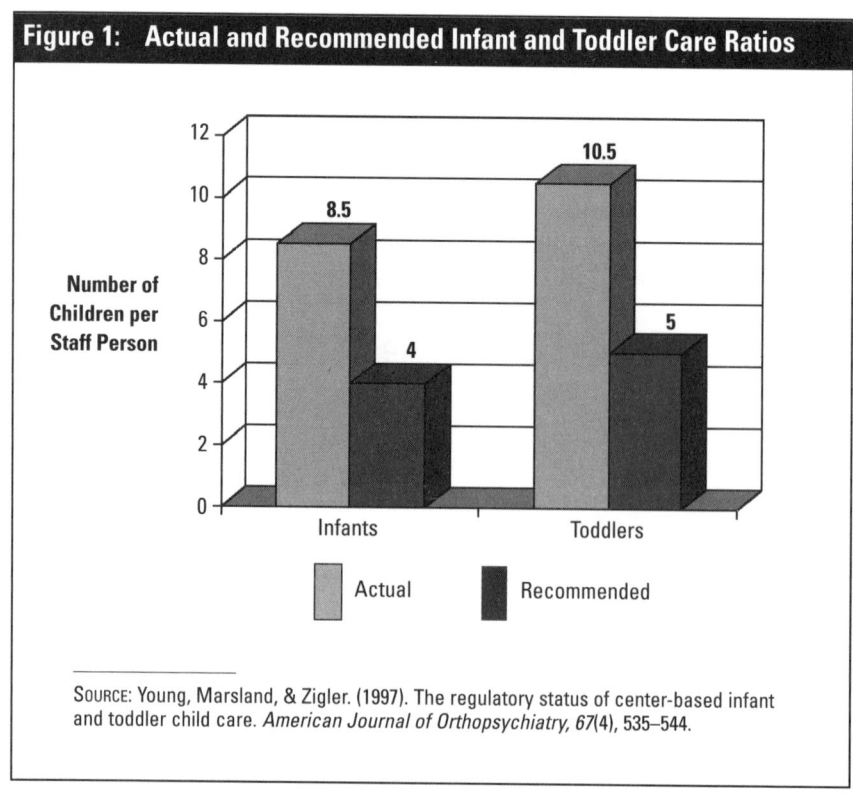

Figure 1: Actual and Recommended Infant and Toddler Care Ratios

Number of Children per Staff Person

Infants — Toddlers

Actual — Recommended

SOURCE: Young, Marsland, & Zigler. (1997). The regulatory status of center-based infant and toddler child care. *American Journal of Orthopsychiatry, 67*(4), 535–544.

factors were found to be key to making child care work for children and families. Those states with the fewest standards had the poorest care. By contrast, states with more demanding licensing standards had fewer poor-quality child care programs [Cost, Quality & Child Outcomes Study Team 1995].

- *Poor families pay disproportionately more for child care.* In 1993, child care for one child accounted for "8% of the median U.S. dual earner family making a before-tax income of $60,000 when both were employed full time" [Cost, Quality, & Child Outcomes Study Team 1995: 44]. By contrast, child care for one child cost almost one-quarter (23%) of the 1993 median before-tax income for lower-income families ($21,000) that were headed by single parents employed full time " [Cost, Quality, & Child Outcomes Study Team 1995].

Cost-Effectiveness

Center child care, even poor care, is costly. The cost, however, would be higher in nonprofit centers if it were not for contributions from foregone wages of staff, donations, volunteer hours, and subsidized rent—which together cover more than one-fourth of the cost of care [Cost, Quality and Child Outcomes Study Team 1995]. There are strong indications that quality care is minimally more expensive than poor care. The Cost, Quality and Child Outcomes Study Team found that better-quality services cost on average just 10 % more than mediocre care. These findings suggest that modest investments, combined with reasonable regulation, could significantly improve the efficacy of early child care interventions [Cost, Quality & Child Outcomes Study Team 1995].

Conclusion

Research indicates that higher-quality center-based child care programs result in favorable benefits for children, including improved cognitive skills in language development and premath, enhanced socioemotional development, and better teacher-child relations. The hallmark of quality center-based child care is high staff-to-child ratios (1:4 for infants and 1:5 for toddlers), well-trained and higher-paid staff, experienced administrators, and a safe, clean, stimulating physical environment. Studies find a scant 8%–14% of children are enrolled in high-quality center-based day care. Stringent state regulation of child care centers would help to improve these percentages.

References

Cost, Quality & Child Outcomes Study Team. (1995). *Cost, quality, and child outcomes in child care centers, Public Report* (2nd ed.). Denver: Denver Economics Department, University of Colorado at Denver.

Galinsky, E., O'Donnell, N. S., Beyea, B., & Boose, J. (1998). *The Florida child care quality improvement study.* New York: Families and Work Institute.

Peisner-Feinberg, E. S., Culkin, M. L., Howes, C. & Kagan, S. L. (1999). *The children of the Cost, Quality, and Outcomes Study go to school: Executive summary.* Online: www.fpg.unc.edu/~ncedl/pages/cqes.htm.

Peth-Pierce, R. (1997). *The NICHD Study of Early Child Care.* Washington, DC: Public Information and Communications Branch, National Institute of Child Health and Human Development. Online: www.nih.gov/nichd/html/new/early-child/Early_Child_Care.htr.

Whitebook, M. Howes, C. & Phillips, D. (1989). *The national child care staffing study: Who cares? Child care teachers and the quality of care in America.* Oakland CA: The Child Care Employee Project.

Young, K. T., Marsland, K. W. & Zigler, E. (1997). The regulatory status of center-based infant and toddler child care. *American Journal of Orthopsychiatry,* 67(4), 535–544.

What Works in Center-Based Child Care

Study Authors	Survey Sample	Research Design/ Outcome Measure	Findings
Cost, Quality & Child Outcomes Study Team. (1995). *Cost, quality, and child outcomes, public report. 2nd edition.* Denver, CO: Economics Department, University of Colorado at Denver.	• Four-state sample of 50 for-profit and 50 nonprofit full day licensed centers • 228 infant/toddler classrooms; 521 preschool classrooms • 826 children and their families	• Administrative data from centers and on-site interviews of center staff • Day-long observations using ECERS and ITERS, Caregiver Interaction and Teacher Involvement Scales and teacher self assessments • Developmental observations of children and teacher ratings of children • Parent surveys	• Child care at most centers in the U.S. was poor to mediocre with one half of the infant and toddler rooms of poor quality; 1 in 7 centers had a level of quality that promoted healthy development; 1 in 8 threatened health and safety; 7 in 10 centers were providing mediocre care that compromised children's school readiness; 40% of infant/toddler rooms endangered children's health and safety; only 1 in 12 centers were providing developmentally appropriate care. • Quality was related to higher staff-to-child ratios, staff education and specialized training, administrator's prior experience, and better teachers' wages. • States with more demanding licensing standards had fewer poor-quality centers. • Children's cognitive and social development were positively related to quality with children displaying better language and premath skills, advanced social skills, more positive attitudes towards child care experience, and warmer relations with caretakers. • Quality of child care was positively related to better child development outcomes across mother's education; quality care was more strongly related to positive outcomes for children at risk. • Good-quality care cost more than poor care, but not significantly more. • Although parents reported they value good quality care, they substantially overestimated the quality of care their children were receiving.

(continued next page)

What Works in Center-Based Child Care (continued)

Study Authors	Survey Sample	Research Design/ Outcome Measure	Findings
Peisner-Feinberg, E.S., Culkin, M.L., Howes, C. & Kagan, S.L. (1999). *The children of the Cost, Quality and Outcomes Study go to school, executive summary, June 1999.* Available: http://www.fpg.unc.edu/ ~NCEDL/Pages/ cqes.html	• Four-year follow-up study, beginning in 1993, of 826 children from the Cost, Quality and Child Outcomes study (See above) • Followed children from end of next to last preschool year until the end of second grade	• Data collected using developmental, teacher involvement, and classroom observational scales; individual child assessments; teacher ratings of children; parent reports of child and family characteristics. • Study measured the impact of child care longitudinally from preschool to second grade.	• Children who attended child care with higher quality had better language and math skills from preschool years into elementary school. Quality of care was associated with better developmental outcomes across the range of family circumstances. • Children with closer teacher-child relationships in child care had better classroom social and cognitive skills, language ability, and math skills into elementary school. These relationships were the strongest predictors of children's social and behavioral skills and were strongly associated with fewer problem behaviors for children and children at risk of school failure and whose mothers had less education.

Reference	Sample	Purpose/Method	Findings
Peth-Pierce, R. (1997). *The NICHD Ssudy of early child care.* Washington, DC: Public Information and Communications Branch, National Institute of Child Health and Human Development. Available: http://www.nih.gov/nichd/html/new/early-child/Early_Child_Care.htr	• 1364 children, starting in 1991 and followed at intervals during first seven years of life in 10 locations; children were from various socioeconomic and ethnic backgrounds. • Children were in a variety of child care settings as randomly chosen by parents. • No attempt was made to control quality or selection of care.	• Study assessed the relationship between child care experiences and characteristics, family characteristics and influences, child care and mother child relationships, and children's developmental outcomes. • Data collected using trained observers, interviews, questionnaires and testing. • Measured child's social, emotional, intellectual, language development, behavior problems and adjustment, and physical health.	• Higher-quality of care over first three years of life was modestly associated with children's cognitive and language development and higher school readiness. • Better developmental outcomes for children were found in child care situations which met guidelines for child-staff ratios, group sizes, teacher training and education, and had care givers who provided more sensitive, responsive and cognitively stimulating care. • Poor and near poor infants were usually cared for either in family day care homes or by family members and were likely to receive relatively lower quality of care than those few children who attended infant centers. Infants who attended child care centers received better care—care comparable to center care received by affluent children. • Children in near-poverty received a lower quality of center care than children in poverty, possibly because they did not qualify for subsidized care. • Family characteristics (mother's education and family income) were strong predictors of children's outcomes. • Insecure attachments were greater in infants who received poor quality of care, were in care more than 10 hours per week, or were in more than one child care setting the first 15 months of life. Their mothers were rated lower in sensitivity. If both mothers and child care providers fell in the bottom 25% of the sample in terms of providing sensitive care, the likelihood that the children would be securely attached was 45% compared to 62% when child care givers and mothers provided more sensitive care.

31

What Works in Home-Based Child Care

Martha G. Roditti

H ome-based child care—both regulated and non-regulated—is the source of 33% of preschool care and over 90% of infant care. With regard to home-based child care, "both parents and providers see a warm, caring, responsive relationship between the child and provider, a safe environment, and good communication between the provider and parent as the crux of quality" [Galinsky et al. 1994: 20]. Yet, home-based care is difficult to define and may range from arrangements that are almost parental to small child care centers in a home.

Child care by kith (friends) and kin (family) can be a source of considerable support to parents [Collins & Pancoast 1976]. Parents appear to choose home-based care because they prefer that familiar people care for their infants and toddlers, it meets difficult and unpredictable scheduling needs, and it is available and affordable [Collins & Carlson 1998].

Quality in Home-Based Child Care

One large three-state study found that providers who were more sensitive and more responsive also were more intentional in their approach to child care [Galinsky et. al 1994]—that is, they were more child-centered and committed in their child care giving. By contrast, caregivers who were adult-centered—that is, providing care primarily to help mothers—were found to be less sensitive and less responsive to children. These providers worked out of a sense of obligation and were less committed to the children for whom they were caring. The study found that the following were associated with providers who were child-centered:

- *Chosen occupation.* Providers offering good or adequate care saw child care as a chosen occupation. Inadequate caregivers, by contrast, saw child care as work they undertook only while their own children were at home.

- *Job commitment.* Providers who were rated as more sensitive saw themselves as committed to child care as an occupation.

- *Professional development.* Providers with more professional preparation in the form of classes or workshops were found to be more sensitive and were more likely to be rated as providing good or adequate care.

- *Planning.* Providers who thought ahead about children's activities were rated as more sensitive and more responsive and were ranked as providing higher-quality care.

- *Involvement with other providers.* Providers who were involved with other family child caregivers in associations or who participated in child care food programs were more likely to be rated as sensitive and responsive and more likely to feel connected to their work.

- *Compliance with regulations.* Although parents ranked regulation as relatively unimportant, the study showed that regulated providers were more involved with other providers, provided more sensitive caregiving, planned more activities for children, became caregivers for child-centered reasons, felt more committed to their jobs, and viewed the job as a chosen occupation.

- *Adherence to standard business and safety practice.* Providers who were regulated were more likely to follow good business practices—such as reporting their income as taxes and having parent-provider contracts—and were more likely to follow standard safety practices.

- *Higher fees.* Only 52% of relative caregivers in the study charged for child care. Providers who had higher incomes from child care, however, were rated as more sensitive. The study found that parents were willing to pay more for quality and that irrespective of the form of child care they used—regulated or nonregulated, relative or nonrelative—the more they paid, the more sensitive to children the provider was [Galinsky et al. 1994].

Challenges in Home-Based Child Care

Although some home-based child care is very good, there are problems:

- *Children's attachment to their providers is low, a pattern similar to that found in child care centers.* One study found that only half of children were securely attached to their home-based providers, a finding comparable to findings from studies of children's attachment to teachers in child care centers. The researchers concluded, "Thus, there doesn't seem to be any difference between care in homes and centers, relatives or nonrelatives in terms of the security of children's attachments" [Galinsky et al. 1994: 79].

- *Infants in care experience multiple caregivers.* A National Insitute of Child Health and Human Development (NICHD) study found that 18% of infants spent the entire first year at home with their mothers without supplemental care, 50% were cared for either by a father/partner or grandparent, 20% were in family day care homes, and 8% received center care. A significant number of infants in child care experience multiple arrangements before their first birthday. "Findings that infants in care typically experienced more than two nonparental arrangements during the first year of life are of concern" [NICHD Early Child Care Research Network 1997: 357]. The stability and continuity of care for infants are critical because they can predict developmental outcomes. Children with more changes in child care arrangements are more likely to be insecurely attached, less competent with peers as toddlers, more withdrawn and aggressive in preschool, and have more social and cognitive problems when they enter elementary school [NICHD Early Child Care Research Network 1997].

- *Relative care is not always quality care.* Research found that "children are not more likely to be securely attached to providers who are relatives than to nonrelatives" [Galinsky et al. 1994: 5]. The same study found that care by unlicensed relatives can be less sensitive and responsive than care by licensed relatives, particularly when the motivation is a sense of obligation rather than commitment. The research found that "60% of relatives became providers for adult-focused reasons—to help out a relative—and less than 25% of them feel that child care is their chosen profession" [Galinsky et al. 1994: 51].

- *Few home-based child care arrangements meet standards of good quality.* In one study, 35% of home-based child care providers were scored as inadequate; 56% were rated in the adequate or custodial range; and only 9% were scored in the good range [Galinsky et al. 1994] (See Figure 1).

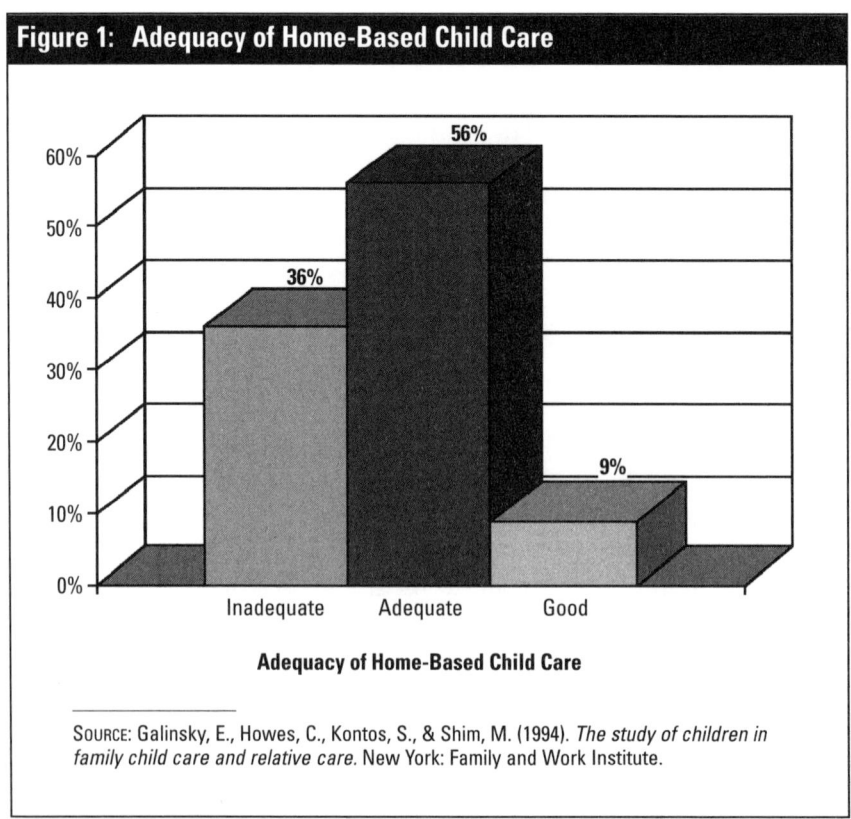

Figure 1: Adequacy of Home-Based Child Care

Adequacy of Home-Based Child Care

SOURCE: Galinsky, E., Howes, C., Kontos, S., & Shim, M. (1994). *The study of children in family child care and relative care.* New York: Family and Work Institute.

- *Home settings provide less high-quality care for poor children than for higher-income children.* The NICHD study found that "children from families in poverty who were cared for in-home received relatively low-quality care" as compared to poor children who attended centers, whose quality of care was comparable to that provided to affluent children [Peth-Pierce 1997: 9]. The study found that low-income families were more likely to use home-based settings and middle-income parents used home-based and center care in equal proportions. Upper-income families were twice as likely to use regulated care, whether in homes or in centers, than unregulated care and that they rarely used relative care [Peth-Pierce 1997].

- *Welfare reform appears to promote poor care for poor children.* With the passage of federal welfare reform legislation in 1996, states have been pressured to expand the supply of child care through unregulated forms of care or through child care that is exempt from licensing children of only one family. Research indicates that these forms of care tend to be of poor quality [Center for the Child Care Workforce 1998].

Cost-Effectiveness

The following factors should be considered with regard to the costs and the cost-effectiveness of home-based child care:

- *Unregulated home-based child care is less costly and of poorer quality, and unregulated providers are less likely to earn a living wage* [Center for the Child Care Workforce 1998].

- *Public funding for unregulated home-based child care, as an approach to the welfare-to-work child care supply problem, is a short-term solution.* Expansion of unregulated home-based care masks the need for greater availability of regulated child care for low-income families.

- *Child care compensation is not always monetary.* Many parents pay for home-based care in other ways than cash, such as through providing groceries or child care exchanges. "In-kind payments are more likely among families who use relatives (49%) than among those who use nonregulated providers (20%) or regulated providers (14%)" [Galinsky et al. 1994: 71].

Conclusion

The vast majority of infants and a significant number of preschoolers receive home-based child care. Research has found that home-based providers who are intentional in their career choice are more committed to the children for whom they care and offer a higher quality of services. These providers usually have more professional preparation, plan activities for the youngsters in advance, and are involved with other providers. Regulated providers are more likely to have these attributes. Of significant concern is the extent to which infants in care experience multiple caregivers, often in poor quality homes. Further, welfare reform appears to be promoting poor care for poor children by supporting the use of available, unregulated home-based care.

References

Center for the Child Care Workforce. (1998). Public funding for unregulated child care: A bad idea on the rise. *Rights, Raises, Respect, 2*(2), 3–5.

Collins, A. & Carlson, B. (1998). Child care by kith and kin: Supporting family, friends and neighbors caring for children. *Children and Welfare Reform: Issue Brief 5.* New York: National Center for Children and Poverty.

Collins, A. H. & Pancoast, D. L. (1976). *Natural helping networks: A strategy for prevention.* Washington, DC: National Association of Social Workers.

Galinsky, E., Howes, C., Kontos, S., & Shim, M. (1994). *The study of children in family child care and relative care.* New York: Family and Work Institute.

NICHD Early Child Care Research Network. (1997). Child care in the first year of life. *Merrill-Palmer Quarterly, 43*(3), 340–360.

Peth-Pierce, R. (1997). *The NICHD Study of Early Child Care.* Washington, DC: Public Information and Communications Branch of the National Institute of Child Health and Human Development. Online: www.nih.gov/nichd/html/new/early-child/Early_Child_Care.htr.

What Works in Home-Based Child Care

Study Authors	Survey Sample	Research Design/ Outcome Measure	Findings
Galinsky, E., Howes, C., Kontos, S. & Shim, M. (1994). *The study of children in family child care and relative care.* New York: Family and Work Institute.	• Three-state survey • Random sample of 820 mothers who used family child care and relative care arrangements • 226 providers (112 regulated, 54 nonregulated, and 60 nonregulated relatives) • 225 children	• Data were collected from interviews with mothers, provider interviews, observations of typical daily activities, self assessments of providers, and child outcomes. • Study measured provider-child relationship and overall quality of care: provider sensitivity and responsiveness, child development in terms of attachment/security, and cognitive development.	• Care in the home was provided by three distinct groups: regulated family child care providers, nonregulated family child care providers, and nonregulated relatives who provided care. • Across all family and provider groups, parents and caregivers agreed that child safety, provider/parent communication, and a warm relationship with provider were most essential. • Intentionality (commitment to caring for children) was an indicator of higher quality. • Only one-half of children in sample were securely attached to providers. • Only 9% of homes were rated as good quality or growth-enhancing, 56% as adequate or custodial, and 35% as inadequate or growth harming. • Children from low-income homes were in lower-quality care than children from higher income families. • Children were no more or less likely to be securely attached to relative providers than to nonrelatives.

32

What Works in Child Care for Maltreated and At-Risk Children

Martha G. Roditti

M altreated and at-risk children can benefit from quality child care programs to compensate for the difficulties they confront in their families [Lieberman 1993]. These families are predisposed to multiple challenges often associated with a combination of factors:

- Pernicious poverty and poor housing;
- Larger than average families, single parenting, and early parenting;
- Domestic conflict;
- Substance abuse;
- Mental illness and emotional difficulties;
- Developmental disabilities;
- Mobility; and
- Isolation [Thompson et al. 1997; Garbarino et al. 1992].

Quality child care can be used as a social support for parents at risk of maltreating their children, as prevention of child maltreatment, and as an intervention service for maltreated children and their families [Miller & Whittaker 1988; Wells & Tracy 1996; Roditti 1995; Thompson et al. 1997; Hershfield 1995]. It is the least restrictive source of emotional nurturing, information exchange, and concrete help for children and families.

Quality Child Care for Maltreated and At-Risk Children

Quality child care centers or family day care homes can offer high-risk families—and all families—the following forms of social support:

- Counseling, advice, parent education, and guidance in their child-rearing concerns;

- Models of effective, nonaggressive forms of discipline and child management—including positive forms of interacting with and engaging children and models of safe and secure environments for children;

- Monitoring of emotional and physical health and well-being of the children in care and competent child abuse and neglect reporting;

- Introductions to other parents for activities that offer support;

- Emergency respite; and

- Access to information on resources and referrals to other forms of community support.

A quality child care environment can be a refuge for a child from a troubled environment. Garbarino and colleagues [1992], in their discussion of resilient children, consider child care to be an important protective factor for children who are exposed to dangerous situations. Child care provides opportunities for children to interact with adult role models who are warm and caring and offers a safe environment with a clear structure, predictable experiences, and developmentally appropriate opportunities to develop self-esteem and coping skills through academic and/or social achievement [Garbarino et al. 1992].

The use and effectiveness of quality day care as an integral part of services to high-risk children have been demonstrated by the Yale Child Welfare Research Program [Seitz et al. 1983] and the Kempe Early Education Project Serving Abuse Families (KEEPSAFE) [Oats et al. 1995]. These studies—while recognizing that quality child care has a similar impact on all children despite differences in maternal education, gender, ethnic background, and type of program—have found nonetheless that at-risk children benefit somewhat more from participation in quality child care programs [Cost, Quality & Child Outcomes Study Team 1995; Oats et al. 1995; Seitz et al. 1983].

The Yale Child Welfare Research Program

The Yale Child Welfare Research Program was a 10-year longitudinal study, beginning in 1971, that compared participating children and families with nonparticipants [Seitz et al. 1983]. Services began during a mother's pregnancy and continued to 30 months postpartum. The program used a range of social support services, including home visiting by social workers, high-quality infant-toddler day care, pediatric care, and individualized psychological services. Child care involved specially trained staff and a child-to-staff ratio of 3:1. Each child had a primary caregiver and received individualized care focusing on the child's emotional and social development. Staff provided continuity between the program and the home, offering advice and developmental information to parents.

After 10 years, children and families in the program had significantly greater strengths in the following areas:

- Social development of children (boys had fewer school problems);
- School adjustment (boys were rated higher by teachers);
- School attendance (boys and girls missed fewer days);
- Parental education (more mothers completed education beyond high school);
- Employment (most families were economically self-sufficient); and
- Child bearing (families waited longer than nonparticipating families to have a second child).

The early interactions with the day care staff appeared to have a long-lasting effect on parent-child bonding. Program families were significantly more active in their children's education and appeared to be more active and competent in their exchanges with schools [Seitz et al. 1983].

The Kempe Early Education Project Serving Abused Families (KEEPSAFE)

KEEPSAFE was a three-year program from 1985 to 1988 that provided therapeutic preschool for 24 physically and sexually abused children. The school provided developmentally focused early education to improve the social skills of children. Child-adult ratios were high and staff turnover was low, resulting in consistent and predictable care. Case management was provided, and the curriculum followed National Association for the Education of Young Children (NAEYC) standards. Each child had weekly or twice-weekly individual sessions with the staff psychotherapist and daily group therapy. Home visiting offered support services to improve the quality of the interaction between the child's primary caregiver and the child. As a result of these services, 79% of the children were able to enter public school, and one-third were placed in regular classrooms [Oats et al. 1995].

Challenges in Developing Quality Child Care for Maltreated and At-Risk Children

A multidisciplinary approach that blends child care and other services appears to be highly effective for high-risk families with young children. There are challenges, however, in providing such services as "the parents in greatest need for supportive assistance from child care providers are likely to be the most difficult, perplexing, and daunting parents to aid" [Thompson et al. 1997: 183]. Child care providers face the following challenges in serving these children and families:

- Child care providers need skills in working with children who have developmental problems as a result of abuse and neglect.

- Child care providers need training and professional support to provide parents with counseling, stress management, and child management education and must understand child maltreatment and its etiology.

- Child care providers need additional training and supportive assistance from supervisors, child protection agencies, and trained consultants to prevent burnout.

- Specialized child care consultation can give providers direction in managing difficult situations.

- Child care programs must be both child-centered and family-focused. Family-focused programming involves the facilitation of peer networks among parents, referral of parents to other community services, meeting with parents on the parents' time, and involving the family in the child care program.

- Child care programs must be part of a network of services for at-risk parents so that the multiple needs of these families—which cannot be addressed by child care programs alone—are met [Thompson et al. 1997]. Any system of care that involves maltreated children should include child care providers.

- Child care programs must be accessible, affordable, and available to foster parents and kin caregivers of maltreated children.

Child care programs that are well-designed, intensive, and parent-focused can help parents develop their abilities to care for their young children. Very few child care programs, however, are funded adequately to offer the weekly or monthly home visits, workshops, and classroom involvement offered by experimental programs like the Yale Child Welfare Research Program and KEEPSAFE [Frede 1995]. In a review of two generation programs which provide child development for children and parenting services to families, the authors noted that "there is substantial evidence that effects on children are best achieved by services aimed directly at children, and effects on parents are best achieved by services to parents. There is only limited evidence to support the indirect method of achieving large effects, that is, achieving effects on children through earlier effects on parents" [St. Pierre et al. 1995: 89–90]. It cannot be assumed that parenting services alone will translate necessarily into improvements in children's lives. High-intensity, quality child care must be part of the equation. Researchers caution that although there is good research concerning quality child care, research is limited on what constitutes a quality parenting, adult education, or job training program [St. Pierre et al. 1995].

Interface With the Child Welfare System

A final challenge in developing quality child care for maltreated and at-risk children is the child welfare system view of child care. Child welfare social workers often consider child care only as a relatively safe form of substitute care and not as a partner in planning for the child's well-being. Research suggests that a partnership between child care and the child welfare system is important for the following reasons:

- *Transitions are traumatic for young maltreated children.* Multiple out-of-home placements can be harmful to children's well-being

[Berrick et al. 1998]. Child care providers can serve as resources to child welfare social workers regarding the child's perceptions and can aid the child in the transition from their family's home to the homes of relatives, foster parents, adoptive parents, or to other permanent placements. Sensitive utilization of child care can be a source of continuity, bridging these moves and providing comfort to the child. Loss of child care can be traumatic for the child and family. When a child moves to out-of-home-care, the child may lose the stability of his or her day care program, including contact with friends and teachers. The parent will lose the child's place in the program, and may not be able to re-enroll the child when the child returns home. At the same time, if the child moves during the out-of-home placement, it may be necessary to find a new child care program with each move.

- *Foster parents and kin caregivers often work and need child care.* Like children's parents, foster families and relative caregivers often must rely on two wage earners to survive. Child care subsidies to these caregivers are, as a result, often essential and represent a cost-effective means of finding and keeping out-of-home caregivers.

- *A coordinated system of care for children and families is needed.* Child care programs, child welfare services, and other services for young children and their families must be coordinated. Communications often break down and children and families may fall through the cracks.

- *Children benefit when child welfare workers share developmental assessments and plans for children with child care providers.* Child care providers, relative caregivers, and foster parents need information on the extent of children's physical, emotional, and developmental problems and the plans that have been developed to meet children's needs. Creative solutions are needed to ensure the appropriate sharing of information, so that confidentiality is maintained but services to children are not short-changed. At the same time, assessments of young children must be completed in a timely manner. When the assessment is delayed, the child may move to a new placement or return home before the child care program receives the information that is essential to meeting the child's needs.

- *Respite child care is a critical resource.* Because 24-hour care for maltreated children can be exhausting, relative caregivers and foster parents need respite programs to temporarily relieve them of their duties. Parents likewise require such assistance, which may be offered in the form of crisis nurseries or specialized family day care homes. Few of these programs, however, are available to families needing them [Access to Respite Care and Help 1994].

Cost-Effectiveness

Quality early intervention using a multisystems model that incorporates child care can enhance parental financial independence and promote child functioning [Seitz et al. 1985]. An investment in the prevention of abuse and neglect and in the treatment of maltreated children results in more favorable outcomes for children and families and decreased costs in relation to child welfare services, including foster care.

Conclusion

Maltreated children can benefit greatly from high-quality child care. Child care providers need extra training, supervision, and consultation to meet these children's special needs. Center and home-based day care can offer high-risk families support through counseling and advice, parent education and guidance in child-rearing concerns, emergency respite, and a network of other supportive parents. A multidisciplinary approach that blends child care with other support services appears to be particularly effective for high-risk families with young children.

References

Access to Respite Care and Help. (1994). *Respite: Prevention, preservation and family support.* Chapel Hill, NC: Access to Respite Care and Help (ARCH), National Resource Center for Crisis Nurseries and Respite Services.

Berrick, J. D., Needell, B. Barth, R. P., & Jonson-Reid, M. (1998). *The tender years: Toward developmentally sensitive child welfare services for very young children.* New York: Oxford University Press.

Cost, Quality & Child Outcomes Study Team. (1995). *Cost, quality and child outcomes in child care centers, public report.* Denver, CO: Denver Economics Department, University of Colorado at Denver.

Frede, E. C. (1995). The role of program quality in producing early childhood program benefits. *The Future of Children, 5*(3), 113–132.

Garbarino, J. Dubrow, N. Kostelny, K., & Pardo, C. (1992). *Children in danger: Coping with the consequences of community violence.* San Francisco: Jossey-Bass Publishers.

Hershfeld, B. (1995, Fall). The role of child care in strengthening and supporting vulnerable families. *The Prevention Report, 2–4.*

Lieberman, A. F. (1993). *The emotional life of the toddler.* New York: The Free Press.

Miller, J. L. & Whittaker, J. K. (1988). Social services and social support: Blended programs for families at risk of child maltreatment. *Child Welfare, 67,* 161–175.

Oats, R. K., Grey, J. Schweitzer, L., Kempe, R. S., & Harmon, R. J. (1995). A therapeutic preschool for abused children: The KEEPSAFE Project. *Child Abuse and Neglect, 19*(1), 1379–1386.

Roditti, M. G. (1995). Child day care: A key building block of family support and family preservation programs. *Child Welfare, 74,* 1043–1068.

St. Pierre, R. G., Layzer, J. I., & Barnes, H. V. (1995). Two-generation programs: Design, cost, and short-term effectiveness. *The Future of Children, 5*(3), 76–93.

Seitz, V., Rosenbaum, L. K., & Apfel, N. H. (1983). Effects of family support intervention: A ten-year follow-up. *Child Development, 56,* 376–391.

Thompson, R. A., Laible, D. J., & Robbenholt, J. K. (1997). Child care and preventing child maltreatment. In S. Reifel, C. J. Dunst, & M. Wolery (Eds.), *Advances in early education and day care: Volume 9* (pp. 173–208). Greenwich, CT: JAI Press, LTD.

Wells, K. & Tracy, E. (1996). Reorienting intensive family preservation services in relation to public child welfare practice. *Child Welfare, 75,* 667–692.

What Works in Child Care for Maltreated and At-Risk Children

Study Authors	Survey Sample	Research Design/ Outcome Measure	Findings
Seitz, V., Rosenbaum, L.K. & Apfel, N.H. (1983). Effects of family support intervention: A ten-year follow-up. *Child Development, 56,* 376–391.	• 10-year study of families from same area from 1971–1981 • Experimental sample consisted of 18 children from 17 families; control sample of 18 children from 18 families	• Data collected during mother's pregnancy and continued to 30 months postpartum; range of social support services offered; data gathered over 10 years through developmental testing, interviews with children's teachers and guidance counselors, and interviews with parents. • Interventions included home visiting by social workers, infant-toddler day care of high-quality, pediatric care, and individualized psychological services. • Outcome measures: social development, school adjustment, school attendance, parental employment, child bearing, and parent-child bond.	• Comprehensive medical and social support services including quality day care, delivered in a personalized, nurturing way to impoverished women resulted in reduced subsequent child bearing and increased maternal return to school. • Almost all of the intervention families were self-supporting compared to one-half of control families. • Intervention mothers waited a median of nine years before having a second child, had higher school attainment and smaller families than control group mothers. • No long-lasting cognitive change in children were found, but experimental children had significantly more positive socialization and school adjustment compared to control children. Experimental group children were rated higher by their teachers, missed fewer days of school, and received significantly less-costly remedial services from schools when compared to control group children. • Parent-child bond was greater in experimental families, as expressed in greater involvement in and communication with children's school (possibly due to earlier positive experience with day care staff). • Early intensive family support intervention had a significant potential for improving long-term family functioning for some poor families.

Services for Adolescents

33

What Works in Promoting Positive Youth Development: Mentoring

Joseph Tierney and Jean B. Grossman

The notion that an unrelated adult can help guide and build the competence and character of a young person by encouraging, challenging, and advising is not a new idea. Over the past two decades, there has been widespread enthusiasm for mentoring programs as a way to address the needs and problems of youth. These programs pair adults with youth to foster relationships that will focus on the young person's needs. Although mentoring programs have burgeoned, there has been no firm evidence that mentoring itself can produce positive results. Some studies have examined programs that combined the presence of a supportive adult with services such as tutoring and college preparation. The most effective of these programs achieve their goals—improved academic performance and attitudes [Cave & Quint 1990; Johnson 1998] and decreased substance abuse [LoSciuto et al. 1996]. Because these programs combined mentoring with other interventions, however, it is unclear whether mentoring alone can confer benefits.

The evaluation of the Big Brothers Big Sisters (BBBS) program, however, provides conclusive evidence that high-quality one-on-one mentoring alone can make a difference in the lives of youth and demonstrates the program practices that make mentoring effective [Tierney & Grossman 1995]. The operational practices and standards of BBBS programs must be noted, however, because many other mentoring programs are not as well-structured or carefully managed and, thus, have not been found to be as effective. Each BBBS agency has a professional staff of case managers who screen and train youth and mentors and supervise each relationship based on national operating standards. These standards govern screening, training, matching, and ongoing supervision and requires that case managers contact the parent, youth, and adult volunteer within two weeks of the match and make monthly contacts during the first year of the relationship.

Findings that Support the Effectiveness of Mentoring

Public/Private Ventures (P/PV) began in 1991 a study of the effects of the BBBS program on adolescents [Tierney et al. 1995]. Eight accredited BBBS agencies participated in cooperation with the national BBBS of America office. Youth between 10 and 14 years old who participated in BBBS programs were compared with those who did not. Youth met with their mentors about three times per month for an average of almost 12 months with each meeting lasting about four hours. The overall findings were positive.

- Mentored youth were 46% less likely than were youth in the control group to initiate drug use during the study period. For every 100 youth who started to use drugs over the study time period, only 54 similar youth with a mentor started using drugs. An even stronger effect was found for mentored minority youth who were 70% less likely to initiate drug use than were similar minority youth in the control group.

- Mentored youth were 27% less likely than were youth in the control group to initiate alcohol use during the study period. Minority girls were only about one-half as likely to initiate alcohol use.

- Mentored youth were almost one-third less likely than were youth in the control group to hit someone.

- Compared to youth in the control group, mentored youth skipped half as many days of school and felt more competent in their schoolwork. Mentored youth showed modest gains in grades. The effect was strongest for girls, particularly minority girls.

- The relationships between mentored youth and their parents improved, primarily as a result of youths' higher level of trust in their parents. This effect was strongest for Caucasian boys.
- Perceived peer relationships improved for mentored youth, particularly among minority boys.
- Measures of self-esteem and self-worth did not indicate improvements for the control youth.

Cost-Effectiveness

These findings from the P/PV study do not mean that the benefits of mentoring occur automatically. Research indicates that screening, training, and supervision are critical in supporting effective mentoring [Sipe 1996], activities which cost approximately $1,000 per year per match [Tierney & Grossman 1995; Fountain & Arbreton 1998]. Research also indicates that mentors must devote several months to gaining the trust of their mentee [Morrow & Styles 1995].

Conclusion

This research presents clear and encouraging evidence that caring relationships between adults and youth can be created and supported by programs and can yield a wide range of tangible benefits. Over the past 15 years, it has become clear that mentoring is not as easy as some believe, nor will mentoring alone enable young people to overcome the myriad of problems many of them face. With responsible practices, sufficient resources and realistic expectations, however, mentoring can augment the resources available to help many vulnerable young people.

References

Cave, G. & Quint, J. (1990). *Career beginning impact evaluation.* New York: Manpower Demonstration and Research Corporation.

Fountain, D. & Arbreton, A. (1998). *The cost of mentoring.* Philadelphia: Public/Private Ventures.

Johnson, A. W. (1998). *An evaluation of the long-term impact of the Sponsor-A-Scholar (SAS) Program on student performance.* Princeton, NJ: Mathematica Policy Research.

LoSciuto, L., Rajal, A. K., Townsend, T. N., & Taylor, A. S. (1996). An outcome evaluation of across ages: An intergenerational mentoring approach to drug prevention. *Journal of Adolescent Research, 11*(1), 116–129.

Morrow, K. V. & Styles, M. B. (1995). *Building relationships with youth in program settings: A study of Big Brothers Big Sisters.* Philadelphia: Public/Private Ventures.

Sipe, C. L. (1996). *Mentoring: A synthesis of P/PV's Research: 1988–1995.* Philadelphia:Public/Private Ventures.

Tierney, J. P. & Grossman, J. with Resch, N. L. (1995). *Making a difference: An impact study of Big Brothers/Big Sisters.* Philadelphia: Public/Private Ventures.

What Works in Positive Youth Development: Mentoring

Study Authors	Survey Sample	Research Design/Outcome Measure	Findings
Johnson, A. W. (1998). *An evaluation of the long-term Impacts of the Sponsor-A-Scholar (SAS) program on student performance.* Princeton, NJ: Mathematica Policy Research.	• 80 youth who were Sponsor-A-Scholar students in 1993 (classes of 1994, 1995, 1996, 1997) • 254 Philadelphia high school students matched to the SAS scholars by race, gender, schools attended, and ninth grade performance	• Matched comparison group design • Data on grade-point average • High school graduation and college attendance was collected annually from 1993–1997. • The evaluation assessed the combination of mentoring, college preparation services, and financial assistance.	• Grades in 10th and 11th grade improved among SAS youth relative to the comparison group youth. • More mentored youth attended college the first and second year after graduation.
Tierney, J.P. & Grossman, J. B. with Resch, N. L. (1995). *Making a dfference: An impact study of Big Brothers/ Big Sisters.* Philadelphia: Public/Private Ventures.	• 1,138 youth ages 10–16 who were eligible for the program in eight cities (Philadelphia, Pennsylvania; Rochester, New York; Minneapolis, Minnesota; Columbus, Ohio; Wichita, Kansas; Houston and San Antonio, Texas; an10p1d Phoenix, Arizona) • Half were randomly assigned to the experimental group and half were excluded from the program for 18 months.	• Randomized pre-/post-test control group design with an 18-month follow-up • The evaluation assessed mentoring alone.	• Mentored youth were less likely to start using drugs or alcohol, skipped school less, felt more competent and earned slightly higher grades, and had better relationships with parents and peers.

(continued next page)

What Works in Positive Youth Development: Mentoring (*continued*)

Study Authors	Survey Sample	Research Design/Outcome Measure	Findings
LoSciuto, L., Rajal, A. K., Townsend, T. N. & Taylor, A. S. (1996). An outcome evaluation of across ages: An intergenerational mentoring approach to drug prevention. *Journal of Adolescent Research, 11*(1), 116–129.	• Each year for three years (school years 1991–1992, 1992–1993, 1993–1994) in three middle schools, one sixth grade class each was randomly assigned to: a control status; the Positive Youth Development Curriculum (PYDC) and community service; or a combination of PYDC, community service, and an older mentor • 199 youth were control youth; 193 were "PYDC and Service" youth; and 180 were "PYDC, Service and Mentor" youth	• Randomized pre/post-test control group design • The study examined the effect on attitudes towards school elders, drug use, reaction to stress, self-perception, well-being, and knowledge about older people.	• Mentored youth fared better than the "PYDC and Service" youth on attitudes toward school, future and elders; knowledge about older people; and frequency of substance abuse.
Cave, G. & Quint, J. (1990). *Career beginning impact evaluation.* New York: Manpower Demonstration and Research Corporation.	• 1,233 high-school juniors were recruited. Half were randomly assigned to the experimental group and encouraged to take part in Career Beginnings. Half were excluded from the program.	• Randomized control group design with follow-up one and two years after random assignment • The study assessed effect of Career Beginnings on college attendance (program combined college preparation services with mentoring).	• Career Beginnings increased the rate of college attendance.

34

What Works in School-Based Substance Abuse Prevention: Interactive or Peer Programs

Miriam P. Kluger and Noelle Gallant

Most adolescents are at risk for substance abuse [Tobler 1992]. Many schools provide students with information about the harms of drugs and alcohol in an effort to prevent substance abuse. Emphasis is placed on intrapersonal skill-building in the areas of self-esteem, coping, and decision-making. These prevention programs are often noninteractive, and little attention is given to the communication of ideas among peers [Tobler & Stratton 1997]. Studies on the efficacy of these prevention programs and programs that target psychological factors, such as self-esteem building and values clarification, have been limited at best.

Research on Interactive or Peer Substance Abuse Prevention Programs

Much research has been conducted on the efficacy of the Drug Abuse Resistance Education (DARE) program with consistent findings of no reduction in drug use behaviors and attitudes [Wysong et al. 1994; Ennett et al. 1994]. As Figure 1 illustrates, Wysong and colleagues found that students who were taught the DARE curriculum were as likely to have used drugs and alcohol in the past year as students who did not receive DARE training. For noninteractive programs like DARE, however, research is needed on both short-term and long-term results.

One strategy that holds some promise of more effective prevention of adolescent substance abuse is interactive or peer programs. The Office of Substance Abuse Prevention [1989] defines interactive programs or group processes as teaching techniques that include active participation of all classroom students in such activities as discussion, brainstorming, or practicing of new behaviors. Interactive programs are based on the theory that adolescents are strongly influenced by their peers [Montemayor 1982].

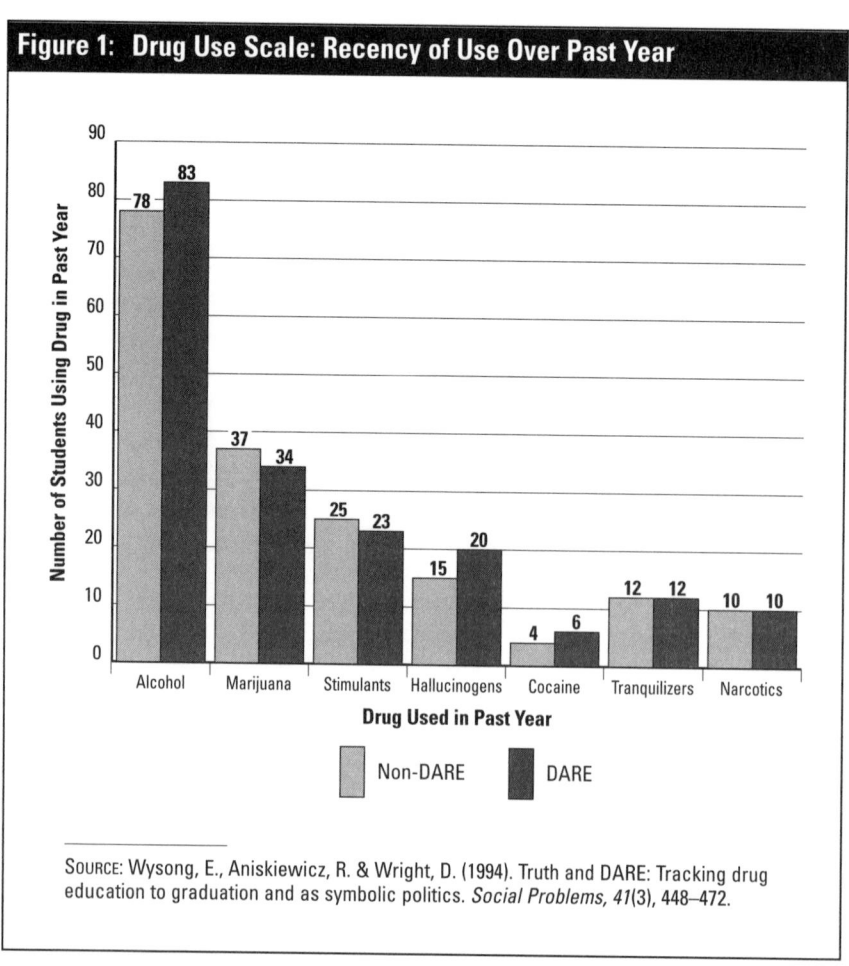

Figure 1: Drug Use Scale: Recency of Use Over Past Year

Source: Wysong, E., Aniskiewicz, R. & Wright, D. (1994). Truth and DARE: Tracking drug education to graduation and as symbolic politics. *Social Problems, 41*(3), 448–472.

Interactive programs are purported to work because peer pressure impacts attitudes and behaviors. In the area of substance abuse, it is believed that as a result of positive peer influence—through peer teaching, peer counseling and other positive interactions—adolescents will be less likely to use drugs and alcohol. Early research suggests that:

- Prevention programs that involve peer groups are more effective than programs delivered noninteractively by teachers or program staff [Schaps et al. 1981];

- Peer students trained to give educational information may be more credible to students than professionals, such as social workers [Botvin et al. 1984]; and

- For small group discussion programs on substance abuse issues, peer leadership is significantly more effective than teacher-facilitation [Perry 1996].

Peer programs have two components: knowledge building about the short and long-term effects of drug use and a group situation that encourages peer support for not using drugs. Peer interaction in the group setting is the important factor in the success of these programs, with an adolescent leader playing a key role in developing a positive peer atmosphere. The more effective adolescent leaders act as guides rather than dominating the group and encourage adolescents to feel empowered to make conscientious decisions. Regardless of the information that is conveyed during the program, peer programs emphasize the interaction and exchange of ideas among peers.

In an analysis of 91 adolescent drug prevention programs, all of which included a control or comparison group of students who received no drug prevention program, peer programs were found to be the most effective when compared with programs that are considered knowledge only, affective only, or a combination of those two program types [Tobler 1992]. The analysis found:

- Half of the peer programs studied decreased cigarette, alcohol, marijuana, and hard drug use following receipt of 10 or fewer hours of the peer program;

- Peer leaders tended to be selected volunteers and older adolescents; and

- Peer leaders were likely to have received training in the program activities and support from teachers who remained with the group to ensure classroom discipline.

In an analysis of 120 school-based programs, Tobler and Stratton [1997] found additional support for the efficacy of peer programs in reducing drug use. These programs—more recently referred to as interactive programs—were found to be successful in reducing adolescent use of a number of substances, including cigarettes, alcohol, and marijuana.

The success rate was based primarily upon self-reported paper-and-pencil tests given confidentially in a classroom setting, although some studies included physical tests such as saliva. Of note, differences between interactive and noninteractive programs held across all adolescent ages, for all racial and ethnic groups, and for all substances examined (cigarettes, alcohol, marijuana, and other illicit drugs). As shown in Figure 2, the effectiveness of school-based programs could be enhanced by as much as eight-fold if interactive/peer groups replaced current noninteractive programs.

Conclusion

All young people are at risk for substance use and abuse. Prevention of adolescent substance abuse has captured national attention, and millions of dollars have been spent on programs such as DARE, although it has not been proven to be effective. Identifying effective approaches to substance use/abuse prevention is of critical importance to protect the health of children while they are young and to improve their odds of living drug-free. From a child welfare perspective, prevention of drug and alcohol addiction allows children to grow up and become drug-free parents. Furthermore, new guidelines from the federal Safe and Drug Free School program administrators require that grantees demonstrate research-based evidence that the strategies and models they choose are effective in preventing or reducing drug use, violence, and disruptive behavior.

Preliminary support is shown for interactive and peer interventions in reducing use of substances. Although more research is needed to determine the long-term efficacy of the interactive approach, the work of Tobler and associates [1997] is very promising. The critical need for effective drug abuse prevention approaches suggests that the current noninteractive, knowledge-based programs be replaced with curricula

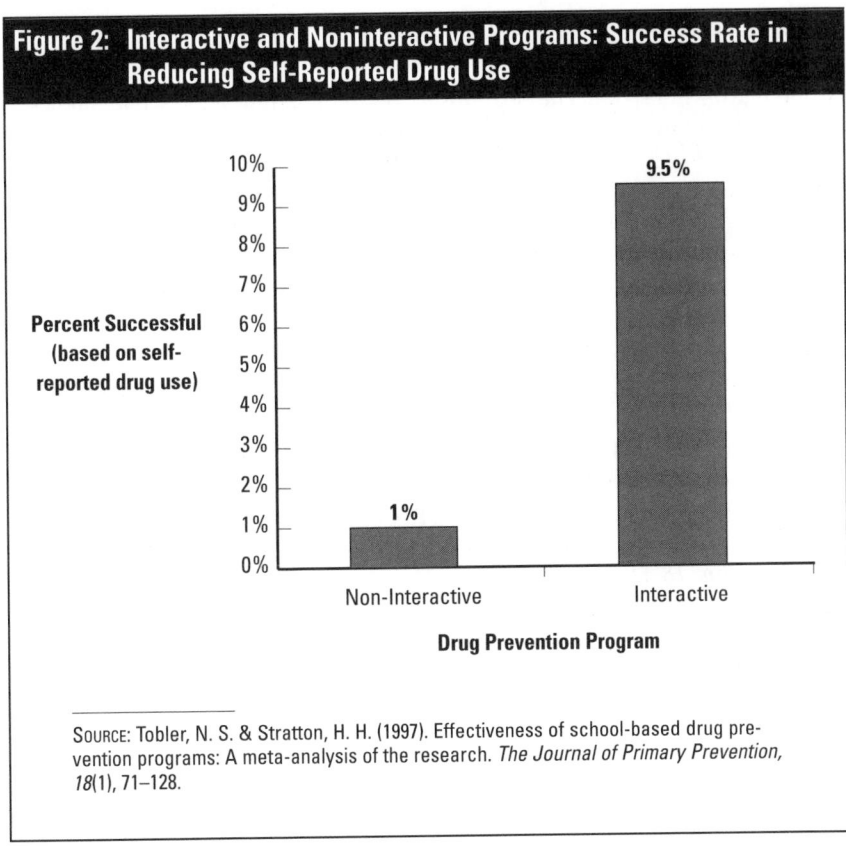

Figure 2: Interactive and Noninteractive Programs: Success Rate in Reducing Self-Reported Drug Use

Source: Tobler, N. S. & Stratton, H. H. (1997). Effectiveness of school-based drug prevention programs: A meta-analysis of the research. *The Journal of Primary Prevention, 18*(1), 71–128.

which include interactive techniques. Because the administrators of the Safe and Drug Free School program are considering adding an interactive component to their new grant guidelines, program evaluators may soon have many more opportunities to investigate this approach.

References

Botvin, G., Baker, E., Renick, N., Filazzola, A., & Botvin, E. (1984). A cognitive-behavioral approach to substance abuse prevention. *Addictive Behaviors, 9,* 137–147.

Ennett, S. T., Tobler, N. S., Ringwalt, C. L., & Flewelling, R. L. (1994). How effective is drug abuse resistance education? A meta-analysis of project

DARE outcome evaluations. *American Journal of Public Health, 84*(9), 1394–1401.

Montemayor, R. (1982). The relationship between parent-adolescent conflict and the amount of time adolescents spend alone and with parents and peers. *Child Development, 53,* 1512–1519.

Office of Substance Abuse Prevention. (1989). Prevention Plus II: Tools for creating and sustaining drug-free communities (DHHS Publication No. ADM 89-1649). Washington, DC: U.S. Government Printing Office.

Perry, C. (1996). Research abstract: Models for effective prevention. *The Prevention Researcher, 3*(1), 1–6.

Schaps, E., DiBartolo, R., Moskowitz, J., Palley, C., & Churgin, S. (1981). A review of 127 drug abuse prevention program evaluations. *Journal of Drug Issues, 1,* 17–43.

Tobler, N. S. (1992). Drug prevention programs can work: Research findings. *Journal of Addictive Diseases, 11*(3), 1–28.

Tobler, N. S, & Stratton, H. H. (1997). Effectiveness of school-based drug prevention programs: A meta-analysis of the research. *The Journal of Primary Prevention, 18*(1), 71–128.

Wysong, E., Aniskiewicz, R., & Wright, D. (1994). Truth and DARE: Tracking drug education to graduation and as symbolic politics. *Social Problems, 41*(3), 448–472.

What Works in School-Based Substance Abuse Prevention Programs

Study Authors	Survey Sample	Research Design/Outcome Measure	Findings
Tobler, N. S. (1992). Drug prevention programs can work: Research findings. *Journal of Addictive Diseases, 11*(3), 1–28.	• 91 drug prevention programs that included drug use measures to demonstrate the programs' ability to prevent or reduce teenage drug use	• Program was the unit of analysis • Dependent variables were outcome measures (drug knowledge, attitudes and values, self-reported drug use, skills, actual behavior). • Effect size was computed for each outcome measure reported.	• Peer programs, when compared to all other strategies, produce the highest effect sizes for all measures except behavior. • Substantial positive gains were achieved in 10 or fewer hours by 50% of the peer programs.
Tobler, N. S. & Stratton, H. H. (1997). Effectiveness of school-based drug prevention programs: A meta-analysis of the research. *The Journal of Primary Prevention, 18*(1), 71–128.	• 120 school-based drug prevention programs that evaluated success on self-reported drug use measures	• Program was the unit of analysis • Independent variables were type of program and program content. • Dependent variable/outcome measures were knowledge, attitudes, drug refusal skills, general skills, school and psychological well-being. • Effect size was computed for each outcome measure reported.	• Interactive programs had an effect size of approximately .20 across all subsets of programs compared to .02 for the noninteractive programs.
Ennett, S. T., Tobler, N. S., Ringwalt, C. L. & Flewelling, R. L. (1994). How effective is drug abuse resistance education? A meta-analysis of project DARE outcome evaluations. *American Journal of Public Health, 84*(9), 1394–1401.	• Eight methodologically rigorous DARE evaluations	• Calculated an effect size to quantify the magnitude of DARE's effectiveness with respect to each of six outcomes that reflected the curriculum's aims	• The DARE effect size for drug use behavior ranged from .00 to .11 across the eight studies. • For all outcomes considered, the DARE effect size means were substantially smaller than those of programs emphasizing social and general competencies and using interactive teaching techniques.

35

What Works in Treatment Programs for Substance-Abusing Youth

Lori K. Sudderth

S ubstance abuse among children and adolescents is a critical problem. It exists, however, among a group of problems that include social and coping skill deficits, family conflict, parental substance abuse, criminal behavior, community risk factors, and academic difficulties [Jenson et al. 1995; Weinberg et al. 1998]. At the same time, dual disorder is especially common among adolescents with substance abuse problems [Stowell & Estroff 1992]. Treatment is further complicated by the fact that most young people who need treatment for substance abuse do not seek it themselves but instead are referred by their parents or the criminal justice system [Connecticut Department of Children and Families 1997; Hubbard et al. 1985]. Treatment for adolescents with substance abuse problems can be complex, as illustrated in Figure 1.

The Center for Substance Abuse Treatment (CSAT) recommends that treatment programs for substance-abusing adolescents should include the following elements:

- Orientation which clarifies the program expectations to clients and includes client contracts that specify treatment goals, time frames, and consequences for violating the rules;

- Daily scheduled activities that encourage skill-building, relapse prevention, diversion from substance-abusing behavior, and academic improvement;

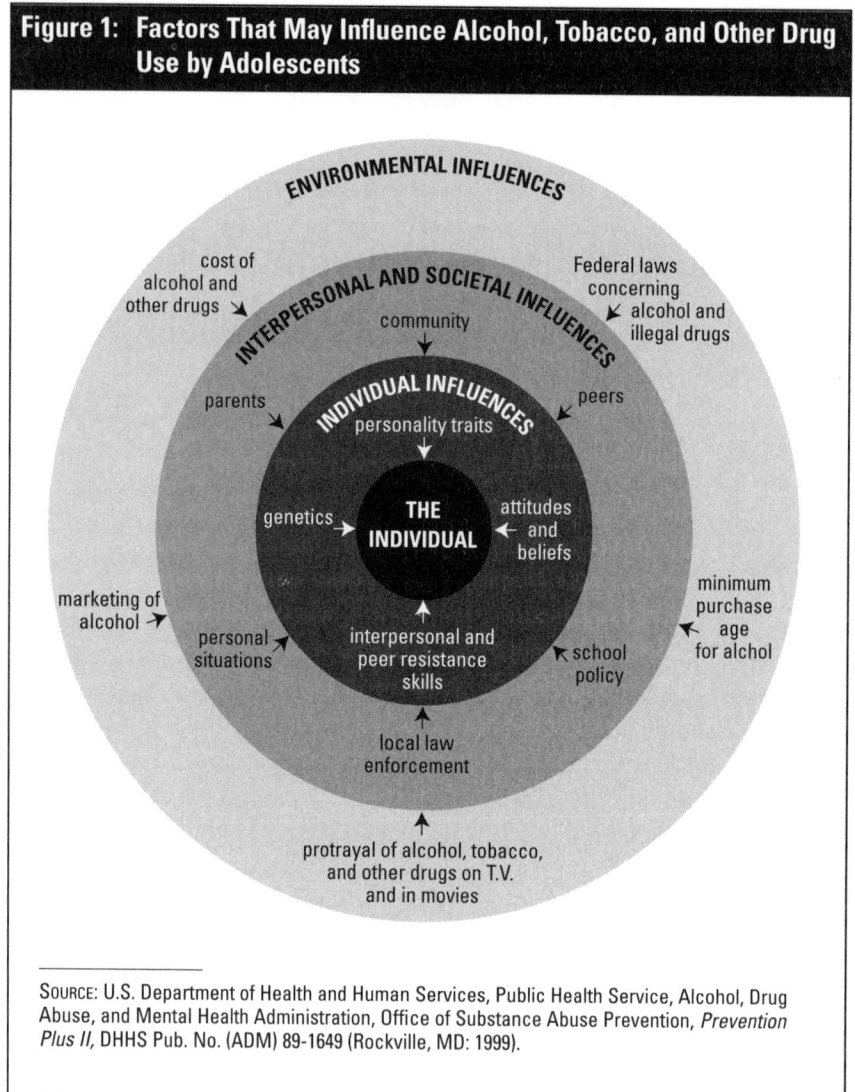

Figure 1: Factors That May Influence Alcohol, Tobacco, and Other Drug Use by Adolescents

SOURCE: U.S. Department of Health and Human Services, Public Health Service, Alcohol, Drug Abuse, and Mental Health Administration, Office of Substance Abuse Prevention, *Prevention Plus II,* DHHS Pub. No. (ADM) 89-1649 (Rockville, MD: 1999).

- Positive peer influence through group activities;
- Clear methods for resolving conflicts that arise between clients and staff;

- Integration of schooling with the treatment program and educational activities that focus on substance use and recovery; and

- Vocational guidance and training.

[U.S. Department of Health and Human Services 1999].

Treatment models may include supportive therapy, cognitive behavior therapy, interactional group treatment, multisystemic therapy, or some combination of these interventions. Supportive therapy encourages expression of feelings and insight into the self and incorporates discussions of drug-related experiences. Cognitive behavior therapy (CBT) involves teaching adolescents skills to deal with problems related to drug or alcohol use (such as family conflict or employment issues), and avoiding alcohol or drug use [MacKay et al. 1991]. Interactional group treatment is short-term, present-oriented group treatment which focuses on self-esteem, affect, self-care, and relationships [Khantzian et al. 1992]. The focus of multisystemic therapy (MST) is on the network of social factors that encourage substance abuse among children and adolescents. Interventions may include cognitive behavioral therapy in individual or group sessions and work with families, teachers, neighbors, police, and peers to impact the youth's environment [Henggeler et al. 1992; Weinberg et al. 1998].

Evaluation of Treatment Programs for Substance-Abusing Youth

There is research demonstrating the effectiveness of CBT and MST in programs for substance-abusing youth. Although both approaches have received empirical support in terms of effectiveness, it is not clear that one is more effective than the other.

Cognitive Behavioral Therapy (CBT)

The effectiveness of CBT has been demonstrated in comparison to other types of short-term therapy [Azrin et al. 1994; Kaminer et al. 1998]. Azrin and colleagues [1994] compared outcomes for 13 to 18-year-old drug-abusing youth in CBT to similar youths in supportive therapy. CBT was found to be more effective in reducing drug use: 27% of the students receiving CBT reported drug use compared to 91% of the students receiving supportive therapy (See Figure 2). Further, there was greater improvement in the students' psychological state and their family relationships as measured by standardized questionnaires. The sample size, however, was quite small (n = 26), and the results should be interpreted with caution.

Multisystemic Treatment (MST)

The National Institute on Drug Abuse (NIDA) sponsored an evaluation of MST on substance use and antisocial behavior among adolescents and the impact of MST on adolescents' relationships with family and peers.

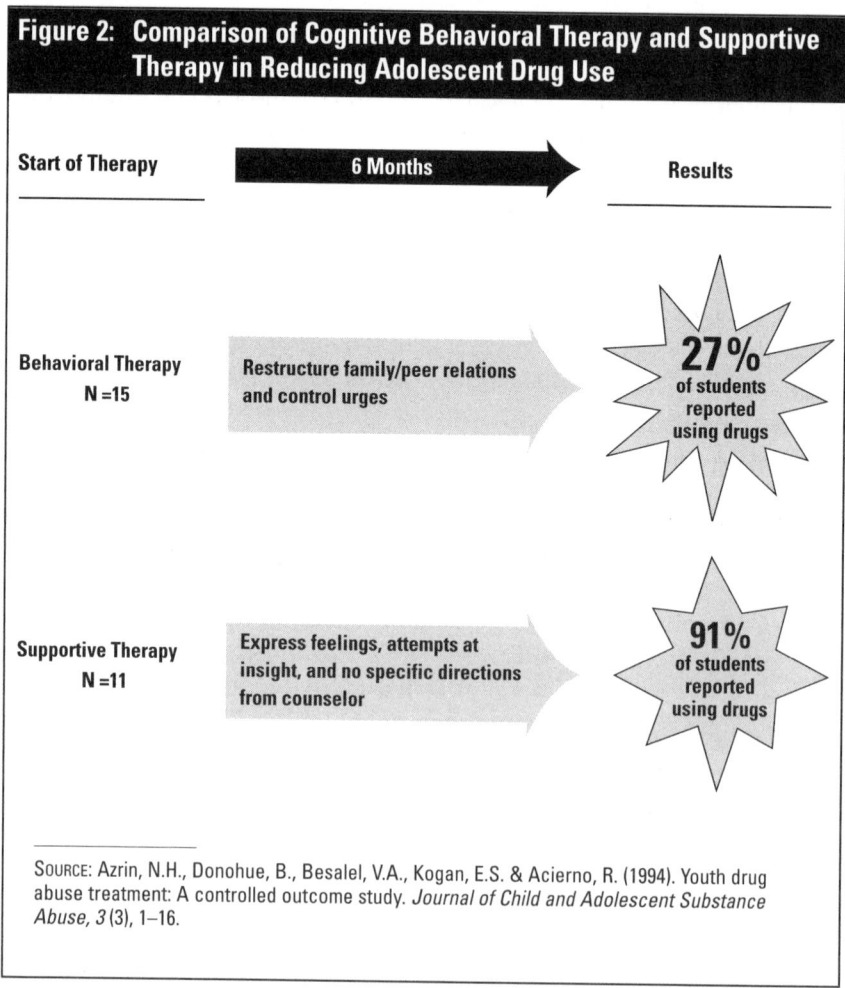

Figure 2: Comparison of Cognitive Behavioral Therapy and Supportive Therapy in Reducing Adolescent Drug Use

Start of Therapy — 6 Months → Results

Behavioral Therapy
N =15
Restructure family/peer relations and control urges
27% of students reported using drugs

Supportive Therapy
N =11
Express feelings, attempts at insight, and no specific directions from counselor
91% of students reported using drugs

Source: Azrin, N.H., Donohue, B., Besalel, V.A., Kogan, E.S. & Acierno, R. (1994). Youth drug abuse treatment: A controlled outcome study. *Journal of Child and Adolescent Substance Abuse, 3* (3), 1–16.

Conducted in Charleston, South Carolina, researchers used controlled trials in which 118 juveniles, 12 to 17 years old, were randomly assigned to either a program using MST or the usual services provided to juveniles. Participants had been referred by the Department of Juvenile Justice and met DSMIII-R criteria for a substance abuse disorder. Testing occurred pre- and posttreatment with a six-month follow-up. Results suggested that MST reduced self-reported alcohol and marijuana use by 46% [Henggeler 1997; Pickrel & Henggeler 1996]. In addition, a one-year follow-up suggested that MST significantly decreased the number of days juveniles spent incarcerated after treatment [Schoenwald et al. 1996]. These positive results extended to the families of the juveniles with parents reporting higher program retention rates and lower alcohol use among adolescents and "increased parental restrictiveness in child management, decreased family conflict, improved dyadic relations in parents, decreased youth conformity to antisocial peer pressure, and improved emotional bonding with peers" [Pickrel & Henggeler 1996: 204]. Support for MST also has been demonstrated in studies examining treatment outcomes for violent and chronic juvenile offenders [Henggeler et al. 1992] and studies comparing outcomes from MST with the results of individual therapy [Borduin et al. 1995].

Cost-Effectiveness

Currently there has been no systematic evaluation of MST in comparison to programs that rely solely on a cognitive behavioral approach. This comparison is critical because MST costs more per client initially than other types of programs [Schoenwald et al. 1996]. Schoenwald and colleagues [1996] compared the cost of MST to that of traditional services for juveniles on probation in South Carolina at the time of service delivery and at the one-year follow-up. They verified that MST initially costs more per client than traditional services ($5,063 per youth vs. $3,369 per youth), but they found that at the one-year follow-up, MST youth had to date an average of 569 incarceration days compared to 1,051 incarceration days for youth who received traditional services. The authors concluded that the long-range savings made the cost of the MST program only slightly more expensive than traditional services. Although MST is more expensive than other approaches, it also was found to reduce time youth spent in residential placements [Schoenwald et al. 1996].

Conclusion

The preponderance of evidence suggests that substance abuse treatment programs for youth should be comprehensive in addressing a range of relevant issues rather than only the substance abuse problem. Substance abuse may be related to emotional problems, criminal activity, violence, academic problems, and teen pregnancy, and treatment programs must address, on an individual basis, all presenting problems.

Cognitive behavior therapy (CBT) has been found to be effective in reducing drug use and improving adolescents' psychological state and family relationships. Multisystemic treatment (MST) has been found to be effective in reducing self-reported alcohol and marijuana use and decreasing the number of days juveniles spent incarcerated. Although CBT and MST have received empirical support in terms of effectiveness, it is not clear that one is more effective than the other. Although MST is more expensive to implement than other approaches, initial results suggest that the long-term benefits of reduced residential placement and incarceration time are worth the investment. Any such implementation should include an evaluation of longitudinal costs to further verify that MST is cost-effective.

References

Azrin, N. H., Donohue, B., Besalel, V. A., Kogan, E. S., & Acierno, R. (1994). Youth drug abuse treatment: A controlled outcome study. *Journal of Child and Adolescent Substance Abuse, 3*(3), 1–16.

Borduin, C. M., Mann, B. J., Cone, L. T., Henggeler, S. W., Fucci, B. R., Blaske, D. M., & Williams, R. A. (1995). Multisystemic treatment of serious juvenile offenders: Long-term prevention of criminality and violence. *Journal of Consulting and Clinical Psychology, 63,* 569–578.

Connecticut Department of Children and Families. (1997). Substance abuse treatment needs of DCF committed youth in placement. Hartford, CT: Substance Abuse Division, Office of Children's Mental Health, Substance Abuse and Health Services.

Henggeler, S. W. (1997). The development of effective drug abuse services for youth. In J.A. Egertson, D.M. Gox, & A.I. Leshner (Eds.), *Treating Drug Abusers Effectively* (pp. 253–279). New York: Blackwell Publishers.

Henggeler, S. W., Melton, G. B., & Smith, L. A. (1992). Family preservation using multisystemic therapy: An effective alternative to incarcerating serious juvenile offenders. *Journal of Consulting and Clinical Psychology, 60*(6), 953–961.

Henggeler, S. W., Schoenwald, S. K., Pickrel, S. G., Rowland, M. D., & Santos, A. B. (1994). The contribution of treatment outcome research to the reform of children's mental health services: Multisystemic therapy as an example. *Journal of Mental Health Administration, 21*(3), 229–239.

Hubbard, R. L., Cavanaugh, E. R., & Craddock, S. G. (1985). *Characteristics, behaviors, and outcomes for youth in the TOPS Study* (Report submitted to the National Institute on Drug Abuse, Contract No. 271-79-3611). Research Triangle Park, NC: Research Triangle Institute.

Jenson, J. M., Howard, M. O., & Yaffe, J. (1995). Treatment of adolescent substance abusers: Issues for practice and research. *Social Work in Health Care, 21*(2), 1–18.

Kaminer, Y., Blitz, C., Burleson, J. A., Kadden, R. M., & Rounsaville, B. J. (1998). Measuring treatment process in cognitive-behavioral and interactional group therapies for adolescent substance abusers. *Journal of Nervous and Mental Disease, 186*(7), 407–413.

Khantzian, E. J., Halliday, K. S., Golden, S., & McAuliffe, W. E. (1992). Modified group therapy for substance abusers: A psychodynamic approach to relapse prevention. *American Journal of Addictions, 1,* 67–76.

MacKay, P. W., Donovan, D. M., & Marlatt, G. A. (1991). Cognitive and behavioral approaches to alcohol abuse. In R. J. Frances & S. I. Miller (Eds.), *Clinical Textbook of Addictive Disorders* (pp. 452–481). New York: The Guilford Press.

Pickrel, S. G. & Henggeler, S. W. (1996). Multisystemic therapy for adolescent substance abuse and dependence. *Child and Adolescent Psychiatric Clinics of North America, 5*(1), 201–211.

Schoenwald, S. K., Ward, D. M., Henggeler, S. W., Pickrel, S. G., & Patel, H. (1996). Multisystemic therapy treatment of substance abusing or dependent adolescent offenders: Costs of reducing incarceration, inpatient, and residential placement. *Journal of Child and Family Studies, 5*(4), 431–444.

Stowell, R. J. A. & Estroff, T. W. (1992). Psychiatric disorders in substance-abusing adolescent inpatients: A pilot study. *Journal of the American Academy of Child & Adolescent Psychiatry, 31,* 1036–1040.

U.S. Department of Health and Human Services. (1999). *Treatment of adolescents with substance use disorders.* Rockville, MD: U.S. Department of Health and Human Services, Substance Abuse and Mental Health Services Administration, Center for Substance Abuse Treatment.

Weinberg, N. Z., Rahdert, E., Colliver, J. D., & Glantz, M. D. (1998). Adolescent substance abuse: A review of the past 10 years. *Journal of American Academy of Child and Adolescent Psychiatry, 37*(3), 252–261.

What Works in Treatment Programs for Substance Abusing Youth

Study Authors	Survey Sample	Research Design/Outcome Measure	Findings
Azrin, N.H., Donohue, B., Besalel, V.A., Kogan, E.S. & Acierno, R. (1994). Youth drug abuse treatment: A controlled outcome study. *Journal of Child and Adolescent Substance Abuse, 3*(3), 1–16.	• 26 subjects recruited through advertising at schools and agencies and in newspapers. • Subjects ranged from 13-18 years old. • Subjects completed at least four treatment sessions.	• Subjects received either cognitive behavioral therapy or supportive therapy. • Subjects provided information on drug usage following treatment. • Psychological state and family relationships were measured by standardized instruments such as the Beck Depression Inventory, the Parent Satisfaction Scale, Youth Satisfaction Scale, and Quay Problem Behavior Checklist.	• Cognitive behavioral therapy was more effective than supportive therapy in reducing drug use and improving the psychological state and family relationships of clients.
Henggeler, S. W., Schoenwald, S. K., Pickrel, S. G., Rowland, M. D. & Santos, A. B. (1994). The contribution of treatment outcome research to the reform of children's mental health services: Multisystemic therapy as an example. *Journal of Mental Health Administration 21*(3), 229–239.	• 118 participants were referred from the Department of Juvenile Justice in South Carolina. • Subjects ranged from 12–17 years and met DSMIII-R criteria for substance abuse disorder.	• Participants randomly assigned to either usual services or MST groups • Pre and post-testing occurred with a six and 12-month follow-up.	• MST was more effective than traditional services through the juvenile justice system: treatment dropout rates, substance use, and criminal behavior were reduced.

36

What Works in Treatment for Delinquent Adolescents: Day Treatment

Jann L. Hoge and Sue Ann Savas

D ay treatment programs allow delinquent youth to live in a home setting while they receive therapeutic and supportive services 5 to 14
hours per day, up to 6 days a week. Services may include group, family,
and individual therapy; specialized educational services; interaction with
participants' home schools; recreational programs; family education and
support groups; crisis response support; and case management services.
Day treatment has been viewed as a less restrictive, less costly alternative
to traditional residential treatment [Comer 1985; Kettlewell et al. 1985;
Rosenthal & Glass 1990; Schutjer 1982; Velasquez & Lyle 1985].

The Effectiveness of Day Treatment Services for Delinquent Adolescents

The efficacy of day treatment services for delinquent youth—and for adolescents in need of mental health treatment—has been examined for over
20 years. Few studies, however, have compared the outcomes of day treatment for delinquent adolescents to more restrictive forms of treatment.
One study of an Indiana day treatment program for adjudicated adolescents [Comer 1985] found, on the basis of the subjective impressions of

staff and self-reports of youth and parents, a range of positive outcomes, including:

- A decrease in chronic behavior problems;
- An increase in self-esteem;
- Improved school attendance;
- Greater family harmony; and
- A higher number of released youth (more than half) remaining in the community.

Three additional studies have explored outcomes of day treatment programs for delinquent youth [Hoge & Savas 1998; Rosenthal & Glass 1990; Velasquez & Lyle 1985]. The principal findings of these studies were:

- *For delinquent youth, day treatment was as likely as residential treatment to lead to a home-based living situation at 12 months after program completion.* A desired outcome of treatment for delinquent adolescents is return to and/or maintenance of a living situation with a parent, guardian, relative, or foster parent, or placement in a supervised independent living arrangement. A Michigan study [Hoge & Savas 1998] found youth in day treatment and youth in residential treatment equally likely to be living in a home-based setting 12 months after release (84% in day treatment compared to 81% in residential treatment, not a statistically significant difference). Similarly, a study of delinquent adolescents in Minnesota [Velasquez & Lyle 1985] found no significant difference between youth in day treatment and youth in residential treatment with regard to their living situations at a 12-month follow-up (32% of day treatment adolescents compared to 39% of residential treatment adolescents, not a statistically significant difference) (See Figure 1).

- *For delinquent youth, day treatment may be more likely than residential treatment to lead to post-treatment schooling.* Twelve months after program completion, 88% of day treatment graduates and 61% of residential treatment graduates in the Michigan study were in school [Hoge & Savas 1998]. The Minnesota study [Velasquez & Lyle 1985] found similar school attendance for both groups at 12 to 22 months follow-up (57% for day treatment youth compared to

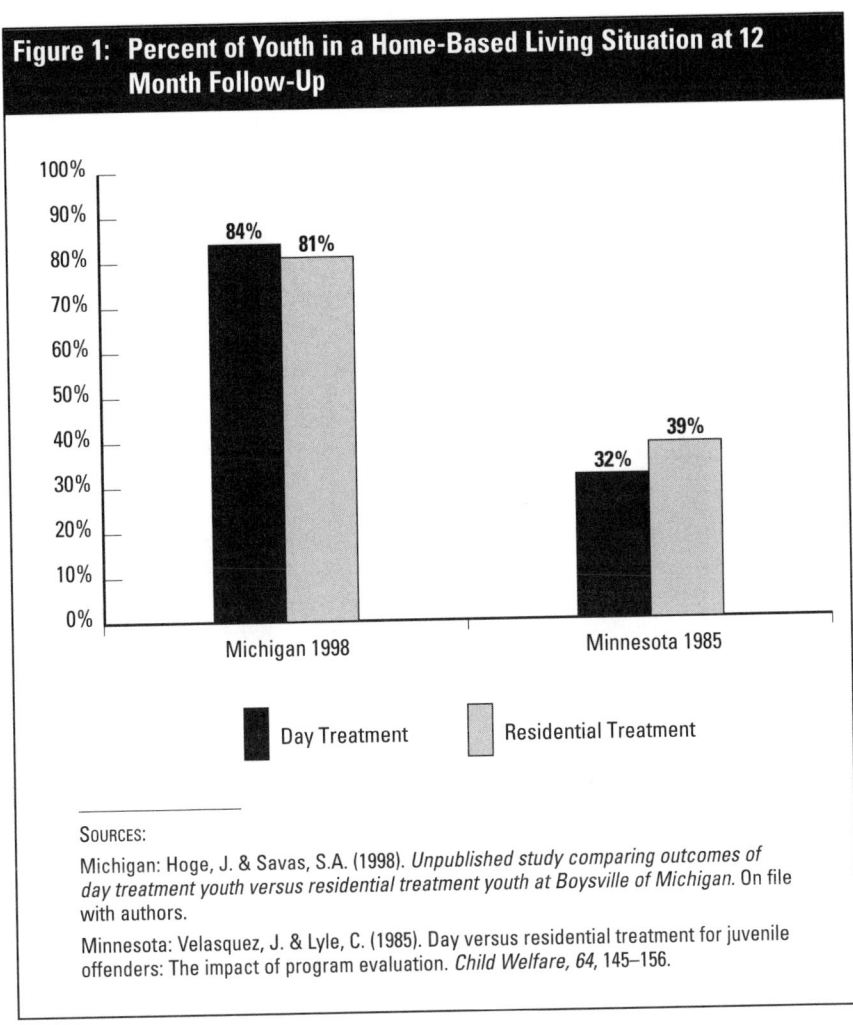

Figure 1: Percent of Youth in a Home-Based Living Situation at 12 Month Follow-Up

SOURCES:

Michigan: Hoge, J. & Savas, S.A. (1998). *Unpublished study comparing outcomes of day treatment youth versus residential treatment youth at Boysville of Michigan.* On file with authors.

Minnesota: Velasquez, J. & Lyle, C. (1985). Day versus residential treatment for juvenile offenders: The impact of program evaluation. *Child Welfare, 64*, 145–156.

50% for residential treatment youth, not a statistically significant difference). In the Colorado study [Rosenthal & Glass 1990], 15% of day treatment youth and 8% of residential treatment youth were attending school two to four semesters after entering the programs (not a statistically significant difference) (See figure 2). Finally, in the Indiana study, day treatment youth and their parents reported improved school attendance [Comer 1985].

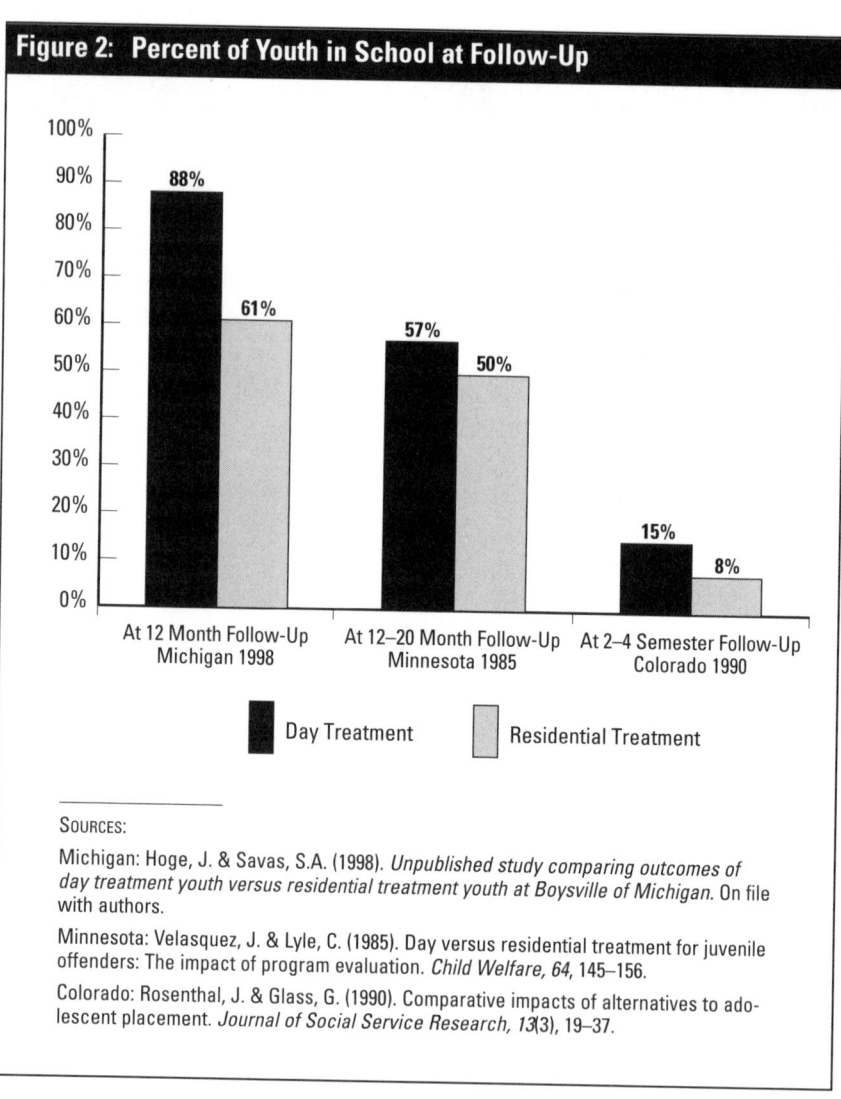

Figure 2: Percent of Youth in School at Follow-Up

SOURCES:

Michigan: Hoge, J. & Savas, S.A. (1998). *Unpublished study comparing outcomes of day treatment youth versus residential treatment youth at Boysville of Michigan.* On file with authors.

Minnesota: Velasquez, J. & Lyle, C. (1985). Day versus residential treatment for juvenile offenders: The impact of program evaluation. *Child Welfare, 64,* 145–156.

Colorado: Rosenthal, J. & Glass, G. (1990). Comparative impacts of alternatives to adolescent placement. *Journal of Social Service Research, 13*(3), 19–37.

- *For delinquent youth, day treatment and residential treatment had similar outcomes regarding participants' illegal activity.* The three studies found no significant differences in delinquency rates for adolescents who had received day treatment compared to those in residential treatment. In the Michigan study [Hoge & Savas 1998],

96% of day treatment youth and 93% of residential treatment youth had no new adjudications at the 12-month follow-up (not a statistically significant difference). The Minnesota study [Velasquez & Lyle 1985] reported that 64% of day treatment youth and 70% of residential treatment youth had committed no new offenses at follow-up (not a statistically significant difference). Although the Colorado study [Rosenthal & Glass 1990] found a higher average number of reported offenses among youth in day treatment compared to youth in residential treatment after 12 months in the programs, they reported no difference between the groups following completion of the programs. Youth in residential programs may have fewer opportunities than day treatment youth to commit offenses during placement, whereas the two groups have equal opportunities for illegal behavior after program completion. Outcomes measured post-program are more informative and can be used to establish sustained treatment effects.

- *Delinquent youth benefited from the less restrictive environment of day treatment.* Day treatment programs allow young people to remain at home and therefore, are less intrusive than residential treatment programs. The Indiana, Michigan, Minnesota, and Colorado studies found that living at home afforded delinquent adolescents opportunities to practice new skills in the home and community environment, while receiving program guidance and support [Comer 1985; Hoge & Savas 1998; Rosenthal & Glass 1990; and Velasquez & Lyle 1985].

Cost-Effectiveness

Day treatment programs generally cost less than residential programs. Figure 3 shows per diem cost comparisons for the three major studies. In the Michigan [Hoge & Savas 1998] and Minnesota [Velasquez & Lyle 1985] studies, day treatment was less costly than residential treatment. In the Colorado study [Rosenthal & Glass 1990], costs were similar. In the Indiana study, Comer [1985] noted that an advantage of day treatment was that funding required for institutional food and lodging could be allocated to program enrichment.

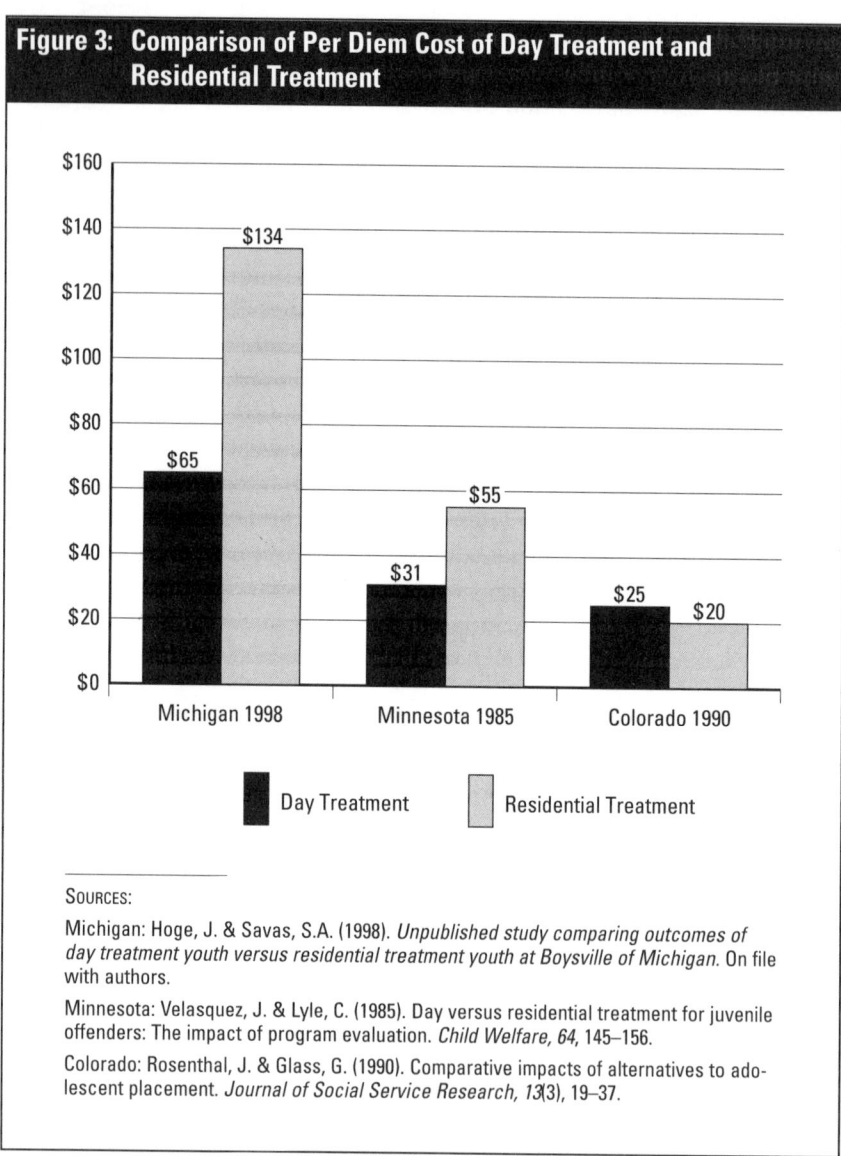

Figure 3: Comparison of Per Diem Cost of Day Treatment and Residential Treatment

SOURCES:

Michigan: Hoge, J. & Savas, S.A. (1998). *Unpublished study comparing outcomes of day treatment youth versus residential treatment youth at Boysville of Michigan.* On file with authors.

Minnesota: Velasquez, J. & Lyle, C. (1985). Day versus residential treatment for juvenile offenders: The impact of program evaluation. *Child Welfare, 64,* 145–156.

Colorado: Rosenthal, J. & Glass, G. (1990). Comparative impacts of alternatives to adolescent placement. *Journal of Social Service Research, 13*(3), 19–37.

Conclusion

Day treatment offers a less restrictive alternative to traditional residential treatment for delinquent adolescents. Research suggests similar outcomes overall for the two services although there is some evidence of better school attendance after day treatment and other benefits associated with keeping young people at home. Day treatment programs usually cost less than residential treatment programs. The day treatment model shows promise as an effective and efficient alternative to traditional residential treatment for delinquent adolescents. Issues requiring further investigation include the role of a multisystemic approach, including intensive family involvement in day treatment services [Clements 1988; Savas et al. 1998; Waugh & Kjos 1992; Kraft & DeMaio 1982; Tolmach 1985]; matching adolescents with program models based on their specific needs [Brandt 1979]; and monitoring current and released program participants [Savas et al. 1998].

References

Brandt, D. (1979). Development of intake criteria in a day treatment program for delinquent boys. *Psychological Reports, 44*, 1028–1030.

Clements, C. (1988). Delinquency prevention and treatment: A community-centered perspective. *Criminal Justice and Behavior, 15*(3), 286–305.

Comer, R. (1985). Day treatment of adolescents: An alternative to institutionalization. *Journal of Counseling and Development, 64*, 74–76.

Hoge, J. & Savas, S. A. (1998). Unpublished study comparing outcomes of day treatment youth versus residential treatment youth at Boysville of Michigan. On file with authors.

Kettlewell, P., Jones, J., & Jones, R. (1985). Adolescent partial hospitalization: Some preliminary outcome data. *Journal of Clinical Child Psychology, 14*(2), 139–144.

Kraft, S. & DeMaio, B. (1982). An ecological intervention with adolescents in low-income families. *American Journal of Orthopsychiatry, 52*(1), 131–140.

Rosenthal, J. & Glass, G. (1990). Comparative impacts of alternatives to adolescent placement. *Journal of Social Service Research, 13*(3), 19–37.

Savas, S. A., Fleming, W., & Bolig, E. (1998). Program specification: A precursor to program monitoring and quality improvement. A case study from Boysville of Michigan. *Journal of Behavioral Health Services and Research, 25*(2), 208–216.

Schutjer, M. (1982). Day treatment for delinquency youth: An alternative to residential care. *Children Today, 11*(1), 20–23.

Tolmach, J. (1985). "There ain't nobody on my side": A new day treatment program for black urban youth. *Journal of Clinical Child Psychology, 14*(3), 214–219.

Velasquez, J. & Lyle, C. (1985). Day versus residential treatment for juvenile offenders: The impact of program evaluation. *Child Welfare, 64,* 145–156.

Waugh, T. & Kjos, D. (1992). Parental involvement and the effectiveness of an adolescent day treatment program. *Journal of Youth and Adolescence, 21*(4), 487–497.

What Works in Treatment for Delinquent Adolescents

Study Authors	Survey Sample	Research Design/Outcome Measure	Findings
Comer, R. (1985). Day treatment of adolescents: An alternative to institutionalization. *Journal of Counseling and Development, 64,* 74–76.	• 41 adjudicated adolescents in a day treatment program in Indiana and their families	• Data collected from youth self-reports, parent evaluations, and staff reports; collected after the first two years of the program. • Outcomes measured were self-esteem, school attendance, family harmony, behavior problems, and remaining in the community.	• Youth and parent evaluations indicated increased self-esteem, improved school attendance, and greater family harmony. • Staff reported that youth had decreased chronic behavior problems. • More than 50% of youth had remained in the community.
Hoge, J. & Savas, S.A. (1998). *Unpublished study comparing outcomes of day treatment youth versus residential treatment youth at Boysville of Michigan.* On file with authors.	• 123 youth from a county in Michigan, who were released from Boysville between 1/1/96 and 5/31/98 after completing either a day treatment program (n = 70) or a residential treatment program (n = 53)	• Data collected from release records and follow-up surveys. • Outcomes measured at time of release were length of stay, graduation from program, living situation, and cost per day. Follow-up at three and 12 months. Outcome measures included living situation, productivity (in school and/or working), and legal lifestyle.	• 84% of day treatment youth compared to 81% of residential treatment youth were in a home-based living situation at 12 months after release. • 92% of day treatment youth compared to 73% of residential treatment youth were in school and/or working at 12 months after program completion. • 96% of day treatment youth compared to 93% of residential treatment youth were living a legal lifestyle (no new adjudications) at 12 months after release.

(continued next page)

What Works in Treatment for Delinquent Adolescents (continued)

Study Authors	Survey Sample	Research Design/Outcome Measure	Findings
Rosenthal, J. & Glass, G. (1990). Comparative impacts of alternatives to adolescent placement. *Journal of Social Service Research, 13* (3), 19–37.	• 93 youth, ages 12–17, who were first-time admissions to long-term residential treatment, day treatment, or family treatment services between September 1, 1980–December 31, 1981 in Colorado: 37 from residential treatment, 23 from day treatment, 33 from family treatment	• Data collected from record review and follow-up surveys. • Outcomes measured were delinquency rates, school performance, and program costs.	• Day treatment youth had highest delinquency rates up to one year after release; delinquency rates in the three groups were similar at 15–30 months post-intervention. • School performance among youth in three groups was similar. • Day treatment had highest program costs due to extensive professional services involved.
Velasquez, J. & Lyle, C. (1985). Day versus residential treatment for juvenile offenders: The impact of program evaluation. *Child Welfare, 64* (2), 145–156.	• 202 delinquent youth, ages 12–19, in a day treatment program (n = 81) or residential treatment program (n = 168) in Minnesota	• Data collected from the public department's computerized information system and a survey of probation officers or social workers. • Outcomes measured were living situation, school attendance, post-treatment offenses, and overall behavior.	• 32%–39% of youth remained in family setting at 6–12-month follow-up, regardless of program. • 49% of residential youth and 57% of day treatment youth were attending school at six- month follow-up (no significant difference). • No difference between groups in overall distribution of offenses prior to and following treatment; for misdemeanors, residential youth had significantly fewer offenses after treatment than before although day treatment youth did not. • A small majority of youth were greatly or somewhat improved in overall behavior after treatment: 55% of residential youth and 44% of day treatment youth (no significant differences).

About the Authors

Gina Alexander, M.S., M.S.W., is vice president of The Villages, a family and children's agency providing child welfare and behavioral health services throughout Indiana and Kentucky. She holds a M.S. in education and a M.S.W. from Indiana University. Much of her work has been in program development and administration in child welfare and children's mental health, with particular emphasis on developing an outcomes orientation for these systems. She directed a comprehensive follow-up study of her agency's residential services, *Caring for troubled children* (with T. Huberty, 1993) and contributed to the development of the IARCCA Outcomes Project, an outcome evaluation study of Indiana children in out-of-home care now in its third year. She currently is serving as coprincipal investigator for the Odyssey Project, a multisite descriptive and prospective study of children in residential group care and therapeutic foster care sponsored by the Child Welfare League of America.

Richard P. Barth, M.S.W., Ph.D., is the Frank A. Daniels Distinguished Professor of Human Services Policy Information in the School of Social Work at the University of North Carolina at Chapel Hill. He was previously Hutto Patterson Professor, School of Social Welfare, University of California at Berkeley. His (coauthored) books include *Adoption disruption: Rates, risks, and resources, From child abuse to permanency planning: Pathways through child welfare services* (Aldine, 1994), *Child welfare research review I and II* (Columbia, 1994; 1997); and the *Tender* *years: Toward developmentally-sensitive child welfare services* (Oxford, 1998). He is on the editorial boards of several research, policy, and practice journals, including *Adoption Quarterly and Children and Youth Services Review.* He was the 1998 recipient of the Presidential Award for Excellence in Research from the National Association of Social Workers.

Susan Belanger, M.A., is a research associate for Jewish Child Care Association. She received her M.A. in developmental psychology from Fordham University, where currently she is a doctoral candidate. Belanger has served on the faculties of Fordham University and Lehman College and has been published in the areas of ethics and moral development, memory, behavior and psychopathology, and foster care.

Lucy Berliner, M.S.W., is the director of Harborview Center for Sexual Assault and Traumatic Stress and clinical associate professor, University of Washington School of Social Work and Department of Psychiatry and Behavioral Sciences. Her activities include clinical practice with child and adult victims of trauma and crime, research on the impact of trauma and the effectiveness of clinical and societal interventions, and participation in local and national social policy initiatives to promote the interests of trauma and crime victims. Berliner, an editorial board member for several journals that deal with interpersonal violence, has authored numerous peer-reviewed articles and book chapters. She also has served on local and national boards of organizations, programs, and professional societies.

Jill Duerr Berrick, Ph.D., is the director of the Center for Social Services Research and associate professor at the School of Social Welfare at the University of California at Berkeley. Berrick teaches courses on social policy, social sciences research, and social work administration. She also conducts research on various topics concerning poor children and families. Berrick has authored or coauthored seven books on child abuse, foster care, and family poverty and has written extensively for academic journals. Her most recent book, *The tender years: Toward developmentally sensitive child welfare services for young children* (Oxford University Press, with Barbara Needell and Richard P. Barth) examines the child welfare system for young children.

Patricia Chamberlain, Ph.D., is the founder and director of the Oregon Social Learning Center's Treatment Foster Care (TFC) programs that have served severely disturbed and chronically delinquent youth since 1983. In 1998, the Oregon TFC model was selected as one of 10 empirically-based violence prevention blueprint programs by the Office Juvenile Justice and Delinquency Prevention and the Colorado Center for the Study and Prevention of Violence. Chamberlain has published numerous articles on TFC, and is currently conducting an National Institute of Mental Health-funded study on the effectiveness of TFC with females referred from the juvenile justice system. A similar study focusing on males was completed in 1995.

Patrick A. Curtis, Ph.D., is the director of research for the Child Welfare League of America (CWLA). He has been a researcher and manager for 20 years in child welfare and related social services with special expertise in the design, funding, and administration of research and evaluation at the national level. Curtis is principal investigator for the Odyssey Project, a national, multisite, descriptive, and prospective study of children and youth living in residential group care, group homes, and therapeutic foster care. The project is comprised of 23 CWLA member agencies representing diverse programmatic content and geographic distribution. Curtis is also principal investigator for the evaluation of the Enhanced Support Services for Kinship Caregivers Project funded by the U.S. Department of Health and Human Services, Children's Bureau, as well as the separately funded Kinship Care Adoptions Project, also supported by the U.S. Department of Health and Human Services, Children's Bureau. His most recent publications are *Child abuse and neglect, A look at the states: The CWLA stat book* (1999) with Michael R. Petit et al.; *The foster care crisis: Translating research into practice and policy* (1999) edited with Grady Dale, Jr. and Joshua Kendall University of Nebraska Press; and "The Beginnings of Child Welfare Research in the United States," (1999) published in the journal *Child and Adolescent Social Work.*

Nan W. Dale is president and CEO of Children's Village in Dobbs Ferry, New York, a multiservice agency providing a range of child welfare and mental health services. She is author of *Safe and Sound: Preventing Child Abuse in Residential Care* and *Conflict Management in Out-of-Home Care,* in addition to journal articles and op-ed pieces for the New York Times. She has also contributed to two films on the Bosnia conflict and served as a commentator on National Public Radio. Ms. Dale was selected as Executive of the Year, 2000, by the National Federation of Nonprofits and currently serves as chair of the Child Welfare League of America National Advisory Council of Executives.

John Eckenrode, Ph.D., is professor and chair of the Department of Human Development at Cornell University and codirector of the Family Life Development Center. His research concerns child abuse and neglect, stress and coping processes, and the effects of preventive interventions. He is a social psychologist (Tufts, 1979), has authored numerous journal articles and chapters, and has edited three books, *Stress between work and family* (with Susan Gore); *The social context of coping; and Understanding abusive families* (with James Garbarino). In 1997, he and his collaborators on the Prenatal/Early Infancy Project received the annual research award from the National Institute for Health Care Management in the maternal and child health care category. In 1995, he received the Robert Chin Memorial Award from the Society for the Psychological Study of Social Issues (SPSSI) for the best paper on child abuse and neglect that year.

Kathleen Coulborn Faller, Ph.D., A.C.S.W., D.C.S.W., is a professor of social work at the University of Michigan. She is also faculty director of the CIVITAS Child and Family Programs, director of the Family Assessment Clinic, and principal investigator on the Interdisciplinary Child Welfare Training Program, a federally funded program to train multidisciplinary, community-based teams to address the needs of complex child welfare cases. All of these programs are at the University of Michigan. She is involved in research, clinical work, teaching, training, and writing in the area of child welfare and is the author of several books, including *Social work with abused and neglected children* (The Free Press); *Child sexual abuse: An interdisciplinary manual for diagnosis, case management, and treatment* (Columbia); *Understanding child sexual maltreatment* (Sage); *Child sexual abuse: Intervention and treatment* (DHHS) and the APSAC study guide: Interviewing children suspected of having been sexually abused (Sage), and approximately 40 research and clinical articles. She is a member of the American Professional Society on the Abuse of Children's Advisory Board. She was formerly a member of the organization's board of directors and executive committee.

William Feigelman, Ph.D., is currently a professor and the chairperson of sociology at Nassau Community College in Garden City, New York. He completed his doctoral studies in sociology at the State University of New York at Stony Book in 1987. With several books and more than 30 journal articles to his credit over the last 25 years, he has been a frequent contributor to the literature on adoptions. In 1983, with Arnold Silverman, he wrote *Chosen children: New patterns of adoptive relationships* (NY: Praeger). His writings have addressed numerous adoption issues including transracial and single-parent adoptions and the search for birth parents among adoptees, among other controversial adoption subjects. His most recent work in the field has been devoted to tracking the long-term adjustment differences between adoptees and their birth-parent raised counterparts. He has received research grant support from a variety of agencies including the National Institute of Mental Health, National Science Foundation, the Research Foundation of the State University of New York, and the California Department of Health Services to pursue these and other areas of sociological research.

John Fluke, Ph.D., joined Walter R. McDonald & Associates, Inc. as director of research in December 1999. From 1992–1999, Fluke was director of program analysis and research for the Children's Division of The American Humane Association (AHA). He has extensive research experience in the area of Child Protective Services safety and risk assessment and has directed or managed many projects including the development of assessment technology in Illinois, Idaho, and Texas. Decision-making research grants include the *Dynamics of Unsubstantiated Reporting and Aspects of the National Child Protective Screening Study* under subcontract to the American Bar Association. Until 1999, he organized the research component of the annual Child Protective Services Risk Assessment Roundtable. He has published widely in the field, presented at numerous national and international forums, and participated on several advisory, policy making, and corporate boards. He received his Ph.D. in organizational decision science from Union Graduate School in 1996 and a master's degree in anthropology from Pennsylvania State University.

Noelle Gallant, M.A., received her degree in anthropology from the University of Connecticut. She currently works as a grants associate for the Village for Families & Children, Inc. of Hartford, Connecticut. Prior to obtaining her position at the Village, she worked as a researcher in a wide variety of areas, including public health, early childhood development, and reproductive health.

Amy Gordon, M.S., is a research associate at the Child Welfare League of America (CWLA), where she serves as the evaluator for a national demonstration project on kinship care. The Department of Health and Human Services Children's Bureau funds this collaborative project between CWLA and the Baltimore Department of Social Services. She also has been involved with research in the areas of family foster care, independent living, residential treatment, and Head Start. She recently authored *Outcome initiatives in child welfare,* (CWLA 1999), a summary of current national and local efforts to measure child welfare outcomes.

Jean Grossman is the vice president of research at Public/Private Ventures (P/PV) and has worked there for 12 years. She is an economist who has written in diverse areas, such as youth mentoring, youth development, youth and adult employment, and evaluation methodology. She is one of the nation's leading experts on youth mentoring. She coauthored *Making a difference: An impact study of big brothers/big sisters* (BBBS), has edited *Contemporary issues in mentoring,* a volume about mentoring and is doing further analysis of the BBBS data to determine in more detail how mentoring works. She is currently heading up P/PV's work on afterschool programs. In particular, she is project director for the evaluation of the Extended Service Schools (ESS) Initiative. This initiative funds 17 cities throughout the country to operate afterschool programs in low-income neighborhood schools. The evaluation will examine the planning issues around using schools as afterschool care facilities, implementation and activity quality issues, the cost and financing of such programs, what types of youth participate, and how participation affects the youth's experiences.

Harold D. Grotevant, Ph.D., is a professor of family social science and adjunct professor of child psychology at the University of Minnesota. He received his B.A. in psychology at the University of Texas at Austin (1970) and his Ph.D. at the Institute of Child Development, University of Minnesota (1977). Grotevant is a fellow of the American Psychological Association and received the Excellence in Research Award from the College of Human Ecology at the University of Minnesota in 1994. His publications focus on relationships in adoptive families and on the development of identity in children and adolescents within their family contexts. His list of over 100 publications includes several books related to adoptive families: *Emotional disturbance in adopted adolescents: Origins and development* (with R.G. McRoy and L. Zurcher, 1988); *Openness in adoption: New practices, new issues* (with R.G. McRoy & K. White, 1988); and *Openness in adoption: Exploring family connections* (with Ruth G. McRoy: Sage, 1998).

Isaac V. Gusukuma, Ph.D., L.M.S.W., is an associate professor, director of the Social Work Program, and head of the Department of Sociology and Social Work at Howard Payne University in Brownwood, Texas. Gusukuma received his B.A. in sociology and M.S.W. from the University of Hawaii at Manoa in Honolulu, Hawaii. He received a Master of Religious Education from Southwestern Baptist Theological Seminary in Ft. Worth, Texas and Ph.D. in social work from the University of Texas at Austin. His social work experience has focused on children and families. He is a licensed social worker in Texas. Gusukuma's research efforts have focused on intercountry adoptions, particularly the adoption of children from Latin America and China by families in the United States.

Jann L. Hoge, Ph.D., A.C.S.W., was previously the program evaluation supervisor with Boysville of Michigan. She currently is a faculty member at Marygrove College in Detroit, Michigan. Hoge received her Ph.D. from the University of Michigan. She has over 10 years of clinical and research experience with delinquent youth and the families, tutoring, and mentoring special needs adolescents, and providing crisis intervention counseling.

Dana M. Hollinshead, M.P.A., M.A., is a program/policy analyst in the Children's Division of the American Humane Association (AHA). Hollinshead is an experienced policy analyst specializing in the areas of child welfare issues and services. She conducts program evaluations, policy analyses, trainings, field interviews, case studies, and focus groups. She also designs, collects, analyzes, and reports quantitative and qualitative research and provides technical assistance to public and private child welfare agencies on child welfare reform issues. Since joining AHA in 1997, Hollinshead spearheaded and wrote division position papers regarding the proposed ASFA regulations and outcome measures, facilitated workshops at AHA's ASFA Roundtable, and authored an article about the impact of ASFA on AOD-affected families in the child welfare system. Hollinshead received a B.A. in psychology from Colby College in Waterville, Maine, in 1989 and, received a Master's in Public Administration and a Master of Arts public policy degree from the George Washington University in Washington, DC.

Todd Klempner, M.S.W., is the former research and policy associate for the Chemical Dependency Initiative at the Child Welfare League of America (CWLA). During his two years at CWLA, Klempner also has worked extensively with the public policy department and in grant development. Klempner coauthored an issue brief in 1999, *Mortality Trends Among U.S. Children and Youth*. In 1998, Klempner received his M.S.W. from the George Warren Brown School of Social Work at Washington University.

Miriam P. Kluger, Ph.D., serves as director of the Village Center for Applied Research & Evaluation, a Division of the Village for Families & Children, Inc. in Hartford, Connecticut. As senior vice president for continuous quality improvement, research and planning services, she also leads the agency's efforts in quality improvement, strategic planning, outcome effectiveness, and accreditation. She received her Ph.D. in applied psychological research and evaluation from Hofstra University in Hempstead, New York. Before joining the Village, Kluger was a health care analyst at Queens Hospital Community Mental Health Center in Jamaica, New York, and held positions in project management training and public relations research at AT&T. She has coauthored several books including *Strategic business planning: Securing a future for the nonprofit organization; Innovative leadership in the nonprofit organization: Strategies for change; and No more partings: An examination of long-term foster family care.*

David Kolko, Ph.D., is an associate professor of child psychiatry and psychology at the University of Pittsburgh Medical Center. At Western Psychiatric Institute and Clinic, he directs the Special Services, a treatment research program for youth referred by the Juvenile Court. He currently is involved in a study to evaluate services for juvenile sexual abusers and a clinical trial examining the effectiveness of multimodal treatments for young children with disruptive disorders. He is serving a second term on the board of directors of the American Professional Society on the Abuse of Children and is cochair of its research committee. His primary clinical research interests involve the evaluation of treatments directed towards child antisocial behavior, including firesetting, adolescent sexual offending, and child physical abuse/family violence.

Patricia Goth Mace, Ph.D., received her doctorate in developmental psychology at the University of Texas in Austin. She has worked as a research associate at the Village for Families & Children, Inc. for 15 years, conducting program evaluations and writing grants to support program development at the agency. In addition, for three years she has worked closely with Connecticut's statewide association of sexual assault crisis services to support their development and evaluation of programs for victims of sexual assault. Her current interests are focused on empirically supported mental health treatments for children and families.

Anthony N. Maluccio, D.S.W., is a professor of social work at Boston College. A frequent consultant to child welfare agencies and schools of social work, he has conducted research in the areas of permanency planning for children and youth, family preservation, and family reunification for children in out-of-home care. He has authored or coauthored a number of books, including *Permanency planning for children: The child welfare challenge—Policy, practice and research; Together again—Family reunification in foster care; Teaching family reunification; and Reconnecting families—A guide to strengthening family reunification.*

Karen McCurdy, Ph.D., is an assistant professor in human development and family studies, at the University of Rhode Island. For over 10 years, she has conducted research on the effectiveness of child abuse prevention programs and currently is examining factors that influence parental engagement and retention in family support programs. She received her Ph.D. in human development and social policy at Northwestern University.

Ruth G. McRoy, Ph.D., holds the Ruby Lee Piester Centennial Professorship in Services to Children and Families and is the director of the Center for Social Work Research at the School of Social Work at the University of Texas at Austin. She also holds a joint appointment in the University of Texas Center for African and African American Studies and is a member of the University of Texas Academy of Distinguished Professors. She has authored or coauthored numerous articles and book chapters on adoptions, and has presented many invited papers at national and international conferences. Her five coauthored books include: *Transracial and inracial adoptees: The adolescent years* (with L. Zurcher, 1983); *Emotional disturbance in adopted adolescents: Origins and development* (with H. Grotevant and L. Zurcher, 1988); *Openness in adoption: New practices, new issues* (with H. Grotevant and K. White, 1988); *Social work practice with black families* (with Sadye Logan and Edith Freeman, 1990); and *Openness in adoption: Exploring family connections* (with H. Grotevant, 1998). Her latest book, *Special needs adoptions: Practice issues* was published in January.

Edmund V. Mech, M.S.W., Ph.D., is a professor of social work and the director of the Foster Youth-in-Transition project at the University of Illinois at Urbana-Champaign. He received a Ph.D. in developmental psychology from Indiana University, and a M.S.W. from Bryn Mawr College. His agency experience includes positions at Family Service of Memphis, the Children's Aid Society of Pennsylvania in Philadelphia, and the Children's Bureau of Delaware in Wilmington. Mech directed the Arizona Welfare Study, sponsored by the Arizona State Legislature, served as director of the Research Center at Bryn Mawr College, and director of the Regional Research Institute at Portland State University. Special appointments include the National Academy of Sciences Panel on Employment and Training, Guest Scholar-Brooking Institution, and Visiting Scholar, Institute of Politics, Harvard University. His research focus has been on the preparation of foster youths for independent living. Publications include numerous research articles on various aspects of foster youth in transition to independent living.

Kristine E. Nelson, D.S.W., is a professor in the Graduate School of Social Work at Portland State University in Oregon. For nearly a decade she was director of research at the National Resource Center on Family

Based Services at the University of Iowa, one of 10 national child welfare resource centers. She has been the principal investigator on six federally funded studies of family preservation services and of child neglect and has participated in several national symposia and expert panels on research and research methodology in these areas. Nelson is coauthor of *Reinventing human services: Community- and family-centered practice* (Aldine, 1995); *Evaluating family-based services* (Aldine, 1995); and *Alternative models of family preservation: Family-Based services in context* (Charles C. Thomas, 1992). She has been a contributing author to several texts on family preservation and has published numerous articles. Nelson earned her doctoral degree at the University of California at Berkeley and holds an M.S.W. from Sacramento State University and a B.A. from Stanford University.

Steven Nichols is completing his Ph.D. in counseling and school psychology at Indiana University in Bloomington where he also is an associate instructor in counseling. He also provides counseling services at the Center for Human Growth on the Indiana University campus.

Kimberly A. Nollan, M.S.W., Ph.D., in social welfare from the University of Washington in 1996. She earned her M.S.W. and B.S. in psychology also from the University of Washington. Nollan began work with The Casey Family Program in 1992. In her current position as a research analyst, she is responsible for the design and implementation of a prospective, longitudinal study investigating the identity formation and attachment relationships of youths in private out-of-home care. She is involved in determining the cost of services and impact of services on youth outcomes. In addition, she is refining the existing Ansell-Casey Life Skills Assessment and developing an accompanying curriculum. Nollan has written various articles on the acquisition of life skills and independent living preparation of youths in out-of-home care. She also presents information and offers training on life skills assessment.

Peter J. Pecora, Ph.D., has a joint appointment as the manager of research for The Casey Family Program and professor in the School of Social Work at the University of Washington in Seattle. He began his career as a line worker and later a program coordinator in a number of child welfare service agencies in Wisconsin. He currently is implementing outcome-oriented case planning systems, collecting data on the progress of children in foster care, and developing instruments for assessing outcomes in child and family services. His books and articles focus on child welfare program design, administration, and research, including *The child welfare challenge* (with J.K. Whittaker, A.N. Maluccio and R.P. Barth, Walter de Gruyter, in press); *Assessing youth behavior using the child behavior checklist in family and children's services* (with N. LeProhn, K. Wetherbee, E. Lamont and T. Achenbach, Child Welfare League of America in press); and *Quality improvement and program evaluation in child welfare agencies: Managing into the next century* (with W. Selig, F. Zirps, and S. Davis (Eds.). Child Welfare League of America 1996).

Barbara A. Pine, M.S.W., Ph.D., is a professor at the University of Connecticut School of Social Work where she currently chairs the Administration Concentration and the Substantive Area on Children and Families. She teaches and writes in the areas of social work management, child welfare, and professional ethics. Her most recent publications in child welfare include *Reconnecting families: A guide to strengthening family reunification services* and *Teaching family reunification: A sourcebook*, both of which were co-authored with Robin Warsh and Anthony N. Maluccio.

Martha G. Roditti, M.S.W., currently is a faculty member of the School of Social Work at San Francisco State University. She teaches and develops curriculum, student workshops, and student field activities for the school's Title IV-E Child Welfare M.S.W. Training program. She also coordinates a Children's Bureau-funded community partnership training project with San Francisco Department of Human Service Child Welfare Program. She previously was executive director of the Children's Council of San Francisco, a child care resource and referral agency. She presents workshops on child welfare and childcare as well as lectures in child welfare policy.

Sue Ann Savas, M.S.W., is the program evaluation director at Boysville of Michigan. She is an adjunct lecturer at the University of Michigan School of Social Work. Savas serves on national program evaluation and research committees, focusing on outcomes and quality improvement processes. Her evaluation experience and publications are in the area of child welfare and juvenile justice.

Elizabeth Schnur, Ph.D., is the director of strategic planning and research for Jewish Child Care Association in New York City. She received
a Ph.D. in developmental psychology from the University of Michigan,
and did post-doctoral work at Educational Testing Service (ETS) where
she worked on the ETS Longitudinal Head Start data set. Schnur has
served on the faculties of Adelphi and Hofstra Universities, and has been
published in the areas of language and communicative development,
Head Start, day care, and foster care.

Katreena Scott is finishing her Ph.D. dissertation at the University of
Western Ontario. Her work has focused on evaluation of batterer intervention programs, on the developmental paths to adolescent and adult abusive behavior, and preventative interventions for youth. She is the recipient
of numerous research awards including the APA Division of the Psychology
of Women Hyde Graduate Student Research Grant and the Social Science
and Humanities Research Council Doctoral Fellowship and she is coauthor of *Alternative to violence: Empowering youth to develop healthy relationships* (with D. Wolfe and C. Wekerle, Sage 1997).

Russell Skiba, Ph.D., is an associate professor in counseling and educational psychology at Indiana University. A member of the School
Psychology faculty, he has worked to develop effective intervention and
consultation strategies for children with emotional and behavioral problems. He was a member of the expert panel and writing team that developed the President's *Early Warning, Timely Response Guide* for school
safety, and is currently writing a book for Guilford Press, *Preventing
school violence: Alternatives to suspension and expulsion.* Skiba has
directed a number of federally funded research projects and published
extensively in management, assessment of emotional and behavioral disorders, and systems change. Skiba is the director of the Indiana
University Institute for Child Study. He is the project director of the Safe
and Responsive Schools Project, a U.S. Department of Education Projects
of National Significance grant working with five schools in two school districts to develop comprehensive and preventive school safety plans.

Lori K. Sudderth, Ph.D., is a research associate at the Village Center
for Applied Research and Evaluation in Hartford, Connecticut. She
received her doctorate in sociology from Indiana University in 1993, and

completed post-doctoral work in mental health services at Rutgers University. Her areas of interest include criminology, mental health, and gender, with an emphasis on evaluation of criminal justice programs.

Joseph P. Tierney is the vice president of greater Philadelphia initiatives at Public/Private Ventures (P/PV). He directs the Community-Serving Ministries Initiative, a project involving faith-based organizations in youth programs such as literacy, violence reduction, job readiness and training, and child care. In addition, he directs P/PV's youth violence-reduction projects, which include providing management and operational support for Philadelphia's Youth Violence Reduction Project (YVRP), an analysis of homicide trends in the city from 1996–1999 and a study of violence through the eyes of some of the YVRP participants. Tierney has conducted research and developed initiatives in the areas of youth violence reduction, literacy, mentoring, employment and training, welfare reform, community development, national service, and youth corps. Among other reports and articles, he has co-authored *Critical issues facing Philadelphia's neighborhoods: Violence reduction* (1999); *Making a difference: An impact study of big brothers big sisters of America* (1995); and *Overcoming roadblocks on the way to work: A bridges to work field report* (1999).

Elizabeth M. Tracy, Ph.D., teaches courses in direct social work practice methods, home-based family intervention, school social work, and child welfare, cochairs the Children, Youth and Family Concentration, and coordinates the School Social Work Certificate Program at the Mandel School of Applied Social Sciences. Tracy is interested in social work models which support families and make use of and strengthen natural helping networks. She has provided training in social support assessment and intervention to a number of programs, and has served on the Executive Committee of the Ohio Association of Family Based Services. Tracy worked with Head Start on an examination of social networks of low-income families, and also with mental health case managers on a training and demonstration project to strengthen support systems of persons with chronic mental illness. She also facilitated the work of a National Family Preservation working group which developed a source book on family preservation teaching. As a faculty fellow under an NIAAA grant, she pursued clinical and research interests with local family-based programs around substance abuse issues in child welfare. Most recently, she completed a qualitative evaluation of a placement prevention strategy, The Family Stability Incentive Fund, operating in 17 Ohio counties.

Robin Warsh, M.S.W., is a lecturer and the project director at Boston College Graduate School of Social Work. She teaches, researches, and consults in the area of family and children's services. She is the coauthor of numerous books and articles on child and family welfare, including *Together again—Family reunification in foster care, Teaching family reunification: A sourcebook;* and *Preparing adolescents for life after foster care.* She is currently principal investigator and project director of a federally funded grant on promoting professional education in child welfare. In addition, she maintains a clinical practice in the Boston area.

James K. Whittaker, Ph.D., is a professor in the School of Social Work at the University of Washington and cochair of the Center for Policy and Practice Development at Boysville of Michigan. His interests and publications are in intervention design, development and evaluation with high-risk youth and families.

Katherine Wingfield, M.S.W., is the special assistant to the executive director at the Child Welfare League of America. She was previously the program manager of CWLA's Chemical Dependency Initiative. During her tenure with CWLA she has worked on a variety of issues impacting children and families involved with the child welfare system including adolescent health, teen pregnancy prevention, and chemical dependency. In 1997, she completed a national study of the policies and programs public child welfare agencies have in place to support chemically affected children and families and has received a grant from the Office of Juvenile Justice and Delinquency Prevention, the Office of National Drug Control Policy and the Center for Substance Abuse Prevention to develop resource materials for child welfare professionals. Wingfield received her bachelor's degree from Wesleyan University and her Master's in Social Work from Catholic University.

David A. Wolfe, Ph.D., is a professor of psychology and psychiatry at the University of Western Ontario, Canada. He is a founding member of the Center for Research on Violence Against Women and Children in London and a fellow of the American Psychological Association. He is the author of numerous articles and books on the broad topics of child abuse and domestic violence including *Children of battered women* (with P. Jaffe and S. Wilson; Sage 1990) and *Child abuse: Implications for child development and psychopathology* (Second Edition, Sage 1999).